THE GREAT
MONSTER MAGAZINES

ALSO BY ROBERT MICHAEL (BOBB) COTTER
AND FROM MCFARLAND

The Complete Misfits Discography: Authorized Releases and Bootlegs, Including Recordings by Danzig, Samhain and The Undead (2019)

Ingrid Pitt, Queen of Horror: The Complete Career (2010; paperback 2018)

Vampira and Her Daughters: Women Horror Movie Hosts from the 1950s into the Internet Era (2017)

A History of the Doc Savage Adventures in Pulps, Paperbacks, Comics, Fanzines, Radio and Film (2009; paperback 2016)

The Women of Hammer Horror: A Biographical Dictionary and Filmography (2013)

Caroline Munro, First Lady of Fantasy: A Complete Annotated Record of Film and Television Appearances (2012)

The Mexican Masked Wrestler and Monster Filmography (2005; paperback 2008)

THE GREAT MONSTER MAGAZINES

*A Critical Study of the
Black and White Publications
of the 1950s, 1960s and 1970s*

Robert Michael (Bobb) Cotter

McFarland & Company, Inc., Publishers
Jefferson, North Carolina

The present work is a reprint of the illustrated case bound edition of The Great Monster Magazines: A Critical Study of the Black and White Publications of the 1950s, 1960s and 1970s, *first published in 2008 by McFarland.*

LIBRARY OF CONGRESS CATALOGUING-IN-PUBLICATION DATA

Cotter, Bobb.
The great monster magazines: a critical study of the black and white publications of the 1950s, 1960s and 1970s / Robert Michael (Bobb) Cotter.
p. cm.
Includes bibliographical references and index.

ISBN 978-1-4766-7898-6
paperback : 50# alkaline paper ∞

1. Monsters in motion pictures — Periodicals — History. 2. Horror films — Periodicals — History. 3. Comic books, strips, etc. — United States — History and criticism. 4. Monsters in literature. I. Title.
PN1995.9.M6C66   2019   791.43′6703 — dc22   2008012158

British Library cataloguing data are available

© 2008 Robert Michael "Bobb" Cotter. All rights reserved

No part of this book may be reproduced or transmitted in any form or by any means, electronic or mechanical, including photocopying or recording, or by any information storage and retrieval system, without permission in writing from the publisher.

Front cover: Artwork by Sebastià Boada for the Skywald publication *Scream*, issue 10, October 1974 (courtesy Gary Brodsky).
Back cover: Advertising art and copy from page 74 of *Monsters Unleashed*, issue 2, September 1973 (courtesy Marvel Entertainment, Inc.).

Printed in the United States of America

McFarland & Company, Inc., Publishers
Box 611, Jefferson, North Carolina 28640
www.mcfarlandpub.com

Dedicated to Dad, Brownie, Carl, Joey Ramone, my wonderful wife Cheryl,
and Lucky the Wonder Dog; E-Gor, Reggie, PT, Mr. Jim, Duff and Bif 3.
With special thanks to Carol Pinkus (Marvel Comics Group),
Leigh Stone (Conan Properties), Gary Brodsky (Skywald),
Ken Kropf and the Eide's crew, Peter Normanton (*From the Tomb*),
and Elvis, who watches over us all.

Table of Contents

Preface: Monsters ... Unleashed!   1
Introduction: Four-Color Fiends   7

ONE — Monster Movie Madness   31
TWO — Creepy Monsters, Eerie Zombies, and Generally Undead No-Goodniks   69
THREE — Invasion of the Vampires, or Bat's Entertainment!   99
FOUR — Conan the Franchise: Monsters, Muscles and Maidens   121
FIVE — Thrilling Savage Adventure Tales: The Bloody Pulps   148
SIX — Crazy Kung Fu Apes Fight Space Wars; or, Jump on In, the Bandwagon's Fine   173
SEVEN — The New Breed: Illustrated Horror, Science Fiction and Fantasy   204

Epilogue   221
Appendix: Publications by Category
   I. Comic Books   223
   II. Movie Monster Magazines   224
   III. Black-and-White Magazines   225
Bibliography   227
Index   229

Preface: Monsters ... Unleashed!

The monster magazine is dead; long live the monster magazine! In the (very late) 1950s, 1960s and 1970s, before video and DVD and the Internet, before comics specialty shops, before fan publications that are as slick as anything produced in that time period, if not slicker, and especially before the lines that separated children from teens and teens from adults became so blurred as to become almost indistinguishable, normal retail outlets such as newsstands, grocery or drugstores, or department stores were haunted by the phenomenon known as the "monster magazine."

Monster magazine is a blanket term, which, for purposes of this study, will be used to describe both magazines that primarily covered horror movies, and magazines that contained stories that featured monsters, illustrated in comic book style but printed in black-and-white rather than color. The key word, then, is not monster, but magazine. They were once very different from regular comic books, and were a primary source of information, entertainment, and inspiration for whole generations of "monster kids" who, in turn, became "monster pros," this author included.

Originally, the present book was planned solely as a history of the brief-but-fertile Marvel Monster Group, the name that the comics giant gave to its line of magazines when it ventured into the field created by James Warren and plowed by various groups and levels of imitators. And while entire excellent books have already been devoted to two of the other big players in the genre (*The Warren Companion* by Jon B. Cooke and David Roach, and *The Skywald Horror-Mood* by Skywald's horror-soul, "Archaic" Alan Hewetson), that phase of Marvel's history seems to have slipped under the radar, which is a shame, because there are all sorts of instances where Marvel proved that it was capable of more than just your basic garden-variety superhero. The above authors, and critics in general, are so dismissive of Marvel's output, you would think they were dismissing the efforts of some fly-by-night used-car salesman, not the number one comic book publisher in the world; as if Marvel's sheer corporate size automatically makes its titles the inferior efforts of work-for-hire hacks, and not "horror specialists" like those at the above companies. This is obviously not the case.

But in the course of research, and just plain reading, whether it is the magazines themselves, or the books devoted to them, two

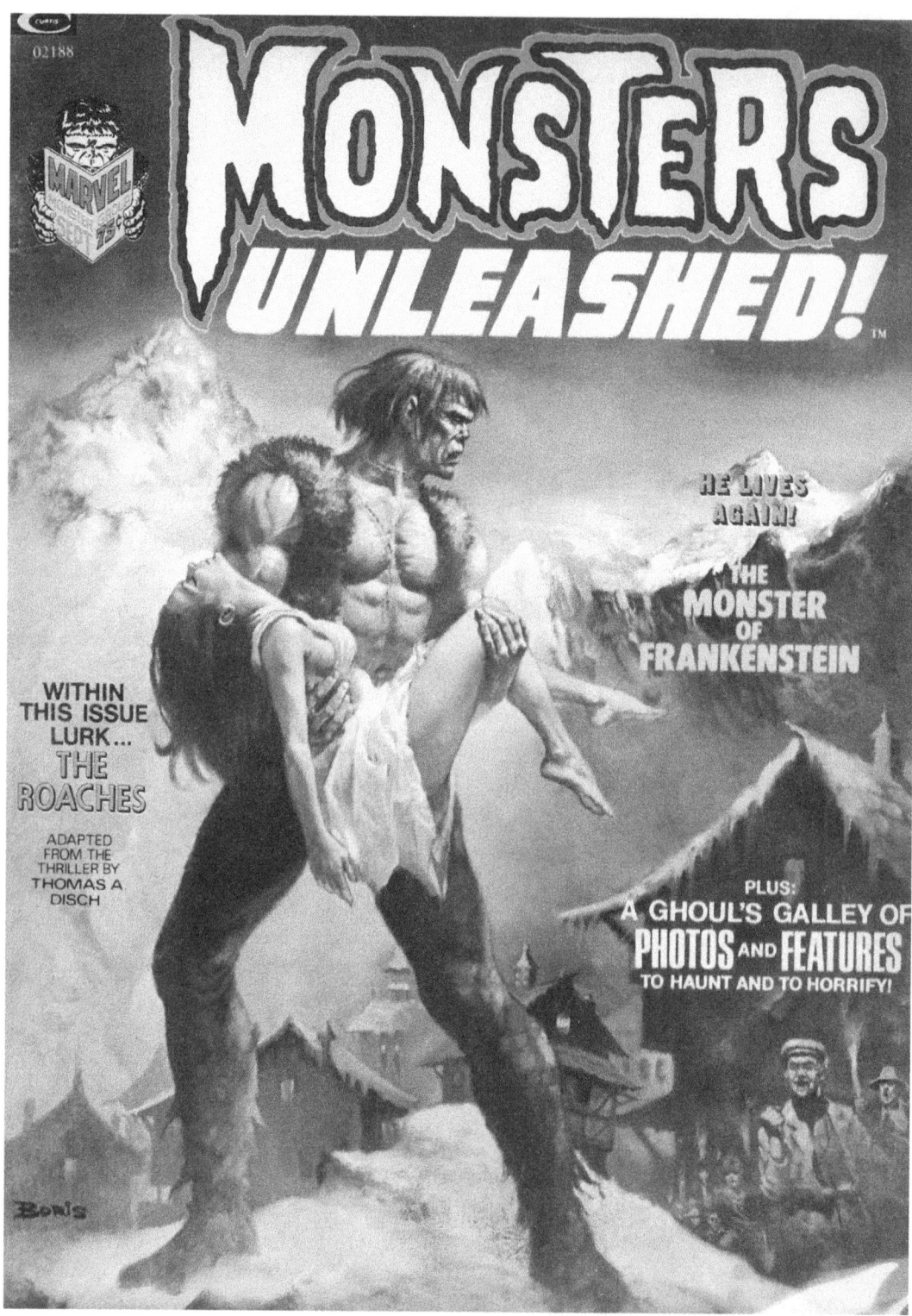

Monsters Unleashed no. 2 (Marvel) — The cover image that has come to symbolize the Marvel Monster Group: Boris Vallejo for *Monsters Unleashed* no. 2 (courtesy Marvel Entertainment, Inc.).

things became apparent. One, perhaps inevitably, is how one-sided such histories can be, dismissing every other company's product as inferior to the book's subject. Two, it's impossible to talk about one without talking about its relation to the others of its kind, and their relationship and contributions to the genre as a whole. So the study will lean in Marvel's direction, not because of favoritism or the opinion that Marvel's products were better than the others, but simply because its magazines have not been as adequately covered as the others mentioned above. Of course, the danger in writing anything about Marvel, especially if it's complimentary, means that the author is likely to be perceived as a "Marvel Zombie," a back-handed term which has been tossed about fandom for years to describe someone who is mindlessly devoted to Marvel product. So while the book is mainly about Marvel Zombies (not the fan kind), it will strive to be as objective and as inclusive as possible, taking the others into account because they are all part of a larger tapestry.

Perhaps this is an appropriate time to clarify just what the book covers, what it doesn't, and why. It doesn't claim to be an exhaustive history of the horror comic, nor of any of the companies discussed, simply their contributions to the monster magazine genre. What qualifies as a monster magazine in this book? The basic description is in the second paragraph, but let's elaborate — it has to be a magazine, not a four-color comic book (although they will obviously be discussed in relation to the magazines) that either features monsters, has a strong fantastic content, or is related to the magazines by dent of influence or artistic connection. For example, the book covers not only the expected monster titles, but also *The Savage Sword of Conan*, as well as, say, *The Deadly Hands of Kung Fu*. It's about the rise and fall of horror, and its subsequent resurrection via those black-and-white magazines. For, as hard as it might be to believe now, publishers couldn't get away with some things, even under the relaxed rules of the comics code (the rise and fall of which is also discussed), and if a comics or horror fan wanted something on a little higher plane (or even just more skin and gore), they had to find it in a magazine.

The book is about the rise and fall of these magazines, the concept of which was born in the '50s, nurtured and grew in the '60s, came to a peak, and crashed, for a period, in the '70s, when *Star Wars*, the resultant mania for science fiction and demand for slick color magazines and ever-gorier horror films made the black-and-white magazines seem as anachronistic as the black-and-white horror movies of which most of them extolled the virtues. The story is told more or less chronologically, as it must be to show why this type of magazine came into existence. The chapters do not deal with particular companies, but rather certain sub-genres to which each publisher's contributions will be evaluated, such as monster movies, zombies and other assorted man-made monsters, vampires, sword-and-sorcery, pulp-type fiction, etc.

The book includes technical credits, especially where such information has not been collected, as in the case of Marvel. An alphabetically arranged appendix groups the works discussed in the text into three main categories — comic books, movie monster magazines, and black-and-white magazines — for quick reference. In the case of publishers whose works have already been extensively indexed, only information which applies to the issue at hand will be included.

What differentiates a comic book from a magazine? The physical dimensions are different, but, the era of publication has a lot to do with that. Times, like children, have changed, and so has the level of what is acceptable in a mainstream comic book. The reasons for the proliferation of monsters in magazine form are that they were for teenagers, college students,

Shock no. 1 (Stanley) — Originally the cover for *Weird Tales of the Future* no. 7 (1953), Bernard Bailey's hellishly unsettling art was used again for a black-and-white illustrated horror magazine that also showcased 1950s tales — produced in 1969.

and maybe even grown-ups, while comics were for kids. The monster movie magazines and the illustrated horror magazines were what you graduated to right after regular comics and before you graduated to girly magazines (at least legally). Monster and horror movies and stories of all types are so commonplace and so accessible in the twenty-first century that it's hard for people to comprehend that they once were harder to come by. For a time, vampires and werewolves were taboo in comic books. Nowadays they hawk breakfast cereal and help children learn arithmetic on educational television shows.

And it's all in blazing, glorious, computer-generated color. Black-and-white comics, like black-and-white films, are no longer a viable option, unless in some sort of "retro" project. Media are omnipresent. Every movie ever preserved is available to view in the home. Personal computers allow access to information, graphics and video like never before. The cynicism and disillusionment that were natural and logical consequences of Watergate and Vietnam have trickled down through the succeeding generations, imparting a pseudo-sophistication and jadedness that have not only blurred the lines, but raised the bar as far as what is acceptable kids' fare. Violence is no longer printed in black-and-white and kept on an upper shelf, it is simply rated "M" and stocked right beside Betty and Veronica.

But in the heyday of horror, things were different. If you wanted a stronger dose of horror than your garden-variety comic book, if you wanted news on the latest monster movies or the classics, if you simply wanted feel the thrill of discovery, expand your horizons, or taste forbidden fruit, you had to reach up a little higher. Sometimes that's all a teenager needs to do, and every teenager needs to do it.

Introduction: Four-Color Fiends

It all starts with EC. Well, not really, although Educational Comics' William Gaines was the son of Max Gaines, who literally did invent American comic books. Gaines Jr. had taken control of the company after the unexpected death of Gaines Sr. in a boating accident, and quickly realized that kids who read comic books did not do so to be educated, but to be entertained, which is why EC's first title, *Picture Stories from the Bible*, did not exactly establish it as a power to be reckoned with. The soon-renamed Entertaining Comics didn't invent monsters, and wasn't the first to publish crime or horror comics, but was unquestionably the best — in fact, EC was so good at what it did, that it endured societal and governmental pressure that no other comics publisher has had to face before or since. The titles of its "new trend" have long since passed into legend — *Tales from the Crypt, The Vault of Terror, The Haunt of Fear, Shock SuspenStories, Weird Science, Weird Fantasy, Weird Science-Fantasy, Incredible Science Fiction, Panic, Frontline Combat, Two-Fisted Tales* and of course *Mad*; and the company's bullpen is a Hall of Fame in itself, the best the field had to offer, all in one place at one time. It's almost impossible to conceive now, especially when flavor-of-the-minute superstar artists come and go as quickly as some of their ill-conceived comics, that so much talent could work together, and for years at that. Frank Frazetta, Wallace Wood, Reed Crandall, Al Williamson, Jack Davis, Johnny Craig, Graham Ingels, Harvey Kurtzman, Bill Elder, Joe Orlando, Bernie Krigstein, Angelo Torres, George Evans, and John Severin all together in their prime, doing their best work. William Gaines encouraged individual styles, and went out of his way to make sure that his artists were noticed — which is precisely what got them in hot water. But we're getting ahead of ourselves — let's backtrack a couple of generations.

After World War I ended, Americans began a decade-long drunk, more kindly referred to as The Roaring Twenties or The Jazz Age, to shut out the limited horrors of war that they had experienced. After World War II, and almost four years of even greater horrors, Americans might have liked Ike and begun moving to the suburbs, but their comics were not so sedate or well manicured. To cope with the horrors of this war, they curiously began to turn out some of the most lurid, yet realistic, crime and horror stories the graphic medium had produced yet! The Americans' involvement in two world conflicts had reshaped sensibilities and exposed Americans to cultures much different than their own, and this new-found worldly sensibility was reflected in the comics. As if unable to deal with their own broadening of views, they turned right around and hypocritically, hysterically, censored them. Or more precisely, threw such a scare into the industry that it censored itself, and in that germ lies the basis for this whole book. It turned out that the real crime and horror wasn't happening in the comics, it was happening to the comics.

Monsters and crime have been a part of comics practically from the beginning. Dick Tracy was an Earthman who fought other Earthmen who looked like monsters; Flash Gordon was a man from Earth who fought alien monsters on Mongo and anywhere else his spaceship carried him; Superman is an alien who fights monsters on Earth and everywhere else in the universe. Batman, in his very first year of adventures alone, fought a mad scientist (Dr. Hugo Strange) and a King Kong copy, and found his ultimate nemesis, the Joker. His hideously grinning countenance was admittedly inspired by the Conrad Veidt film *The Man Who Laughs*, and, not so admittedly, by a 1936 pulp story, "The Grim Joker," by sometime–*Shadow* scripter Ted Tinsley. The Spectre was the ghostly super-hero alter ego of murdered cop Jim Corrigan; not only were his unearthly powers arguably even greater than Superman's, but his requisite cape was more like a hooded shroud. The original, and still the greatest, Captain Marvel (Shazam!) waged an epic battle with the Monster Society of Evil. Hillman's *Airboy Comics* featured a supporting strip called "Sky Wolf," which in turn spawned the immortal Heap. (For more on the Heap, see the Heap section below.) The seventh issue of *Prize Comics* (September 1940) featured the first of many installments of Dick Briefer's beloved "Frankenstein," the first monster in history to star in his own ongoing series, a series that was so popular, the monster got his own title as well, thereby also becoming the first classic monster to get his own book. Briefer's Frankenstein did a reverse; it started out as a humor strip, and then became a straight horror series. While EC may have had a monopoly on talent, it didn't have the horror field to itself.

Besides titles that included strong elements of fantasy and horror in ongoing characters, the most popular format for delivering horror was the anthology title, a format which EC would perfect. It was a format with a lot of competition; at one time, it seemed as if there were as many horror, science-fiction and fantasy comic books as there were comic books themselves. They included Fawcett's legendary *This Magazine Is HAUNTED*, with its equally legendary horror host, Doctor Death, and *Worlds of Fear*. Crestwood created its own legend with *Black Magic* by Joe Simon and Jack Kirby. Also popular were American's *Adventures into the Unknown, Out of the Night, Forbidden Worlds* and *Unknown Worlds*; Avon's *Eerie* (which appeared twenty years before the Warren mag of the same name and became *Strange Worlds* with number eighteen) and *Witchcraft*; Fiction House, like Timely, carrying high the flag of pulp tradition with *Planet Comics* and *Ghost Comics,* with monsters and cheesecake (the feminine kind) being prerequisite cover and story ingredients. Youthful scared a few years' growth out of readers with *Chilling Tales*. Merit shed light on *Dark Mysteries*. Ajax offered up *Haunted Thrills, Strange Fantasy* and *Voodoo*. Mister Publications scored with *Mister Mystery*, which also happened to be the host's name. Issue 12 features one of the infamous injury to the eye covers which later so provoked and stimulated Doctor Wertham. Charlton offered *Mysteries of Unexplored Worlds, The Thing* (which was not related to the movie of the same name, but was a prime target for Wertham's wrath because of its excessive violence), and *Unusual Tales*. Harvey, who published the supernatural kids' classics *Hot Stuff the Little Devil*, *Wendy the Good Little Witch*, and *Casper the Friendly Ghost*, played it straight just as well with *Alarming Tales*, *Black Cat Mystery*, *Tomb of Terror* (which became *Thrills of Tomorrow*) and *Witches' Tales*. Story went on *Mysterious Adventures*; Star startled with *Startling Terror Tales;* Toby tipped in with *Tales of Horror*; Quality, living up to its name as usual, spun a *Web of Evil*. Ace did likewise with *Web of Mystery* and puzzled over *Baffling Mysteries*, St. John served up *Weird Horrors* and gave us a *Nightmare*, Gillmore shocked with *Weird Mysteries*, and S.P.M. looked ahead in *Weird Tales of the Future*.

And then there was Timely. Timely was the name adopted for the comics wing of Martin Goodman's Marvel Publishing Company, heretofore a producer of pulp magazines (*see* Chapter Five). Goodman had entered the business in 1932 with *Complete Western*. So Marvel was Timely before it was Marvel, but it was actually Marvel before it was Timely. The pulp *Marvel Science Stories* was published in 1938 (the first Goodman magazine to use the word "Marvel" in its title); *Marvel Comics* no. 1 was published the following year. Timely, which later morphed into Atlas (between being Marvel), built its foundation on monsters. Its very first major superheroes in its very first comic book were monsters. *Marvel Comics* no. 1 featured both the Human Torch and the Sub-Mariner; one issue featured two of the three characters that would become the backbone of Marvel's line. DC Comics' Superman was the ultimate symbol of virility. Bruce Wayne might have dressed like a bat and fought monsters, but underneath the cowl he was still a handsome millionaire playboy. Timely's Human Torch, on the other hand, was not even human to begin with — he was an android who burst into flames! The Torch learns to control this pyro-power, and is soon inventing all sorts of clever ways to use his flame to maim and kill, especially when faced with the twin menace of the "Japs" and "Ratzis" in the war that soon followed his creation. The enemy now literally became the monsters, hideous, grotesque, fanged freaks whose features and limbs were as twisted as their souls and deeds. The non-propagandist menaces he faced were equally as hideous, if somewhat redundant: The Underground Demons, The Masked Fiend, The Masked Horror, The Werewolf Horror, The Purple Ghost, The Ghost of Shadow Manor, The Asbestos Lady, and The Walking Corpse. He had the obligatory (for most) teenage sidekick named Toro, who was neither a bull nor an android, but a human orphan who just happened to be impervious to flame. How the Torch taught him to actually burst into flame was never explained, and perhaps it was best left unsaid.

Prince Namor, the Sub-Mariner, had actually seen action before that first issue of *Marvel Comics*; the same story that appeared in that issue had already been published (six months previously) in the first issue of the theater giveaway comic book *Motion Picture Funnies Weekly*. Comic books had just been invented, and were already in reprint! (But, to be fair, that's the way comics in general started out, and even the first issue of *Superman* was composed of reprints of stories from *Action Comics*). The Sub-Mariner, created by the legendary "Wild" Bill Everett (one of the true architects of comics' golden age), has been called comics' first anti-hero, and while he was no outright monster, he was certainly different. He may have had a swimmer's physique, but he also had pointed ears (for a modern reference point, think *Star Trek*'s Mr. Spock in a pair of Speedo swim trunks). And while Captain America sported wings on his cowl, the Sub-Mariner grew them, Mercury-like, from his ankles. Actually, the most monstrous thing about him was his temper. A seagoing scoundrel named McKenzie knocked up Namor's mom and then left her, an act that understandably caused Namor to be angry with the surface world. The only reason he doesn't kill all humans is because the bad guys who want to do the same thing keep getting in his way. His opponents were just as monstrous as the Torch's: the Dead Who Swim, the Flying Dutchman, the Shark, the Sea Wolf, and the World Destroyers, with whom he might have allied, except they had Atlantis in their sights, too. One thing took the edge off Namor's menace — he had a propensity for some of the most embarrassing oaths ever uttered by a superhero. "Sufferin' shad!" and "great pickled herring!" were probably the worst offenders, though he had oceans more. The Sub-Mariner's fire vs. water battles with the Human Torch are some of comics' earliest and most fondly remembered hero vs. hero slugfests. To this day, the Sub-Mariner can't make up his mind, and has alternately been reinvented as hero and villain; one incarnation in the '70s saw him billed as the "Savage Sub-Mariner," and he even shared the top spot in *Super Villain Team-Up* with Doctor Doom. Nowadays he's labeled Marvel's first mutant, in order to get a little piece of that X-Men action.

And speaking of Captain America, the third and most iconic member of Timely's "big three" spent a great deal of time fighting monsters before he turned his attention to the Japa-Nazis, an activity to which he returned when World War II ended. In fact, the book was even re-titled *Captain America's Weird Tales* for the last two issues before the original title was cancelled. Indeed, for practically the first ten issues drawn by the legendary Joe Simon and Jack Kirby team, Cap fought practically nothing but the most hideous fiends that the duo could conjure up. A casual reader perusing the contents page of the latest issue of the "star-spangled avenger" might well have had to double-check to see that he hadn't actually picked up a copy of the original *Weird Tales* pulp. "Horror Played the Scales!" "The Hotel of Horror!," "Patient in the Horror Hospital!," "The Hunchback of Hollywood and the Movie Murders!" and "The Queer Case of the Murdering Butterfly and the Ancient Mummies" were just a few of the exclamatory and long-winded adventures from Cap and his teenaged sidekick, Bucky Barnes. The individual villains were as gruesome as the story titles: Fang, the Arch-Fiend of the Orient, the Black Witch, the Black Talon, the Phantom Hound of Cardiff Moor, Dr. Necrosis, the Seven Sons of Satan, the Mad Torso, the Leopard Woman, the Murdering Mummy, and his most famous arch-foe, one which, unlike the others, refused to stay in his grave: the Red Skull. In his first appearance, the Red Skull was supposedly revealed as George Maxon, traitorous aircraft manufacturer and designer, but after his return, no mention was ever made again of that alternate identity, intimating that the Skull was exactly what he appeared to be.

But the Titanic Trio didn't have all the monsters to themselves. *The Angel* was a standard-issue dashing hero; he wasn't a monster (although he had a moustache, which is pretty horrifying in itself), but many of his exploits centered on the fantastic, weird, and just plain grotesque. "Horror in the Haunted Cathedral," "The Wolf Man Terror," "The Weird Ghost of Amber Swamp," "The Case of Professor Torture," "The Banquet of Blood," and "The Tangled Web of Death" all attempted to infuse gray hairs into the Angel's moustache. *The Terror* wasn't the Boris Karloff movie, but an accident victim injected with the blood of a mad dog. This, er, fairly common medical practice allows the victim to survive, but at what price? When he gets close to a crime, he transforms into a Mr. Hyde–like monster. *The Whizzer* was mainlined, too, except in his case, it was mongoose blood, which not only turned him into Timely's version of the Flash, but also christened him with one of the most embarrassing monikers in the entire history of comics. (On a personal note, the author wishes to assure one and all that he will never write a book that does not somehow find a way to shoehorn *The Whizzer* into its pages. That also goes for *The Fin*, his other favorite minor-league golden-age hero. *The Fin* was not a five-dollar bill, but an underwater hero who, like the Sub-Mariner, was the brainchild of Bill Everett. *The Fin* wasn't a mutant like the Sub-Mariner, and he wasn't out to destroy the surface world, but he did have a costume with a fin on the head.)

After World War II, superheroes fell out of fashion faster than a speeding bullet. Superheroes, despite having killed fifty times the actual number of enemy casualties in the funny pages, had done absolutely nothing for the real war effort, and weren't doing much for crime on the streets either. So instead of fantasies of good-types long-underwear vs. bad long-underwear types, the genre turned to stories involving more realistic criminals. They were dark, frank, seedy, cynical; real people doing real nasty things to other real people, just like the real world. Monsters underwent a change, too, with the new and exciting addition of radiation as a danger. The bomb infected even the classic monster types, and now monsters symbolized runaway science in a way undreamed of before, as cold-war paranoia was also added to the stew. Never before had monsters been created by a force that could also drop on your head at any moment. It was this atmosphere of fear-mongering that led critics of comic books to target the medium with a venom that is still almost impossible to believe. Of course, comic books were an incredibly easy target, and publishers capitulated with supplication that was just as hard to believe. But it wasn't just the monsters and the crooks that scared people; it was intelligence, and not the governmental kind. Crime and horror comics provided an ugly enough mirror of ourselves, but the third and last straw showed even more unpleasant truths than the crime and horror comics — and that straw was humor. The men and women who had their horizons broadened were now asking pointed questions about the society to which they had returned, questions that had only been sparingly asked before, questions about commodity fetishism and governing institutions and racial equality and the true nature of capitalism. And when you go asking questions about things like that, naturally, the people responsible for maintaining the illusion get very uncomfortable. The two people made most uncomfortable were Dr. Frederic Wertham of New York University, and Mr. John Goldwater, head of Archie Comics.

Wertham needs no introduction, as his name will forever live in infamy of the hearts of comic fans, although it should be noted that he was not, as many believe, the organizer of or a participant in the formation of the Comics Code Authority. He was merely a publicity-seeking headshrinker who saw a golden opportunity to lend credence to his questionable theories. His unscientific method of proving his hypotheses was roundly attacked in medical journals. But his book *Seduction of the Innocent* scared practically every mother in America. He was the originator of the ridiculous "Batman and Robin are homosexuals" theory, and had god-fearing moms everywhere convinced that comic books, particularly those specializing in crime and horror, were responsible for every perverse act, sexually or morally, that was being perpetrated by their sons and daughters. Although in later life he was to express regret at the methods he used, and the scorn with which he was treated by comics fans, there can be no denying that his was the hand that fanned the flames of comic book burnings. He claimed that it was never his intention to have comics censored; he merely wanted a ratings system like that of movies which kept more adult material out of the hands of impressionable youngsters. But if that was truly the case, it seems he wouldn't have gone about things the way he did. Still, he was hardly in a position to enforce his wishes, and while Wertham took care of the mobsters and the monsters, he left the humor out of the equation — an easy thing to forget. Cue John Goldwater. As Les Daniels hypothesizes in his seminal *COMIX: A History of Comic Books in America* (Bonanza Books, 1971):

> Voices still whisper in undertones that *Mad* might have been happier had [Harvey] Kurtzman and [Bill] Elder never spit in the face of a certain buck-toothed creature with a granite grin topped by carrot-colored crisscross marks. Such suggestions may mean nothing, but it is interesting to note that John Goldwater, the spearhead of the Comics Code Authority, was in his spare time the owner and manager of that perennial champion of tasteless conformity, Archie. Billed as "America's Typical Teenager," he has remained steadfastly behind the times. When *Mad* parodied his career as "Starchie," he was transplanted from the cardboard world of suburban one-upmanship into the Blackboard Jungle. After unreal adventures among Elder's famous metropolitan junkyards, Starchie was jailed for running a high school protection racket. Goldwater was presumably not amused. This much is clear: the Comics Code Authority which he headed inspired marketing pressure which drove certain comic books out of business. [For more on *Mad, see* Chapter Six]

What was this Comics Code Authority, and why do fans keep saying terrible things about it? The Comics Code Authority was like the Patriot Act of comic book history, a self-imposed cowardly capitulation by comic book publishers, a hysterical reaction to right-wingers determined to impose their moral standards and what they deemed acceptable on the public whether the public wanted it or not. The Comics Code was adapted on October 26, 1954, and proudly presented itself as one of the most oppressive, puritanical agents of censorship since the Hays Code. It was welcomed with open arms and closed minds. For all its bluster, it had no legal authority. Let's examine the standards of the Comics Code as originally adopted. The Code for Editorial Matter General Standards Part A reads:

1. Crimes will never be presented in such a way as to create sympathy for the criminal, to promote distrust of the forces of law and justice, or to inspire others with a desire to imitate criminals.
2. No comics shall explicitly present the unique details and methods of a crime.
3. Policemen, judges, government officials and respected institutions shall never be presented in such a way as to create disrespect for established authority.
4. If crime is depicted, it shall be as a sordid and unpleasant activity.
5. Criminals shall not be presented so as to be rendered glamorous or to occupy a position which creates a desire for emulation.
6. In every instance good shall triumph over evil and the criminal shall be punished for his misdeeds.
7. Scenes of excessive violence shall be prohibited. Scenes of brutal torture, excessive and unnecessary knife and gunplay, physical agony, and gory and gruesome crime shall be eliminated.
8. No unique or unusual methods of concealing weapons shall be shown.
9. Instances of law enforcement officers dying as a result of a criminal's activities should be discouraged.
10. The crime of kidnapping shall never be portrayed in any detail, nor shall any profit accrue to the abductor or kidnapper. The criminal or the kidnapper must be punished in every case.
11. The letters of the word "crime" on a comics magazine cover shall never be appreciably greater in dimension than the other words contained in the title. The word "crime" shall never appear alone on a cover.
12. Restraint in the use of the word "crime" in titles or subtitles shall be exercised.

General Standards Part B continues:

1. No comic magazine shall use the word "horror" or "terror" in its title.
2. All scenes of horror, excessive bloodshed, gory or gruesome crimes, depravity, lust,

sadism, and masochism shall not be permitted.
3. All lurid, unsavory, gruesome illustrations shall be eliminated.
4. Inclusion of stories dealing with evil shall be used or shall be published only where the intent is to illustrate a moral issue and in no case shall be presented alluringly nor so as to injure the sensibilities of the reader.
5. Scenes dealing with, or instruments associated with walking dead, torture, vampires and vampirism, ghouls, cannibalism and werewolfism are prohibited.

General Standards Part C says: "All elements or techniques not specifically mentioned herein, but which are contrary to the spirit and intent of the Code, and are considered violations of good taste or decency, shall be prohibited."

Rules governing dialogue were as follows:

1. Profanity, obscenity, smut, vulgarity, or words or symbols, which have acquired undesirable meanings, are forbidden.
2. Special precautions to avoid references to physical afflictions or deformities shall be taken.
3. Although slang and colloquialisms are acceptable, excessive use should be discouraged and wherever possible good grammar shall be employed.

About religion, the code says, "Ridicule or attack on any religious or racial group is never permissible."

Clothing was addressed thusly:

1. Nudity in any form is prohibited, as is indecent or undue exposure.
2. Suggestive or salacious illustration or suggestive posture is unacceptable.
3. All characters shall be depicted in dress reasonably acceptable to society.
4. Females shall be drawn realistically, without any exaggeration of physical qualities.

NOTE: It should be recognized that all prohibitions dealing with costume, dialogue, or artwork applies as specifically to the cover of a comics magazine as they do the contents.

Marriage and sex rules included:

1. Divorce shall not be treated humorously nor represented as desirable.
2. Illicit sex relations are neither to be hinted at nor portrayed. Violent love scenes as well as sexual abnormalities are unacceptable.
3. Respect for parents, the moral code, and for honorable behavior shall be fostered. A sympathetic understanding of the problems of love is not a license for morbid distortion.
4. The treatment of love/romance stories shall emphasize the value of the home and the sanctity of marriage.
5. Passion or romantic interest shall never be treated in such a way as to stimulate the lower or baser emotions.
6. Seduction and rape shall never be shown or suggested.
7. Sex perversion or any inference to same is strictly prohibited.

The code even spells out rules for advertising matter:

These regulations are applicable to all magazines published by members of the Comics Magazine Association of America, Inc. Good taste shall be the guiding principle in the acceptance of advertising.

1. Liquor and tobacco advertising is not acceptable.
2. Advertisements of sex or sex instruction books are unacceptable.
3. The sale of picture postcards, "pin-ups," "art studies," or any other reproduction of nude or semi-nude figures is prohibited.
4. Advertising for the sale of knives, concealable weapons, or realistic gun facsimiles is prohibited.
5. Advertising for the sale of fireworks is prohibited.
6. Advertising dealing with the sale of gambling equipment or printed matter dealing with gambling shall not be accepted.
7. Nudity with meretricious purpose and salacious postures shall not be permitted in the advertising of any product; clothed figures shall never be represented in such a way as to be offensive or contrary to good taste or morals.

8. To the best of his ability, each publisher shall ascertain that all statements made in advertisements conform to fact and avoid misinterpretation.
9. Advertisement of medical, health, or toiletry products of questionable nature are to be rejected. Advertisements for medical, health, or toiletry products endorsed by the American Medical Association, or the American Dental Association, shall be deemed acceptable if they conform to all other conditions of the Advertising Code.

This much was also clear: comics had about three choices: conform, die, or go underground. Some companies, like Timely and DC, conformed and survived, even though they too underwent some tense fiscal periods, although DC was in a better position because it always had Superman and Batman, who seem to thrive no matter what permutation is performed on their characters. Strangely, Timely's short-lived revivals in the 1950s of its most popular heroes, the Torch, Sub-Mariner and Captain America, did not capture the public's imagination they way they had a decade earlier. But perhaps this wasn't so strange: instead of fighting hideous monsters and brutal, inhuman Jap-a-Nazis, they turned to fighting plain old crooks and drab communists. EC died, except for one title, *Mad*, which would rise, phoenix-like, from the ashes, as a regular magazine. In doing so, it would not only become the first to attempt to circumvent the Comics Code (which in turn would inspire James Warren to do the same), it would raise the kids (who later were nurtured by Warren) that would become that underground. (Gaines also tried to do an end-run around the code with what he called picto-fiction magazines, like *Terror Illustrated*, which were more like pulps than black-and-white comic magazines, in that they featured text stories with spot illustrations. Although they delivered some fine stories, with art by EC greats, they failed to catch on because of the format.) In turn, the underground publications would use the code's restrictions as a to-do list, and would not only have an effect on what was permitted in mainstream comics (even the black-and-whites), but would also have far-reaching effects on creators' rights and work-for-hire policies.

The immediate result of the Comics Code Authority, besides the death of imagination for a time in mainstream comics, was that all of those comics that wished to remain in the mainstream and achieve coveted newsstand space and nationwide distribution now had to carry a small white postage stamp–shaped seal in the upper right-hand corner of the cover that read "Approved by the Comics Code Authority." Comics that did not were subject to immediate refusal from the distributor on. It simply didn't pay to put out a comic that didn't feature that stamp — unless, of course, you were Dell Comics. Dell Comics was the pre-eminent purveyor of funny animal fables, its main stars being the Disney characters. They were naturally beyond reproach, Disney being as much a paragon of tasteless conformity as Archie. Archie Comics never produced anything but Andy Hardy/Henry Aldritch–type zany and safe teenage goings-on. At least Dell contributed, in the guise of Donald Duck as written and drawn by Carl Barks, some of the finest adventure stories, bar none, that the medium has ever seen.

EC did try at first to get with the program. The new direction of books like *Piracy, Valor, Incredible Science Fiction*, and *Aces High* had replaced the new trend of classic titles, but the magic was gone. Fiction House and Quality characters like Sheena and Blackhawk, robbed of their sex appeal and sophisticated storytelling, withered, and although some survived through virtue of being bought by DC, their magic too disappeared, and their original parent companies went under. Fawcett went under, too, but ironically, not because of the Comics Code Authority. Obviously, the mighty Captain Marvel and family would have had absolutely no problem whizzing past the code guidelines, but DC, in one of the supreme moments of guile and hypocrisy in the history of the comics, sued Fawcett for The Big Red Cheese's supposed copyright infringement of Superman, when in fact its only crime was to sell more issues than the Man of Steel. Conveniently overlooked was DC's copyright infringement of Fawcett; DC's Superboy, Supergirl, etc., being direct rip-offs of the Marvel family — Captain Marvel, Jr., Mary Marvel, and even Hoppy the Marvel Bunny, a forerunner of Krypto the Super-Dog. DC put Fawcett and the Captain out of business — and then turned around and bought the rights to the character. DC even had the nerve to have Superman introduce the character on the cover of his comeback title in the '70s, which was titled *Shazam!* (Although DC had copyrighted the contents of the stories, somehow it didn't actually copyright the name "Captain Marvel" itself, and Marvel naturally snagged it — an ignoble fate for perhaps the purest comic book character of all time but not nearly as ignoble as the way DC has butchered the character since then).

DC had no problems submitting to the code, because its bread and butter, even in the relatively superhero-less Fifties, was still Superman, Batman, and Wonder Woman, and all DC had to do was make sure that Batman and Robin hung out with girls more and Wonder Woman hung out with girls less. With Timely, it was a bit more problematic — its whole approach to comics was a fiery, pulpy, no-holds-barred intensity. DC fantasy tended to fall into two categories: either hard science science fiction stories, restrained and cerebral, or endearingly goofy cases like "The Space Cabbie," "The Atomic Knights," or the "Bizarro" Superman. But some defied description, like The Creature Commandos (*Weird War Tales*), which featured a man-made monster, a vampire, a werewolf, a medusa and G.I. Robot as a crack team of operatives in World War II. Knowingly or unknowingly, this borrows the premise of 1942's *The Mad Monster*, in which mad scientist par excellence George Zucco hopes to create a werewolf army for the United States to take on the Nazis. Like the Culhanes of Cornfield County, they weren't silly, merely foolish.

Perhaps DC is not usually thought of as a monster haven, but that historically low-key approach (altered forever with the introduction of its Vertigo mature line) has produced healthy competition for Marvel. DC produced titles like *House of Mystery, Tales of the Unexpected* (which became simply *The Unexpected* with no. 105, and lasted for over a hundred more issues), *Tales of Ghost Castle, Sword of Sorcery, The Phantom Stranger, Stalker* (a demonic sword and sorcery hero by Wallace Wood and Steve Ditko), *Beowulf, Claw the Unconquered, House of Secrets, (Do You Believe in) Ghosts, Time Warp, Doorway to Nightmare, Strange Adventures, Weird War Tales, Weird Mystery Tales, Weird Western Tales,* and *Weird Worlds* (featuring Edgar Rice Burroughs heroes like John Carter of Mars, Carson Napier of Venus and David Innes of Pellucidar at the Earth's Core). Other titles included *Secrets of Haunted House, Secrets of Sinister House (The Sinister House of Secret Love!), Forbidden Tales of Dark Mansion, Doorway to Nightmare, Mystery in Space, The Witching Hour, Swamp Thing,* Jack Kirby's legendary Fourth World series' *The New Gods, The Forever People, Mister Miracle* and his insane makeover of *Jimmy Olsen* (including a miniature world inhabited by classic monster types, and a Don Rickles clone), not to mention *Black Magic*, which reprinted Simon and Kirby's classic Crestwood horrors from the '50s. "King" Kirby, who had relocated (or returned, depending on how you look at it) to DC, also created other classic series in *The Demon*, which featured more Kirby takes on classic monsters and myths, and *Kamandi, The*

Last Boy on Earth, Kirby's version of *Planet of the Apes*.

Although Timely had plenty of experience with monsters, it didn't actually publish a full-fledged horror title until 1949 (*Amazing Mysteries* no. 32). That was the first issue, but in the time-honored comic book and magazine tradition, the numbering was continued from the comic book formerly known as *Sub-Mariner*; all of a sudden, one was, and the other wasn't. The shift in focus from superheroes to horror was just as abrupt across the entire Timely line; even the venerable *Captain America Comics* became *Captain America's Weird Tales* for two issues before it finally bit the dust altogether. The title that had laughed itself all the way to the bank as *Joker Comics* with 42 issues became *Adventures Into Terror* with the next. *Marvel Mystery Comics* turned into *Marvel Tales* after 92 issues, although the replacement name is rather less exciting, so it's hard to see why. *Teen* grew up overnight into *Journey Into Unknown Worlds*. The year 1951 brought even more changes and more fun new titles; *Marvel Boy* became *Astonishing*, along with three actual number ones: *Mystic, Space Squadron,* and the seminal *Strange Tales*. All of these titles carried into the next year, which added *Adventures Into Weird Worlds, Mystery Tales, Spellbound,* and *Uncanny Tales*, plus another title that would survive into the new Marvel age, *Journey Into Mystery*. Titles like the previous, and *Strange Tales*, which had risen out of the ashes of the superhero or had replaced him or her entirely, would ironically turn into showcases for the new breed of Marvel superhero. Before it became Marvel, however, Timely itself changed names again, this time into Atlas, and it was as Atlas that it would (just barely) survive the 1950s.

Meanwhile, 1953 and 1954 rung in with only two new titles added to the existing lineup, *Menace* and *Speed Carter, Spaceman*. These were the golden years of Atlas Horror, Fantasy and Science Fiction in the hearts and minds of many historians and fans; unfortunately, they were also the golden years of the comic book witch hunt and comics code, and Atlas output suffered accordingly. Still, with EC and all those other publishers out of the way, Atlas should have pretty much had the field all to itself, and for a couple of years, it did. This, in turn, was what nearly did the company in. In an echo of the technique that would both characterize and deep-six the black-and-white line twenty years later, Atlas flooded the market. Other Atlas Horror/Sci-Fi/Suspense titles included *Suspense, Venus, Space Worlds, Adventures Into Mystery, World of Fantasy, Strange Stories of Suspense, Strange Tales of the Unusual, World of Suspense, World of Mystery, The Yellow Claw, Strange Worlds,* and *Amazing Adventures,* which became *Amazing Adult Fantasy,* which became *Amazing Fantasy*. But the now second-rate quality of the stories began to catch up with them, and the overwhelming mediocrity caused the readership to stay away in droves. The company fell, and nearly didn't get up; it canceled all but a very few titles and fired all but one employee: Stan Lee, Goodman's nephew. But the Marvel name and its own real superhero revival were still a few years away, and Atlas needed to survive. Stan was stuck, but then conceptual (for the comics) and financial (for the company) salvation, for the time being, came in the form of a four-hundred-foot tall Japanese lizard.

Godzilla was certainly not the first giant movie monster to ravage civilization, but the character caught the worldwide public's fancy in a way that dwarfed even Godzilla. Lee noted the enthusiasm, and also found a loophole in the code: although it forbade man-made and man-like monsters of every type, it said absolutely nothing about dinosaurs or similar oversized beasts. And so Stan and a small art staff composed of Jack Kirby, Steve Ditko, Don Heck and Paul Reinman set about re-making the few fantasy titles that had survived like *Strange Tales* and *Tales of Suspense* showcases for giant monsters of every conceivable origin, sporting some of the most wonderful names that have ever passed into comic book legend.

By far, the most legendary is Fin Fang Foom, a four hundred foot tall Chinese lizard (or dragon, if you will) who is awakened from a centuries-long slumber. But instead of stomping Taiwan, he does the right thing and stomps a bunch of godless Commies. The legion of giant monsters included Groot, the Tree-Monster from Planet X who is defeated by termites. There was the Glop, Taboo ("The Thing from the Murky Swamp!"), Mummex, Gomdullah, Grottu ("King of the Insects!"), Grog, the Blip, X ("The Thing That Lived!"), Goom and Googam, son of Goom, Gorgolla ("The Living Gargoyle!"), Vandoom ("The Man Who Made a Creature!"), Moomba, Bombu, Kraa ("The Unhuman!"), Gargantus, Zzutak ("The Thing That Shouldn't Exist!"), Orrgo, Klagg, Monstrollo, Oog, Sporr ("The Thing That Could Not Die!"), Gorgilla, Krang, Zog, Titan ("The Amphibian from Atlantis!"), Gigantus ("The Monster That Walked Like a Man!"), Monstro, and last but not least, a huge hairy booger called the Hulk. He actually made a return appearance, but by the time he did so, Marvel's other Hulk had come on the scene, so Marvel renamed him the Titan.

As might be expected, the well for these literally titanic tales would soon run dry too, but not before two very important things happened. The giant monsters not only put the company back on solid financial ground, but gave it the keys to the secret of Marvel's eventual mega-success: the ability to produce exciting material within the code's restrictions, and not-so-super heroes. More often than not, the leading male in the giant monster tales was a guy with a problem, most often being not being accepted by his peers for a variety of reasons. By story's end, he has defeated the menace and redeemed himself. Marvel made this the basis for its whole line of superheroes — they weren't handsome alien supermen or handsome millionaire playboys; they were nerdy teenagers who were bitten by radioactive spiders, or nerdy scientists who were changed into monsters, or crippled doctors who changed into Norse gods. This decidedly different approach to the long-underwear boys made Marvel a mint, and, like a couple of decades earlier, the change was pretty abrupt — although this time it worked in reverse: now the superheroes were, and horror wasn't. The trademark giant Kirby monster did make one final grand gesture, appearing on the cover of the first issue of *The Fantastic Four* (whose lineup contained a smaller Kirby monster, the Thing), as if to pass the "torch" on to a new generation (and to make sure readers knew that it was a comic book from the same company). The nerdy scientist who changed into a monster was the Hulk, a gamma-ray variation on the Jeckyll/Hyde theme where the monster looks like Frankenstein and speaks like Johnny Weissmuller's Tarzan, and not coincidentally, DC's Frankensteinian Solomon Grundy. The Hulk went on to become one of Marvel's most popular superheroes, and even had his own black-and-white magazine for a while.

The incredible success of Marvel has been well documented, and that success gave them the clout and public support needed to do something none of the other majors had even attempted — they defied their code-conspirators and published three comics without the Code seal of approval, sending shockwaves throughout the industry and fandom as well. But it wasn't merely a case of defiance on Stan's part — he had actually been approached by the United States department of Health, Education and Welfare to do a drug abuse story; they knew how many people would be reached through the pages of Marvel. And so Marvel published numbers 96, 97 and 98 of *The*

Fantasy Masterpieces no. 2 (Marvel) — The immortal Fin Fang Foom is easily the most popular Marvel giant monster of all time — his name is legend (courtesy Marvel Entertainment, Inc.).

Amazing Spider-Man, the first mainstream four-color superhero comics not to bear the Code seal since that organization's inception.

As a result, the Code began to undergo periodic revisions. The first came in 1971 — "narcotics or drug addiction" were once again permitted to be depicted, as long as they were depicted as "a vicious habit." Also making a welcome return to color comics were "vampires, werewolves and ghouls, when handled in the 'classic' tradition, such as *Frankenstein*, *Dracula*, and other high-caliber literary works" that were "read in schools around the world." In another instance, in 1989, the ban on homosexuality was reversed to allow non-stereotypical portrayals of gays and lesbians. In 2001, Marvel withdrew from the association completely and established its own ratings system. As of 2008, DC and Archie were the only major comic publishers still submitting books for code approval, and not even all of DC's books, at that.

Was the implementation of the Comics Code Authority successful? In terms of rival publishers allegedly putting certain targeted companies out of business, of course it was. Did it have a profound effect on how comics were both produced and perceived? Again, yes. But thankfully, times change, and by the time that Marvel forced the issue, the Code was already archaic, and afterwards, although still nominally in power, the Comics Code Authority was well and truly shown up for the paper tiger it had always been. Of course, *Mad* had been figuratively (and literally, at one point) giving them the finger for years, and as for vampires, werewolves and ghouls, well — James Warren never had any use for the Code, either.

James Warren originally wanted to be Hugh Hefner. The Philadelphia-born Warren's first pro publishing venture was a men's magazine modeled on *Playboy* entitled *After Hours* (*see* Chapter Six). Unfortunately for Warren, it was no *Playboy*, and lasted only four issues, but that fourth and last issue contained the seed from which Warren's entire publishing empire would grow, and the seed was horror. Two articles by science-fiction fan supreme and sometime literary agent Forrest J Ackerman (he doesn't punctuate the middle initial), "Confessions of a Science-Fiction Addict" and "Scream-o-Scope Is Here!" provided the inspiration for the unexpected smash success *Famous Monsters of Filmland*, which subverted the minds of almost as many impressionable youngsters and outraged as many parents and teachers as EC had and *Mad* still did. (For more on *Famous Monsters*, see the following chapter). By the mid-'60s, the world was in the midst of a full-blown monster movie revival; everybody, it seemed, had gone monster mad. Publishers wanted to get some of those monsters down off the screen and back on to the comic book pages. But there was still the matter of the code, so like Gaines before him and Stan Lee after, Warren said to hell with the code. He was a lifelong comics fan, and like so many others, had loved EC. He decided that the time was right to revive the EC brand of illustrated horror, but since he still couldn't do that in a newsstand comic, he took the Gaines route, and made it a black-and-white comics magazine instead. *Creepy* was born, was another smash, and spawned not only companion publications, but invented a whole new form of expression for horror comics. And that was the most important thing — horror comics were finally back from the grave. Utilizing the enormous writing talents of Archie Goodwin and the cream of the EC bullpen, Warren unleashed a torrent of zombies, ghouls, werewolves, vampires, and other assorted maniacs, whose like had not been seen for ten years, on an unsuspecting and grateful public.

Marvel took note of Warren's success with monsters in black-and-white, and since the code had liberalized its guidelines in the face of Spider-Man's defiance, one of Stan Lee's first moves was to return monsters to the four-color pages. This time around, however, monsters and horror were not the sole property of anthology titles. In the tradition of the great Universal and Hammer monsters (not to mention the Marvel tradition of continuing characters), all of the classic monster types were given their own series, plus all sorts of new variations on those themes, not to mention the constant creature parade in the pages of *Conan the Barbarian* and the other books.

Although *Marvel Spotlight* no. 2, featuring the first "Werewolf by Night" story was actually on the stands two months before *Tomb of Dracula,* the comic starring the Lord of the Vampires was intended from the beginning to be Marvel's flagship horror title. (It was originally planned as a black-and-white; *see* Chapter Three for more details). No tryout strips in already-existing anthology titles to test fan reaction, no guest shots in *Spider-Man* or *Daredevil* to test the waters. Dracula got his own title right off the—bat, with the first issue dated April 1972. The series lasted until 1979, and the fact that this was a pet title of Lee's is evidenced by the top-rank artist selected for the launch (Gene Colan, by his own admission working on his dream job), who was retained for the entire 70-issue run. It took a few issues to settle on a writer (Marv Wolfman) and inker (Tom Palmer), but once teamed with Colan, they, too, stayed till the very end. After re-establishing Drac's popularity, though, it seemed as though you couldn't pick up a Marvel comic that didn't feature Dracula. He started popping up in superhero titles and made appearances in Marvel's other monster comics. He would finally get a black-and-white title as well (*see* Chapter Six). The Dracula family got its Mary Marvel/Vampirella in the lithe form of Lilith, Dracula's daughter, who made her first appearance in *Giant-Size Chillers* no. 1 (which changed its title to the more commercial *Giant-Size Dracula* with no. 2). Surprisingly, Marvel didn't create a son for Dracula, and Atlas/Seaboard hopped on that one. Blade, the Vampire Slayer was introduced in *Tomb of Dracula* no. 10, and proved such a popular adversary that he not only remained for the duration of that series, but headlined a couple of his own, and eventually made the leap to the big screen in the person of Wesley Snipes, who already has three Blade films under his belt. Dracula popped up at Warren in a number of stories (both solo and as a guest) and a short series or two, and though some of these were very well done (i.e. "The Coffin of Dracula" by Archie Goodwin and Reed Crandall, *Creepy* 8 and 9), somehow Dracula was never really able to make it at Warren.

The creature created by the fertile mind of Doctor Frankenstein (or Mary Shelley, if you will) must tie with Dracula as fiction's most popular and enduring fiend, and has, like Dracula, become an iconic figure. Their longevity and popularity, like Tarzan's, has been in great part perpetuated by their cinematic incarnations, which can differ wildly from their source novels. Many of their cinematic permutations improve on those sources simply by moving. Obviously, both *Frankenstein, or the Modern Prometheus* and *Dracula* contain some brilliant ideas and scenes, and both are fairly scary, but *Frankenstein* in particular is a turgid, plodding piece, whose best ideas were much more eloquently explored by films. Sometimes they were even more eloquently expressed in a comic book, which brings us to Marvel's *The Monster of Frankenstein* (Retitled *The Frankenstein Monster* with issue no. 7). The art in the first six issues was handled by one of Marvel's finest monster go-to guys, Mike Ploog, who brought the monster to vivid

Opposite: Werewolf by Night no. 15 (Marvel) — Mike Ploog, one of Marvel's top horror talents in the '70s, provides this classic take on two of Marvel's top horror stars of the '70s (courtesy Marvel Entertainment, Inc.).

Introduction

illustrated life. The first four issues adapted Shelley's novel, and performed the near-impossible task of making the thing readable. Frankenstein's monster had his own black-and-white strip, too, in *Monsters Unleashed* (*see* Chapter Two). The color title had its share of notable artistic contributors besides Ploog, including Neal Adams and John Buscema (who also did the black-and-white version), but only stuck around for seventeen issues.

The Man-Thing took the opposite tack from most of the other Marvel monsters — while most of the others got their start in four-color titles and were then pressed into double-shifts on the magazine line, the Man-Thing got his start in a black-and-white, the first issue of *Savage Tales* (*see* Chapter Five). The story was simply entitled "Man-Thing," with a script by Roy Thomas and Gerry Conway from an idea by Stan Lee, and, as always, with superlative art by Gray Morrow. Actually, the script is more Conway than Thomas, as Roy recounted in an interview for *Back Issue* no. 6:

> Stan, back when we decided to do *Savage Tales*, decided he wanted one of the features in there to be what he called "Man-Thing." He had a couple of sentences: "a guy is cooking up chemicals in a swamp. He falls in, and comes out as this monster." That was about it. I took it and fleshed it out into a two-page plot. I didn't want to write it, so I gave it to Gerry Conway, who I assume wrote a script in advance for Gray Morrow. By the time the story was done, it kind of had three writers, in a sense.

Actually, four, if you want to get technical and include Harvey Kurtzman. Stan's two-sentence idea was exactly what happened in a hilarious parody of the Heap ("Heap!") in an early *Mad*, minus the laughs. Marvel got a lot of mileage out of this story. Not only was it reprinted (with color added) to launch Man-Thing's first solo series (in *Fear* no. 10), but then again only about a year later to re-launch Man-Thing's black-and-white career in *Monsters Unleashed* no. 3. Man-Thing has also gone Hollywood, in one of the worst comic book movies ever, bar none, and this is taking into account all the bad Marvel TV-movies of the '70s. For more info on Marvel's carrot-nosed stalker of the swamps, see the *Monsters Unleashed* section of Chapter Two. For a comic book that explores the theme to its fullest and beyond, see DC's *Swamp Thing* and, for that matter, the original Heap (see below).

The Living Mummy was featured in *Supernatural Thrillers*, Issues no. 5 and 7 through 15. *Supernatural Thrillers* had previously been an anthology title showcasing the works of great authors like Theodore Sturgeon, H.G. Wells and Robert E. Howard (an adaptation of his "Valley of the Worm" by Roy Thomas and Gil Kane appeared in issue no. 3 and was later reprinted in *The Savage Sword of Conan*). Gil Kane also supplied most of the covers for the Living Mummy series, which achieved the heretofore-unimaginable feat of making a shambling 3,000 year-old reanimated corpse a dynamic monster of action! The series ended with the cancellation of the title. Warren had a Mummy series, too, in *Eerie* ("The Mummy Walks"). The twist to Warren's was that instead of the more typical and traditional life-in-death cursed prince or warrior, the mind of a modern man, Jerome Curry, was trapped inside the walking corpse. Although fairly well done, it didn't last as long as the Living Mummy, despite a couple of great covers by Sanjulian on which the Mummy looks just like Karloff — covers that certainly wouldn't have been out of place on *Famous Monsters*. The collage cover to *Eerie no. 50* also featured Sanjulian renditions of Paul Naschy's werewolf "El Hombre Lobo" and Christopher Lee as Dracula — not that any of them looked like the characters in the strips themselves, but it sure was a cool cover.

As already mentioned, the Werewolf by Night began howling in *Marvel Spotlight* no. 2 (December 1971), but soon graduated to his own title. The first cover for *Marvel Spotlight*

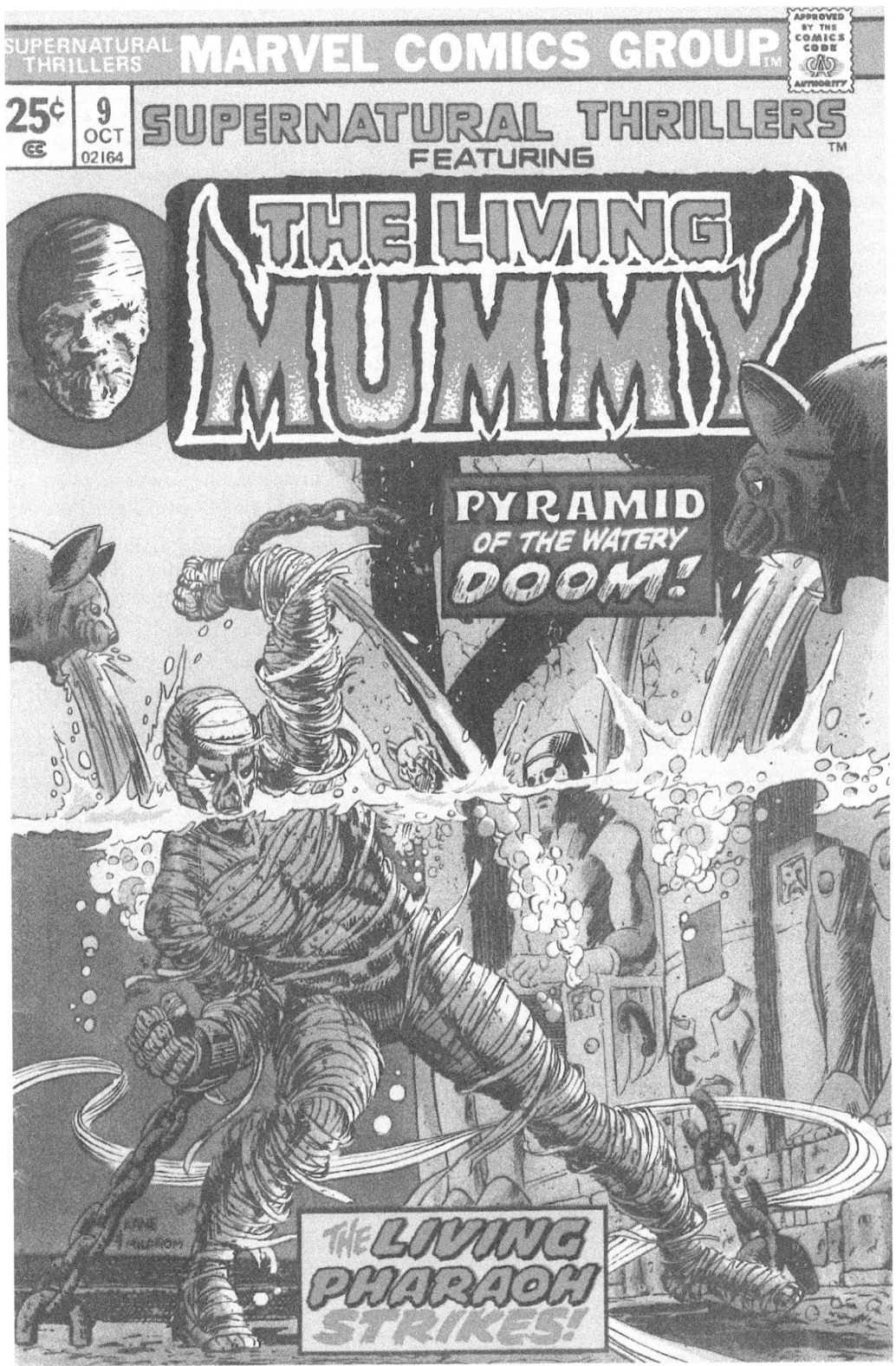

Supernatural Thrillers no. 9 (Marvel) The Living Mummy — Man of Action! Gil Kane does the cover honors for *Supernatural Thrillers* no. 9 (courtesy Marvel Entertainment, Inc.).

was by Neal Adams (who had also done *Tomb of Dracula* no. 1's cover), but the artist who really breathed un-life into the strip was, once again, Mike Ploog. Ploog was a former employee and protégé of Will Eisner ("The Spirit"), who used Eisner's expressive technique as a springboard for his own unique style. Ploog's superb cover for *Werewolf by Night* no. 15 is reproduced in this volume, a stunning piece that not only showcases that unique style, but also fondly recalls and somewhat pays tribute to Frazetta's classic "Duel of the Monsters" cover for *Creepy* no. 7. As in so many other comic book cases, the art redeemed the stories which, while generally entertaining, left no lycanthropic cliché unturned, although they did manage one neat little joke — the unfortunate young man who became a wolf when the moon was full and bright was, perhaps, pre-destined by his name — Jack Russell! But if that makes you wince, consider the name of the protagonist of Warren's competing werewolf series: Arthur Lemming. The Warren Werewolf series also appeared in *Eerie*; entitled "Curse of the Werewolf," it was neither any relation to the Hammer film of the same name starring the late, great Oliver Reed nor any competition to the Marvel series, Ploog's superior artistry lifting the Marvel man-beast head-and-shoulders above its counterpart.

"It! The Living Colossus" was an odd choice for a series. Werewolves and vampires are sexy, and at least have enough emotional upheaval to motivate a series of stories or films, but a huge stone behemoth? This kind of giant monster was great for a one-off story in the Atlas phase but not a continuing feature. One of the globs that Marvel threw at the wall that didn't stick, it didn't even last long enough for readers to get tired of it, and even a titanic tussle with Fin Fang Foom didn't help; It ate up space for a mere four issues (21–24) of *Astonishing Tales*, the new and improved version of the original *Astonishing*.

Another odd series star was "The Golem," a four-issue *Strange Tales* filler (174–177). The silent films starring Paul Wegener are classics; on the other hand, they are regarded so mostly by hardcore horror fans and/or historians. The four-color fiends were victims of the same kind of thinking that characterized (and ultimately killed) the black-and-white line: flood the market. Once the code restrictions were relaxed, anything remotely horrible got page space. Most any publisher will pick quantity over quality any day. As far as The Golem goes, readers are advised to see the movies, but forget the comic book.

"The Ghost Rider" was originally the moniker of a 1950s western hero published by Magazine Enterprises, who affected a beautifully simplistic costume: an all-white, luminous outfit, including Stetson, boots and mask. His persona was from beyond the grave, but he confronted his earthly foes with earthly six-guns. The character, inspired by both the Vaughn Monroe song "Ghost Riders in the Sky" and the Disney film *The Headless Horseman*, was extremely popular, appearing not only in fourteen issues of his own title, but *Best of the West, Black Phantom,* and *Great Western* (all of which, including his own book, were issued under the umbrella title of *A-1 Comics*). He also appeared in guest strips in *Bobby Benson Comics, Tim Holt Comics*, and *Red Mask* (the comic formerly known as *Tim Holt*). A number of original Ghost Rider covers were masterfully rendered by Frank Frazetta, thereby insuring the character's place in popular iconography. The Ghost Rider was eventually admitted into Marvel's stable of cowboy heroes that included the Rawhide Kid, Kid Colt-Outlaw, and their original saddle pal, the Two-Gun Kid, and immediately distinguished himself, not only with his history and costume, but by the fact that he wasn't called 'Kid' something-or-other and that Marvel got his original artist, "Darlin'" Dick Ayers, to delineate his new adventures.

Marvel, though, wasn't about to let a great name like "The Ghost Rider" be wasted on a character that few people were going to read, so they gave it a patented Marvel makeover, and the former Avenging Phantom of the Plains traded in his great white stallion for an iron horse — a motorcycle. Gone, too, was the white mask and outfit that simply glowed in the dark — as a matter of fact, gone was his whole face, replaced by a flaming skull (no doubt inspired by the Flaming Skulls biker gang, who never sued). Marvel would publish both the western and modern versions of the character for a while, but the Masked Rider of the Plains was soon eclipsed by his mod counterpart, and faded into oblivion. The original Ghost Rider is periodically reprinted under various titles like *Night Rider* and *The Haunted Horseman*, but it seems as though he is cursed to share the same fate as the original Captain Marvel, relinquishing the name they made famous. The modern version got off to a great start, with Gary Friedrich and Mike Ploog shepherding him through some wild adventures, but suffered the all-too typical fate of many a Marvel hero in becoming just another number in the production line, falling victim to increasingly silly villains and lackluster creative teams. The Ghost Rider was most decidedly a second-string hero the first time around, although he managed to hang on for ten years and 81 issues, finally expiring when the demon left Johnny Blaze, G.R.'s original alter ego. But he came back in a big way in the 1990s, with another alter ego, as one of Marvel's new grim and gritty psycho heroes inspired by the Punisher; his legally questionable methods of extracting justice from a situation include beatings with a flaming chain, sucking out a criminal's soul with his Penance Stare, and exclaiming "Feel the pain!" This brings to mind the comments made about the first James Bond film, *Dr. No*, by Thomas Wiseman in Britain's *Sunday Express*, who opined that "Bond's methods and morals were indistinguishable from the villains.'" That has become even truer in an increasingly ruthless world. Still, anyone with a flaming skull for a head can't be all bad, and the character was the subject of a big-budget movie in 2007, which featured Nicholas Cage as Johnny Blaze. The movie even manages to work the western Ghost Rider into the tale, and one of the film's highlights is a scene where both Ghost Riders speed side by side across the plains, to the tune of Vaughn Monroe's signature song.

Creatures on the Loose was the color comic that Marvel's sword and sorcery heroes gravitated towards, or graduated from; the first King Kull was printed there (no. 10), and it was also home to Gullivar Jones — Warrior of Mars and Thongor, Warrior of Lost Lemuria. Gullivar Jones was the John Carter–like hero of *Gullivar of Mars* by Edwin L. Arnold, which was the sole novel of Gullivar's extra-terrestrial exploits. Thongor was a Conan rip-off by L. Sprague DeCamp's Conan collaborator Lin Carter (for much more on Conan, DeCamp and Carter, *see* Chapter Four). For more on Gullivar, see the *Monsters Unleashed* section of Chapter Two, although note that all six of Gullivar Jones's adventures in *Creatures on the Loose* had gorgeous covers; five by Gil Kane and one by Jim Steranko, who also did the next one, the introductory cover for the Thongor series. Actually, you'd be hard pressed to find a Marvel comic in this time period that didn't, at one point or another have a series of covers and/or interior art by Kane. Gil Kane, who fused the raw energy and dynamism of Jack Kirby with the grace and Adonis-like musculature of Burne Hogarth, is one of the true masters of the form, and his output for Marvel is even more staggering when one considers he was working for himself and everybody else, too. As at ease with crowded battle scenes as he was with more intimate set pieces, his signature trick was what fans will forever fondly remember as the "up the nose" shot, a dramatic angle he used countless times; fans would look for it and be upset if they didn't see at least one "up the nose" shot. The interior art for the Gullivar strip was bolstered not only by the hand of Kane and a battalion of inkers, but that of former master Superman artist Wayne Boring and Gray Morrow as well. Kane also worked on Marvel's version of that other Martian warrior, or in this case warlord, *John Carter, Warlord of Mars*, which took its title from Burroughs's third Martian novel. It ran a decent 28 issues, and featured not only Kane's dynamic yet faithful interpretation of Burroughs's monsters and heroes, but also some fine work by Rudy Nebres.

After inspiring all of those giant Marvel monsters, twenty years later Godzilla himself would join Marvel's four-color lineup in 1977; around the same time, he would also hit the Top 40 charts as the subject of a Blue Oyster Cult song. The song, a good-time heavy metal stomp, lasted for only a few minutes and was very cool; the comic lasted for twenty-four issues and wasn't. Rather than exploiting the elements that made Godzilla popular in the first place, Marvel instead tried to shoehorn the creature into its universe, bringing in characters like the Fantastic Four and S.H.I.E.L.D. The series was written by Doug Moench and drawn by veteran *Incredible Hulk* artist Herb Trimpe, and caught on with the younger kids at whom it was aimed, although it was neither's best work. Trimpe is an artist of no fixed style who needs a strong inker, and when coupled with someone like John Severin, as he was on a memorable Hulk run, he was capable of very good work. But he didn't have the same luck with his stint on Godzilla. Although the series proved popular enough, the decision to cancel it was made when Toho Studios asked for a substantial raise in Godzilla's licensing fees, and Marvel didn't feel the extra investment was worth it.

Not all of Marvel's monsters would get their own series right away. Morbius, The Living Vampire, began his career as a Spider-Man villain, and was actually the first vampire to appear in comic books with the relaxation of the code restrictions. His enthusiastic reception by the fans cemented Marvel's decision to go right to the source and do *Tomb of Dracula*. Morbius was introduced in the memorable story arc in which Doctor Kurt Connors (a.k.a. the Lizard), in trying to cure Spider-man, gave poor Peter six arms instead, making him a very real spider-man, which naturally ratcheted up the strip's already considerable quotient of angst. Into the middle of all this mess flaps Morbius, and it is he who ultimately returns Peter to normal by putting the bite on him, relieving him of the extra appendages, but curiously, not turning him into a vampire-man. Only in the comics: a guy who's been bitten by a radioactive spider seeks help from a guy who can turn himself into a lizard, and gets returned to "normal" by a vampire bite. Morbius graduated to a starring role in *Vampire Tales* (see Chapter Three), and also replaced Man-Thing as the lead feature in *(Adventures into) Fear* for eleven issues (no.'s 20–31) when the Man-Thing got his own title.

Not all of Marvel's monsters were successes. For every Dracula there was a Mordred the Mystic or Skull the Slayer or Bloodstone; for every Ghost Rider, there was a Son of Satan or Tigra the Were-Woman or Man-Wolf. The last was the astronaut son of *Daily Bugle* editor J. Jonah Jameson who went into space a man and came back a werewolf. The aforementioned titles and monsters were by no means all—*Tower of Shadows, Crypt of Shadows, Chamber of Chills, Dead of Night, Where Creatures Roam, Monsters on the Prowl, Creatures on the Loose, Where Monsters Dwell, Weird Wonder Tales, Fantasy Masterpieces, Worlds Unknown, Chamber of Darkness, Tomb of Darkness, Vault of Evil,* and a re-launch of *Journey Into Mystery* helped the now mighty Marvel to dwarf the output of its golden Atlas phase in quantity, if not always in quality.

Charlton Comics produced some very

underrated horror comics, both pre- and post-code. Pre-code, it served up the gore with the best of them, and post-code became as watered down as the rest of them. The best thing about them in any era was Steve Ditko, the artist who had breathed life into Spider-Man and Dr. Strange, and who, along with Jack Kirby, had been the backbone of the Atlas fantasy line. He became the undisputed top dog at Charlton, which might have paid him less than Marvel, but gave him complete creative freedom, which was what he craved (and would take to the hilt independently with enigmatic, dogmatic and controversial works like *Mister A* and *Avenging World*). He even worked on Charlton's monster movie adaptations like *Gorgo, Reptilicus* (whose name was changed to *Reptisaurus*), and *The Return of Konga/Konga's Revenge. Monster Hunters, Scary Tales, Haunted (Baron Weirwulf's Haunted Library), The Many Ghosts of Doctor Graves, Ghost Manor, Ghostly Haunts, Haunted Love, Ghostly Tales, Midnight Tales,* and *Tales of the Mysterious Traveler* featured not only the talents of old pro Ditko, but (at the time) rising young stars like Mike Zeck, Joe Staton and John Byrne, all of whom used Charlton's creative freedom to further their talents and gain valuable experience.

Skywald's legend and reputation was built on its black-and-white horror magazines, and deservedly so, but it also published a (very) short-lived line of color comic books which are overlooked by most fans and collectors — and deservedly so. The color line proved to be too much of a drain on Skywald's budget, and was quickly discontinued, but frankly, if most of the comics had been any good, they might not have been such a drain. The only one with any potential was, of course, a horror comic, Skywald's resurrection of comics' original swamp monster, *The Heap* (although it must be noted that, like some of DC's and Marvel's resurrected superhero names, this was not the original Heap). The creative team on the revived *Heap* — Robert Kanigher, Tom Sutton and Jack Abel — on the lead (and only Skywald color) Heap story, "Shadows of Satan" was solid, as was the story, but this turned out to be the only issue. The Heap had already appeared in Skywald's black-and-whites, and would return there for quite a few more adventures (see succeeding chapters for more info on both Skywald and their various magazines).

The original Heap was one of comics greatest monsters, and also turned into one of its most complex characters. The Heap was introduced, as noted, in the "Sky Wolf" strip in *Air Fighters* comics, and soon eclipsed the series' actual star to such an extent that he was given his own strip. The Heap was a World War I German ace, who, when shot down, crashed in a swamp. But the crash doesn't kill him; the elements of the swamp mix with his own chemistry to create a thing. A thing that could only be called — a Heap! The smash-hit character's mythology then began to grow dense indeed, with The Heap taking on Christ-like connotations as the series progressed. Clearly, not your garden-variety swamp monster, and modern comics fans that are awed by DC's "adult" version of its Swamp Thing really ought to check out the inspiration.

But like Atlas/Seaboard a few years later, the rest of the color Skywald comic books were derivative with a capital "D": *Jungle Adventures* featured the requisite Tarzan rip-off, Zandar, along with JoJo, King of the Congo, Taanda the Jungle Princess, and the Blue Gorilla. Skywald also published not one, but two separate comic books based on the characters from the film *Butch Cassidy and the Sundance Kid*, each in his own title (*Butch Cassidy* and *Guns of Death Featuring the Sundance Kid*), but even if it had only been one, the results would have been the same. More owlhoots plied their frontier trade in *Wild Western Action featuring the Bravados*, but this oater bore even less of a resemblance to its source film than the others. *Tender Love Stories* tearfully told "tales of heartbreak and romance." Most of the stories in Skywald's color comic books were reprints from the '50s, with the lead story in each book being the only new offering, and even the reprints weren't that great.

Atlas/Seaboard and its history, like Skywald, will be discussed in succeeding chapters. Atlas had a black-and-white line, but unlike Skywald, Atlas/Seaboard's main focus was color comics, although it couldn't budge Marvel, DC, Mickey Mouse or Donald Duck off the newsstands any more than Skywald or Tower or any other company could. And like Skywald again, Atlas's use of derivative characters didn't help. *The Brute* is often cited as a Hulk rip-off, but actually it's more like the movie *Trog*. True, both comics feature big, strong monsters that cause much destruction of property, but whereas the Hulk has been turned into a monster by gamma rays, the Brute was a thawed-out caveman — not that this made much of a difference to comic book fans. *Demon Hunter, Fright (featuring Son of Dracula), The Grim Ghost, Moorlock 2001, Planet of Vampires, Tales of Evil*, and *Weird Suspense* rounded out Atlas/Seaboard's gore group, with *Planet of Vampires* the best of the bunch. Like every other Atlas/Seaboard title, it was derivative, but like A/S's *The Scorpion*, it mixed its influences in a more creative manner than just slavish imitation. *Planet of Vampires* mixed elements of *The Omega Man*, the *Planet of the Apes* movies and the movie of the same name to create one of the few titles that made fans sorry to see Atlas/Seaboard go. *Moorlock 2001* pilfered both Wells and Clarke for its title, but its living plant hero didn't grow on anyone. It was still not as silly as *The Grim Ghost*. Despite some sharp Ernie Colon artwork, it couldn't overcome its basic concept, a rip-off of the Spectre, but instead of a cop, a highwayman becomes an undead avenger. *Demon Hunter*, like the Scorpion, would turn up at Marvel under a different name.

And speaking of comics that turn up at different companies with different names, let's consider a similar situation which seems to involve two different comic book companies. Some explanation is necessary when dealing with Dell/Gold Key, as many people consider them to be two separate companies, which they were and weren't. Most assume that Gold Key simply took up where Dell left off, but it's not quite as clear-cut as that. Both Dell and Gold Key comics were produced by the Western Printing and Lithograph Company, which also owned the rights to the characters. Dell was a publisher of many other kinds of periodicals in addition to comic books, and Dell, from 1938 until 1962, bought its comics from Western, and distributed them under the Dell imprint. When Dell and Western had a financial disagreement, Western simply continued to print the same comics, but distributed them under the Gold Key or Whitman imprint. Dell then began its own comic book line, which went out of business in 1973. So the Dell name genuinely belongs to Dell Comics published from 1962 to 1973. Others were actually Western, whether Dell or Gold Key.

Dell/Gold Key (or Western), like Charlton, is not often mentioned in the same breath as Marvel or DC, but truthfully (and quite unlike Charlton), Dell/Gold Key outsold them both. Dell/Gold Key outsold everybody. Captain Marvel and Superman were very, very popular characters (at one point Captain Marvel was coming out every two weeks just to satisfy the demand), and Lev Gleason boasted (or alleged) that his *Crime Does Not Pay* sold a million copies of every issue, but *Walt Disney's Comics and Stories* moved over two million issues a month, sometimes closer to three.

Dell/Gold Key's adventure and fantasy comics were like the second leading men of movies — dependable, solid, always there when you need them, and sometimes capable of brilliance, like pretty much anything Russ Manning worked on. Manning is one of the true giants of comic art; his ultra-clean and seemingly supernatural sense of composition enhanced the Tarzan newspaper strip for many years, ably continuing (and some say surpassing) the superlative artistic tradition established by Burne Hogarth and Hal Foster. Manning's newspaper strips, as well as new work, appeared in *Tarzan* and *Korak, Son of Tarzan*. Manning turned *Magnus — Robot Fighter* into a cult classic, his imagination never flagging in the face of the challenge of constantly creating so many variations on a theme, and he turned in some of the coolest robots ever to appear in comics. *Boris Karloff Tales of Mystery* was originally titled *Boris Karloff's Thriller*, after the television series, but was changed when the series was cancelled. In the comic as in the show, Boris played the benign host, and was featured on the premiere issue's photo cover; a small inset photo of Karloff appeared on every cover after that. *Star Trek*, as can be imagined, was quite the popular book, and ran for nearly four times as many years as the original television series. *The Occult Files of Dr. Spektor* and *Doctor Solar, Man of the Atom* both came out of Western, along with *UFO Flying Saucers*. *Doc Savage* and *G-8 and his Battle Aces* were attempts at pulp revivals that unfortunately lasted for only one issue each; the Doc Savage comic (a well-done adaptation of "The Thousand-Headed Man") was particularly eye-catching because of the reprinted paperback cover art by James Bama. The first issue of *Buck Rogers in the 25th Century* was published in 1964, and the second didn't come out until 1979. The first issue didn't catch on, and the remainder of the series (another 15 issues) didn't begin publication until the release of the terrible movie which also bore the title of the comic. Awful though it was (one of the historical inspirations for *Star Wars* had become just another in a long line of clones of that movie, even down to cute robots), it spun off into a television series, although this didn't help Western. Western also published *Movie Comics — Beneath the Planet of the Apes, Fantastic Voyage, First Men in the Moon, King Kong, 20,000 Leagues Under the Sea,* and *X—The Man with X-Ray Eyes*. These adaptations were not nearly as neat as Dell's *Movie Classics*, which is discussed in the following paragraph.

After almost thirty years with Western, Dell was on its own. Most of its post–Western output consisted of titles devoted to television shows like *The Beverly Hillbillies, Bewitched* and *The Monkees,* with its fantasy output negligible or downright ridiculous. *Kona, Monarch of Monster Isle* ripped off Burroughs and Pellucidar for 21 issues, *Ghost Stories* stuck around for 37, *Tales from the Tomb* was a one-shot "Dell Giant" from '62, and *Melvin Monster* and *Millie the Loveable Monster* were aimed at the younger set. As for the downright ridiculous, Dell had adapted *Frankenstein* and *Dracula* for its *Movie Classics* series. The response was good, so Dell decided to give them series of their own — but since this was well into the era of the Comics Code, technically, Dell wasn't allowed to do a monster series. So what was Dell's solution? One of the most ill-conceived and jaw-dropping ideas ever to hit comics. Dell turned the Undying Monster and the Lord of the Vampires into costumed superheroes. The results were as bad as the idea sounds, and both series ended quickly. Dell's *Movie Classics* was an ongoing series that adapted one movie per comic, and Dell made some excellent choices in the monster category, including *Jason and the Argonauts, The Raven, Tales of Terror, Die Monster Die, The Creature (from the Black Lagoon), Frankenstein, Dracula, The Wolfman, Jack the Giant Killer, Mad Monster Party, Masque of the Red Death, Santa Claus Conquers the Martians, The Tomb of Ligeia, Twice-Told Tales, Two on a Guillotine, Valley of Gwangi,* and *War Gods of the Deep*. All of them had great covers, whether they were photos taken from the films or paintings, with *Frankenstein* and *The Creature* featuring the best in the painted category. Dell might not have had much success with its comic line after it split with Western, but its movie comics, at least, were superior to those that Western had produced.

The Comics Code is alive and well in the new millennium; if you squint hard enough, you can still see the stamp on mainstream comics, although it's purely cosmetic. Admittedly, there still seem to be some limits; you probably won't see Mary Jane flashing her fully bare breasts at Peter Parker anytime soon or see the graphic details of their sex life, but other than that, anything else seems fair game. In an odd way, comics have finally followed Dr. Wertham's alleged suggestions and groups of books aimed at adult or mature readers that cannot be sold to readers under the age of 18. They are clearly marked as such, although that designation grows as confusing as the times.

The Spirit

The Spirit was one of the most influential strips of all time, by one of the most influential storytellers in the history of the graphic art medium, Will Eisner. Private eye Denny Colt was shot and left for dead; nursed back to health in Wildwood Cemetery, his identity as Colt is kept dead and he begins a new crime-fighting life as the Spirit. Warren's repackaging of the character's adventures began a revival of interest that continues unabated to the present day, with a strip that began life as a cheap newsprint supplement now collected in expensive hardbound editions. Eisner forsook the character, but continued to work in the field until the time of his death, producing new covers (but never again a new story) for Spirit reprint comics and award-winning graphic novels. But although his artistic ability and gift for cinematic compositions and characterizations remained without peer, his desire to make a big statement often gave his work an air of self-importance that detracted from the overall impact. When he put his pretensions on the back burner and concentrated on telling a tale, there were very few others that could touch him, and as a result, the Spirit remains his monument.

The Spirit no. 1 (April 1974)

Cover: Basil Gogos/Will Eisner
Frontispiece: Introduction by Will Eisner, photo of Eisner
"The Last Trolley"—Will Eisner, John Spranger/Eisner
"Escape"—Will Eisner
"Li'l Adam"—Will Eisner
"The Criminal"—Will Eisner
"El Spirito"—Will Eisner
"The Killer"—Will Eisner, John Spranger/Eisner
"Granule of Time"—Will Eisner, John Spranger/Eisner
"The Partner"—Will Eisner

The Spirit had been languishing in relative obscurity until Warren decided to bring him back. The gem of the issue is "Li'l Adam (The Stupid Mountain Boy)," which neatly anticipates *Mad* with its brutally funny parody of popular newspaper strips and their creators. Eisner not only skewers Li'l Abner (obviously), but Little Orphan Annie and Dick Tracy, and the villain receives his comeuppance from a real-life version of one of his cartoons.

• ONE •

Movie Monster Madness

Movie monsters, like comic book monsters, have been with us ever since their respective genres began — in fact, the second theatrically released film was a monster movie, a version of Robert Louis Stevenson's *Dr. Jeckyll and Mr. Hyde.* Many of the pioneering special-effects films of Georges Méliès were of a fantastic nature, like *The Conquest of the Pole* and his most famous, *A Trip to the Moon.* "The great profile" himself, John Barrymore, took delight in distorting his classic features for roles like Captain Ahab in *Moby Dick* and his own take on Stevenson's creation. His makeup as Hyde was truly creepy, even spidery, a resemblance hammered somewhat heavily handed home by an image of him transforming into a huge spider while hovering over the heroine's bed. And, of course, there was Lon Chaney Sr., who was not merely a horror star, but one of the truly towering acting talents of the silver screen, etching unforgettable characterizations as Quasimodo in 1923's *The Hunchback of Notre Dame,* as Eric in *The Phantom of the Opera,* and as Dead Legs Flint in *West of Zanzibar,* among many others. His tragic death in 1930 allowed the world only one chance to hear his equally towering voice in a talkie, a remake of the silent *Unholy Three,* and also deprived the world of a chance to see him as Dracula. But his departure opened the door for another actor, who would hitch a ride on the little train that could. The actor's name was Bela Lugosi, and the little train was Universal Studios. Never on a level playing field with the big boys like MGM, Universal was looked upon as a reliable source of cheap thrills, mostly of the western variety. All of that changed with its production of *Dracula* (1931), which immediately cast Universal in the role of the industry's number one purveyor of horror, and, for better or worse, permanently linked Lugosi's name with that of Stoker's vampire. Universal's next monster production, *Frankenstein,* was to cement its position as the top studio for horror, and inadvertently created yet another star when Lugosi turned down the role: Boris Karloff.

During the next five years, Universal (and some other studios, some big, some small) created nearly every one of the creatures that would become not only the face of the company, but the classics, the cornerstones of fantasy filmdom. It was the golden age of Hollywood, and Hollywood horror as well. *Dracula* and *Frankenstein* were followed by *The Mummy, White Zombie, Island of Lost Souls, Murders in the Rue Morgue, King Kong, The Black Cat, The Raven, The Werewolf of London, Mad Love* and *The Bride of Frankenstein.* Despite the creation of a code that regulated the content of motion pictures, MGM pushed the limits ever farther with the Kraft-Ebbing sexual deviance of *Mad Love* (with Peter Lorre as the original "creep"—a term that Lorre invented) and, Universal, the Poe-inspired torture devices of *The Raven*. In fact, the studios had become so adept at purveying the gruesome that British censors instituted the famous horror film ban of the late '30s, a foreshadowing of the fate that would befall comic books of the same nature twenty years later.

Of course, they came back. Monsters always do. After an enterprising theater owner ringed spectators around the block with a triple-feature of *Dracula*, *Frankenstein* and *King Kong*, Hollywood got back into the horror business in a big way, but soon encountered a foe even more terrifying than the loss of British profits—World War II. The war meant that everything was scaled back. Gone were the days when the Mummy or the Frankenstein monster commanded "A" budgets and talent. Fast-paced, escapist thrills were the order of the day, and Hollywood horrors filled the bill admirably, culminating in the last hurrah of the classic monsters, the much-loved (and rightly so) *Abbott and Costello meet Frankenstein*. Then "classic" monsters went into hibernation again, not because of censors, but because of public tastes. America was entering its great Populuxe phase. This brought not only of conspicuous consumption, but, more importantly, previously unheard-of mobility and forward momentum, not only in outlook but also in design. This was the atomic age, and, as the world was affected by the atom bomb, so were the monster movies. It was the beginning of the space race, and, as the world was consumed by the quest for the planets, so were the monster movies. New monsters were not the product of just one mad scientist and his crackpot theories, but of science itself gone horribly wrong. Cold war paranoia created a thriving genre for alien invasion movies. But just as movie monsters were reaching for (or coming from) the stars, across the pop culture divide, Supreme Court justices were reaching for their gavels. After the cowardly creation of the Comics Code by frightened publishers many types of monsters disappeared from the newsstands for a good fifteen years. Curiously, the public outrage that greeted the subjects of crime and horror in the comics did not extend to movies, or if it did, had a much less noticeable effect. Some of the most hardboiled and nightmarish *film noir* classics were made in this time period, and monsters just kept getting nastier. Kids were no longer allowed to observe entrails being removed on the printed page, but Herschell Gordon Lewis was plying his bloody trade for any youngster that could sneak or lie his way into the movie theater. Perhaps this was the reason the movies proliferated—monster fans just didn't have anywhere else to go to get their monster fix. Pretty soon, they would, in spades.

The monster boom of the late '50s and early to mid-'60s was an amazing phenomenon. It was precipitated by the baby boom after World War II. In America, the growing families resulting from all that post-war sex were now not only an emerging social force, but an economic one as well, and a large number of monster movies began to cater to that segment of the population. By the mid-'60s, monsters really were everywhere. There were monster games and monster toys; there were the inimitable, much-beloved Aurora monster models, with magnificently rendered box art by the inimitable, much-beloved Doc Savage paperback artist James Bama. (One of his paintings, for the Big Frankie model, featuring Glenn Strange as the Frankenstein monster, was later used as the cover for the 1965 *Famous Monsters Yearbook*.) Bama did another great Frankenstein portrait, for a Bantam paperback edition of Mary Shelley's novel. This time the monster bore a suspicious resemblance to his Doc Savage cover model, former TV Flash Gordon Steve Holland. ("Doc

Frankenstein"? Oddly enough, that would become the title of a real comic book a generation later.) There were monsters on TV, and not just on the late, late show. There was TV's First Family of Fright, *The Munsters*, as well as the live action version of Charles Addams' darkly humorous cartoons *The Addams Family*. Other entrants included *The Twilight Zone*, *The Outer Limits*, and *Lost in Space*. There was even an episode of *Leave It to Beaver* that centered on the trouble Beaver and his pals got into at school for wearing their horrible, Big Daddy Roth–inspired monster sweatshirts. There were monster trading cards, and even monster bubble bath (Soakee Toys, as they came to be remembered in popular legend). There were monster Valentine's Day cards.

But the monster boom didn't just happen because American teens had more disposable income; rather, it was the converging of several divergent factors. Both England and Mexico chose this time period to start their ambitious programs of re-making classic monsters. The older horror films were released to TV as part of the Shock Theatre package, introduced to a whole new generation of fans via horror hosts such as Zacherley, Vampira, Ghoulardi, M.T. Graves, and "Chilly Billy" Cardille. And it also happened because of one, and only one, magazine. *Famous Monsters of Filmland* struck the newsstands like one of the bolts of lightning that animated Frankenstein's monster, and its impact and influence cannot be underestimated. It has become fashionable, in recent years, to try and discount that impact, alleging that *FM* wasn't serious enough, or in-depth enough. Not true. *FM* created a rallying point for fans which in turn led to horror-film criticism. *FM* was a beacon around which monster fans could gather and see that there were others like them. And how about publisher James Warren's anti–Vietnam editorial? Or his omnipresent anti-smoking ads? Or Forrest J Ackerman's avowed atheism? These were stands which could well have alienated a significant part of Warren's audience. (Indeed, the anti–Vietnam stories in *Blazing Combat* did alienate people; *Blazing Combat* was banned from Army bases, thereby effectively causing its cancellation.) These examples show that *FM* could indeed be very serious, even to its own possible detriment. And it was only supposed to be a one-shot, a quick cash-in on the newfound popularity of monster movies, both new and old, but as it turned out, *FM* not only perpetuated the genre, but became its leading exponent.

As he would do with *Creepy* a few years later, Warren virtually created a genre, and he catered wonderfully to the cravings of the newborn nation of monsterkids. As could be expected, the bandwagon began to fill up rather quickly: *Monster Parade, World-Famous Creatures, Mad Monsters, Horror Monsters, Modern Monsters, Monsters and Things, Monsters and Heroes, Chilling Monster Tales, Shock Tales, Thriller, Shriek, Suspense, Werewolves and Vampires,* even *3-D Monsters*. A few, although initially inspired by *Famous Monsters*, went on to become credible contributors to the field in their own right, like *Castle of Frankenstein, Fantastic Monsters of the Films, Monster Mania,* and later *The Monster Times* and Marvel's *Monsters of the Movies* (see below). But most of the above listed were fly-by-night; obviously produced by people who had little or no knowledge and even less love of the genre.

In these days of instantly accessible knowledge via the Internet, chat-room groups and video/DVD technology, it's difficult for some people to conceive that there was once a time when these things simply did not exist. If you were a monster fan, you couldn't just run to the local video store or go online and pick up virtually anything. Once you heard about it, you might have to wait for years for it to show up on TV; network TV, at that. There were no cable channels that catered to specialized audiences. And then you had to be sure to stay up to see it because you didn't know when

"Is it Gorgo by Gogos, or Gogos by Gorgo?" asked the contents page for one of *Famous Monsters*' most famous covers.

you would ever get to see it again. This was long before Carlos Clarens's *Illustrated History of the Horror Film*, or Everson's *Classics of the Horror Film*, or any other book that dealt with monster movies, again, books which would not have been possible without *FM* to consolidate the audience or to foster the idea that such films were worthy of serious studies. The tone may have been light, personified by editor Forrest J Ackerman's predilection for pusillanimous puns, but if you look closely enough, it was obvious that nobody loved monsters the way Forry did. This enthusiasm, which proved extremely infectious, was perhaps his greatest lasting contribution to the genre. And if a fifty-page filmbook of *Bride of Frankenstein* isn't in-depth enough for you, in the days before home video, issues like that were the closest thing to owning the film. *Famous Monsters of Filmland* wasn't simply at the head of the class; it was and is in a class by itself. Even more than that, it created the class.

True, it did take a few issues to find its sea legs, as most magazines do, but all of the crucial elements were there from the beginning. They just needed to be refined. The lightness of style, the puns were there from the beginning — this was seen as necessary to soften the horrible subject matter for the impressionable young minds at whom the magazine was aimed. Of course, when those young fans became older fans, it might not have been necessary, but by then, that was just the *FM* style. Had it changed, it might have dropped off the face of the earth. Critics can assert that *Castle of Frankenstein* or *Monster Mania* were better, more serious publications, but how long did they last? What can't be debated was that *Famous Monsters* was always the best of the monster magazines, bar none, in terms of design and graphics. Beautiful full-page photos balanced by blocks of lettering and text. Soon it would be so bold as to have just the title of an article take up an entire page, but the font was always so cool that the reader didn't care, because it was just part of an overall great design. The basic cover layout was there from the start, too — the title, blazoned across the top with the word "Monsters" most prominent, in bold, "horror" lettering. The features were listed on the left-hand side, the right being occupied by a monster. Now, for the first two issues, it was James Warren in a monster mask. I kid you not. With the third, the classic *FM* painted monster portrait cover began to gel. Although it wasn't Jim Warren in a fright mask, it was one of his paintings, a rather fine rendering of Chaney Sr. as the opera phantom. It was the only time his artwork would figure so prominently in one of his own magazines, unless you count the time it was reprinted on issue 102. French artist Albert Neutzell handled the next few — his portrait of Lugosi from *Island of Lost Souls* for no. 5 is especially evocative.

With issue no. 9, however, Warren struck gold; that issue featured the first in a long line of magical portraits by the man who would come to be as identified with *FM* as Frazetta is with Conan, or James Bama is with Doc Savage: Basil Gogos. Just as *Vampirella* needed Jose Gonzalez to bring her to artistic life, so *FM* needed the touch of Gogos. The brush strokes were bold and assured, but what really set Gogos's work apart from others was his use of light and shadow, and the vivid colors in which he rendered those lights and shadows. As with Frazetta, he was as realistic as he needed to be, but also knew when detail was merely superfluous. His first cover was Vincent Price as Roderick Usher, made even more striking by being set against a snow-white background. Many more incredible covers were to follow: *Curse of the Werewolf* (no. 11), Zacherley (no. 15), The Colossal Beast (no. 23), Karloff as Frankenstein (no. 56), Karloff as the Mummy (no. 58), Frederic March as Mr. Hyde (no. 62), Lon Jr. as the Wolfman (no. 99), King Kong (no. 108), Mr. Sardonicus (no. 126). The list goes on and on. *Famous

Monsters would feature other talented cover artists over its span of issues, like Ken Kelly and Ron Cobb, but none could ever touch Gogos for technique, inspiration, and fan adoration.

Famous Monsters of Filmland, in its glory days, was a joy to behold and required reading for every true monster fan. But just what were its glory days? Some fans divide the magazine's peak into just two phases: pre– and post–*Star Wars*. Others are more specific. For some, the best issues were any before 1970, but that is to ignore an amazing mid–'70s run (no. 99–135), which features some of Basil Gogos's and Ken Kelly's best cover work, along with some of the heftiest and most info-filled issues of the magazine ever. An admittedly fallow period came in the (issues numbered) mid–'60s through the mid–'90s, when *FM* reprinted covers and articles with abandon, but this was at a time when the whole Warren line was on very shaky financial ground, and all of its titles suffered accordingly, although *FM* kept its end up rather better than the other Warren titles during those dark days. (Although the numbering makes the time seem longer than it actually was, keep in mind that there was no issue 70–79 of *FM*—see the *Monster World* entry for more information on this odd gap.) When *FM* began, it began a genre; indeed, it inspired the people responsible for *Star Wars*. But when it hopped on the *Star Wars* bandwagon, it did so with such abandon that it reduced the magazine to little more than an almost monthly catalog of that movie's merchandise. The words "Star Wars" were often larger than the title itself, causing the readers to wonder whether the magazine was called *Star Wars* or *Famous Monsters*, and those wonderfully colorful painted covers by Gogos and Kelly were replaced, more often than not, by photos from George Lucas's films. The *Star Wars* covers undoubtedly sold more magazines, but something had been lost—instead of being a trendsetter, *FM* became a trend-follower.

In a way, it was supremely ironic. In fact, to quote a line from *Star Wars*: "Once, I was the pupil, now I am the master." *Famous Monsters* was going out of its way to promote a film (admittedly inspired by the serials, classic monster movies and comics which *FM* fervently featured) that would, along with other slick, colorful manifestations of pop culture, ultimately kill *FM*. *Star Wars* was *Flash Gordon* for a new generation, Darth Vader was the *Fantastic Four*'s Doctor Doom in outer space. The movies were in color, with snazzy new state-of-the-art (at the time) special effects, and soon magazines would follow suit. But *Star Wars* was not the only reason for the shift in priorities; it was merely the most visible. The other factor was the emergence of the slasher and gore films. Gore was nothing new to horror films; Gory scenes had been used for shock effect in films like *The Brain That Wouldn't Die* and *The Monster from Piedras Blancas*. Herschell Gordon Lewis had been plying his trade since the '60s, and Hammer Films and other countries took it even farther in the '70s. But in an increasingly cynical, brutal and violent society, the advent of films like *Halloween* and *Friday the 13th* was perhaps inevitable. Brutal violence and gore became the rule rather than the exception, and the monster magazines more or less required the vivid color in which these acts were committed.

FM would try to compete (although it never went to color), featuring more of the new crop of films and television shows inspired by the success of Lucas's film and the slasher films: *Close Encounters of the Third Kind*, *Battlestar Galactica*, *The Fog*, *E.T.*, *Poltergeist*, *Jaws*, *Gremlins*, the banal feature remake of *Flash Gordon*. Occasionally, *FM* would slip in a new or reprinted Gogos cover, or use the hype about the new films as an excuse to run some accompanying article or photos about the films that inspired them, but, by and large, classic horror took a backseat to the new kids in town. It still does (though not in *FM*), but with the advent of home video and later the Internet, classic horror would once again have a voice and a firm fan base that would become its future (*see* Chapter Seven).

The effect *Star Wars* has had on pop culture has been both good and bad. I like, but don't love, the original trilogy, and certainly prefer those films to the second series. I never bought into the hype, although I should have bought into the merchandise to sell later. They're good, sometimes very good films, and appreciation of the source materials adds an extra dimension of enjoyment, although this is certainly not required. *Star Wars* is an easy target, of course. In the days before the Internet, *Star Wars* was the apex of media saturation, manipulation and hype. It was as everywhere as anything could be in those days. Nothing in the fantasy film genre had inspired this kind of attention and adoration in ages. People lined up around the block several times a day to see it; they would walk out of the theater and immediately get right back into the line. The first time I stood in line to see it, the fans on either side of me had already seen it 12 and 14 times, respectively. Again, this was both good and bad. It certainly gave the genre a much-needed shot in the arm, and brought mainstream attention to the merits of the fantasy (film and otherwise) genre in general, but of course, that meant an immediate rash of imitators and the usual cynical hacks trying to cash in. It seemed there were more magazines trying to cash in on the *Star Wars* phenomenon than there were *Famous Monsters* imitators, and the plethora of titles that sprang up in *Star Wars*'s wake were as unimaginatively titled as the contents were unimaginative — *Science Fiction, Horror and Fantasy, Science Fiction Illustrated* (the title of which might lead one to believe it contained comic stories, but such was not the case), *Space Stars, Space Trek, Space Wars, Star Battles, Starblazer, Starburst* (which has admittedly stood the test of time), *Star Encounters, Star Force, Star Invaders,* and *Star Warp*. The phenomenon meant merchandising that was unprecedented, even taking into account Davy Crockett and Beatlemania. While the glut of Star Wars toys may have been overwhelming and ultimately led to movie-making by committee and an industry where the toy lines are put into production and the movies are made to support them, it also led to a culture where exist practically every monster you've ever wanted to see as a model or in a comic book or in any other manifestation of pop culture. While this increasing specialization can be viewed as society's further disintegration into factions that exclude one another, it's still pretty neat to be able to buy a model of the She-Creature. (For more remarks on *Star Wars* and the resultant effect on society and pop culture, *see* Chapter Seven.)

Famous Monsters itself would come back. Fans are still arguing, and will continue for some time to do so, whether the second incarnation should be considered as part of the official run. Of course, Warren does not publish it, so technically, no; but it continues the name, the numbering, the style, and the content, so technically, yes. In fact, one of the most heated debates in monster fandom in recent years (even more so than "who's better, Lugosi or Lee?") has been whether or not to accept the new *Famous Monsters*—although I suspect that those who protest the loudest are still the ones buying every issue in order to have a complete collection. The source of this acrimony is the situation that arose between current publisher Ray Ferry and *FM*'s original editor, the beloved Forrest J Ackerman. When *Famous Monsters* renewed publication, it was under the auspices of Ferry's Dynacomm, with Forry returning to his original post of editor. The move was revealed at the 1993 *Famous Monsters* convention, (also staged by Dynacomm) and was more than enthusiastically received by the attending crowd, who couldn't believe it —*FM* was back! They also enthusiastically received the next few issues, and had already accepted the new *FM* as part of the canon. But then things got ugly. Ferry and Forry parted ways with more than a little acrimony, and began a nasty court fight. Ferry continued to publish *FM*, exactly in the canonical style he had been, but not without being pilloried constantly. Politics aside, the finished product is obviously still a labor of love. Of course, it's not a patch on the original, but it's assuring to know that, if you need it, *Famous Monsters* is still there, and that Ferry, despite innumerable obstacles, has kept the faith. If there is any problem at all with Cooke and Roach's *The Warren Companion*, it is that they gloss over *Famous Monsters*, particularly in the index, claiming that titles for individual articles would mean very little to the reader, and citing a lack of author credits. Forry Ackerman has provided fans with plenty of *Famous Monsters* history in his books, but unless the titles are just outright puns that have no connection to the article (which was not as often as one may think), then they are actually quite helpful in informing fans as to the contents of an issue they want more information about. The issues singled out for examination in this section will have complete content listings, with titles explained where need be, and authors listed whenever and wherever possible.

Monster World (Warren 1964–1966)

Monster World was not just an attempt to capitalize on the success of *Famous Monsters*; it was practically the same magazine. The only difference was the title and some of the department names. For instance, instead of "You Axed For It!" the reader-requested photo section was entitled "IT asked for YOU!" It was really just *FM* in the months that *FM* didn't come out, more or less, and there was simply no point to its existence, unless it was just so that Jim Warren could secure copyright on another catchy title. *Monster World* does score points in one important department. The covers, well-rendered as they were, were not Gogos, but they did feature cool subjects that had heretofore escaped the spotlight in *Famous Monsters*. These included *The Addams Family* and *The Munsters*, and, most surprisingly of all given his enormous cult of followers, Tor Johnson! The most puzzling thing about *Monster World*, other than its publication in the first place, was the fact that it belatedly admitted that it was simply *FM* by another name by adding the total of *Monster World* issues to the numbering of *Famous Monsters*—four years after the title was cancelled. So in October of 1970, a month after the publication of *Famous Monsters* no. 69, readers are terribly confused by the appearance of *Famous Monsters* no. 80. And this wasn't the last time that *FM* played fast and loose in the numbers game—the last issue that Warren Magazines published was no. 192, but when Dynacomm revived the title, the first issue published was no. 200! They needn't have added *Monster World* to the total. Most of the material eventually made its way into *FM*, like the aforementioned She-Creature material, or the photo of Hammer's "The Reptile," which first graced the cover of *Monster World* no. 10, and again saw duty six years later as the cover of the 1972 *FM* "Fearbook."

Monster World no. 1 (November 1964)

Cover: The Wolfman
Frontispiece: "Birth of a Monster!"—Photo collage
"Lurking Ahead: Monster Movies to Come"—(Previews)
"Battle of the Frankensteins"—(Photo/text feature)
"It Asked for You!"—(Photo feature)
"The Maddest Doctor"—(Filmography)
"The Mummy"—Russ Jones, Wallace Wood

"*The Black Sleep*: 6 Monsters for the price of one!"—(Text/Photo feature)
"Terror Talk: News from the Ghoul Gazette"

Monster World no. 1 was important for two historical aspects: one, the first issue contained Warren's very first black-and-white horror comic, an adaptation of Universal's classic *The Mummy* by Russ Jones and Wallace Wood; and the "Fang Mail" logo drawn by Frank Frazetta, his first published work for Warren. "The Maddest Doctor" is a filmography of that most malevolent malpracticioner Lionel Atwill, while the "Battle of the Frankensteins" reveals some very obscure information about not only Mister Magoo's encounter with the undying monster, but a comedy play from 1887 by Richard Henry. There were no photographs from that play, but there was a wealth of equally obscure Frankenstein monster photos from a variety of sources.

Famous Films (Warren 1964–1965)

Famous Films was not another carbon copy of *Famous Monsters*, but a series of three issues that featured lengthy Italian-style *fumetti* adaptations of monster movies both classic (*Curse of Frankenstein/Horror of Dracula* and *The Mole People*) and psychotronic (*The Horror of Party Beach*). (*Fumetti* is a type of comic strip that uses photos with word balloons instead of illustration.) In the pre-videotape/DVD days, these issues, like the *FM* filmbooks, were the next best things to owning a copy of the film! Sharp-eyed comics fans will spot the legendary Wallace Wood in two capacities in *The Horror of Party Beach*—not only does he do the lettering in that distinctive Wood style, but he also inserts himself into the stills from the film itself, sneaking in a cameo as a newspaperman! All three editions are graphically gorgeous, inspired and inspiring, from the poster-like covers through the choice selection of film images to the rare ad art on the back covers, with the *Curse of Frankenstein/Horror of Dracula* issue having particular eye appeal. Russ Jones did the covers for all three along with the story adaptations, and showed why he was such a valuable member of the Warren team before he fell out of Jim Warren's good graces. Like Paul Blaisdell, after his departure Russ Jones's name would never again be mentioned in a Warren magazine, even in reprinted stories! When Warren held a grudge, by George, he held it.

Famous Monsters of Filmland no. 56 (July 1969)

Cover: Basil Gogos
"Last Respects" (Pt. I)
"Karloff in the Magic Castle"—Paul Linden
"This Was His Life"—Victor Morrison
"Last Respects" (Pt. II)
"The King and I"—Forrest J Ackerman
"Last Respects" (Pt. III)
"Karoffilms Checklist"—Filmography
Frankenstein—Filmbook
"Last Respects" (Pt. IV)
"The Graveyard Examiner"—News/fan page
"Mystery Photo"
"You Asked for Him"

This is one of the most famous issues ever of the most famous monster magazine ever. The incredible Basil Gogos portrait of Karloff has become one of the magazine's defining images, and the issue as a whole, a tribute to Boris Karloff, is considered by many to be the single greatest issue of *FM* ever published. Anyone who ever accused FM of a lack of depth would have his argument sorely put to the test with this issue, as complete and informative a tribute to Karloff in magazine form as has ever been put on the newsstands.

Famous Monsters of Filmland no. 87 (November 1971)

Cover: Ron Cobb
Frontispiece: Photo from *Yog, Monster from Space*

The Abominable Dr. Phibes—Film preview
"Girls and Ghouls Gallery"
"The Curse of Frankenstein"
The She-Creature
"Ask Professor Gruebeard"
"Footsteps of Frankenstein"—Archie Goodwin/Reed Crandall
"Mystery Photo"
"The Graveyard Examiner"—News/fan page

FM no. 87 is a great example of the Warren line as it stood in that time period. The cover was by early *FM* workhorse Ron Cobb, who handled a fair number of covers between Gogos stints. It was a great painting of the She Creature—which actually had appeared ten years before, on the cover of the third issue of *FM*'s short-lived sister title, *Monster World*. The article that accompanied it was also a reprint. The cover trumpeted the "23-page Special Photo Story" of *The Curse of Frankenstein*; but neglected to add that it had also originally appeared ten years before, in the *Famous Films* series, coupled with a like treatment of *Horror of Dracula*. Fans were also promised "New Monster Comics," but the story, "Footsteps of Frankenstein," by Archie Goodwin and Reed Crandall, was only new to those who had missed not only its original appearance, in *Eerie* no. 2, but also its previous appearance in *Famous Monsters* no. 49, only three years previously! About the only new thing in the issue was a preview of the now-classic *Abominable Dr. Phibes* starring Vincent Price. It wasn't bad stuff, but fans really had seen it all before, and with issues like this, it's easy to see why companies like Marvel and Skywald thought it would be easy to move in on the territory.

Famous Monsters of Filmland no. 147 (September 1978)

Cover: Basil Gogos
"Pinnacle of Terror?"—Randy Palmer
"Starry-Eyed Warrior"—Joseph LaCour
"1978 *Star Wars* Contest"
"Benign King Boris"—Ronald N. Waite
"Weird Encounters"
"Mystery Photo"
"Death of a Vampire"
"Vampire Jokes Contest"—Forrest J Ackerman
"Mr. Special Effects"
"How to Communicate with an Alien"—William F. Temple
"You Take the Cake"
"Rare Treats (You Axed for It)"
"Graveyard Examiner"

Issue no. 147 is from the so-called decline period of *FM*, and it's hard to argue with that. *Star Wars* has come to completely dominate the mag by this time (even the fine Basil Gogos cover is a Tusken Raider from the films), and even though the articles were new, they started to seem like reprints because the same info and hype was endlessly rehashed, and the articles on classic horror seemed listless and uninspired. There's not even that much variety in the Captain Company ads at this point, which became a *Star Wars* merchandise catalog.

Famous Monsters of Filmland no. 215 (March 1997)

Cover: Arlis Cagney
Staff Writers: Frank Bresee, Eric L. Hoffman
Comedy of Terrors
"The Magic Kharis-tian"
"The Spellbinding Art of *White Zombie*"
"Riddler on the Roof"
"You Axed for It"
Frankenstein's Daughter—(Text/photo feature)
"The Horror Hall of Flame"

Let's take a look at the Ray Ferry/Dynacomm era of *Famous Monsters*, since none of the purists will, and refuse to consider them part of the official canon. The contents haven't changed all that much—classic horror is still the main item on the menu, although modern monster-influenced rock stars like Alice Cooper have sneaked onto covers and into articles, and the puns still fly fast and furiously, although they have yet to achieve Forry velocity in terms of wordplay. One of the biggest differences graphically between the old and new *FM* is the use of modern technology for screen captures from the films covered, opening up a whole new range of photos besides the normal studio stills. The covers aren't Gogos, but some, like this issue's Mummy cover by Arlis Cagney, are as good or better than some by the old second-stringers, like Ron Cobb or Vic Prezio.

MARVEL MOVIE MONSTER MAGAZINES

Monsters to Laugh With/ Monsters Unlimited

Monster Madness

Stan Lee obviously and admittedly loves monsters, but Marvel's initial monster magazine offering misfired. Marvel's attempt to cash in on the monster boom, *Monsters to Laugh With*, was also an attempt to cash in on an unfortunate vein of that boom, the "funny" monster. Warren was also responsible for this approach in a way — as already noted, *Famous Monsters* presented its monstrous subjects with sheen of wit and humor in order to soften the impact for the magazine's younger readers. But in the rush to cash in on *FM*'s monstrous popularity (and rip off its style), most of the other guys missed an important point — *FM* wasn't laughing at the monsters, it was laughing with them. *FM*'s humor, though sometimes painfully corny, was nonetheless respectful and clever, where most of the imitators were merely crass and ill-informed on the subject matter, using the monster photos as cheap vehicles for present-day humor. Again, Stan Lee loves monsters, and had created some great ones in his time — but the quips that accompany some truly great photos of classic movie monsters (full and many double-page spreads, which make those about the size of a lobby card) in both of these series read like he took even less time to think them up than it took him to glance at the photo.

Monsters to Laugh With changed its title to *Monsters Unlimited* with issue no. 4, but didn't change its cheesy style, and only lasted three more issues. Despite the lack of success with the format the first time around, one of the magazines that Lee chose to spearhead Marvel's return to black-and-white format was *Monster Madness*, which was to *Monsters to Laugh With* what *Monster World* was to *Famous Monsters*; a virtual carbon copy, except with newer, hipper, more topical gags, many based on popular advertising slogans of the day, some that border on politically incorrect. *Monster Madness* didn't last half as long as its forerunner, collapsing after only three issues. Perhaps Marvel should have just published a mag called *Frankenstein Funnies*; not only did Mary Shelley's most famous offspring adorn four of the seven *Monsters to Laugh With/Monsters Unlimited* covers, but all three of *Monster Madness*. In the interest of history, or just for kicks, then, let's look at a representative issue of the three — the contents of the first issue of *Monster Madness* (entirely written by "Sinister" Stan). This will be a long list, but it's complete, and gives evidence of the massive selection of classic and rare stills to be found in its pages — and the questionable gags that accompany them.

Monster Madness no. 1 (1972)

Cover: Boris Karloff/*Frankenstein*—"Mabel, Mabel, the Ajax turned blue!"
Frontispiece: Lon Chaney Sr./*The Phantom of the Opera*—"Man, THAT was a belch!"
Bela Lugosi, Helen Chandler/*Dracula*—"You mean you're NOT Jewish?"
Christopher Lee/*The Curse of Frankenstein*—"I was a mess before I had my nose job."
The Ymir/*20,000,000 Miles to Earth*—"Let me make one thing perfectly clear!"
The Mole People—"Men! You're all the same!"
E.E. Clive, Boris Karloff/*The Bride of Frankenstein*—"Try it, you'll like it."
Glenn Langan/*War of the Colossal Beast*—"Hey Charlie, there's a busted pipe in the sauna!"
Lon Chaney Sr., Mary Philbin/*The Phantom of the Opera*—"Smile, you're on *Candid Camera*!"
Beverly Garland, Richard Crane/*The Alligator People*—"Melvin! You've changed!"
The Cyclops (with spear in chest)/*The 7th Voyage of Sinbad*—"Ouch!"
Virginia Christine, Lon Chaney Jr./*The Mummy's Curse*—"Selma, Uncle Bernie needs a Band-aid."
The Beast from 20,000 Fathoms—"I can't believe I ate the whole thing."
Boris Karloff, O.P. Heggie/*The Bride of Frankenstein*—"I'd like to marry your daughter." "You've made me an offer I can't refuse!"
The Ymir/*20,000,000 Miles to Earth*—"Why does company always drop in when the place is a mess?"
Henry Hull/*The Werewolf of London*—"Breck means beautiful hair."
Boris Karloff/*Frankenstein*—"Yoo Hoo! Good Humor Man!"
Jimmy Hunt, Lock Martin/*Invaders from Mars*—"You're in good hands with All-State."
Andree Melly/*Brides of Dracula*—Can Julie and Tricia come out to play?"
Bug-Eyed Monsters/*Invasion of the Saucer Men*—"You'd be a nice guy if you'd learn to relax."
King Kong (atop the Empire State)—"Hey Herbie, toss me that can of Raid!"
The Mole People—"I KNOW you love me, but I don't BELIEVE in mixed marriages!"
Lon Chaney Sr./*The Phantom of the Opera*—" I SAW it, I tell you, I SAW it! There's a white tornado in the kitchen!"
"Fill in the caption" contest—Lon Chaney, Sr./*London After Midnight*
Patrick Knowles, Bela Lugosi/*Frankenstein Meets the Wolfman*—"Now that I've got you here ... let's try an afro this time."
The Mole People—"You mustn't love me for my looks alone."
Frankenstein's Daughter—"You're asking ME what's good for a headache?"
Tom Tryon/*I Married a Monster from Outer Space*—"Sorry, you'll have to go behind the bushes like the rest of us."
Carroll Borland, Bela Lugosi/*Mark of the Vampire*—"At last you know my secret." "Yes. You forgot to pay the electric bill!"
The Monster from Piedras Blancas—"Bubble gum on the banister! That's two demerits!"
Elsa Lanchester/*The Bride of Frankenstein*—"Only my hairdresser knows for sure."
Lon Chaney Jr./*The Wolfman*—"Now for our next charade...."
The Colossus of New York—Daddy! Daddy! Only one cavity!"
Glenn Strange (leering)/*Abbott & Costello Meet Frankenstein*—"Hey, man, got any head shops in this town?"
Ape and Mad Scientist from "unknown silent film"—"We can't go on meeting this way—people are beginning to talk."
Patsy Ruth Miller, Lon Chaney, Sr./*The Hunchback of Notre Dame*—"Finders, keepers—losers, weepers!"
Tom Tyler/*The Mummy's Hand*—"Sorry, I already gave at the office!"
Beverly Garland, Richard Crane/*The Alligator People*—"Can't you wait 'til we get home?"
Charles Ogle/*Frankenstein* (1910)—"Quick! Where's the john?"
Henry Hull/*The Werewolf of London*—"If your deodorant doesn't do the job, try ours."
Ilona Massey, Lon Chaney, Jr., Bela Lugosi/*Frankenstein Meets the Wolfman*—"Sam, you made the sleeves too short!"
Ray "Crash" Corrigan/*It! The Terror from Beyond Space*—"Darn those harsh washday detergents!"
Bela Lugosi/*Abbott and Costello Meet Frankenstein*—"Come, Mr. Whipple, you must learn what happens to those who defy me—after tonight, never again will you squeeze the Charmin!"
Christopher Lee/*The Curse of Frankenstein*—"Like, I'm gonna buy me a new Gillette."
King Kong/*King Kong vs. Godzilla*—"Come alive! You're in the Pepsi generation!"

Lon Chaney Sr./*The Phantom of the Opera*—"If anyone calls, I'll be at the beauty parlor."

Lionel Atwill, Glenn Strange/*The House of Dracula*—""One small step for man, one giant leap for mankind."

Lon Chaney Sr./*The Phantom of the Opera*—"You should have seen me BEFORE I went to charm school."

Inside back cover: Ray "Crash" Corrigan/*It! The Terror from Beyond Space*—"Let's go. You deserve a break today — at MacDonald's."

Back cover: Jack Pierce (makeup artist) and Boris Karloff on the set of *The Bride of Frankenstein*—"Did you read the latest copy of *Monster Madness*?" "Please, I just ate!"

Well, Stan, you said it, we didn't.

Monsters of the Movies

Monsters to Laugh With/Monsters Unlimited and Monster Madness may have been smashing un-successes, but Marvel's third stab at a monster magazine was just what the mad doctor ordered. *Monsters of the Movies*, or *MOM*, as it affectionately came to be referred to, would only last slightly longer than *Monsters to Laugh With/Monsters Unlimited*, eight issues (well, nine if you count the King-Size Annual). It was not only the equal of most other monster movie mags on the stands, but a couple of single issues almost beat *FM* at its own game. But as a whole, *MOM* came nowhere near the level of *FM*, especially in terms of influence, but then again, with the exception of single issues, no other magazine did either. But *Monsters of the Movies* appeared at a time when Warren appeared to be down for the count, and none of Warren's publications at that time were operating at the quality level they had several years previously; if Warren was indeed finished, someone had to be ready to step into the breech. For that period of time, it wasn't hard to match Warren's quality if a publisher tried. Some did, many didn't. It was nice to see the results when one did, because fans had to know where to get their monster fix if Warren wasn't going to supply it. Of course, Warren would rebound, and would outlast this new crop of young Turks, but not before they put a few more gray hairs on Jim Warren's head. It was especially irksome to him when Warren regulars began to appear in the pages of the direct competition.

Monsters of the Movies no. 1 (June 1974)

Cover: Luis Dominguez
"King Kong: Monarch of Monsters"—Doug Moench
"Jeff Rice: The *Night Stalker* Papers"—Al Satian/Heather Johnson (Interview)
"Horrorscoop"—Carla Joseph (Film previews)
"Out of the Mouths of Ghouls"—Stan Lee (Text/photo feature)
"Monsterscope"—(Reviews and previews)
"Karloff at the Raven's Castle"—Ron Haydock (Interview)
"Monsters of the Radio"—Jim Harmon
"The Demon That Devoured Hollywood!"—Roy Thomas, Barry Smith/Dan Adkins
"The Weird World of Real-Life Monsters"—Ron Haydock
"Out of the Mouths of Ghouls"—Stan Lee (Text/photo feature)
"The Dracula Rip-offs"—Don Glut
"Keep Your Coffin Dry, Nevada"—Jim Harmon
"The Many Sons of Kong"—Eric Hoffman
"The Life Story of King Kong"—Jim Harmon

Like the first issue of *Famous Monsters*, the first fear-fraught issue of *Monsters of the Movies* was a solid entry into the field that promised even better things to come, especially in the cover department. Not as inherently cheesy as Jim Warren in a monster mask, the cover introducing *MOM* disappointed in a different way. Luis Dominguez, a Warren mainstay, turned in an effort that fails, mostly because it's too busy. Like a monster rally movie, he tries to shoehorn so many characters in (King Kong, Dracula, Frankenstein, the Mummy, the Wolfman) that none really get a good representation. But at least it was trying to give the reader a hint as to the variety inside, and once the pages were turned, no. 1 didn't disappoint, showing an appealing amount of breadth and scope for a first try.

Of course, the usual suspects were present — Kong, Boris, Bela, Lon Jr., Lee, but there was also coverage of "Night Stalker" author Jeff Rice, monsters on the radio, "the real world of real-life monsters," and, of course, it being a Marvel publication, a six-page comic story (reprinted in black-and-white from *Tower of Shadows*) written by Roy Thomas and drawn by Barry Smith. (This was before he became Barry Windsor-Smith, and while he was still drawing like Jack Kirby instead of Aubrey Beardsley.) The only out-and-out dud was "Out of the Mouths of Ghouls" by Stan Lee which featured (you guessed it) more monster photos with "funny" captions! This was, at least, the last feature appearance of this drivel, although it still snaked its way into story introductions from time to time in various titles.

On the plus side of the horror hotel ledger, in addition to stellar efforts by regular Marvel bullpen members like Doug Moench (another ex–Warren employee), *Monsters of the Movies* featured informed talents like Jim Harmon and Donald Glut (also both ex–Warren), whose co-authored work *The Great Movie Serials* will always be required reading for devotees of that genre, as well as Ron Haydock, a real rock-and-roll monster fan and player. When he wasn't busy interviewing Karloff or Chaney Jr., he was fronting his own combo, Ron Haydock and the Boppers, responsible for the garage-punk classic "99 Chicks." He also starred in various low-budget films like Ray Dennis Steckler's *The Choopers*. He was represented in the first issue of *MOM* with part one of the aforementioned Karloff interview, "Karloff at the Raven's Castle," as well as the also-aforementioned "Real World of Real-Life Monsters." Harmon contributed the "Monsters on the Radio" piece, which examined classic shows like "Lights Out," "I Love a Mystery" (which featured a pre–Felix Unger Tony Randall), and "Inner Sanctum," plus "Keep Your Coffin Dry, Nevada," a text piece that sought to invoke the spirit of those shows. Glut weighed in with "The Dracula Rip-Offs," and together, these three were the backbone of *Monsters of the Movies*. The Thomas/Smith/Adkins tale "The Demon That Devoured Hollywood" was a reprint from *Tower of Shadows* no. 7, yet another in the line of horror-actor-lets-his-roles-get-to-him stories, but with Thomas and Smith at the controls, enjoyable nonetheless.

Monsters of the Movies no. 2 (August 1974)

Cover: Bob Larkin
"The Life and Death of Frankenstein"—Jim Harmon (Text)
"Karloff Speaks"—Ron Haydock (Interview)
"Monsterscope"—Ron Haydock (Reviews and previews)
"Master and Slave"—Alan Hewetson, Syd Shores
"Dracula's Last Stand"—Don Glut (Text)
"The Myths of Frankenstein"—Ron Haydock (Text)
"The Last of the Frankensteins"—Jim Harmon (Interview)
"Big Monsters in Big Little Books"—Jim Harmon (Text)
"Rondo: The Purest of Them All"—Richard O'Brien
"Count Yorga: The Vampire for Here and Now"—Eric Hoffman (Text)
"Count Yorga Speaks"—Al Satian/Don Glut (Interview)
"Horrorscoop"—Carla Joseph (Film previews)

As *Famous Monsters* had its Karloff/Frankenstein tribute issue (no. 56), so did *MOM*. Bob Larkin's first cover for the series is also one of his best, and one of the finest portraits of Karloff (and Colin Clive) ever to appear on a monster magazine. In addition, the supporting articles hold up their end quite informatively. "The Myths of Frankenstein" brought some little-known facts to light, which today are common knowledge, but at the time showed that Marvel was indeed serious about its monster mag. "Master and Slave" is a reprint Frankenstein with a twist in the tale, courtesy of Alan Hewetson and Syd Shores, although for some reason all of the Frankenstein monster faces have been redrawn by John Romita. And even with all of this Frankie, there's still room for articles on Big Little Books, Rondo Hatton, and the coolest vampire of the '70s, Count Yorga.

Monsters of the Movies no. 3 (October 1974)

Cover: Bob Larkin
"Bela Lugosi: His Life and Undeath"— Ron Haydock (Text)
"Barnabas: Dark Shadows in Bright Afternoon"— Don Glut (Text)
"Monsterscope"— Ron Haydock (Reviews and previews)
"Inside Hammer Films"— Russ Jones (Text)
"The Making of *Dark Star*"— Bob Greenberg (Text)
"What's Up, Doc Frankenstein?"— Don Glut (Text)
"Variations on a Vampire Theme"— Don Glut (Text)
"Case File: Blacula"— Eric Hoffman (Text)
"Barr Atwater: The Night Stalker in His Lair"— Al Satian/Heather Johnson (Interview)
"The Blood Is the Life"— Barry Atwater (Text)
"The Life Story of Dracula"— Jim Harmon (Text)

The terrifying third issue of *MOM* showed the magazine had, again, quickly found its own style by focusing on the many different manifestations of one type of monster for the cover features, and all sorts of interesting exotica for the in-betweeners. No. 3 boasted the second great Bob Larkin cover in a row, which included not only the obligatory audience-grabbing portraits of Christopher Lee as Dracula and Jonathan Frid as Barnabas Collins, but William Marshall as Blacula, an honor rarely accorded the veteran actor. Ron Haydock kicked things off with a good mini-bio of Bela. Don Glut scored a hat trick (that's three goals, for all you non-hockey fans): his overview of the cult hit soap horror soap opera "Dark Shadows" and his exploration of cinema vampires not named Dracula were very good, but his highlight score was a piece called "What's Up, Doc Frankenstein?" Along with spotlighting the work of Robert "Beany and Cecil" Clampett, and other high and obscure points in animated horror, Glut also revealed that Bela Lugosi had been the model rotoscoped by Disney animators for the actions of the Demon of Bald Mountain in the "Night on Bald Mountain/Ave Maria" sequence in *Fantasia*.

Special guest columnists included ex–Warren staffer, ex–*Monster Mania* editor, and ex–Hammer Films employee Russ Jones, who provided an inside look at the inner workings of the Hammer Films. There was an article on the making of the sci-fi film satire "Dark Star" by its special effects man, Bob Greenberg, and an article by the Night Stalker himself— or, at least the actor who portrayed him in the movie— Barry Atwater, entitled "The Blood is the Life." Atwater was also an interview subject for Al Satian and Heather Johnson in that issue, and Eric Hoffman (also ex–*FM*) wrote an insightful piece on the above-mentioned William Marshall and his two "Blacula" films. Fantasy fans also fondly remember Marshall, who passed away in 2006, for his roles as "The King of Cartoons" on the TV series *Pee-Wee's Playhouse* and as "Jah-Doo" in the TV adaptation of Ray Bradbury's "The Jar," from the hour-long Alfred Hitchcock series.

Monsters of the Movies no. 4 (December 1974)

Cover: Bob Larkin
"Mystery of the Universal Werewolf"— Ron Haydock (Text)

"Superheroes vs. the Monsters in Distant Lands"—Don Glut (Text)
Crazed Vampire—Ron Haydock (Movie review)
"Lon Chaney: Beyond the Wolfman"—Ron Haydock (Text)
"Beware *The Bat People*"—Ron Haydock (Movie review)
"Werewolves: Part-Time Monsters"—Don/Maggie Thompson (Text)
"Make-Up Man: From *Schlock* to *The Exorcist*"—Al Satian/Heather Johnson/Don Glut (Interview)
"The Wolfman of Spain"—Eric Hoffman (Text)
"Monsterscope"—The staff of *Monsters of the Movies*
"Bello Ordloff Is a Monster!"—Jim Harmon, Mike Royer
"Lon Chaney: Sire to a Dynasty of Terror"—Jim Harmon (Text)

Anyone who has read my book *The Mexican Masked Wrestler and Monster Filmography* knows that this particular issue of *MOM* ("The Super-Sinister Werewolf Issue!") is a sentimental favorite, because it's the monster magazine that introduced me to the wonderful filmic exploits of El Santo, Blue Demon, and Mil Mascaras, in the "Superheroes vs. the Monsters in Distant Lands" article. One of the best things about *Monsters of the Movies* was the prominence it gave to subjects more or less under the other mags' radar; true, *Famous Monsters* had covered Mexican films, but, and I hate to use this phrase, but never in much depth, and particularly not the wrestler/monster films. Even *FM* had a few weak points. *FM* certainly did let petty jealousies get in the way. After Forry had a falling out with ace American International Pictures monster-maker Paul Blaisdell over *Fantastic Monsters of the Films*, he never mentioned Blaisdell's name in the magazine again (although he continued to run countless articles on the films and photos of his monsters). Warren Publishing as a whole was notorious for turning on former employees who had the nerve to start their own magazines or work for competitors.

A quick scan of the credits reveals that Ron Haydock really shouldered the load this time around, his byline appearing on no fewer than two major articles and two movie reviews. Don and Maggie Thompson of *The Comic Buyer's Guide* provided a handy-dandy guide to wolfmen not named Larry Talbot in "Werewolves: Part-Time Monsters," while another little-covered lycanthrope named Waldemar Daninsky got the royal treatment in "The Wolf Man of Spain." Daninsky, of course, is the human name of the werewolf character "El Hombre Lobo" created by the great Paul Naschy. He has appeared in more movies than even Lon Chaney's "baby." (The term "El Hombre Lobo" was used in many Mexican monster movies, but it was only a blanket term for a werewolf, and never a continuing character.) *Werewolf vs. the Vampire Women*, which sounds like a sequel to the Santo movies but isn't, is the best of a very good and certainly distinctive series made by someone with a genuine interest in, and fondness for, the subject matter.

The only real weak spot in the issue is the comic story, "Bello Ordloff is a Monster!" by Jim Harmon and Mike Royer. Royer was an assistant to Russ Manning, and inked a great deal of Jack Kirby's legendary "Fourth World" saga (*New Gods, Forever People, Mister Miracle*, etc.) for DC, but his artwork here, although clearly showing the Manning influence, was nowhere near as inspired as his mentor's. But art-wise, Bob Larkin made up for it with his best cover ever for *MOM*, a beautifully rendered, very atmospheric portrait of Lon Jr. as Universal's Wolfman. Larkin would always throw in nice little secondary elements that gave his paintings character, like the skull in the foreground of the werewolf cover for the magazine-sized *Haunt of Horror* no. 1; here, it's the real wolf howling at the moon in the background, like the extra little critters that decorated the bases of the Aurora model kits.

Monsters of the Movies no. 4 (Marvel) — A prime example of Bob Larkin's photo-realistic painting technique for Marvel's *Monsters of the Movies* no. 4 (courtesy Marvel Entertainment, Inc.).

Monsters of the Movies no. 5 (February 1975)

Cover: Bob Larkin
Frontispiece: Various featured monster photos — Godzilla, The Creature from the Black Lagoon, Dracula (Lugosi), *Bride of Frankenstein*
"Godzilla — Tokyo's Greatest Nemesis" — Don Glut
"Monsterscope" — The staff of *Monsters of the Movies*
"Tod Slaughter: Master of Villainy" — Manuel Weltman
"The Golden Days of Frankenstein: Elsa Lanchester" — Jim Harmon/Frank Bresee (Interview)
"I'm Sorry, the Bridge Is Out, You'll Have to Spend the Night" — Don Glut
"Vampires of Radio" — Jim Harmon
"Monster Masquerade" — (Photo feature)
"Hunting Dinosaurs for Fun (If Not Profit)" — Ron Haydock/Jim Harmon
"Frankenstein's New Monster from Hell" — Eric Hoffman
"The Creature Features" — Don Glut

Bob Larkin's cover subject (and nominal lead feature) for the fifth fright-filled issue of *MOM* was Godzilla, but for the first time in the series, it failed to inspire. The painting, technically, was beyond reproach, as always, but the composition (normally a Larkin strongpoint) was weak. In opting for a full-figure view of Tokyo's favorite son doing what he does best (stomping the city), the cover leaves very little room for striking lighting effects or dramatic tension, unless you count the girl in the foreground with her blouse straining against her breasts. In terms of articles, whereas Ron Haydock had ruled the roost in the previous number, Don Glut and Jim Harmon hog practically this whole issue, ending up with three stories apiece. Actually, Harmon had four if you count the "Bullpen West" editorial. No. 5's Glut trilogy included "Godzilla: Tokyo's Greatest Nemesis"; a review of "I'm Sorry, the Bridge is Out, You'll Have to Spend the Night," a stage play written by Sheldon Allman and Bobby "Boris" Pickett (of "The Monster Mash"), which featured, among many others, Dracula, Frankenstein, the Wolf Man and the Mummy; and another mini-history, "The Creature Features," which, as you might guess, focused on the films of the Creature from the Black Lagoon.

Harmon's hat trick was assisted on one play by old-time radio aficionado Frank Bresee. "The Golden Days of Frankenstein" was actually not about Frankenstein on the radio, but an interview with the "Bride" herself, Elsa Lanchester. On Harmon's second piece, "Hunting Dinosaurs for Fun and Profit," Ron Haydock pitched in for an overview of oversized lizard movies. His third saw him go solo with, finally, the expected historical radio piece called "Vampires of Radio." Manuel Weltman's "Tod Slaughter: Master of Villainy" was a great introductory piece for readers unfamiliar with England's foremost star of homegrown horror films before Cushing and Lee. Rounding out the issue was a preview of *Frankenstein and the Monster from Hell* by Eric Hoffman, with many great photos of Peter Cushing and David Prowse in his "hairy, stitched-up golem-looking" monster from hell makeup.

Monsters of the Movies no. 6 (April 1975)

Cover: Luis Dominguez
"The Mummy Chronicles" — Ron Haydock
"Next Week" — Don Glut
"Monsterscope" — Ron Haydock, Jim Harmon, Eric Hoffman
"Man Who Made Monsters" — Tony Isabella
"*Young Frankenstein*: The Uncensored Version" — Jim Harmon
"Frankenstein's Monster" — Mar Amongo, Rico Rival (Illustrations)
"Abby: A Woman Possessed" — Al Satian/Heather Johnson (Interview)
"William Castle: The Skeleton in His Closet" — Ron Haydock
"The Mummy's Hammer" — Don Glut

Although ostensibly a special Mummy issue, *MOM* no. 6 featured only two measly (although well-done) Mummy articles, and a lackluster Luis Dominguez cover. The subject matter was diverse, which was one of *MOM*'s strong points, but, in the first few issues, even most of the secondary features had been tied into the issue's theme. That's not to say the features aren't good, it's just to point out that there's no common thread; from serials to Mel Brooks to blaxploitation (*Abby* star Carol Speed is interviewed).

Monsters of the Movies no. 7: *Horror of Dracula* filmbook (June 1975)

Horror of Dracula and *Curse of Frankenstein* had been a great double feature in Warren's *Famous Films*, but Marvel went one better with this magazine-length filmbook of *Horror*, as complete as any similar Warren treatment had ever been. The only drawback is the cover, which is not only poorly composed, but lacking in accuracy in the depictions of the faces of Lee and Cushing, particularly Lee.

Monsters of the Movies no. 8 (August 1975)

Cover: Bob Larkin
"Peter Cushing: Thespian Terror Titan" — Doug Moench
"Enter the Madhouse" — Film review by Ron Haydock
"Dr. Frankenstein, I Presume" — Don Glut on Cushing's Frankenstein
"The Hammer Films of Cushing/Lee" — Jim Harmon, Eric Hoffman
"Inside Amicus" — Russ Jones
"Golden Vampires" — Film review by Eric Hoffman
"Once Upon a Time There Was a Vampire" — Jonathan Frid interview by Chris Claremont

Sadly, this was the last real issue of MOM (the obligatory all-reprint annual was to follow), and although not billed as such, a special Peter Cushing issue. He shares a great Bob Larkin cover with Barnabas Collins, and gets the lead article and a bio, and also gets to "Enter the *Madhouse*" (in which he co-starred). A survey of his portrayals of Frankenstein followed, along with a filmography of his appearances with Christopher Lee. In fact, the only article that doesn't feature Cushing is the Jonathan Frid interview. It might have been the last issue, but the magazine sure went out in style. The strange thing about the annual was that it had a cover that featured Mr. Spock from Star Trek, which was slightly misleading — the magazine had never featured a Star Trek article, which surely disappointed those that the cover drew in.

Marvel Movie Premiere

Marvel Movie Premiere (featuring *The Land That Time Forgot*) no. 1 (September 1975)

Cover: Nick Cardy
Frontispiece: Photo from the title movie
The Land That Time Forgot (Adapted from the film of the novel by Edgar Rice Burroughs) — Marv Wolfman, Sonny Trinidad
"Lost Lands, Forbidden Cities" — Lin Carter (Text feature)
The Land That Time Forgot — Movie photo feature

The Land That Time Forgot was a much-ballyhooed production, but when it finally appeared, it remained solidly anchored in the "B" film harbor, due to the hokey-looking dinosaurs and Doug McClure's earnest but stilted acting style (which is why it's a cult favorite). The Marvel version is actually better than the film, because we get the best of both worlds — the dinosaurs look a lot better, and we don't have to watch McClure act. Nick Cardy, long-time Batman delineator, contributes a great painted cover, a slick piece from an artist who had certainly done his share of dynamically drawn covers, but not in oil.

More Vintage Movie Monster Magazines

For Monsters Only

For Monsters Only no. 9 (September 1971)

Cover: Jeff Jones
Frontispiece: Photo of Jonathan Frid as Barnabas Collins (*Dark Shadows*) Inside back cover: Photo from *Trog*
Trog—(Photo/text movie feature)
"Quick Quiz"
"The Howls Are Here"
"Whatever Happened To...?"
"The *House of Dark Shadows* Movie"—(Photo/text movie feature)
"Exhibit Six"—Story/art by Martin J. Arbunich
"Let's Meet the Ladies"—(Photo/text feature)
"Monster Laughs"
"More Fiendish Delights"
Taste the Blood of Dracula—(Photo/text movie feature)
"Killer Dillers"
"Big Things Do Their Thing"—(Photo/text feature)
"John Carradine: Master Villain"
"The Wacky Weirdos"
Back cover: John Severin

For Monsters Only was another magazine that could never figure out exactly what it wanted to be when it grew up. The entry into the monster magazine competition from the publishers of second-rate *Mad* imitation *Cracked* is hard to call a *Famous Monsters* imitation, because, in the first few issues, it played strictly for laughs. Also like *Cracked*, its only redeeming feature was the always first-rate artwork of EC, by Warren and Marvel veteran John Severin. But with issue no. 6, it suddenly shifted gears—sort of. Gone was the outwardly humorous approach, starting with the covers, like this issue's classic by Jeff Jones. Inside were some great, straight monster articles, mostly slanted towards more recent product like *Trog, House of Dark Shadows* and *Taste the Blood of Dracula*. Also of note was a feature on master villain John Carradine, with some great rare photos of the ultra-gaunt master thespian. Unfortunately, the rest of the contents were of the monster photos with funny captions variety, or like the back cover, which showcased "Great Moments in Horror," classic monsters running in fright from Tiny Tim. (Tiny Tim was, amazingly, a very popular entertainer in the late '60s and early '70s who had shoulder-length hair and a huge nose, and sang Rudy Vallee and Al Jolson songs in a high-pitched voice. He had a Top 40 hit with a song called "Tiptoe through the Tulips," and was the subject of TV's first reality wedding when he married his sweetheart, Miss Vicky, on a talk show.) John Severin drew it, but as Bela Lugosi said to a female singer in *You'll Find Out* when complimenting her on her voice, "It's criminal to waste it on such trash!" which more or less sums up Severin's entire career at *Cracked*. The format change did nothing to increase its audience, and the magazine folded a couple of issues later. *Cracked* published a few other funny monster specials, and even tried it again years later with *Monsters Attack!* But that only lasted a few issues as well; the publishers could never get it right, and apparently didn't try very hard.

Mad Monsters

Horror Monsters

Mad Monsters and *Horror Monsters*, both published by Charlton, were from the first wave of *Famous Monsters* imitators, jumping on the bandwagon in 1961. They published a grand total of ten issues each in five years, thereby setting an example for *Castle of Frankenstein*. They tried hard for the *Famous Monsters* look, especially in their page layouts, but like so many others, simply didn't have the depth of talent that made *FM* what it was. But they at least get points for a using a couple of the more obscure and cool monsters as cover subjects. These include the titular creature from *I Married a Monster from Outer Space* (*Mad Monsters* no. 7) and from Ray Dennis Steckler's *The Incredibly Strange Creatures, or How I Stopped Living and Became a Mixed-Up Zombie* (*Mad Monsters* no. 10), and the Head on the operating table from *The Brain That Wouldn't Die* (*Horror Monsters* no. 8). This is not to say the covers are any good; in fact, they're all pretty mediocre. The likenesses are always just short of capturing their models, and it's hard to decide whether they're that way because the artist couldn't nail the image or he was rushed. Probably a little of both.

Horror Monsters no. 2 (1961)

Cover: Painting of teenage Frankenstein
I Was a Teenage Werewolf
"Ghouls and Gags"—(Photo/text feature)
"Teenagers Muscle In on Monster Racket"— (Photo/text feature)
The Pit & the Pendulum
"Edgar Allan Poe"—(Biography)
Gigantis the Fire Monster
"Atrocious Art Gallery: The Weird Drawings of Joseph Krucher (The Bela Lugosi of the Brush)"—(Art portfolio)
"Dulliver's Travels"—(Photo/text feature)
"They Died Laughing"—(Photo/text feature)
The House of Fright

The second haphazardly constructed issue of *Horror Monsters* was its typical grab bag of press releases and gags; the "Atrocious Art Gallery" was well-titled; a fan by the name of Joseph Krucher was billed as a Bela Lugosi (but this guy wasn't even a Sammy Petrillo) of the brush! The issue apparently ran the *Gigantis* press release as was, and didn't even mention the name Godzilla, or that this was a sequel.

Horror Monsters no. 5 (1962)

Cover: Painting of severed Peter Lorre head
Frontispiece: Photo of Boris Karloff
Tales of Terror
"Through the Upper Intestine"—(Photo/text feature)
"Shock Theatre"—(Photo/text feature)
"Peter Lorre: The Little Giant of Monsterdom"— (Photo/text bio feature)
The Head
"Will the Real Frankie Please Stand Up?"— (Photo/text feature)
"Female Fiends"—(Photo/text feature)
Burn Witch Burn!
"Pin Up Parade"—(Photo/text feature)
"They Died Laughing"—(Photo/text feature)

In a field littered with unfunny "funny" monster mags and gags, Horror Monsters was probably the worst offender. By the fifth issue, its content had been slightly upgraded, but its humor remained strictly stupid. Witness this contents page wit: "*Horror Monsters'* Sad Staff: Editor—Sanzar Quasatoad; Ass. Editor—Quaszar Sanatoad; Art Director—Santoad Zorquasar; Ass. Art Director—Zarsatoad Sanqua; SPFX—Toadzar Quasasar; Sandwiches—Meyer." I kneel in awe of such sublime comic genius. No wonder they didn't use their real names.

Mad Monsters no. 9 (Winter 1964)

Cover: *Masque of the Red Death* poster art
Frontispiece: "Cult of Horror" ad
Goliath and the Vampires
"Mad Monsters Photo Quiz"
The Bat
"John Carradine"
"Fiend File"—She-Creature Photo
"Coffin Capers"
Masque of the Red Death
"You'll Wonder Where the Fellow Went...."
Devil Wolf of Shadow Mountain—Vin Saxon
"Ghoul Giggles"
"Fiend File"—Boris Karloff photo

Mad Monsters and *Horror Monsters* are like *Famous Monsters* and *Monster World* in the sense that they're carbon copies of one another, but whereas the latter pair was a case of trying to milk a good thing, the former pair make one wonder why anybody would want to put out one magazine like that, much less two. That said, this was one of the more interesting issues of *Mad Monsters*, especially with the indie film coverage by Vin Saxon, better known as Ron Haydock. The humor wasn't any funnier, but at least there was less of it.

The Monster Times

Technically, *The Monster Times* wasn't a magazine, it was a newspaper, and its unique (for monster mags) format allowed graphic possibilities that simply couldn't be done in a standard-format mag, like more imaginative page layouts, and best of all, a huge poster for the centerfold. It could also come out more often, and maintained a bi-weekly schedule until budget constraints forced it to scale back. Each issue was centered on one theme, and *The Monster Times* had some great themes: *Planet of the Apes*, EC, Dracula, Frankenstein, Bad Movies, Martians, and several about Godzilla. Its tone could often be tongue in cheek, but it never seemed patronizing because the editors knew their stuff and were having fun with, not making fun of, the subject matter.

The Monster Times no. 9 (May, 1972)

Cover: Photo/Metaluna Mutant from *This Island, Earth*
This Island, Earth— Mark Frank (Filmbook)
"Science Fiction in the Comix"— Gary Brown
"The Making of *2001: A Space Odyssey*"— Gary Gerani
"Not Bad for a Buck!"— Joe Brancatelli
"Spaced Out!"— Joe Thomasino, Don and Maggie Thompson (Book reviews)
"Doin' the Buck 'n' Flash!"— Allan Asherman
Centerfold Poster — *This Island, Earth*
"Mushroom Monsters, or, The Day the World Ended and Ended, Part Five"— Joe Kane
Science Fiction in the Cinema—(Book review)
"Mutant Species"— Paul Neary
"The *Monster Times* Teletype"—(News and reviews)
The Space Giants— Allan Asherman (Review)

As evidenced by the contents, the theme for this issue was science fiction. The Metaluna Mutant makes a well-deserved cover appearance and graces the huge poster/centerfold as well; *This Island Earth* is the subject of a well-done filmbook. There's something for everybody in this issue, even comics, an early effort by British artist Paul Neary, who would go on to make quite a name for himself at Warren.

ATLAS/SEABOARD

Marvel was not the only competition for Warren (in the aesthetic sense, that is — obviously, in the larger picture, Warren was no competition for Marvel at all), or vice versa, in the monster magazine and black-and-white illustrated monster sweepstakes. Curiously, DC/National never figured into the equation. It certainly had its share of code-relaxed four-color monsters, but the sum total of its contribution to the magazine field was an issue each of *The Spirit World* and *In the Days of the Mob*. Newer or smaller companies would generally concentrate their efforts in one area or on a select group of publications. Although from time to time an outfit would appear that looked as if it might challenge the big two, like Tower

The Monster Times no. 9 (TMT) — The cover for the special Science Fiction Issue of the world's first monster newspaper, *The Monster Times*, featured the Metaluna Mutant from *This Island Earth*.

Comics, ultimately the challengers just couldn't match the resources at Marvel or DC's disposal. Ironically, the very man who built Marvel into a near-immovable object started the company that would try it in the mid-'70s.

The short story of Atlas/Seaboard Publications boils down to basic plot elements: spite and revenge. In 1968, Marvel publisher Martin Goodman sold Marvel to Cadence Publishing for $15 million, out of which Marvel editor and public face Stan Lee got nothing, not even a Christmas bonus. Goodman also wanted his son Chip essentially to take over Marvel and Stan's job, although he had absolutely no qualifi-cations. In 1972, when Stan's contract was up for renewal, Cadence, realizing his importance to the company for both his comic book savvy and public relations, not only re-signed him with a significant raise, but also promoted him to publisher — leaving Martin Goodman out in the cold. Martin and Chip decided they would try to beat Marvel at its own game; risky business in any case, but the revenge that was the motivation behind the venture backfired. They had top men working for Atlas, some of whom were lured away from Marvel and DC by the promise of better pay, return of artwork, and most importantly, and what was a revolutionary consideration in those days, creators' rights — ownership of the characters they created. No more would they "work-for-hire." But they frittered away good intentions and better talent by thinking that the way to beat Marvel was by being as close to a carbon copy of Marvel as possible, but had mostly concepts that weren't even good enough to be called rip-offs.

It was too much too soon — instead of letting the talent they had pirated away from the big boys have their heads and create some really different characters because they had a personal stake in wanting them to succeed, and nurturing a small number of quality titles, the Goodmans made the same mistake as Marvel did with the magazine group. They saturated the market. They spread themselves too thin. Atlas published a four-color comics line and a line of black and whites as well. Atlas threw every genre conceivable from Kung Fu to Gothic romance at the wall, hoping something would stick. Nothing did. The professionals tried. Some came through with some genuinely fresh concepts, but they were hampered from above by the editorial insistence that the characters be as Marvel-like as possible. For instance, Howard Chaykin created the Scorpion, typical hard-edged and sexy Chaykin, related pulp-style in the milieu of the '30s. Chaykin quit when the powers-that-were decreed that pulp was passé and demanded that the hero be turned into another Spider-Man. This made less sense than most of their decisions, since they already had a bunch of Spidey rip-offs. With an editorial policy like that, it's not hard to see why Atlas went under, but in its tumultuous existence, it did manage to leave behind a few examples that show that, given time and newsstand space, Atlas could have been a contender. Those examples are covered in this chapter and chapters 3 and 4.

Movie Monsters no. 2 (February 1975)

Cover: Greg Theakston
2001: A Space Odyssey
1 Million Years B.C.
"The Celluloid Superman"
"Monster Bugs"
Frankenstein
"*Planet of the Apes* Scrapbook"
Rodan
"Remembering Bela"
"*Doc Savage* Scrapbook"

The second issue of Atlas/Seaboard's longest-lived black-and-white title (a whopping four issues!) showed that not only had "Uncle Forry" taught his pupils well in preparation for putting out their own monster magazines, but that the students reached even farther. Forry, a man who had a way with a pun, never tried anything as naughty as the caption which accompanies a still from "Rodan" on page 60: "Rocket fire turns Rodan's home into a flaming ash hole."

The actors and films discussed within its pages are not always treated with the reverence that most fans had come to expect from *Famous Monsters*. Although it must be noted here that *FM* was not the uncritical cheerleader that many people still characterize it as. *FM* ran future director Joe Dante's "50 Worst Films" article years before such things became fashionable. Indeed, post–Watergate, the fashion (and necessity) to question the institutions that govern our lives extended down to the nascent field of horror film criticism. Whether this was a good thing depends on how one feels about the institutions being questioned.

For instance, everybody agrees that *2001: A Space Odyssey* is a classic, right? Well, not everybody, and the *Movie Monsters* article's author (no individual credits are given) really takes this most overrated of science fiction films to task; so much so, in fact, that editor Jeff Rovin felt it necessary to run a disclaimer after the article, assuring readers that, indeed, it certainly was a classic. But the author rightly attacks the paucity of the storyline, and concludes that, like *Destination: Moon* or *(The Shape of) Things to Come*, other science fiction films with (at the time) state-of-the-art special effects, *2001* would ultimately be regarded as the same, "losing the race with progress." He was right in that sense as well, although it's not just outdated special effects that still make the film one of the most-disputed classics of the science fiction film genre.

Although perhaps running a poor third to such burning fan queries as "Who's faster, the Flash or Superman?" or "Who's stronger, the Thing or the Hulk?" the question "Who's the better Dracula? Bela Lugosi or Christopher Lee?" was (and still is) a hot topic. The article "Remembering Bela," although titled as though it were a fond tribute, not only chooses Lee, but even tries to topple Lugosi as one of the great horror icons. The author clearly didn't know much about Lugosi. Take this statement, for example: "When one stops to consider Lugosi's request of being buried in a large 'Dracula' cape, a few things finally started taking shape. He was bananas!" He also opines that *Abbott & Costello Meet Frankenstein* "seemed to typify all that Lugosi and his twenty-odd years of film acting stood for — canned ham." One would have to wait another twenty-odd years for *Poverty Row Horrors* to find such a virulent hatchet-attack on "poor Bela."

Other pieces in the magazine aren't as troublesome, and in general, it's well done, with a nice selection of subjects and stills. The trendy *Planet of the Apes* cover is a fine portrait of Dr. Zaius by Greg Theakston, who would later go on to produce the legendary pinup digest *The Betty Pages*, and initiated the search to uncover the whereabouts of the reclusive former pin-up goddess. "The Celluloid Superman" is a good overview of the character in serials, film and television, including a very rare still from the unsold pilot "The Adventures of Super Pup." More apes were to be had in the "*Planet of the Apes* Scrapbook," which featured photos from three of the movies, including *Battle for the Planet of the Apes*, which thankfully hid gnome-like pop songwriter Paul Williams under orangutan makeup. And if Marvel could have a Doc Savage magazine aided by the publicity of the film, why then, Atlas/Seaboard would just have a feature on that movie, too.

Movie Monsters no. 4 (August 1975)

Cover: George Torjussen
Twenty Million Miles to Earth
"A Chip Off the Old Block?"
"The Loch Ness Monster"

"Disney: The Monster Factory"
The Thing
"The Day the Earth Stood Still"
"The *Star Trek* Phenomenon"

The (unfortunately) last issue of *Movie Monsters* was another solid effort, and made one regret that Atlas/Seaboard didn't last a little longer, and have time to iron out the wrinkles. Rovin and his merry band of followers, Gary Gerani, Carl Macek and Keith Morris turned in another solid effort, though the lack of individual credits was still frustrating for those who either wish to heap praise or lay blame. The cover artist was George Torjussen, who also did the cover art for the second issue of A/S's Vampirella/Satana rip-off, Devilina. He only did these two covers for Atlas, and his batting average was .500. The Devilina cover is some rather substandard good (or bad) girl art, but his painting here is right on, a somewhat radical take on the title monster from *The Thing* (spotlighted in this issue) that really works.

Hitting a solid leadoff is a fact-filled feature on master animator Ray Harryhausen's classic *Twenty Million Miles to Earth*, with very nice illustrations, and a couple of rare stills. Like *Monsters of the Movies* no. 4, *Movie Monsters* no. 4 also featured a Lon Chaney Jr. feature, "A Chip Off the Old Block?"—but note the question mark. While the *MOM* piece was a straight tribute (although not fawning), the *MM* article was more in the spirit of its Lugosi "tribute" in issue no. 2, although the magazine wasn't quite as rough on Junior as it was on poor Bela. Of course, both Bela and Lon Jr. had their flaws as actors, and both appeared in movies that are way off the radar. Real fans recognize and perhaps even relate to these flaws in their heroes' off-screen lives and their on-screen personas, while realizing that these flaws do nothing to detract from their iconic status and may even contribute to it.

The "real life monster" feature was devoted to the creature that inhabits Loch Ness. Although the feature unearthed no startling new revelations, it did have some awfully nice artwork by Walt Simonson. More fantastic art followed, this time captured from the cells of the animated cartoons released by "Disney: The Monster Factory!" The article rightly pointed out that, for a company with such a wholesome image, Disney had made some striking contributions to the cinema of the fantastic—*Fantasia* and *Snow White* are among the animated features discussed, along with Disney's live-action masterpiece *20,000 Leagues Under the Sea*. More classics from the 1950s were on hand, with lengthy pieces on both *The Thing* and *The Day the Earth Stood Still*. There's an article that attempts an objective look at "The *Star Trek* Phenomenon," apparently written when such things were still possible. As for the "fan page," while *Famous Monsters* had "The Graveyard Examiner," *Movie Monsters* featured "Creaturealm," and any similarity to the former was only natural, as Jeff Rovin, when he was at Warren, was the editor of "The Graveyard Examiner." Photo scrapbooks of lost world movies and the Flash Gordon serials completed the well-rounded issue, but it was all for naught, as the company folded soon thereafter.

Monster Mania

Monster Mania was a legendary, unfortunately very short-lived (although not from lack of quality) effort from former Warren staffer Russ Jones, dedicated mostly to Hammer films. It would take ten more years and Hammer's home country to produce another magazine (*House of* Hammer, see below) that covered the company as well. *Monster Mania* (a wonderful title, and a perfect description of the results of the monster boom) offered very solid but very unpretentious, straightforward, informed coverage of horror films, and a selection of stills and other graphics that were nearly on a par with *Famous Monsters*. *Castle of Frankenstein* was serious, but sometimes a little too serious for its own good. *Monster Mania* only lasted for three issues, but they were three very, very good issues. It was a tragic casualty in the battle for the planet of the monster magazines.

Monster Mania no. 2 (February 1967)

Cover: Frank Frazetta
Frontispiece: Photo of Christopher Lee from *Corridors of Blood*
"Horror Is My Business"—(Interview with Terence Fisher)
"Mania Film Review—*One Million Years B.C.*"
"The Intriguing World of Hammer Films"— Chris Fellner
"What's New in Monsterdom"— Film previews
Christopher Lee: Hammer's Prince of Horror"— Chris Fellner
"The Peter Cushing Story (Pt. 2)"
Subscription ad — Mort Drucker art

This was one of the best single issues of a monster magazine ever published, almost as intriguing for its editorial comments as its contents. To begin with, Frank Frazetta packages it in a breathtaking wraparound cover, the only one he ever did for a monster movie magazine. It is Frazetta's vision and version of the subject of the magazine's lead article, a review of the Hammer film *One Million Years B.C.* It features gnarled gnazghouls, a patented Frazetta battleship-bootied babe, and toothy pterodactyls and titanic T-Rexes, similar to his equally atmospheric and powerful stone-age paintings for Ace's Edgar Rice Burroughs "Pellucidar" series. The entire issue, in fact, is a special tribute to Hammer films, and covers the subject inside and out with a lengthy Terence Fisher interview, a company retrospective, and in-depth, informative biographies of both Christopher Lee and Peter Cushing. Photos and graphics are plentiful, as is the information, and all are presented in well-balanced layouts in which the elements never fight each other. The magazine even had its subscription ad drawn by another comic book legend, second generation *Mad* magazine mainstay, Mort Drucker.

In retrospect, however, it was the words from Russ Jones's editorial desk that proved even juicier than Raquel Welch in her fur bikini from *One Million Years B.C.* It does more than state his desire to produce a quality publication; it's more like a State of the Union Address for monster magazines that not only addresses the competition overall, but singles out *FM* and Jim Warren, not to mention *Castle of Frankenstein*. Although he doesn't go so far as to name names, the intended targets of his barbs are clear:

> It seems that most publishers of monster magazines care not what kind of material is reproduced within the pages of their publications. How many more times can the "Frankenstein Story" be told? How many more times will the same stock shots of the immortal Bela Lugosi as Dracula be printed? How many more times will we see Willis O'Brien's Kong holding Fay Wray? How many more articles on Shock Theater? Heaven only knows. I personally am very fond of the above mentioned, and I was also a robust fan of most of the monster publications, but what has happened? This field has been over-exploited by hack publications, which through the grapevine heard that monsters were big, so they sat down and threw together a monster book, re-wrote their copy from old press books, and went out and bought a handful of stills. This is not a good magazine. It hurts the ones with merit. How many monster magazines do you think your local store will put on sale every month? Somebody has to suffer.
>
> At one time, there was a fairly good monster book, edited by a real pro, a man who has lived in and loved this field, an expert who, with a free hand, could have created an institution, but now even his magazine has dropped to the cellar quality-wise, and offers next to nothing to the serious fan. We trust this is not the editor's doing, but most likely the vast short-sightedness of one of his superiors.
>
> There is another quite good monster mag, which every now and then comes out, usually bi-annually if that; but a mag with no frequency offers very little to the energetic fan.

Monster Mania will be different. It will stand alone, for it is the only trade publication for the real monster enthusiast.

Brave words, and certainly very opinionated, but the best laid plans of mice and monster magazine publishers often go awry, and *Monster Mania* would only last one more issue. The editorial is interesting in that it's not simply the kind of sniping that had been going on practically since the beginning of organized fandom; even when dressed in spiteful language, most of the words are true. It might have been the golden age of monster magazines, but there was about the same amount of trash, percentage-wise, published in the '60s as in the next decade, and Jones is correct in pointing this out. The "mag with no frequency" is obviously *Castle of Frankenstein*, but again, Jones is right. And even when he's attacking *Famous Monsters*, he's careful not to criticize Forry so much as Jim Warren. Forry did have more or less a free hand, and although it's well known that he would rather that *FM* had been called *Wonderama*, and that he ultimately was always answerable to Jim Warren, he did create an institution. The comments were also made at a time when Warren Publishing was beginning to experience the also well-known financial difficulties that almost sank the company, and even Forry and Jim Warren will admit to the drop in quality, so of course they must be given credit for persevering. But everybody also knows there was no love lost between Warren and Jones, so all in all, it's a fascinating little time capsule.

Monster Mania no. 3 (April 1967)

Cover: Photo of Peter Cushing/*Frankenstein Created Woman*
Frontispiece: Photo of Boris Karloff as the Frankenstein monster
"Mania Film Review and Preview"—Film reviews and previews
The Wolf Man—Richard Bojarski (Text/photo feature)
"What's New in Monsterdom"—More film previews
The Revenge of Frankenstein—Chris Fellner (Text/photo feature)
"Monster Mania Fan Club Page"—Annette Florance (Text feature)
Subscription ad—Wallace Wood art

The cover for this issue was nearly as satisfying as the second, although in a different way. It was a photo, but a great one—the famous promo shot of Peter Cushing caressing a skull from *Frankenstein Created Woman*. The photo was later parodied by Skywald for the cover of *Scream* no. 6, for which Cushing is decked out more like the result of one of his experiments! Film reviews and previews are no mere title listing or one or two paragraph affairs; each film gets one or even two pages of text and photos; the cover feature, *Frankenstein Created Woman*, which also featured former Playboy playmate Susan Denberg as the sexy monster, gets six, not to mention more color shots on the back cover. Other films covered are *The Brides of Fu Manchu*, starring Chris Lee, *Chamber of Horrors*, and the classic *A Study in Terror*, in which Sherlock Holmes meets Jack the Ripper. Poster art for *The Brides of Fu Manchu* also gets a spot all to itself later in the issue, and it's worth the price of admission for the tagline alone—"Better Dead Than Wed!"

The two filmbook articles, for *The Wolf Man* and *The Revenge of Frankenstein*, are standouts, with *The Wolf Man* in particular receiving the red carpet treatment. The information is copious, as are the ad art graphics and rare stills, including moody studio portraits of each of the players in its all-star cast. There was the obligatory back-pages catalog of monster merchandise for sale, and the issue is capped off with the added bonus of a Wallace Wood–drawn subscription ad, which was already a moot point, since this was, unfortunately, the last issue.

Castle of Frankenstein

Castle of Frankenstein was a monster magazine that could be excellent and irritating at the same time — sometimes even on the same page! Created as a "serious" counterpart to *Famous Monsters*, it certainly had an "A" list of contributors, many of whom would go on to become leading lights in the field of horror film scholarship, like William Everson (*Classics of the Horror Film, More Classics of the Horror Film*), Ken Beale and Richard Bojarski (*The Films of Boris Karloff*), Chris Steinbrunner, and Jim Harmon. Also appearing were Larry Hama before he became a comic book artist, and even Joe Dante before he became a director. Dante had been at this kind of thing literally since he was a kid — an early issue of *Famous Monsters* printed his "50 Worst Horror and Science Fiction Movies of All Time," written when he was all of fourteen. And even though one might disagree with any or all of his choices, at least the precocious little guy was thinking about it (and had the idea many years before the self-righteous, self-serving and ill-informed Medved brothers). Joe took the time to watch the actual movies before rendering his verdicts, unlike the Medveds.

True, the *Castle of Frankenstein* writers knew their stuff. At times, though, this depth of knowledge backfired, lapsing into smugness and self-importance, a sort of "oh, look how clever and intellectually sophisticated we are, look how much we know" kind of attitude that could be more than mildly off-putting. True, each and every issue was jam-packed with info and great photos — but often at the expense of the layout; photos and text don't complement each other, they wage a battle of supremacy for each and every page. The magazine had its own cover style (title, main picture, then a film strip at the bottom inset with faces from the other features in the mag) just like *FM*, but with one problem — the covers weren't as good, especially the first few covers are by Larry Ivie. The covers did get better once Ivie left. Ivie started his own magazine, *Monsters and Heroes*, which featured both his ideas and his artwork very prominently. It sank after seven issues and a little over a year of publication.

Actually, *Castle of Frankenstein* only published twenty-four issues — over thirteen years. That was the most maddening thing about *CoF*— even if you were an ardent fan, you never knew when the next issue was coming out. This was mostly due to the caprices and finances of its editor, Calvin T. Beck, who was also the publisher. And in a way, the pseudonym he chose for that role was the most telling thing about both the magazine and the man. In the role of publisher, he referred to himself as "Charles Foster Kane," which was, of course, the boy-wonder, rich-kid newspaper tycoon portrayed by Orson Welles in the seminal film *Citizen Kane*. In terms of the magazine, it was great if you got the joke. It was a nice little wink in the direction of people who were into more than just monster movies — but, as Stan Lee said, you can never assume anything. Stan's credo was that every comic book was somebody's first, and you should never assume that they already know what happened in the previous issue. Not that you should repeat the story in every issue (although some would accuse Marvel of doing just that), but you should make sure everybody is in the loop. Beck tried to stuff the magazine as full of contents as the filmic Kane tried to stuff his home full of artifacts. In terms of his personality, it was an indication of the heights to which he aspired but would not be able to reach, maybe even knowing full well he never would. Sadly, artistic vision and business acumen rarely hold hands, and while Beck had more than enough love for the genre, he never had the personality or drive that made Warren's vision work.

Castle of Frankenstein no. 6 (1965)

Cover: Photo from *The Gorgon*
Frontispiece: Photo of Lon Chaney Jr. from *Tales of Tomorrow*
"Frankenstein TV Movie Guide"—(Film reviews)
"Frankenstein Munster"—(Text/photo preview)
"The Return of Christopher Lee"—Michael Parry
"Son of Chaney"—Richard Bojarski
"Fantasy Fest"—Bhob Stewart
"Oldies but Goodies"—(Photo feature)
"Brzezinski's Frankenstein"—John Benson
"A Hitchcocktail Party"—Bhob Stewart
"Horror on the Air"—Bhob Stewart
"Bok"—Martin Jukovsky
"Movie Noose Reel"—(Film reviews)
The Masque of the Red Death—(Text/photo preview)
"Frankenstein TV Guide"—(Film reviews)
"Frankenstein Movie Guide"—(Film reviews)
"Fables of Heroic Fantasy and Eldritch Horror"—Charles Collins
Inside back cover: Poster art from *The Ghost of Frankenstein*
Back cover: Photo of Bela Lugosi from *Dracula*

Castle of Frankenstein no. 23 (1974)

Cover: Marcus Boas
Frontispiece: Virgil Finlay with quote from Shakespeare
"Apes"—Paul J. Wishinsky
"Bok"—Calvin T. Beck (Book review)
"George Pal's *Doc Savage: The Man of Bronze*"—Edward Felipe
"Return to the Planet of the Apes"—Edna Bennington
Alphaville—J. Ramsey Campbell
"King of Horror: Roger Corman"—Steve Myer (interview)
Not of this Earth—Abbie Herrick
"Frankenstein at Large"—(Film reviews)
Around the World Under the Sea—Joe Dante (Film review)
Inside back cover: Photo from *Monster Zero*

Castle of Frankenstein 1967 "Fearbook" Annual

Front/back cover: Russ Jones
Frontispiece: Photo of Lon Chaney Sr. from *The Phantom of The Opera*
Inside back cover: Photo of Adam West and Burt Ward as Batman and Robin
"Frankenstein Movie Guide"—(Current film reviews)
"Boris Karloff, Master of Horror"—Ken Beale
"*CoF* Goes to a Superhero Convention"—John Benson
"The Early Years of Frankenstein"
Blood of the Vampire—Calvin Beck (Film review)
Terror in the Crypt—Alan Dodd (Film review)
"Frankenstein TV Movie Guide"
Darby O'Gill and the Little People—(Film review)
Jonny Quest—(Series preview)
"*CoF*anaddicts"—(Fan Club page, mixed media reviews)

A fan favorite, possibly the best single issue of the magazine ever published, the 1967 *Castle of Frankenstein* "Fearbook" is the perfect example of the first statement of this section. (The term "Fearbook," although often thought to have been invented by Forry Ackerman was actually first used here; *Famous Monsters* later co-opted the phrase and made it its own, but here Calvin Beck actually beat Uncle Forry to a pun.) To illustrate the point, let's take a look at what the magazine had to say in its one-page feature on the classic animated series *Jonny Quest*:

> JONNY QUEST—Curious mixture from the Hanna Barbera cartoon factory which, in the past, has turned out many items notable for their unusual lack of imagination and wit. *Jonny Quest*, a departure for the company, is a realistic cartoon, which somehow gives the impression of an animated comic book. Jonny is the 11-year-old son of a famous scientist; his adventures are exotic, to say the least. The storylines, straight out of B-Movies, are neither interesting nor funny. One was a seeming parody of the old Mummy series, complete with the convenient collapsing cavern to get rid of the monster and the heavy, a high priest type. The animation is erratic, but sometimes unusual and creative, though often out of proportion

and mismatching previous sequences. Dialogue is read well enough, but is ludicrously stilted and unreal. But it is a new kind of children's cartoon — an entire story each episode, with characters a little closer to reality than most.

As Sgt. Hulka (Warren Oates) says in *Stripes*: "Lighten up, Francis!" Joseph Hanna and William Barbera, creators of the much-loved *Tom and Jerry*, among countless others, headed up one of the most successful cartoon studios in history; and while it will always be argued whether they advanced the science of animated cartoons, one thing they were almost never short on was wit or imagination. *Johnny Quest* had more monsters and gadgets than you could shake a stick at — giant crab monsters, pterodactyls, mummies, Yetis, werewolves, creatures from lagoons, mad scientists, robot spies. You name it, it menaced Race Bannon, Hajji, and the Quests. "The storylines, straight out of B-Movies..." (like half the ones that *Castle of Frankenstein* covered) are actually often rather better than the movies that inspired them, with better pacing and, relatively speaking, more elaborate special effects. As for being funny — well, the show was intended to be relatively serious, but Bandit, the canine comedy relief and spiritual, as well as vocal, ancestor of Scooby-Doo (Don Messick did the voices for both dogs) obviously isn't included for "sophisticated" *New Yorker* humor. The show was for children, after all — and provides some charming moments for both children and dog lovers. The editors seem to forget the comedy relief in the classic horrors, some of which was much harder to take. The "parody of the old Mummy series," was the third episode, "The Curse of Anubis," and is played completely straight; straighter, in fact, than *Abbott & Costello Meet the Mummy*. All the basic rules and conventions of mummy movies are observed, respected and exploited, so it's hard to see where the parody comes in. "The convenient collapsing cavern" was hardly a cliché (it would have been more cliché to have the mummy burn up or crumble to pieces), and gosh, aren't the "high priest types" usually the heavy in a mummy movie? It would be difficult to call a cult that keeps a murderous monster alive through the centuries anything else. Even when the magazine tries to say something positive, it can't, like it'll be kicked out of the monster club if it admits to liking the show. Oh well, quality will out, as they say, and forty years after the fact, the original *Jonny Quest* continues to enthrall new generations, while the original *Castle of Frankenstein* is but a cherished memory in the hearts and minds of a relatively few collectors.

Mayfair Publications

Monster Fantasy

In the '70s, Mayfair Publications jumped on the monster mag bandwagon with *Monster Fantasy* and *Monster World*. Warren's title was long defunct, but Warren still wasn't having that, so Mayfair changed the title of the latter to *Quasimodo's Monster Magazine* (see below).

Of the two titles, *Monster Fantasy* was actually rather well done. Theme issues (no. 1, Dracula, Vampires; no. 2, Mummies; no. 3, Sci-Fi; no. 4, Lon Chaney Jr.) had better cover art (collages of the featured subjects), but still had an annoying tendency towards carelessness that mars the overall presentation. With a little more effort, this could have been a solid monster magazine. Why it should differ so wildly in quality from its companion publication is a mystery, and why the other magazine lasted twice as long is an even bigger mystery.

Monster Fantasy no. 2 (June 1975)

Cover: Gentile
"*Monster Fantasy* Movies"—(Film reviews)
"*Monster Fantasy* News"—(Film previews)
"The Mummy Book"—Florence Brown, Gary Gerani
"*The Mummy*"—(Filmbook)
"At Last! A Real Disaster!"—(Film review)
"Rondo Hatton: Hollywood's Monster Without Makeup"
Freaks—(Film history)
"The Strange Death of Lon Chaney"
"Elsa Lanchester: First Lady of Horror"
"The Witchcraft Movies"—Deborah Sherwood
"The Witchcraft Series They Forced Off TV!"
"Encore for a Monster Maker"—(Photo feature)
"The Thing That Was Killing the Girls"—(Prose fiction)
"Monster Pin-Up of the Month: Bela Lugosi"—(Photo feature)

Monster Fantasy no. 3 (August 1975) (No. 4 on the contents page.)

Cover: Gentile
"*Monster Fantasy* Movies"—(Film reviews)
"*Monster Fantasy* Bookshelf"—(Book reviews)
"Laird Cregar: The Tragic Life of Hollywood's Haunted Jack the Ripper"
"The Space Monster Book"—Florence Brown, Gary Gerani
This Island Earth—(Filmbook)
"Monsters from *The Outer Limits*"—(Photo feature)
"The Monsters of *Star Trek*"—(Text/photo feature)
"*Barbarella*—A Space Fantasy"
"Lionel Atwill—Maddest of the Mad Scientists!"—(Text/photo feature)
"A *Monster Fantasy* Masterpiece: *The Phantom of the Opera*"—Max Miller (film history)

"Alfred Hitchcock—Master of Movie Chills"—S.M. (Text/photo feature)
"Bloody Bargains"—Catalog

Monster World/ Quasimodo's Monster Magazine

Quasimodo started out as *Monster World* and tried to play it (relatively) straight at first; early issues' covers feature passable renderings of Bela Lugosi and Christopher Lee's Dracula, and Lon Chaney Sr. as the Hunchback of Notre Dame, and articles on the obligatory old and new subjects. No. 6 has a passable good/bad girl painting, but the last two issues (possibly because they were the last ones) went the total humor (at least in someone's estimation) route. No. 7 has a cover painting of the Wolfman shaving, and the last is described below. The worst thing was, as noted with the example issue below, the muddy photo reproduction and the printing, which was especially cheap. Even if there had been something worth reading, it was hard to see.

Quasimodo's Monster Magazine (Vol. 2 no. 8, May 1976)

Cover: "Ibis"
"The Mummy through the Years"—Ron Weiss
"The Mummy, or: All Dressed Up and No Place to Live, or Gosh, You Don't Look 2,000 Years Old"—Script/art: "Ibis"
"How to See Transylvania on Only 3 Pints of Blood a Day"—Joe Kiernan (Text feature)
"A Look at the Invisible Man"—Lauri Weiss
"The Invisible Man, or: What Did His Wife See in Him?"—Joe Kiernan, Norman Nodel
"*Star Trek* Hall of Fame"—Tony Tallarico (Photo/bio feature)
"Star-Wrecked vs. Spaced-Out 1999 1/2"—Joe "Flash" Kiernan, Tony "Buck" Tallarico
"Shark Fever: The World Is En-Jaw-ing *Jaws*"—Don Wigal

"Monster Madness"
"Continued Next Issue (Pt. 3): Heroes and Horrors"—Ed O'Connor
"Forgotten Horror Films of the Past: *The Spider*"—Cast list, synopsis
"Visions of Tomorrow"—Interview with Edward Edelson by Ed O' Connor

Quasimodo's Monster Magazine was the kind of monster mag that gives monster mags a bad name, and makes something like *For Monsters Only* seem like the collected works of Shakespeare. From cover to cover, it's a shoddy job. The printing and reproduction are still terrible. The cover painting is a joke, literally—a befuddled-looking Mummy receives an eviction notice. Understandably, the responsible party was too embarrassed to sign his or her real name. Fortunately, other responsible parties did choose to sign most everything else, so we know exactly whom to blame for the various atrocities, because the jokes don't stop with the cover. Even more so than *For Monsters Only*, by this time the whole magazine is treated as a joke, and in the couple of selected instances where it attempts a little scholarship, it gets major facts wrong. For example, a history of Mummy movies and leads off with a shot of Boris Karloff from *The Ghoul* labeled as a still from *The Mummy*. The comics are badly written and drawn, and are just stupid—not clever stupid, just dumb stupid. The magazine even has a monster-photo-with-funny-captions feature called "Monster Madness," which Stan Lee probably would have despised if he'd given it any thought. The whole magazine reeks of inauthenticity and condescension, and was evicted from the newsstands with this issue.

EERIE PUBLICATIONS

Revenge of Dracula (1977)

Cover: Photo of Bela Lugosi as Dracula
Frontispiece: Photo of Bela Lugosi as Dracula
"Vampires—The Walking Dead"—John Thomas Church
"Dracula—King of the Vampires"—John Thomas Church
"Female Vampires—Deadlier Than the Males"—Prose/photo feature
Inside back cover: Photo of Bela Lugosi as Dracula
Back cover: Photo of Bela Lugosi as Dracula

Revenge of Dracula was a one-shot magazine published in 1977, a companion to the previous year's *Dracula Classic*. Both were quite well-done packages, doubly surprising when one considers who put them out: Eerie Publications, famed purveyors of 1950s reprints housed under incredibly gruesome new cover art (*see* Chapter Three). The cover for the first is a medium shot of Bela hypnotizing with his hands. The cover here is a simple, tastefully tinted (in shades of green), classic full-face photo of Lugosi giving that patented arched-eyebrow stare. There are no foot-long fangs added, no gallon of blood oozing down his chin, and he's not beheading a female mummy vampire girl in bondage. The whole magazine, like the previous effort, is copiously illustrated with photos of Lugosi, Christopher Lee, William Marshall, and Ingrid Pitt among others, although sadly in this edition they find no space for German Robles and *El Vampiro*. The first article is historical, dealing with the facts and legends that begat and are associated with the vampire. The second deals with vampire movies, and contrary to the prevailing attitude of the time, treats Lugosi with the respect he deserves. Though it makes note of *Dracula*'s flaws, it doesn't simply pass it off as camp and champion the Lee interpretation. There's nothing new in the way of information concerning his career, but the magazine is a real treat for Lugosi fans, with its wealth of photos and that great cover. "Female Vampires — Deadlier Than the Males" is not a history of female vampires, nor the films they inhabit (although plenty of stills from them were used to illustrate the story), but rather a cover exploitation title for Sheridan LeFanu's "Carmilla," on which the film *Countess Dracula*, among others, is based. Like the reprinting of Stoker's "Dracula's Guest" in *Dracula Classic*, it's quite a nice little literary surprise, given Eerie's usual shock tactics with its comics magazines. A few more magazines like these, and a few less magazines with the same cover, would have raised Eerie's standing in the field considerably.

King Kong

Long before the visually stunning (but hideously overlong, poorly acted and cast) Peter Jackson remake of *King Kong* once again made the big ape a household name, the master of Skull Island was the subject of another big-budget remake. This was the 1976 production, which ditched painstaking stop-animation techniques for Rick Baker (literally) in a monkey-suit, a move that misfired by almost cosmic proportions (even though it was a well-designed monkey suit). But what really sunk the movie was its "NOW" topicality, making Ann Darrow a trendy women's libber who gets to spout embarrassing lines like, "Let go of me, you male chauvinist ape!" The only good thing about it was that it got the original (and still the mightiest) version re-released and re-demonstrated that film's superiority; that in turn entailed a number of one-off specials that were hastily produced and looked it. At least they were more or less obligated to make reference to the original, and more stills from the greatest fantasy/adventure/monster movie ever made is never a bad thing, especially if they make more people want to see the original movie. As he did with *The Revenge of Dracula*, John Thomas Church wrote the entire magazine.

Kong: The Most Famous Monster of All Time (1976)

Cover: Unaccredited King Kong painting
Frontispiece: Photo from *King Kong* (1933)
"The Monster of Skull Island"
"The Making of *King Kong*"
"*King Kong*: The Greatest Horror Film of All Time"
"From King Kong to Godzilla"
"Monsters We've Known and Loved"
Inside back cover: Photo from *King Kong* (1933)
Back cover: Poster art from *King Kong* (1976)

House of Hammer/ Halls of Horror (UK)

The year 1976 was tumultuous for Great Britain. The country was suffering from sweltering heat, a garbage strike, massive unemployment and social unrest, from which sprang the British version of American punk rock. The Damned released the first British punk record, "New Rose," and the Sex Pistols swore on Bill Grundy's television show, stirring up a cultural frenzy in a country already on the brink. It was small wonder, then, that the publication of the now legendary *House of Hammer* failed to create a national stir, except of course among monster fans — including punks. There were parallels between the two art forms — punks often made themselves up to resemble something out of *Night of the Living Dead*, identifying with monsters as outcasts of society. Indeed, The Damned's lead singer, former gravedigger Dave Vanian, resembled nothing so much as Count Dracula—and *House of Hammer* covered the movies that inspired the lot.

House of Hammer was masterminded by the James Warren of British monster mags, Dez Skinn (although he might wince at the comparison; more on that shortly). While he was employed by IPC (International Publishing Company), he pitched the idea of a weekly horror comic called *Chiller* that became an annual, *The Buster Book of Spooky Stories*. After moving on to Top Sellers Ltd., he oversaw eight issues of *Monster Mag*, an eight-page magazine that folded out into a big poster. Dismissing the format as too impractical, and still wanting to do horror comics, he did what Marvel and every other publisher had done, and combined comics and movies. The result was *House of Hammer*. Oh, and about that wincing between Warren and Skinn. It seems that when Dez wanted to find an American distributor, the one he contacted thought that his magazine's title sounded too much like a carpentry periodical, so the distributor changed the name to *House of Horror* and proudly announced it to the press. Warren, upon reading the report, produced one of his patented overnight ashcans in order to secure copyright on that title. Naturally, this caused Skinn many hassles, but no matter what the title or format, *Hammer* never caught on over here anyway, despite the quality of the material, which was generally excellent.

House of Hammer no. 5 (June 1977)

Cover: Brian Lewis
"Moon Zero Two"—Story/art by Paul Neary
"Media Macabre"—(News)
"Terrible Monsters"—John Brosnan
"The Coming of Dracula"—Denis Gifford
"Hammer Answer Desk"

Deranged—John Fleming (Film review)
"Mexican Monsters"—Barrie Patterson
"Van Helsing's Terror Tales: One Man's Meat!"—Story/art by Martin Asbury

This issue features a literally eye-popping spaceman cover from Brian Lewis that makes the decomposing astronaut from the cover of Creepy no. 64 look positively sedate. *Moon Zero Two* is the film adapted in this issue, with both the writing and art being handled by homegrown talent Paul Neary, who had also garnered an American following due to his work at Warren. Two of Britain's most respected genre authors contribute articles, and there is even an article on Mexican monsters. Besides the illustrated movie adaptations, *House of Hammer* contained a cracking backup strip that starred Van Helsing (in the person of Cushing) as both host and player for new adventures featuring the world's greatest vampire-hunter. The early issues can be a tough pull, but are well worth the effort.

House of Hammer no. 10 (January 1978)

Cover: Brian Lewis
Frontispiece: Photo of John Carradine from *The Sentinel*
"Curse of the Werewolf"—Steve Moore, John Bolton
"Media Macabre" (News and previews)
"Media Macabre Review"—Tony Crawley (*The Sentinel*)
Shadowman—Sidney Falco (film review)
"The Year of Fu Manchu: 1932"—Denis Gifford (text/photo feature)
Close Encounters of the Third Kind—Film preview
"The Monster Gallery"—Photo feature
"Kong's Kind"—Steve Moore (Text feature)
Curse of the Werewolf—John Brosnan (Text/photo feature)
Back cover: *Curse of the Werewolf* poster art

This is one of the best-remembered issues. Brian Lewis's *Curse of the Werewolf* cover was one of his finest efforts, even rivaling Basil

Gogos's similar inimitable piece for *Famous Monsters* no. 12. *House of Hammer* had a unique way of presenting the filmbooks for the lead feature — comic strip adaptations, rather than the usual photo/text combination. The practice resulted in some unique adaptations, particularly this issue's interpretation of *Curse of the Werewolf*, in which Brian Lewis proved once again that he was as adept with a pen as he was with a paintbrush, at the head of the class from the Graham Ingels/Bernie Wrightson school. There's a good balance of old and new, and there's more *Curse of the Werewolf* info and photos courtesy of John Brosnan, making it a very nice item for fans of the film.

House of Hammer no. 13 (April 1978)

Cover: Brian Lewis
Frontispiece: Photo from *Star Wars*
"Plague of the Zombies"— Steve Moore, Trevor Goring/Brian Bolland
"Media Macabre" (news and previews)
"Media Macabre Review"— John Brosnan (*The Uncanny*); John Brosnan (*War of the Monsters*); Tise Vajimaji (*The People That Time Forgot*)
"Special Preview: *Star Wars*"— Alan Frank
"Fantasy Film Festival"— Jean-Marc Lofficier
"The Dead That Walk"— Tise Vajimaji
"Van Helsing's Terror Tales: The Curse of Cormac"— Steve Parkhouse, Brian Lewis
Back cover: *Plague of the Zombies* poster art

By now, the *Star Wars* bug had bitten even *House of Hammer*, but the magazine didn't give itself over to the trend as completely as FM did. The Hammer classic *Plague of the Zombies* gets a rare cover spot and the lead feature. Brian Bolland, who would find fame with "Judge Dredd" and much work for DC, lends inks to Trevor Goring's pencils for the moody black-and-white adaptation of the film. "The Dead That Walk" was the title of an article that prefigured the title of a book by fellow Briton Leslie Halliwell, which covered all of the major classic monster series. The book is informative but dry.

House of Hammer no. 15 (June 1978)

Cover: Brian Lewis
"The Mummy's Shroud"— Donnie Avenell, David Jackson
"Media Macabre" (News and previews)
"Media Macabre Review"— John Brosnan (*The Island of Dr. Moreau*); Tony Crawley (*Blue Sunshine*); Alan Frank (*Audrey Rose*)
"*House of Hammer* Exclusive: *Fanatic*"— John Fleming
"Beyond the Living Dead: An Interview with George A. Romero"— Tony Crawley
"The Shadow of the Sphinx"— Alan Frank
"Special Preview: *Victor Frankenstein*"
"Van Helsing's Terror Tales: Wilbur's Whisky"— Story/art by Dave Chester
Back cover: *The Mummy's Shroud* poster art

This is two issues later, and not a wookie in sight! Instead, *House* moves into the future by mixing the new and the classic, but not giving inordinate amounts of space to any one product. Brian Lewis contributes his usual fine cover, his take on *The Mummy's Shroud*, but the inside adaptation is not nearly as successful. This, however, is redeemed by the back-cover inclusion of the art for the one-sheet for the film, which bears the immortal tagline: "Beware the beat of the cloth-wrapped feet!"

Hammer's House of Horror no. 1 (March 1978)

Cover: Brian Lewis
Frontispiece: Photo from *The Gorgon*
"Curse of the Werewolf"— Steve Moore, John Bolton
"The Golden Age of Horror: Boris Karloff"— Denis Gifford
Witchfinder General— John Fleming (Film review)

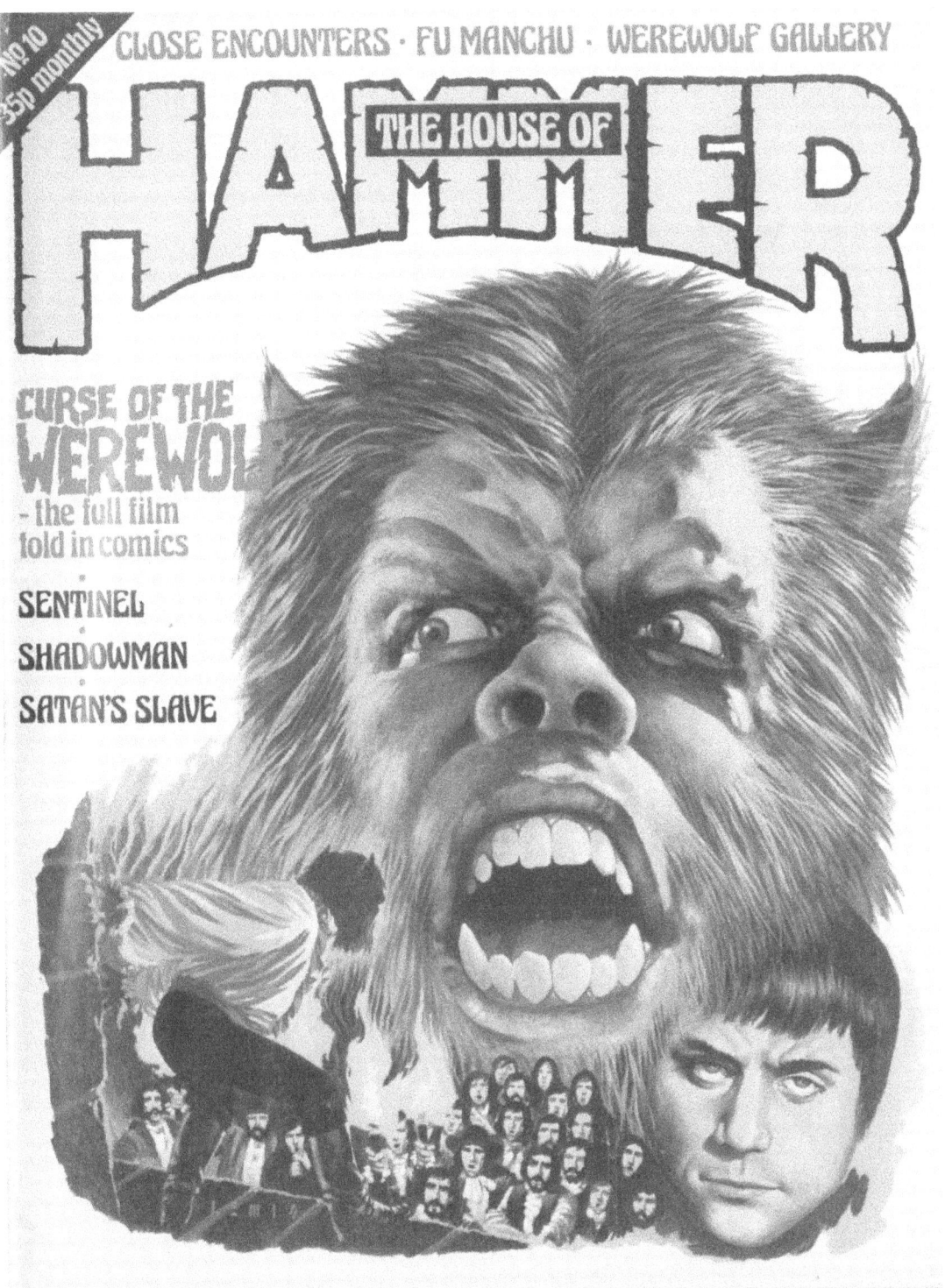

House of Hammer no. 10 (HOH) — one of England's everlasting contributions to monster movies was Hammer Films, which made an everlasting contribution to the monster magazine genre. Cover by Brian Lewis (courtesy Dez Skinn and Comics International).

"Beyond the Living Dead: An Interview with George A. Romero"— Tony Crawley
Curse of the Werewolf— John Brosnan (Text/photo feature)
Psycho— Tony Crawley
"History of Hammer" (Pt. 1)— Bob Sheridan
"Van Helsing's Terror Tales: A Spot of Blood"— Donnie Avenell, Patrick Wright
Back cover: *Curse of the Werewolf* poster art

    This was the issue that caused so much friction between Warren and Skinn. Skinn skirted the problem by adding "*Hammer's*" to the *House of Horror* as soon as the shipment got to the states. There was little else he could do, since copies were already in transit when the Warren news came through. Created for American consumption, it was a collection of the best the magazine had offered up to that point, but despite the excellence on display and the wonderful, iconic Brian Lewis Vampire Girl cover, it still failed to find more than a cult audience — great for its rep, but lousy for sales figures. *Witchfinder General* was the British title for the Vincent Price film released in the U.S. by AIP as *The Conqueror Worm* in an attempt to cash in on the popularity of its Poe series.

Shriek!

Shriek! no. 3 (Summer 1966)

Cover: Unaccredited painting of generic Snake People
"Christopher Lee: The Loneliness of Evil"—(Interview)
Dracula, Prince of Darkness—(Review)
The Face of Fu Manchu—(Review)
"Blood Galore"—(Photo feature)
The Reptile—(Review)
"The Zombie A–Z"—(Text/photo feature)
The Plague of the Zombies—(Review)
Onibaba—(Review)
"The Psychopath"— Robert Bloch
Rasputin, the Mad Monk—(Review)
The Reptile—(Review)
"Monstrous Memories"—(Photo feature)

    Shriek was an early solid entry into the monster mag sweepstakes that failed to develop an identity, and therefore an audi-ence. Most of the content consisted of photos and reviews of the movies listed therein. Fortunately the filler shied away from the fun-ny stuff. This issue features almost as much Hammer info as monster mania, and would be more highly regarded if it were not for the exceedingly generic and sloppy cover art.

• Two •

Creepy Monsters, Eerie Zombies, and Generally Undead No-Goodniks

As Warren Publishing began the genre of black-and-white illustrated horror, so it does this chapter, as it must. There wouldn't be a genre, or chapter (or the book, for that matter) if it weren't for James Warren. His publications' effect on the graphic story medium is incalculable. The genesis and history of Warren's efforts in this field have been well documented in *The Warren Companion*, required reading for anyone with any interest in the company. So the Warren section of the chapter will focus more on individual issues and accomplishments; the various themes and types of monsters found in those issues, and how they compare and contrast with the publications that their success spawned.

WARREN PUBLISHING

Creepy

This was the original, and still the greatest, black-and-white horror comic ever published. *Creepy* was the first of its kind, the standard-bearer for the entire genre, which it created. Its early issues featured a collection of talent unseen since the glory days of EC; in fact, Warren employed many former top EC talents. Warren's entire line foundered when the company experienced financial trouble in the late '60s, and the quality of every magazine was severely compromised. Warren rebounded, but his illustrated horror magazines moved away from the EC look, towards the more illustrative style of the many Spanish artists, and the more progressive styles of the new wave of American artists. This alienated some of the older fan base, but enough remained, or were generated anew, to keep the title on the stands for 18 years. Its influence on the illustrated horror medium is incalculable, continuing to resonate almost fifty years after it first appeared.

Creepy no. 15 (June 1967)

Cover: Frank Frazetta
"City of Doom!"—Archie Goodwin, Steve Ditko

"Adam Link, Champion Athlete"—Otto Binder, Joe Orlando
"The Adventure of the German Student!" (Washington Irving)—Archie Goodwin, Jerry Grandenetti
"The River!"—Johnny Craig
"*Creepy*'s Loathsome Lore!"—Archie Goodwin, Gil Kane
"The Terror Beyond Time!"—Archie Goodwin, Neal Adams

Put on a blindfold and stick a pin in a stack of early *Creepy* (well, not really, heaven forbid, but you get the point) and you'll hit a winner. Where else were you going to find a magazine (in this case, for instance) featuring Goodwin, Frazetta, Ditko, Craig, Kane and Adams all at once, and doing some of their most memorable work? Frazetta's monochromatic Neanderthal cover has become iconic, and Ditko's Warren output is some of the most accomplished of his career. Gil Kane gets to visualize a variety of monsters for his spot, and Neal Adams gets to visualize Ultimate Evil for "The Terror Beyond Time," which resembles, in Adams's words, nothing so much as a "Hot Fudge Sundae!" (writing in *The Warren Companion*).

Creepy no. 64 (August 1974)

Cover: Vaughn Bode/Larry Todd
Frontispiece: Bernie Wrightson
"Forgotten Flesh"—Doug Moench, Vincente Alcazar
"Mates"—Doug Moench, Esteban Maroto
"High Time"—Steve Skeates, Paul Neary
"Only Losers Win!"—Rich Margopolous, Howard Chaykin
"One Autumn at Arkham"—Tom Sutton
"To Sleepy Hollow Returned"—Jeff Rovin, Leo Summers
"An Angel Shy of Hell"—Jim Stenstrum, Richard Corben

Monster moviemakers, American International Pictures in particular, would often design a killer poster first, and then make the movie based on the poster. James Warren would do this on occasion as well—he would get a piece of art he liked so much he would then build an issue around it. Each creative team would get a look at the art, and then do a story, each offering its own unique take; very seldom did the same painting suggest the same ideas. One such instance was this issue of *Creepy*. The cover art, which is indeed iconic, was penciled by Vaughn Bode and colored by Larry Todd, and features a spaceman in the advanced stages of decomposition; a gruesomely beautiful image that is at once revolting and riveting.

Creepy no. 75 (November 1975)

Cover: Ken Kelly
Frontispiece: Bernie Wrightson
"The Escape Chronicle"—Budd Lewis, Jose Ortiz
"Phantom of Pleasure Island"—Gerry Boudreau, Alex Toth
"Snow"—Bruce Bezaire, Rich Buckler Sr./Wallace Wood
"Death Expression"—Jim Stenstrum, John Severin
"Thrillkill"—Jim Stenstrum, Neal Adams

This was another notable issue of *Creepy*, not so much for the heavyweight art lineup, but for the first appearance of the devastating, truly chilling, intense "Thrillkill" by Stenstrum and Adams, an all-time fan favorite, and possibly the best single story ever published by Warren. It does not feature traditional monster, but is scarier and more horrifying than a thousand other stories containing armies of fiends. It unfortunately eclipses some of the other very fine work in the issue, particularly the stories drawn by Toth and Buckler/Wood, which contain some pretty hard-hitting moments of their own. It's so good that both Stenstrum and Adams could've retired then, their reputations assured—but fortunately, they didn't.

Creepy no. 120 (August 1980)

Cover: Jeff Jones
Frontispiece: Rudy Nebres

"Deathwatch" — Roger McKenzie, Leo Duranona
"Hell House" — Alabaster Redzone (Jim Stenstrum), Jesus Blasco
"Black Rainbow" — Budd Lewis, Ruben Yandoc
"One Mind, Closed for Alterations" — Gerry Boudreau, Jess Jodloman
"A Taste for Heroes" — Gerry Boudreau, Carmine Infantino/Pablo Marcos
"Winterbeast" — Budd Lewis, Val Mayerik
"Black Snow" — Jeff Rovin, Herb Arnold

Even at this late stage of the game, Warren was capable of some great offerings, like this issue's great zombie cover by Jeff Jones. The irony of it was that Atlas/Seaboard had rejected it for its *Weird Tales of the Macabre*. In these later years, Warren Magazines reused a couple of previously published Skywald and Atlas/Seaboard covers, something that would have been unthinkable when Warren was exercising a firmer controlling hand.

Creepy 1968 Yearbook

Cover: Jack Davis, Frank Frazetta
Frontispiece: Frazetta
"Duel of the Monsters" — Archie Goodwin, Angelo Torres
"Return Trip" — Arthur Porges, Joe Orlando
"Abominable Snowman" — Bill Pearson, John Severin
"Werewolf" — Larry Ivie, Frank Frazetta
"The Thing in the Pit" — Ivie, Gray Morrow
"Vampires Fly at Dusk" — Archie Goodwin, Reed Crandall
"Sand Doom" — Archie Goodwin, Al Williamson
"Hot Spell" — Archie Goodwin, Reed Crandall

This first *Creepy Yearbook* is a staggering collection of the talent at Warren's disposal in the magazine's salad days, a true comic artists' hall of fame. The same can't be said for all the writers, although these are all solid efforts. The best, of course, was written by real-life superhuman Archie Goodwin, who did so much more for comics than simply write great stories and be an editorial example for all to follow. If anything, the collection is just a hair short of being perfect. If you're going to have an early *Creepy* story by Goodwin and Al Williamson (and one that would have fit very comfortably, both in style and tone, in *Tales from the Crypt*), you really must include "Success Story," the horribly comic tale of cartoonist Baldo Smudge, a tale especially beloved by comics fans because all of the main characters resemble real-life Warren contributors, including Goodwin and Warren himself. It wouldn't be the last time Warren was used as the model for the villain of a story (for example, see the awesome Neal Adams adaptation of Harlan Ellison's "Rock God" in *Creepy* no. 32). He was reportedly always a good sport about it.

But the art — from cover to cover, it's the best of the best. One of Warren's vaunted galleries showcases four out of the first five covers, all masterpieces by Jack Davis and Frank Frazetta. It's also Frazetta's last published comic book story, "Werewolf," a feature alone worth the price of admission. It's two monsters for the price of one by Angelo Torres, in the story that was pictured so memorably on the cover of *Creepy* no. 7, in "Duel of the Monsters." It's Joe Orlando in a real "Return Trip" to the EC days. It's John Severin and Gray Morrow and Al Williamson doing wonderful monsters, and Reed Crandall with his trademark unsurpassed draftsmanship. It's a shining example of everything horror comics were and can be, and some of the most brilliant usage of the black-and-white medium ever seen.

Eerie

With the runaway success of *Creepy*, the field was wide open and ripe for another magazine like it, so a couple of years later, Warren published it. *Eerie* was to *Creepy* what *Monster World* was to *Famous Monsters*; more of what the fans couldn't get enough of, except that the stories were narrated by the repulsively rotund Cousin Eerie instead of the gaunt, cadaverous

Uncle Creepy. Realizing the redundancy, Warren's solution was to turn *Eerie* into a magazine for continuing series, while *Creepy* continued to publish stand-alone tales. *Creepy* and *Eerie* would have the field to themselves for a few years, and it's interesting to note that no real competition appeared until it looked as though the Warren magazines were in trouble. But although they had plenty of competition for a time, and some of it very, very good, at the end of the battle for the planet of the monster magazines, *Creepy* and *Eerie* were the last ghouls standing.

Eerie no. 12 (November 1967)

Cover: Dan Adkins
Frontispiece: "*Eerie*'s Monster Gallery!" — Roy G. Krenkel
"The Masque of the Red Death" (adapted from Edgar Allan Poe) — Tom Sutton
"Vampyrus!" — Jeff Jones
"... Nor Custom, Stale..." — Johnny Craig
"Escape!" — Joe Orlando
"Portrait of Satan!" — Rik Estrada
"The Past Master" (adapted from Robert Bloch) — Craig Tennis, Al McWilliams

Published just on the cusp of Warren's "dark years," the decline in fortunes can already be observed by the notable absence of Archie Goodwin's name from the writing credits. Most of the stories' artists write as well as draw. This issue is memorable and popular for its Dan Adkins cover, a faithful, accomplished rendering of Lon Chaney as the Mummy that would have sat well on *Famous Monsters*.

Eerie no. 53 (January 1974)

Cover: Sanjulian
"Wart Monster of Tennessee" — Doug Moench, Rich Buckler Sr./Bill DuBay
"The *Eerie* Eye" — Sanjulian biography with portrait by Bill DuBay
"The Mummy Walks: Enter Mr. Hyde" — Steve Skeates, Jaime B. Remohi
"Curse of the Werewolf: To Save a Witch's Soul!" — Al Milgrom, Martin Salvador
"Hunter" — Rich Margopolous, Paul Neary
"Schreck: First Night of Terror!" — Moench, Vincente Alcazar/Neal Adams
"Fathom Haunt: Spawn of the Dread Thing" — Tom Sutton

Lon Chaney's Mummy had graced the cover of *Eerie* no. 12, and Boris Karloff's Mummy checked in with two appearances, no. 50 and this issue, a stunning Sanjulian portrait. The magazine had settled into its continuing character phase by now. The best of the storylines was the post-apocalyptic adventure series "Hunter" by Margopolous and Neary, who was Warren's most popular and talented British import.

Eerie no. 70 (November 1975)

Cover: Sanjulian
Frontispiece: Bernie Wrightson
"Coffin: The Final Sunrise" — Budd Lewis, Jose Ortiz
"Hunter II: Goblin Thrust" — Budd Lewis, Paul Neary
"Code Name — Slaughter Five" — Gerry Boudreau, Leopoldo Sanchez
"El Cid: Crooked Mouth" — Lewis, Gonzalo Mayo
"Oogie and the Junkers" — Bill DuBay, Esteban Maroto

This featured yet another great cover that had people wondering why it wasn't on *Famous Monsters*. Sanjulian's masterful painting might have been intended to represent the "Coffin" character, but it was "The Colossal Beast," from *War of the Colossal Beast*, just as sure as the turning of the earth. "Hunter II" is not merely the second phase of the character's adventures; the writers actually killed the first one.

Eerie no. 81 (February 1977)

Cover: Frank Frazetta
Frontispiece: "Introducing Exciting *Eerie* 81!"

"Goodbye, Bambi Boone"—Cary Bates, Carmine Infantino/Dick Giordano
"The Comic Books"—Joe Brancatelli (Text feature)
"The Taking of Queen Bovine"—Gerry Boudreau, Ramon Torrents
"The Bride of Congo"—Bill DuBay, Carmine Infantino/Gonzalo Mayo
"You're a Big Girl Now" (color)—Bruce Jones, Richard Corben
"Starchild"—Louise Jones/David Michelinie, Jose Ortiz
"The Giant Ape Suit"—Roger McKenzie, Luis Bermejo
"Golden Girl"—Nicola Cuti, Leopoldo Sanchez

This was another concept issue centered on a cover, Frazetta's last original piece published by Warren. Frazetta had originally done it for Wallace Wood for a science fiction magazine that Wood was creating for Warren called *Pow*, but when the plans fell through, the painting ended up on the cover of *Eerie*, much to Frazetta's surprise. Regardless of the circumstances, it remains one of his most whimsically imaginative and best-loved pieces, and inspired some imaginative stories for the issue as well.

MARVEL

Tales of the Zombie

Zombie! The word itself, used to describe the walking dead, is almost more horrible than "monster," carrying with it the very stench of the grave. Zombies, as a pop culture phenomenon, were initially encountered in William Seabrook's *The Magic Island*, published in 1929. Seabrook based his work on allegedly eyewitness accounts of voodoo ceremonies at which zombies were actually animated, and his description follows:

> Neither a ghost, nor a person who had been raised Lazarus-like from the dead, the Zombie is a soul-less human corpse, still dead, but taken from the grave and endowed by sorcery with a mechanical semblance of life. It is a dead body that is made to walk and act and move as if it were alive. People who have the power to do this go to a fresh grave, dig up the body before it has had time to rot, galvanize it into movement, and then make of it a servant or a slave — occasionally for the commission of some crime, more often simply as a drudge around the plantation or farm, setting it dull and heavy tasks, and beating it like a dumb beast if it slackens.

The cinematic equivalent of the reanimated corpse has produced two distinct strains. Until 1968, movie zombies all had been of a type, according to the guidelines laid down by Seabrook: they have a grave-like pallor and vacant stare, and are content to shamble slowly along until their victims, like those of the Mummy, back themselves into a convenient corner, and the zombies perform the dirty deed. Cinemas presented poetic masterpieces like *White Zombie*, and Noble Johnson's truly scarifying turn as a zombie in the second greatest horror-comedy of all time, *The Ghostbreakers*, with Bob Hope and Willie Best ("Is you in there, zombie?"), and great B-movies like *King of the Zombies* (Mantan Moreland). But the zombie never really caught on with audiences, and was soon relegated to a prop in comedies like *Zombies on Broadway*. The zombie as occasionally useful prop continued through the '50s and early '60s in B productions like *The Zombies of Mora-Tau* and *The Four Skulls of Jonathan Drake*, the latter featuring old pro Henry Daniell as the voodoo master and Paul G. Wexler (*see* chapter 4) as a zombie henchman with the physical stature and look of Christopher Lee. Naturally, Hammer Films took it a step further. In *Plague* of the Zombies, the monsters were much scarier and nastier, although they still shambled. This was all to change very shortly.

In 1968, Pittsburgh filmmaker George Romero unleashed his revolutionary (and even socially relevant) *Night of the Living Dead*, and the notion and the image of the zombie permanently changed. No longer satisfied with looking and acting vacant, zombies became not only more athletic, but capable of the most extreme kinds of nastiness, including exhibiting a distinct predilection for human flesh. Zombies were now a hot commodity worldwide, finding expression in such diverse forums as the films of Lucio Fulci, Amand D'Ossorio's "Blind Dead" series, which themselves had been inspired not only by Romero, but by Mexico's "Mummies of Guanajuato" series. Other singular Mexican entries into the zombie sweepstakes were *La Invasion de los Muertos* ("The Invasion of the Dead"), which featured masked wrestling legend Blue Demon battling an army of the undead, who, among other things, could fly helicopters, and *Santo contra Los Zombies*, wherein fellow masked legend El Santo takes on remote radio-controlled zombies who can be blown up when their usefulness is at an end.

Marvel's Zombie, Simon Garth, is a combination of both types of zombie — nearly indestructible and certainly athletic although still prone to shambling, and his adventures were certainly gorier than those of the old-school zombies, although he didn't go in for flesh-eating, as it's rather hard to sell a hero who's a cannibal. But sell him they did, and *Tales of the Zombie* was perhaps Marvel's most consistent black-and-white horror magazine. For image, Marvel looked to the past — the Zombie was inspired directly by a Stan Lee–scripted and Bill Everett–drawn monster in the Atlas story "Zombie!" That story itself is reprinted as the second chapter of Garth's origin story in the first issue. What started as a tribute to Everett's design and artistic genius sadly became a memorial tribute in *Tales of the Zombie* no. 2, as the man responsible for the Sub-Mariner, the Fin, and a host of wonderful weird comics passed away shortly before it went to press. But the writing and social situations in which the Zombie found himself were pure '70s, and the series' chief writer and architect, Steve Gerber, (not to mention the readers) reveled in his anti-establishment potshots, delivered with as much zest as in the other comics Gerber scripted. He fortunately resisted the temptation to bring in Howard the Duck. Like Tony "Iron Man" Stark, Simon Garth is an industrialist, and Gerber seems to take delight in his predicament even as he's trying to make a zombie a sympathetic character. A lead character, no less, and one who can't even speak at that, but Gerber pulled the whole thing off by making the Zombie's thoughts a sounding board for, not only his, but the supporting characters' opinions and thoughts. And with Gerber's writing, there was never a shortage of oddball supporting players.

Gerber is part of the consistency mentioned in the preceding paragraph. Of ten regular issues, he wrote the Zombie's tales for seven, plus a prologue/epilogue for an eighth. The consistency also spread to the covers. The first four were by Boris Vallejo, the rest, plus the annual, by Earl Norem, so at times the Zombie vaguely resembled an undead Conan. The inside art was also consistent. Other than the Bill Everett/John Buscema/Tom Palmer/Syd Shores team from issue no. 1, and quick bits by Alfredo Alcala and Virgil Redondo, Filipino workhorse Pablo Marcos delineated the bulk of "The Man Without a Soul" stories. Marcos, like Graham Ingels and Bernie Wrightson, had an affinity for rotting corpses, and though the others left their mark, Marcos pretty much claims the Zombie as his own.

Tales of the Zombie no. 1 (1973)

Cover: Boris Vallejo
"Zombie: Altar of the Damned"— Steve Gerber, John Buscema/Tom Palmer

Tales of the Zombie no. 1 (Marvel) — Boris Vallejo was the Marvel Magazine Group's premier talent, contributing covers to nearly every title (courtesy Marvel Entertainment, Inc.).

"Zombie!" — Stan Lee, Bill Everett
"Iron Head" — Stan Lee, Dick Ayers
"The Sensuous Zombie" — Tony Isabella (Text feature)
"The Thing from the Bog" — Kit Pearson/Marv Wolfman, Pablo Marcos
"The Mastermind" — Tom Sutton
"Zombie: Night of the Walking Dead" — Gerber, Buscema/Syd Shores

"World Screamiere! Fantastic Fear-Filled First Issue!" blared the typical Marvel cover hype, and it really was fantastic. *Tales of the Zombie*, along with *Dracula Lives*, *Monster Madness*, and *Monsters Unleashed* was in the first wave of the Marvel Monster Group, and was a very solid debut. Vallejo contributed a striking, dramatic cover, and his Zombie is an awesome creature. Like his covers for *Savage Sword of Conan* and the other Marvel horror titles, his paintings were not only the magazine's public face, but gave the public a taste of artistic ability previously reserved for higher-priced hardcover books or paperbacks, which was one of the great things about all the monster and black-and-white horror mags. Of course, while Vallejo would abandon Marvel and the world of comics in a few years for paperbacks, books and beyond, he did work that not even a later sophistication in technical style could top. Curiously, as his style became more refined, his figures became even stiffer. Most other artists loosen up the longer they're at it. His work for Marvel was breezy when compared to his later style.

John Buscema is one of that select group of comic book artists for whom no genre is off-limits; superhero, western, horror, sword-and-sorcery, sci-fi, war — he handles every subject with consummate skill and panache, and his gift for composition and dramatic storytelling is equaled by but a few. Hence, he was the best choice to shepherd the Zombie artistically on his introductory shamble. The reader can practically feel the Zombie's clammy flesh, and the sweaty bayou setting (Buscema has a particular gift for atmospheric landscapes) is so fully realized, they might even find they reach for a handkerchief to mop their brows while reading. Buscema did the layouts on the first and third chapters of the Zombie's origin. Though the finished art was by, respectively, Tom Palmer and Syd Shores, Buscema's stamp is everywhere. Certainly Palmer and Shores were fine artists in their own right, but without Buscema's gift for composition, the stories would have been told much differently. Of course, they were all working from the template provided by Bill Everett. It was ironic in hindsight to find out that such a "hippy" looking Zombie (long hair, tattered jeans, necklace, amulet, vest, bare feet) had been created in the 1950s.

Even the second-line features were very good. "Iron-Head" was another Atlas reprint with some great Dick Ayers artwork, and the Zombie's future delineator Pablo Marcos did a gruesomely great job on what was probably his "scream test" for the main feature, "The Thing from the Bog." Tony Isabella's article "The Sensuous Zombie," is not at all what its rather slippery and necrophiliac title might suggest, but rather a photo-filled history of zombie movies up to and including *Night of the Living Dead*, although curiously, that groundbreaker is only given a cursory paragraph, an oversight that would be corrected in spades later. As noted previously, Marvel had access to a great library of horror movie stills, and when it wasn't burdening them with *Monster Madness*-style captions, Marvel used them to set the tone for the illustrated story to follow. This was particularly effective and appreciated in *Tales of the Zombie*, as zombie movies, at that time, were more obscure, with good stills hard to find.

Tales of the Zombie no. 2 (October 1973)

Cover: Boris Vallejo
"Zombie: Voodoo Island" — Steve Gerber, Pablo Marcos
"Voodoo Unto Others!" — Tony Isabella, Win Mortimer

"Acid Test" — Stan Lee, George Tuska
"Introducing Brother Voodoo" — Tony Isabella (Text feature)
"Twin Burial" — "Chuck Robinson" (Don McGregor), Ralph Reese
"From Out of the Grave" — Gene Colan
"Voodoo: What's It All About, Alfred?" — Chris Claremont (Text feature)
"Zombie: Night of the Spider" — Steve Gerber, Pablo Marcos

Another superb cover by Boris Vallejo, and the first appearance of Pablo Marcos as the regular Zombie artist are among this issue's highlights. "Voodoo Island" was also the name of a Boris Karloff film, and there's an article hyping Marvel's newest sensation, Brother Voodoo. Why Don McGregor used a pseudonym for "Twin Burial" is puzzling — it wasn't like he was writing the whole issue or anything, and the story is certainly nothing to be ashamed of. It was even selected for the annual.

Tales of the Zombie no. 3 (January 1974)

Cover: Boris Vallejo
"Zombie: When the Gods Crave Flesh" — Steve Gerber, Pablo Marcos
"With the Dawn Comes ... DEATH!" — Chris Claremont (Fiction)
"Net Result" — Stan Lee, John Romita
"Warrior's Burden" — Tony Isabella, Vincente Alcazar
"*The Night of the Living Dead* goes on ... and on and on" — Don McGregor (Film review)
"I Won't Stay Dead!" — Stan Lee, Bill Walton
"Jilimbi's World" — Doug Moench, Enrique Badia

The title of Don McGregor's critique could imply two things. Either it refers to the influence the movie exerted, or he's just tired of the whole thing, which would have even been more curious since this was written before any of the sequels came out. It's actually an objective look, and not the reverential treatment one might expect. He argues for its modern-day classic status while taking note of its flaws.

Tales of the Zombie no. 4 (March 1974)

Cover: Boris Vallejo
Inside front and back cover: Pablo Marcos
"Zombie: The Law and Philip Bliss (Pt. 1)" — Steve Gerber, Pablo Marcos
"James Bond Meets Baron Samedi, or *Live and Let Die* Revisited" — Don McGregor (Movie review)
"The Drums of Doom" — Gerry Conway, Rich Buckler Sr./Vic Martin/Winslow Mortimer
"Neo Witchcraft" — Lin Carter (Text feature)
"Courtship by Voodoo" — Tony Isabella, Ron Wilson
"Night Filth Rising" — Doug Moench, Winslow Mortimer
"Four Daughters of Satan" — John Albano, Ernie Chua
"Zombie: The Law and Philip Bliss (Pt. 2)" — Steve Gerber, Pablo Marcos

Boris Vallejo's Zombie is at his most pumped on Boris's last cover for the series. As with *Savage Sword of Conan*, when the Boris era ended, the Earl (Norem) era began with the next issue. Steve Gerber gets in some pointed barbs at the legal profession in "The Law and Philip Bliss," as a homeless man from whom the lawyers have taken everything gains control of the Zombie and uses him for revenge against those lawyers. Roger Moore's first outing as James Bond is dissected. The Baron Samedi with whom he meets was played by Geoffrey Holder, a fine, accomplished actor possessed of a deep, musical voice, who is primarily remembered for his 7-Up commercials, much the same way that many people only know Orson Welles from his wine commercials, rather than his many brilliant films.

Tales of the Zombie no. 5 (May 1974)

Cover: Earl Norem
Inside front and back cover: Pablo Marcos

"Zombie: Palace of Black Magic"—Steve Gerber, Pablo Marcos
"*White Zombie*: Faithful Unto Death"—Doug Moench (Text feature)
"Who Walks with a Zombie?"—Stan Lee, Russ Heath
"With the Dawn Comes ... DEATH! (Pt. 2)"—Chris Claremont (Fiction)
"Brother Voodoo Lives Again!"—Doug Moench (Text feature)
"Voodoo War"—Tony Isabella, Syd Shores/Dick Ayers/Mike Esposito
"Death's Bleak Birth"—Doug Moench, Frank Springer

"Who Walks with a Zombie?" has art by Russ Heath, and reprint or not, anything by him is always a welcome sight. The magazine finally gets around to covering the classic Lugosi film *White Zombie*, and there's also another piece on Brother Voodoo, who hadn't exactly set the world on fire in *Strange Tales*. He lasted all of four issues. Not even a year later, he was back at the door of *Tales of the Zombie*, Humfro in hand and looking for a comeback. His run was so short there wasn't all that much to come back from.

Tales of the Zombie no. 6 (July 1974)

Cover: Earl Norem
Frontispiece: Pablo Marcos
"Zombie: Child of Darkness"—Steve Gerber, Pablo Marcos
The Plague of the Zombies—Gerry Boudreau (film review)
Sugar Hill—Jim Harmon (Film review)
The Compleat Voodoo Man"—Chris Claremont (Text feature)
"End of a Legend"—Doug Moench/Len Wein, Gene Colan/Frank Chiaramonte
"The Voodoo Beat"—Carla Joseph (Film previews)

This issue includes film reviews of not only the Hammer classic *The Plague of the Zombies*, but of the ultra-hip, cult classic, blaxploitation zombie movie *Sugar Hill*, which inspired a record label (Sugar Hill) and a group (The Sugar Hill Gang).

Tales of the Zombie no. 7 (September 1974)

Cover: Earl Norem
Frontispiece: Alfredo Alcala
"Zombie: The Blood Testament of Brian Collier"—Doug Moench, Alcala (Prologue and epilogue: Steve Gerber, Pablo Marcos)
"Voodoo in the Park"—Kenneth Dreyfack (Text feature)
"Haiti's Walking Dead"—Doug Moench, Winslow Mortimer
"Inside *Inside Voodoo*"—Chris Claremont (Book review)
"A Second Chance to Die"—Carl Wessler, Alfredo Alcala

Due to heavy workloads, the regular Zombie team of Gerber and Marcos was only able to contribute a frame to the main story, which was handled by the more-than-adequate replacement combo of Doug Moench and Alfredo Alcala. Moench's tone is different from Gerber's; grimmer and less playful, but no less effective, and Alcala's lush style complements it perfectly. The opening scene is both horrific and action-filled; and if a battle to the death between a zombie and an alligator in a swamp can be called a thing of beauty, then this is just gorgeous.

Tales of the Zombie no. 8 (November 1974)

Cover: Earl Norem
Frontispiece: "Voodoo Killers"—Tony Isabella, Mike Kaluta
"Zombie: A Death Made of Ticky-Tacky"—Steve Gerber, Pablo Marcos
"Jimmy Doesn't Live Here Anymore"—David Anthony Kraft (Fiction)
"Night of the Hunted"—Larry Leiber, Ron Wilson/Esposito/Giacoia

"Tales of the Happy Humfro" — Chris Claremont (Text feature)
"Makao's Vengeance" — David Anthony Kraft, Alfredo Alcala

Alfredo Alcala returns, only for a back-up story, but his style lifts it above all the other second features. Gerber and Marcos return as well in fine form for the Zombie story, whose title unfortunately makes it sound like Death by Hard Candy; it also marks their swan song on the series.

Tales of the Zombie no. 9 (January 1975)

Cover: Earl Norem
Frontispiece: "Was He a Voodoo Man?" — Tony Isabella, Winslow Mortimer
"Zombie: Simon Garth Lives Again!" — Tony Isabella, Virgil Redondo/Alcala
"Zombie: A Day in the Life of a Dead Man" — Tony Isabella/Chris Claremont, Yong Montano/Alfredo Alcala

This issue marks the title character's swan song in the series. The mag would only last one more issue anyway, but for some reason the publishers decided to wrap up the Zombie's saga in this one, leaving the last issue of *Tales of the Zombie* without a Zombie, or at least Simon Garth (see below). The art is fine; Alcala inks both stories, but although the closure to the Zombie's adventures is satisfactory, the road taken by Isabella reads a little more like the typical Marvel soap opera than Gerber's offbeat storytelling.

Tales of the Zombie no. 10 (March 1975)

Cover: Earl Norem
Frontispiece: Tom Sutton
"The Resurrection of Papa Jambo" — Doug Moench, Tony DeZuniga
"Eye for an Eye, Tooth for a Tooth" — Gerry Conway, Virgil Redondo/Rudy Nebres
"Malaka's Curse" — Carl Wessler/John Warner, Vincente Alcazar
"Grave Business" — Tom Sutton

Talk about indignities — it's bad enough to be a zombie, but then to be pushed out of your own magazine and before the last issue! Even when Vampirella didn't have a strip in her own magazine, she got to play the hostess with the ghostest and introduce the stories, which, admittedly, would have been hard for the Zombie, not being able to speak and everything. At least he got on the misleading cover, another fine Earl Norem painting.

Tales of the Zombie Annual no. 1 (Summer 1975)

Cover: Earl Norem
Frontispiece: Pablo Marcos
"Zombie: Altar of the Damned" — Steve Gerber, John Buscema/Tom Palmer
"Zombie!" — Stan Lee, Bill Everett
"Zombie: Night of the Walking Dead" — Gerber, Buscema/Syd Shores
"Twin Burial" — "Chuck Robinson" (Don McGregor), Ralph Reese
"Warrior's Burden" — Tony Isabella, Vincente Alcazar
"Jilimbi's World" — Doug Moench, Enrique Badia
"Death's Bleak Birth" — Doug Moench, Frank Springer
"A Second Chance to Die" — Carl Wessler, Alfredo Alcala

When the majority of the Marvel black-and-white line ended, most of the titles were wrapped up with an "annual" that reprinted the best from the run of the title. *Tales of the Zombie* was one such title, but it really didn't get the proper send-off. You would think that an annual would be a perfect place, like a lot of the Warren yearbooks, to give the fans a concentrated shot of their favorite character or artist, but no such luck here. All Simon Garth fans get is the "Zombie Trilogy" from the first issue, and five other mostly filler tales from the rest. It doesn't appear as though a lot of thought or care went into deciding the contents for this issue.

Monsters Unleashed

Monsters Unleashed began as a pure anthology title; the first issue contained a wide variety of monsters and some notable contributors, including Roy Thomas (adapting a Robert E. Howard story, naturally), Ralph Reese, Gene Colan and Doug Wildey. The series characters, in the misshapen forms of the Frankenstein Monster and the Man-Thing began with the second, and it was soon obvious where the attention was being focused, with more Atlas reprints appearing as no-cost filler and the secondary strips being handled by secondary talent. The Frankenstein Monster and Man-Thing alternated cover honors for the first eight issues, but then they were pushed aside in favor of newer, shinier monsters that were as forgettable as their names.

The immortal Frankenstein Monster was pulling double shifts at Marvel, appearing in a color comic (*see* Chapter One), as well as co-headlining *Monsters Unleashed*, but to Marvel's credit, it wasn't just more of the same in a different format. The four-color *Monster of Frankenstein* was a period piece, adapting the original novel and keeping it in that period. The version that appeared in *Monsters Unleashed*, taking its title cue from the Karloff-starring *Frankenstein 1970*, was set in modern times, and followed the classic premise and pattern of the Universal series: the monster is indestructible, and after the death of his original creator, wanders in and out of situations where he is used for evil ends by various evil people, or abused by yet another over-zealous mad scientist. Regular Sgt. Fury scripter Gary Friedrich wrote the first few stories and then the equally talented Doug Moench got the assignment. Likewise, the art chores were at first handled by the ubiquitous John Buscema and a slew of inkers; the torch (or brush, if you will) was then passed to Val Mayerik, another apparent graduate of the Graham Ingels school. But unlike Pablo Marcos, he was equally at home with muscled living corpses as he was with shriveling dead ones.

Monsters Unleashed's other co-starring feature, like Frankenstein, had his own color comic, and made his initial appearance at virtually the same time as Swamp Thing, making it nearly impossible to determine who came up with the idea (although The Heap preceded both). Both ideas were interesting takes on the original, and each had its own distinctive creative team — Gerber and Ploog on Man-Thing, and Len Wein and Bernie Wrightson on Swamp Thing. Swamp Thing first appeared in *House of Mystery* no. 92, and was also a smash hit. After a couple of masterful years under the watch of the legendary Wein/Wrightson team, the series underwent a stagnant period, but then Alan Moore got hold of it, and the Swamp Thing's mythos grew as dense as the Heap's. He was reinvented not so much as a monster, but a force of nature, less a swamp thing than a swamp god. Man-Thing didn't experience the same kind of creative evolution or consistency, although he appeared in some fantastic individual stories and issues, in particular *Giant-Size Man-Thing* no. 1. The title of the comic alone has become a fan favorite, and snickering is once again permitted, because that's obviously what the guys putting out the book were doing, and everybody got a kick out of it. Snickering was also permitted, nay, encouraged, on the lead story, which had a hilariously cynical script by Steve Gerber and even better than usual art by Mike Ploog. Man-Thing takes on a rival swamp monster who started out the story as a human villain that looked just like Richard Nixon! Eventually, just as The Heap had eclipsed Sky Wolf in popularity, Man-Thing was shunted to the sidelines in his own title by another Gerber creation, Howard the Duck. Howard the Duck was enormously popular, and later became the subject of an acrimonious legal battle between Marvel and Gerber over the subject of creators' rights.

Howard got his own book, a newspaper strip, and a black-and-white magazine, and even ran for President; in fact, he was so popular that he even rated a feature film, which was so bad that it dealt the character's popularity a permanent deathblow.

There was one other series character in *Monsters Unleashed* that did not appear in every issue, "Warrior of Mars," otherwise known as Gullivar Jones. He had lost his lead spot in *Creatures on the Loose* to Thongor. The Warrior of Mars series that had appeared in color was well done, but not well received; his stories in black-and-white were not well done, and did nothing to revive interest in the character.

Monsters Unleashed! no. 1 (1973)

Cover: Gray Morrow
"The Man Who Cried Werewolf" (adapted from Bloch) — Gerry Conway, Pablo Marcos
"The Thing in the Freezer" — Marv Wolfman, Syd Shores
"Vampire Tale" — Stan Lee, Doug Wildey
"Skulls in the Stars" (adapted from Robert E. Howard) — Roy Thomas, Ralph Reese
"Portrait of the Werewolf as a Young Man" — Tony Isabella (Text)
"One Foot in the Grave" — Stan Lee, Tony DiPreta
"The Fake"
"World of Warlocks" (adapted from Gardner F. Fox) — Roy Thomas, Gene Colan

Monsters Unleashed! no. 1 was a solid debut for the title, although it was still grasping for a direction. A direction, of a kind, would emerge with the introduction of two continuing characters in the misshapen forms of the Frankenstein Monster and the Man-Thing in the next issue, but the term "direction" here is used in the context of the contents. There's a slightly disjointed feel to begin with, as the title itself was basically a catch-all for any monsters who didn't have their own themed titles, like zombies, or Dracula, plus it was a mixture of comics, articles, and, in lieu of horror hosts, monster movie photos adorned with Lee's corny captions which introduced the stories. The magazine would soon abandon the corn, but continue to use movie photos as lead-ins, which actually worked when the still fit the story at hand.

Gray Morrow's cover is well rendered, but lacks impact. Almost literally a werewolf chasing a girl in a nightgown up a tree, it doesn't have a strong central image, and isn't quite up to the standards he'd achieved at Warren, or even on other Marvel mags, such as his stunning piece for the digest version of *Haunt of Horror* no. 1. "Monsters Unleashed!" screamed the letters in bright yellow tones, the "Monsters" part of it bearing a suspicious resemblance to a more famous magazine that included that word in its title. Cover blurbs trumpet — well, either the wide spectrum of subjects covered ("Warlocks! Moor-Monsters! Vampires! Things that go bump in the night!"), or that previously mentioned lack of focus, depending on your point of view.

The moor-monster is featured in an adaptation of a Robert E. Howard story about Puritan swashbuckler Solomon Kane, written by Conan-meister Roy Thomas and drawn by Wallace Wood protégé Ralph Reese. Reese's Wood influence is obvious, although he had his own style as well, and was not as much a clone of Woody as Wayne Howard (no relation to Robert E.). The only bad thing he inherited from Wood (and, truly, the only possible quibble with Wood's own style) was a stiffness of figures that sometimes did not flow as rapidly as the story action. This is a minor quibble, though, indeed, and does little to take away from the story, which is a contender for the best one in the magazine. Inclusion of a Sword and Sorcery story also shows that Marvel thought it completely appropriate to the title (and would include other S & S stories in its other monster titles). And whatever one thinks of Marvel, it can't be denied that Marvel, as

Robert E. Howard's comic book champion in the '70s and '80s, did as much as even Frazetta or Lancer Books to rescue the author from literary obscurity.

Besides Howard, the first issue of *Monsters Unleashed* also featured "The Man Who Cried Werewolf!" from the powerful pen of Robert Bloch, author of *Psycho* and *Asylum*, and "World of Warlocks" by Gardner Fox, who created his own Conan pastiche with "Kothar of the Magic Sword." The stories are adapted by, respectively, Gerry Conway and Roy Thomas, and both stories employ top-shelf artists—Pablo Marcos on the former, Gene Colan on the latter. Marcos does a fang-tastic werewolf, and Colan's work, always superlative, is easily the equal of any of the black-and-white stuff he did for Warren, on a tale that would also have fitted easily into *Savage Tales*, *Unknown Worlds of Science Fiction*, or even Warren's *Blazing Combat*.

Monsters Unleashed! no. 2 (October 1973)

Cover: Boris Vallejo
"Frankenstein 1973"—Gary Friedrich, John Buscema/Syd Shores
Karloff: The Man, the Monster, the Movies—Tony Isabella (Book review)
"Lifeboat"—Gerry Conway, Jesus Blasco
"The Madman"—Stan Lee, Bill Everett
"The World's Most Wanted Monster"—Martin Pasko (Text/photo feature)
"Sword of Dragonus"—Frank Brunner
"The Roaches" (adapted from Thomas Disch)—Gerry Conway, Ralph Reese

Monsters Unleashed no. 2 is among the top ten single monster magazine issues ever published by Marvel. The company may have flooded the market with too many titles too soon, but if they had all been this good, that wouldn't have mattered. It's as good as anything Warren was putting out that month, and even had a bit of Warren's Spanish flavor with a story illustrated by the talented Jesus Blasco ("Lifeboat"). Starting off with the truly iconic Boris cover (which would later be used as the cover for a collection of Marvel's Frankenstein stories), where a muscular Frankenstein Monster faces off against the iconic angry villagers bearing torches. Victor Frankenstein's "son" was the lead story for the issue, the Marvel story that brought the monster into current times, although the basic plot was as old as the Universal or Hammer movie series: a wayward scientist revives the monster for his own ends, and ends up paying with his life. The only difference was that the mad scientist in this tale had long hair and sideburns. Solid scripting and (naturally) solid artwork by John Buscema make the character's debut in this format as enjoyable as in the color comics. As noted above, the inspiration for the series title was the Karloff movie *Frankenstein 1970* (the only movie in which Karloff actually portrayed a member of the Frankenstein family). The Frankenstein Monster's greatest screen portrayer had two articles devoted to him in this issue, one a review of the (then) newest book on Karloff's life and career, and the other, more on the movies, making it almost as much of a special Frankenstein issue as the second issue of *Monsters of the Movies* had been.

The secondary stories are all first-rate. Dragonus was a barbarian character created by Frank Brunner, who also appeared in the over/under/sideways-ground comic classic *Star*Reach* (see Chapter Six). Although some might think the story more appropriate for *Savage Tales*, it actually served to strengthen the connection between the two genres. "The Roaches" was a Ralph Reese specialty, showcasing his particular talent for revealing just how creepy God's normal little creatures can be, as usual with gut-wrenching results. "The Madman" was the obligatory (but only) reprint, but some thought actually went into its selection. When Marvel actually put some thought and care into how its black-and-white magazines looked, it produced issues like this one.

Monsters Unleashed! no. 3 (December 1973)

Cover: Neal Adams
"Man-Thing"— Roy Thomas/Gerry Conway, Gray Morrow
"The Cyclops"— Stan Lee, Jack Davis
"Frankenstein A.K. (After Karloff)"— Martin Pasko (text/photo feature)
"The Death-Dealing Mannequin"— Kit Pearson/Tony Isabella, Winslow Mortimer
"Contact"— Tom Sutton
"Swamp Girl"— Stan Lee, Tony DiPreta
"Preview: The Son of Satan"— Carla Joseph (Promo feature)
"The Cold of the Uncaring Moon"— Steve Skeates, George Tuska/Klaus Janson
"Birthright"— Roy Thomas, Gil Kane/The Crusty Bunkers

The previous issue was great, and the third is not far behind. The only problem with it is that three of the stories (two are the first two in the magazine, no less) are reprints, so it's a good thing that the quality is high among all three. That being said, the origin tale of the Man-Thing was making its third appearance in two years. This fact is almost offset by the absolutely stunning Neal Adams Man-Thing cover, one of the best he ever did for Marvel, but the fact remains. The other reprints are the golden Atlas oldies "The Cyclops," with some powerful Jack Davis art, and "Swamp Girl." "Frankenstein A.K." was a look at some of the movies featuring the monster after Karloff had vacated the character's asphalt-spreader's boots. "Contact" is a grand retro tale in the finest EC twist-ending tradition, and "Cold of the Uncaring Moon" was a non-series werewolf strip lifted above the level of average by the art team of old pro George Tuska joined by (then) newcomer Klaus Janson, who would become a household name as part of the team responsible for *The Dark Knight Returns*. Marvel saved the best for last, and even though "Birthright" might have seemed like a reprint, it wasn't. With a script by Roy Thomas and flawless artwork by Gil Kane and the Crusty Bunkers, it reads like a sci-fi version of the recent adaptation of Robert E. Howard's "Valley of the Worm," right down to the hero's climactic confrontation with a giant worm, so it at the very least produces a distinct feeling of déjà vu. Still, it's a cracking tale, with its own nice little sting in the end.

Monsters Unleashed! no. 4 (February 1974)

Cover: Luis Dominguez
"Frankenstein 1973: The Classic Monster"— Gary Friedrich, John Buscema, Syd Shores/Winslow Mortimer
"The Hands"— Stan Lee, Gene Colan
"Our Martian Heritage"— Chris Claremont (Text/photo feature)
"Gullivar Jones, Warrior of Mars: Web of Hate"— Tony Isabella, Dave Cockrum
"Gullivar Jones: First Man on Mars"— The Bullpen (Text); Jim Steranko (Illustration)
"A Monster Reborn"— Steve Gerber, Pablo Marcos
"The Monster Maker: A Review of *Ray Harryhausen's Film Fantasy Scrapbook*"— Tony Isabella (book review)
"The Killers"
"To Love, Honor, Cherish–'Til Death!"— Chris Claremont, Don Perlin
"In Memoriam: Lon Chaney Jr."— Martin Pasko

Luis Dominguez's cover for the fearsome fourth issue of *Monsters Unleashed* is one great piece of work, a werewolf painting that rivals either of Bob Larkin's for *Haunt of Horror* no. 1 and *Monsters of the Movies* no. 4 for sheer imagination and werewolfery. An added bonus is that the face of the lycanthrope bears a striking resemblance to that of Steven Ritch in the underrated *The Werewolf* (Columbia, 1956). In terms of Dominguez's other horror magazine covers, it is surpassed perhaps only by his stunning cover for *Famous Monsters* no. 93. But, overall, the high standard, which had characterized the first three issues, seemed to start to slip a bit. Frankenstein, of course, was still in the capable hands of Friedrich, Buscema and company; Gene Colan is beyond reproach, and Pablo Marcos was always a plus, as was the review of the Harryhausen book, which once more succeeded in mixing monster articles with monster comics. But the rest of the issue's features lack punch. The Gullivar Jones is illustrated by a Dave Cockrum that had yet to hit his stride, and Don Perlin's style was just plain unsuited to the genre, a mistake that Marvel would increasingly repeat in its black-and-white line.

Monsters Unleashed! no. 5 (April 1974)

Cover: Bob Larkin
Inside covers: Man-Thing Poster
"Man-Thing: All the Faces of Fear"—Tony Isabella, Vincente Alcazar
The Golden Voyage of Sinbad—Gerry Conway (Film review)
"Peter Stubb: Werewolf"—Tony Isabella/Ron Wilson
"The Dark Passage"—Stan Lee, Ogden Whitney
"Glenn Strange, Frankenstein: Monster of Dodge City"—Don Glut (Text)
"Demon of Slaughter Mansion"—Don McGregor, Juan Boix/Pablo Marcos
"Monsters in the Media"—Carla Joseph (Previews and reviews)
"The Werewolf Tale to End All Werewolf Tales!"—Stan Lee, Paul Hodge
"Frankenstein 1974: Once a Monster..."—Gary Friedrich, John Buscema/Win Mortimer

The first Bob Larkin cover for the title was a doozy, with the Man-Thing locked in fierce battle with a snapping crocodile while holding a girl dressed like Daisy Duke aloft. Who came first, Man-Thing or Swamp Thing? Who cares? The original swamp monster, the Heap, inspired both, and both were the recipients of some fine stories and artwork, in this issue courtesy of Tony Isabella and Vincente Alcazar. Alcazar could be maddeningly inconsistent—one moment turning in subtle, atmospheric work, with smart placing of blacks, scratches and washes; the next, looking like the pen barely touched the paper. This could have a lot to do with deadlines, and this story shows him at the top of his form. Isabella had another story in the issue, a mini-story, as it were: Marvel's version of "Creepy's Loathsome Lore." The one-pager, a "strange ... but true?" type, is as interesting as the original, but is not served well by the art, Ron Wilson being a superhero artist who was unsuited to the subject matter.

The most-hyped story in the issue was "Demon of Slaughter Mansion," although in retrospect, it's hard to see why. Promised for the previous two issues as a "tale too hot to handle" (editorial quote from the letters page), it turned out to be a rather ordinary stock tale of vengeance from beyond the grave. Far more enjoyable in an outlandish way is the "Frankenstein 1974" installment "Once a Monster..." in which the standard Frankensteinian plot element of brain transferal is taken to possibly the most ridiculous extreme ever, and that includes *Frankenstein Meets The Space Monster*.

The three horror film features are all solid, with nice selections of photos. They might not have had *Famous Monsters*'s style, but, to Marvel's credit, its monster movie news and reviews were always informative. When Marvel actually devoted a whole magazine to the effort (see *Monsters of the Movies*, Chapter 1), it was much better than anyone would have expected. "The Dark Passage" is not Marvel's version of the Humphrey Bogart film where Bogey walks around wrapped up like a mummy, but more vengeance from beyond the grave, only this time in a reprint. Romance specialist artist Ogden Whitney turned in a superlative work, and, as vengeance from beyond the grave stories go, this moldy oldie beats "The Demon of Slaughter Mansion" hands down. Whitney did a ton of horror and romance comics, and is also fondly remembered by comics fans for his work on Tower Comics's legendary "T.H.U.N.D.E.R. Agents" series and characters, particularly the android NoMan.

Monsters Unleashed! no. 6 (June 1974)

Cover: Boris Vallejo
Frontispiece: "Thunderbird"—Tony Isabella, Ernie Chua
"Frankenstein 1974: ... Always a Monster!"—Gary Friedrich, Val Mayerik
"Monsters in the Media"—Carla Joseph (Previews and reviews)
"The Strange Children"
The Dinosaur Dictionary—Alan Gold (Book review)
"Dark Flame"—Gerry Conway, Carlos Freixas
"Werewolf by Night: Panic by Moonlight"—Gerry Conway (Prose); Mike Ploog (Illustrations)
"The Maggots"—Stan Lee, Hy Rosen
"The Waters of Werewolves"—Doug Moench, Winslow Mortimer
"The Scrimshaw Serpent"—Doug Moench, Alfonso Font

This was Boris Vallejo's last cover for this particular title, always a sad note, but the pain is eased by yet another nutty installment of Frankenstein '74, and Mike Ploog art for the "Werewolf by Night" prose story. Don Glut's highly informative *Dinosaur Dictionary* is reviewed, but the issue had no monster movie review.

Monsters Unleashed! no. 7 (August 1974)

Cover: Val Mayerik
"Frankenstein 1974: A Tale of Two Monsters"—Doug Moench, Val Mayerik
"Werewolf by Night: Madness Under a Midsummer Moon"—Gerry Conway (Prose); Pat Broderick/Klaus Janson (Illustrations)
"The Bleeding Stones"—Doug Moench, Vincente Alcazar
"The Burning Man"—Tony Isabella, Ernie Chua (Chan)
"Monsters in the Media"—Carla Joseph (Previews and reviews)
"The Frankenstein Legend"—Don Glut (Text feature)
"Blind Man's Bluff"—Gerry Conway, Carlos Freixas
"Monster in the Mist"—Stan Lee, Al Williamson

Val Mayerik's cover features a generic (albeit well done) demon swamp monster that looked as though it stepped right off a *Savage Sword of Conan* cover, and he once again contributes a super Frankenstein job. The "Werewolf by Night" feature misses Mike Ploog's illustrations, but is still a fun read. Only one Atlas reprint this time around, but it's a thriller.

Monsters Unleashed! no. 8 (October 1974)

Cover: Earl Norem
Frontispiece: "Monsters from the Sea"—Tony Isabella, Ernie Chua (Chan)
"Frankenstein 1974: Fever in the House of Freaks"—Doug Moench, Val Mayerik
"Man-Thing: Several Meaningless Deaths"—Steve Gerber (Prose); Pat Broderick/Al Milgrom (Illustrations)
"Swamp Stars of the Silver Screen"—Don Glut (Text feature)
"One Hungers"—Neal Adams, Adams/Dan Adkins
"Gullivar Jones, Warrior of Mars: A Martian Genesis"—Tony Isabella/ Doug Moench, George Perez/Duffy Vohland/Rich Buckler Sr.

The best thing about *Monsters Unleashed* No. 8 is the wonderfully pulpy bondage and torture cover by Earl Norem, the Frankenstein Monster and sexy girl menaced by an even more monstrous-looking fiend brandishing a red-hot poker. You don't really need any more than that, but the insides are a solid lot—Frankenstein and The Man-Thing are both on hand, as well as Gullivar Jones, the Warrior of Mars attempting a comeback in the magazine line after having failed to catch on in color comics.

Monsters Unleashed! no. 9 (December 1974)

Cover: Earl Norem
Frontispiece: "The Atomic Monster"—Tony Isabella, A. Jones/D. Vohland

"Frankenstein 1974: The Conscience of the Creature"—Doug Moench, Val Mayerik
"The Jewel That Snarled at Slight Greed"—Doug Moench, Don Perlin
"Man-Thing: Several Meaningless Deaths" (Pt. 2)—Steve Gerber (Prose); Pat Broderick/Al Milgrom (Illustrations)
"Wendigo: Snowbird in Hell"—Chris Claremont, Yong Montano

Only two issues to go after this one. Frankenstein and Man-Thing are still around, but the cover spot is claimed by the Wendigo, a monstrous adversary of the Hulk's whose main claim to fame was that the issues he appeared in also contained the first appearance of mega-popular superhero Wolverine. Gerber's prose on the Man-Thing entry is as twisted as usual, but the illustrations let it down.

Monsters Unleashed! Annual no. 1 (Summer 1975)

Cover: Ken Bald
Frontispiece: "Thunderbird"—Tony Isabella, Ernie Chua
"The Cold of the Uncaring Moon"—Steve Skeates, George Tuska/Klaus Janson
"They Might Be Monsters"—Tony Isabella, Pablo Marcos
"World of Warlocks" (Fox)—Roy Thomas, Gene Colan
"Lifeboat"—Gerry Conway, Jesus Blasco
"Demon of Slaughter Mansion"—Don McGregor, Juan Boix/Pablo Marcos
"Birthright"—Roy Thomas, Gil Kane/The Crusty Bunkers
"To Love, Honor, Cherish—'Til Death!"—Chris Claremont, Don Perlin
"All the Faces of Fear"—Tony Isabella, Vincente Alcazar
"Thunderbird"—Tony Isabella, Ernie Chua
"Monsters from the Sea"—Tony Isabella, Ernie Chua (Chan)

Although the Frankenstein Monster and the Man-Thing had been the most featured stars and had carried the title throughout its run, for some odd reason neither were represented in this best-of collection, which would have been okay if it had contained all of the best non–Frankie or Manny material, but it didn't. *Monsters Unleashed!* had dispensed with the film articles by the last few issues, and did here as well, so it didn't have the balance that characterized the early issues of the run, nor was it a true representation of the title.

The Legion of Monsters

The Legion of Monsters no. 1 (September 1975)

Cover: Neal Adams
Frontispiece: Pablo Marcos
"The Frankenstein Monster: The Monster and the Masque"—Doug Moench, Val Mayerik/Dan Adkins, Marcos
"The Manphibian: Vengeance Crude"—Tony Isabella, Dave Cockrum/Sam Grainger
"The Legion Report"—Don/Maggie Thompson (Film previews)
"The Flies"—Gerry Conway, Paul Kirschner/Ralph Reese
"Dracula, Chapter Seven: Death Be Thou Proud"—Roy Thomas/Dick Giordano
"Monster Madness"—Stu Shwarzberg
"Monster Gallery"—Hermoso Pancho, Pete Lijuaco, Gray Morrow (Illustrations)

The Legion of Monsters was, like *Masters of Terror*, an inventory title, except that in this case the existing inventory was unused new stories instead of reprints (Marvel had to find a place to use stories created for the now mostly-aborted black-and-white line). Frankenstein and Dracula are featured, the seventh chapter of Roy Thomas and Dick Giordano's Stoker adaptation finally finding a home. Also featured is the Creature from the Black Lagoon-styled Manphibian. Ralph Reese is represented by perhaps his most stomach-churning tale ever, and Neal Adams contributes a solid cover, but the catchall title did nothing to revitalize the Marvel Monster Group as we knew it.

The Legion of Monsters no. 2 (Unpublished; partial contents announced in no. 1)

"Morbius: The Madman of Mansion Slade"— Doug Moench, Sonny Trinidad
"Satana: Night of the Demon, Night of the Damned"— Chris Claremont, George Evans
"Dracula, Chapter Eight: Hour of the Wolves"— Roy Thomas/Dick Giordano

Partial contents for the second issue were announced in the first, but when *The Legion of Monsters* did about as well as *Savage Tales* no. 1 in terms of sales, plans were dropped. *Marvel Premiere* no. 28 featured a Legion of Monsters composed of Marvel's most popular supernatural superheroes, Ghost Rider, Man-Thing, Morbius, and Werewolf-by-Night, but even this all-star team failed to make the name catch on.

Haunt of Horror

The Haunt of Horror was actually a twice-told title for Marvel. The first incarnation was in the digest prose-fiction format, making it the closest link to the actual pulps that Marvel would ever publish, since the pulps themselves had morphed into those selfsame digests. The link was strengthened by the inclusion of true pulp heavyweights like Robert E. Howard and Fritz Leiber, and the format of the stories themselves — two columns of text with full-page and spot illustrations throughout. The presentation (the first issue had a particularly striking Gray Morrow cover) and the format were good, but the experiment was a failure. Apparently the book fell between a crack — too "comic book" (merely because Marvel had produced it) for the serious horror, science fiction and fantasy fans, but too "serious" (because there were so many words unconnected to balloons) for comic book fans. The title was revived as a full-size, black-and-white magazine. Like the digest, at first, it was an anthology, even retaining a couple of those illustrated stories. But Marvel felt, rightly or wrongly, once again, that a successful magazine needed a continuing character on which to hang its hat. The company should have stayed with the anthology format, because the series character Marvel came up with was a particularly lame twist on a popular theme of the '70s, exorcism, due to the popularity of the movie *The Exorcist*. (For more trends, *see* Chapter Six.) In that box-office smash, Max von Sydow plays the priest who casts out Linda Blair's demons. Marvel's variation on the already played-out theme was known as "Gabriel, Devil-Hunter," and looked exactly like the character Nick Fury of S.H.I.E.L.D. (who had been a sergeant in the Big One and then turned into James Bond). Gabriel only blew his horn for the three issues that the magazine had to live. The title was used again for an issue of *Marvel Preview*. Once again, it failed to catch on. It was successfully revived 30 years later for a mini-series adapting Poe, illustrated by old pro Richard Corben.

The Haunt of Horror no. 1 (June 1973)

Cover: Gray Morrow
"The Unspoken Invitation"— Editorial
"Conjure Wife" (Pt. 1)— Fritz Leiber; John Romita, Gene Colan (Illustrations)
"The First Step"— John K. Diomede; Frank Brunner (Illustrations)
"Neon"— Harlan Ellison(r); Barry Smith (Illustrations)
"Loup Garou"— A.A. Attanasio; Mike Ploog (Illustrations)
"In the Wind"— Previews of next issue
"Seeing Stingy Ed"— David R. Bunch
"The Lurker in the Family Room"— Dennis O'Neil
"A Nice Home"— Beverly Goldberg
"Ghost in the Corn Crib"— R. A. Lafferty; Dan Green (Illustrations)
"Night Beat"— Ramsey Campbell

"Boo Kreview"—Baird Searles (Book reviews)
"Authors' Page"—Author biographies
"Usurp the Night"—Robert E. Howard

As Roy Thomas would so candidly admit in the first issue of the magazine-size *Haunt of Horror*, the first issue of the digest of the same name flopped. It's a shame it didn't catch on, as there's always a place for good horror stories whose pictures are mostly created in the mind. Fritz Lieber, with his classic "Conjure Wife" and Robert E. Howard represent the old guard, with young Turks like Harlan Ellison raising the banner for the new, and the mix provides for some great reading. The best of the illustrations are by Gene Colan, who provides some really pulp-like work, and Mike Ploog, whose werewolf on the title page of "Loup Garou" bears more than a passing resemblance to Jack Russell, the Werewolf by Night—not that there's anything wrong with that.

The Haunt of Horror no. 2 (August 1973)

Cover: Frank Kelly Freas
"Devil Night"—Dennis O'Neil
"Pelican's Claws"—Arthur Byron Cover
"Finders Keepers"—Anne McCaffrey
"Kilbride"—Ron Goulart
"Mono No Aware"—Howard Waldrop
"The Jewel in the Ash"—John K. Diomede
"Conjure Wife" (Pt. 2)—Fritz Leiber

Despite an excellent bondage cover by Frank Kelly Freas and some solid stories ("Devil Night," "Finders Keepers," and of course the second half of the classic "Conjure Wife"), this was the last issue of the title for the time being.

The Haunt of Horror no. 1 (May 1974)

Cover: Bob Larkin
Frontispiece: Alfredo Alcala
"The Rats"—Gerry Conway, Ralph Reese
"Heart Stop"—Gorge Alec Effinger (Fiction), Walt Simonson (Illustrations)
"The Last Man"—Stan Lee, Russ Heath
"His Own Kind" (Disch)—Roy Thomas, Val Mayerik/Mike Esposito
"The Nightmare Patrol"—Gerry Conway, Ernie Chua
"In the Shadows of the City"—Steve Gerber, Vincente Alcazar

The first magazine issue of *The Haunt of Horror* looked like a winner. Bob Larkin's cover is among his finest paintings ever; a full-figure shot of a werewolf literally howling at the moon, '70s-style cutie cowering in fear, and what really ices the cake, a grinning skull in the foreground in the right-hand corner. As with all of Larkin's best pieces, the colors are vivid and contrast well, the subjects photo-realistic and the composition simple and strong. And to top it off, this was the first cover he did for the magazine—talk about hitting a homer your first time at bat. The frontispiece by Alfredo Alcala is equally wonderful, featuring an assortment of evil women, ghastly ghouls and other things that go bump in the night, rendered in the lush style that make his work so memorable. "The Rats" again saw Ralph Reese finding horror in normal animals; "The Last Man" is strong, too. Even if it was a reprint, it was a solid story, with especially moody Russ Heath art. "Heart Stop" by George Alec Effinger recalls the digest version of the magazine with its prose fiction, stunningly illustrated by Walt Simonson.

The Haunt of Horror no. 3 (September 1974)

Cover: Jad
"Gabriel, Devil-Hunter: House of Brimstone"—Doug Moench, Billy Graham/Pablo Marcos/Frank Giacoia/Mike Esposito
"The Restless Coffin"—Moench, Pat Broderick/Al Milgrom
"The Exorcist Tapes"—Chris Claremont (Text feature)

"Flirting with Mr. D"—Moench (Text feature)
"The Swamp Stalkers"—Larry Lieber, Lieber/Winslow Mortimer
"They Wait Below"—Bernie Krigstein

Gabriel the Devil-Hunter might have been able to save souls, but he wasn't able to save *The Haunt of Horror*. The magazine was already on the back burner. The two issues that were released after this one were quite late, and quite lame. The one remaining bright spot was this issue's great zombie cover by Jad. Too bad that the feature "The Swamp Stalkers" doesn't quite live up to that cover.

Masters of Terror

Masters of Terror was what's known in the trade as an "inventory title," a book which consists entirely of reprints, or existing inventory. It costs nothing to produce, except to perhaps commission a new cover, and the publisher only worries about original material if and when the title catches on. *Masters of Terror* didn't catch on, but as a short-lived showcase for some of Marvel's best horror adaptations, it's hard to beat, and shows that, with a little more focus (instead of flooding the market), Marvel could have indeed produced a title that could rival Warren at its best. Even if the stories were all reprints, they're still collections that are brimming with the results of superior talent.

Masters of Terror no. 1 (July 1975)

Cover: Gray Morrow
Frontispiece: Gil Kane/Tom Palmer
"It" (Theodore Sturgeon)—Roy Thomas, Marie Severin/Frank Giacoia
"The Horror from the Mound" (Robert E. Howard)—Gardner F. Fox, Frank Brunner
"The Terrible Old Man" (H. P. Lovecraft)—Roy Thomas, Barry Smith/Dan Adkins/John Verpoorten
"Master-Pieces"—Tony Isabella (Text feature)
"The Drifting Snow" (August Derleth)—Tony Isabella, Esteban Maroto
"The Shambler from the Stars" (Robert Bloch)—Ron Goulart, Jim Starlin/Tom Palmer
"Time Out for Terror"—Don and Maggie Thompson (Text feature)
"Terror Toons"—Stu Shwarzberg
"Yours Truly, Jack the Ripper" (Robert Bloch)—Ron Goulart/Roy Thomas, Gil Kane/Ralph Reese

The fine sort-of-new front cover for *Masters of Terror* no. 1, illustrating "It" by Theodore Sturgeon (reprinted from *Supernatural Thrillers* no. 1), was by Gray Morrow, and was based on a previous cover to the same comic by Steranko. "It" is an unforgettable horror tale in the grand old Heap tradition, and Marvel does justice to another clear inspiration for its own muck-monster series, the Man-Thing. For once, Roy Thomas does not handle a Robert E. Howard adaptation, but Gardner Fox steps up to the plate with his take on "The Horror from the Mound," which had originally appeared in the four-color *Chamber of Chills* no. 1. The real gem of the issue, though (as it had been in its original appearance in *Vampire Tales* no. 4; see the following chapter for a fuller description), is "The Drifting Snow," a haunting tale by August Derleth. It features unusually sensitive handling in the script department by Tony Isabella, and an art job by Esteban Maroto which is one of his finest. Equally masterful effort was put into the Robert Bloch short "Yours Truly, Jack the Ripper," an order so tall it took Roy Thomas teaming up with Ron Goulart to do justice to the words, and Gil Kane teaming up with Ralph Reese to bring those words to chilling illustrated life. From the grim, dramatic splash page, where the eyes of a dead girl stare out at the reader, to the last, a POV shot that reveals all, the reader is gripped. Bloch also gets a cinematic treatment in "The Shambler from the Stars," a Lovecraftian piece that is a virtual textbook on how to achieve a maximum variety of shots in a set number of identically

Haunt of Horror no. 1 (Marvel) — Another fine example of Larkin's work, his first cover for Marvel (courtesy Marvel Entertainment, Inc.).

sized panels. Nothing personal against Stu Shwarzberg, but the "Terror Toons" are neither very well drawn, nor very funny. (For example, two men are marooned on an island. One is turning into a werewolf while the other is staring the other way into the sunset saying, "So, what did you used to do at night for kicks, pal?") Unnecessary filler.

Masters of Terror no. 2 (September 1975)

Cover: Dan Adkins
Frontispiece: Gil Kane/Tom Palmer
"The Invisible Man" (H.G. Wells) — Ron Goulart, Val Mayerik/Dan Adkins
"The Man Who Cried Werewolf" (Bloch) — Gerry Conway, Pablo Marcos
"Master-Pieces" — Tony Isabella (Text feature)
"Dig Me No Grave" (R.E. Howard) — Roy Thomas, Gil Kane/Tom Palmer
"Terror Toons" — Stu Shwarzberg
"The Music of Erich Zann" (H.P. Lovecraft) — Roy Thomas, Johnny Craig
"Pickman's Model" (H.P. Lovecraft) — Roy Thomas, Tom Palmer
"Time Out for Terror" — Don/Maggie Thompson (text feature)
"The Roaches" (Thomas Disch) — Gerry Conway, Ralph Reese

Again, a fine, fine cover (by Dan Adkins this time around), again based on a previous painting by Steranko. The frontispiece, by the dynamic Gil Kane/Tom Palmer team, had previously appeared as the cover to the first issue of the revamped *Journey into Mystery*, and it illustrated the Howard story "Dig Me No Grave," which Kane and Palmer drew as well. Roy Thomas, naturally, scripted the story, one of his most successful non–Conan Howard adaptations. Howard's horror stories are often overlooked in favor of his sword and sorcery epics, but at his best, Howard was easily as frightening to read as Lovecraft. Speaking of Lovecraft, he gets served up twice in this first issue. Roy Thomas proves as adept at handling Lovecraft as he does Robert E. Howard on both tales, "Pickman's Model" (which was also a great episode of *Night Gallery*) and "The Music of Eric Zann." He is lent more than able assistance by Tom Palmer solo on the former, and EC/Warren legend Johnny Craig, who sure hadn't lost his stuff, on the latter. H.G. Wells's "Invisible Man" was re-done from Steranko for the cover by Dan Adkins, who also inks the pencils of Val Mayerik on the adaptation inside. Although not nearly as effective as the 1933 film of the novel featuring Claude Rains, it's still a good read, with able scripting by Ron Goulart. Robert Bloch is back with "The Man Who Cried Werewolf," adapted by Gerry Conway and Pablo Marcos, whose werewolves are almost as scary as his zombies. Last, but certainly not least, is a genuinely creepy version of Thomas Disch's short story "The Roaches," which had originally appeared in *Monsters Unleashed* no. 2. Gerry Conway's story chills and repulses, and is aided perfectly by the art of Ralph Reese, whose realistic style makes the normal creatures he invests with such menace all the more unsettling. "Master-Pieces," in both issues, was a couple of pages of short biographies of the featured authors, for readers who might want to know more. Bravo then, good filler.

Skywald

Ah, Skywald. You either love it or you hate it — and even then it seems to be a case of extremes. Those who love it, really love it, and those who hate it, despise it. The appraisals of Skywald's legacy (not too mention the rise in value in the collector's market) find a fitting parallel in the critical evaluations of "B" movies, especially since the advent of monster magazines. Before monster magazines, there was no scholarship in the field of horror films; most of the magazines didn't even treat their subject seriously as Warren proved, though there was a big difference between laughing with the monsters and at them. But from *FM* on down the line, the prevailing critical attitude was, if it was an "A" picture, an acknowledged classic (*Frankenstein, Dracula, The Mummy*, etc.) then that's the way it was treated. But anything like Lugosi's Monogram or PRC films, or most other low-budget productions, were scorned outright, when they were discussed at all. Even some of the classics did not escape the Grim Purist's scythe —*Abbott & Costello Meet Frankenstein*, now rightly considered to be the greatest horror-comedy of all time, was once lumped in with *The Ape Man* or *Plan 9 from Outer Space*. Where the films of fringe directors such as Edgar Ulmer or Edward D. Wood were once looked upon as nothing more than oddball trash, they are now considered to be the work of an auteur. Which brings us back to Skywald.

Until the last generation or so, Skywald, like the late Rodney Dangerfield, "didn't get any respect at all." In the best light, its products were seen as third- or fourth-rate imitations of Warren mags (especially by Jim Warren, but in all honesty, in the beginning they were). The worst-case look saw them lumped in with really third- and fourth-rate stuff like the Eerie Publications. Succeeding generations have seen a virtual 180-degree shift in opinion, to the point where some quarters consider Skywald to be the pre-eminent exponent in the field of horror magazines, bar none. The truth, of course, lies somewhere in between.

It helps to try and put it in perspective. Begun at a time when it looked as though the quality of Warren magazines was beginning to slip, Skywald looked to move in on a market that might possibly be up for grabs. Warren's financial problems of this time period have been well documented. Most of the cream of the artistic crop may have jumped ship in the wake of Archie Goodwin's departure, but Warren still had a small, solid core of contributors. And it could still reprint the cream it had already collected, and Frazetta or Ditko the second (or even third!) time around was still better than anything else anybody could offer up. Skywald, Stanley, and Eerie Publications all had the opportunity to claim a piece of the action, but none could capitalize.

Skywald had too little, too late. Founded by former Marvel man Sol Brodsky and Israel and Herschel Waldman (the "Sky" and "Wald," respectively, of the company name), it stumbled out of the starting gate by producing magazines that were not even up to Warren's diminished capacity. Even Skywald's most hardcore fans have to admit that the first year or so each of *Psycho* and *Nightmare* were Warren imitations, and feeble ones at that. By the time former Marvel and Warren man Alan Hewetson took over the ship and steered it into his legendary "Horror-Mood" phase, Marvel had entered the fray and pushed nearly everybody else off the newsstands. Skywald, which hadn't exactly been on every corner to begin with, found its already-low distribution cut back to the point where it simply had to throw in the towel. Which was a real shame, because, by that time, Skywald had developed a distinct identity, hit its stride, and was producing some genuinely fresh and offbeat material. At its best, Skywald's stories evoked a true sense of dread, and gave the reader exactly what he came for: palpable horror.

Was it better than Warren or Marvel? In selected instances, yes, in others, no; but practically every publisher reviewed in this book did something better than somebody else at some point, so it has to be taken on a case-by-case basis. Did it produce or create a series character that has the timeless, iconic appeal of a Conan or Vampirella? No. Did it create stand-alone horror tales that favorably compared with (or even bettered) similar material being produced by the competitors? Yes. Did it leave a legacy as large as Warren or Marvel? Only time and critical opinion will tell, although in recent years, the tide (and collector's market) seems to be turning in favor of Skywald. In terms of collecting, it's not like people don't want *Famous Monsters* or *Creepy* anymore; they have always been highly regarded and valued, and will probably remain so. Time was when you could go to any comics shop or flea market and Skywald was a dime a dozen. Literally. Nobody had wanted it in the first place, which is why it was in the bargain bin. In the new millennium, prices on Skywald magazines have risen dramatically. Is it because curious, quality-seeking readers have discovered a hitherto untapped vein of solid gold? Or do they just need something new to collect? Maybe it's both, and even more at that.

Is it a question of aesthetics? If so, it is indeed a tricky question, because, in many cases, aesthetics are as varied as the opinions which form them. Is it a punk aesthetic, which denounces its forebears as fools? Is it as former Ramones manager Danny Fields said in *Mojo (The Music Magazine)* in February 2005: "The punk catechism said: 'It's this, not that [Deep Purple]. We may be terrible by your standards, but we're fabulous by the new standards that we've invented.' And that's inarguable." Mostly, I'd agree with that statement — art is nothing if not a challenge to preconceived notions. Elitism is art's worst enemy, and the fact that art can inspire such elitism is not art's fault, but the elitists'. It's like politics or religion, or anything else that gets codified and mystified, when it becomes the property and propaganda of a select few rather than something that everyone can understand and/or participate in. Taste may be subjective, but true talent is not. A different point of view may be as valid as the established notion, but to dismiss an established notion completely simply because it is established is as elitist as the standard which stifles new ideas in the first place. One may prefer the artwork of one of the Skywald staffers to that of Frazetta or Boris or Neal Adams, but to deny those men's talent would be ignorant as well as foolish.

Perhaps the punk rock analogy is apt: if Warren was classical, and Marvel was mainstream pop, then Skywald was punk. Punk, in its purest notion, is a de-mystification, if not destruction, of the established order; questioning, if not completely rejecting, authority — a radical alternative. And Skywald's style was indeed radical, especially compared with Marvel. Warren may have pushed at the outer edge of the envelope, but Skywald opened it up, its "Horror-Mood" concept providing some truly mind-boggling work. It also provided some mind-boggling nonsense, but that's going to be the case with any publisher. The point is that in its short lifespan, Skywald provided the majors with some healthy and inspired competition. It's a shame there ultimately wasn't room for everybody. Of course, that still doesn't make it any easier to shell out thirty bucks for a copy of *Scream*.

So just what, pray tell, is a "Horror-Mood?" "Archaic Al" attempts to describe it, in his own archaic, inimitable, and ellipse-filled way, on the contents page of *Psycho* no. 8, and

Scream no. 5 (Skywald) — This wonderfully manic zombie cover was rendered for *Scream* by Fernendo, and typifies the company's intense approach to illustrated horror (courtesy Gary Brodsky).

in issue no. 13 of the same title (they are punctuated and capitalized exactly as they appeared):

> Psycho 8 starts here, where the mind begins to boggle and wonder and slide over contents sometimes sane and sometimes not... here is where the maniacal miracles are announced and pronounced ready for your consumption... now... may we suggest you quiet your screaming within... for another world is about to enter you... this proud macabre gathering of gargoyles, crypts, black raindrops, thousands of faces and filthy little houses; destined we hope — to rock your primal spinal, eagerly awaits you to turn the page to where the freaky fun of this issue REALLY BEGINS... TO SHRIEK... AT YOUR HORROR-MOOD...
>
> ... Horror is a WEIRD word that CONFUSES As it TEASES... for it means MANY things... and many things mean HORROR... it is a word slightly BEYOND DEFINITION, for HORROR is PEOPLE and EMOTION and EXPRESSION... HORROR is PEOPLE... VAMPIRES... WEREWOLVES... CORPSES... OBSCURE MONSTERS... but in EFFECT... it is YOU... afraid of what such BEASTS and FIENDS might DO to YOU... HORROR is EMOTION, therefore... the unnamable, indescribable FEAR that OVERCOMES you when you are presented with something you can neither UNDERSTAND nor ACCEPT in your MIND, which is why HORROR is incurably linked to MADNESS and LUNACY... HORROR is an EXPRESSION of inner knowledge BURIED at the BACK of your BRAIN... for you KNOW... that FIENDS, MONSTERS, and your FEAR of the UNKNOWN are SECONDARY horrors... the REAL HORROR is YOU... and the UNBRIDLED, BRUTAL ALTER-EGO MADMAN INSIDE YOU who is capable of HORRORS far more EVIL than the WORLD now KNOWS... what is HORROR? YOU ARE!

Now, it should be OBVIOUS to ALL that that the ABOVE was WRITTEN by a man who REALLY LOVES his WORK and — oh, sorry, got caught up in the moment. But, indeed, this was the basic appeal of Skywald — not just its approach to illustrated horror, but the way it was able to communicate that to, and with, its fans. Because Skywald, even more than Warren, needed a strong fan base to survive. It was certainly developing that, but it's hard to develop new fans when your magazines can't be found, and it's just as hard to keep the old ones for the same reason. And if nobody can find your magazines, they can't buy them, and then you go out of business, which is precisely what happened to Skywald. Still, in its all-too-brief existence, it achieved a rapport with its fans unlike Marvel or even Warren, who were no slouches at fan-friendliness. Skywald (and Alan Hewetson in particular) loved what it was doing. The fans loved what Skywald was doing. They felt that the Skywald magazines were created just for them, and Hewetson reciprocated the feeling. Love 'em or hate 'em, there will never ever be another like 'em.

Psycho no. 5 (November 1971)

Cover: Boris Vallejo
Frontispiece: Bill Everett
"Let the Dreamer Beware"— Jerry Siegel, Ralph Reese
"Power of the Pen"— Doug Moench, Doug Wildey
"The Heap: Cavern of Doom"— Ross Andru, Andru/Mike Esposito
"The Vampire"— Allan Asherman (Text/photo feature)
"The Unholy Satanists"— Alan Hewetson, Serge Moren
"Out of Chaos, a New Beginning"— Marv Wolfman, Rich Buckler, Sr.
"Frankenstein: The Sewer Tomb of Le Suub"— Sean Todd

Psycho no. 5 is a prime example of pre–Horror Mood Skywald. Most people like to call the early Skywald a feeble Warren imitation (Jim Warren certainly thought it was). Truth to tell, it looks a lot more like the Marvel black-and-whites, due to the depth of that talent that had been utilized by Marvel, like Boris Vallejo, Ralph Reese, Doug Moench,

Marv Wolfman, Allan Asherman, Rich Buckler the Elder, Hewetson himself, and the real coup, Bill Everett. Everett contributes a giant monster frontispiece that shows, even shortly before his death, he had not lost an iota of skill. In fact, Everett was one of the rare artists who continually refined his style, where most others reach a certain plateau and then begin to coast or take shortcuts. Everett was never like that, and the world of comics is much richer for his dedication. And, yes, the Jerry Siegel listed in the credits is indeed the creator of Superman, and his contribution is pretty twisted compared to your average Man-of-Steel adventure, even further elevated by some outstanding Ralph Reese art. It is, in fact, the cover story, and is illustrated by a gorgeous Boris painting, one of his finest for any company from this period.

The art for the whole issue is first-rate, in fact, with one or two glaring exceptions. Doug Wildey lends his immense talent to a Doug Moench script, and gets in a nice tribute to his pal and all-around good-guy Archie Goodwin by making the hero of the story look just like him. Up next is The Heap. The art is handled by veteran team Ross Andru and Mike Esposito, and Andru writes as well, although not nearly as well as he drew. That's the main problem with the tale — despite the inherent pathos of a still-functioning human mind trapped inside the body of a hideous monster, Andru elicits no sympathy for the creature. Sad to say, neither does the original man-inside-a-monster, Frankenstein, who is even less well served in a story that makes *Frankenstein Conquers the World* look like an attempt at serious art. "The Sewer Tomb of Le Suub (Frankenstein: Chapter Three)" is both written and drawn by Sean Todd, whose art and writing are neither amateurish enough to be endearing nor stylized enough to be charming, and is a prime example of a case where Skywald detractors are right: this is shock value and gore for their own sake. Shock value abounds in the Al Hewetson/Serge Moren "The Unholy Satanists," but it is Hewetson's brand, which makes a world of difference, and is only a taste of future Horror-Mood (the term had not yet been adopted at this point) delights in store.

Psycho no. 8 (September 1972)

Cover: Jose Mirelles
Back cover: Pablo Marcos
"A Gargoyle, a Man!" — "Hervelson" (Alan Hervelson), De la Rosa
"Devil's Woman" — Marv Wolfman, Ross Andru/Mike Esposito
"Have You Ever Seen the Black Rain?" — Alan Hewetson, Juez Xirinius
"The Filthy Little House of Voodoo" — Hewetson, Ramon Torrents
"Bad Choke" — Don Glut, Juez Xirinius
"City of Crypts" — "Howie Anderson" (Alan Hervelson), Villanova

The Horror-Mood literally starts here. The term is first used here and in *Nightmare* no. 9, although neither used it on the covers. That would start with the next issue of each. The cover for this issue is exceedingly well done, and a treat for Hammer film fans — the woman on the cover is Maggie Kimberly in a famous pose from *The Mummy's Shroud* (except this time she's menaced by a particularly crazed vampire). "A Gargoyle, a Man!" was the first installment of Skywald's cult hit "Human Gargoyles" series, in which a family of stone gargoyles come to life were used to illustrate man's inhumanity to man and to gargoyle. Having worked at Marvel, Hewetson knew the value of a good solid series character, and worked hard to create distinctive characters and series. Andru and Esposito are back in tandem for the cover story, "Devil's Woman." But Andru didn't write the story this time, Marv Wolfman did, while Andru and Esposito are let loose to deliver some truly over-the-top gore, clearly enjoying themselves after so many sanitized superhero adventures for the majors. In fact, the gore meter runs in the red the entire issue, but it's so completely outlandish, and done with such wit and skill and imagination, that it only offends those who are too sensitive. It's not merely gore for gore's sake, with no meter or rhyme. The issue doesn't dwell on gore, but uses it at precisely the right time and place in each story for maximum shock effect. Undoubtedly the high point of the issue was "The Filthy Little House of Voodoo," illustrated by Warren mainstay Ramon Torrents, who works in a wonderfully moody wash style, quite unlike his usual, highly decorative, fine-line Warren style. Al Hewetson handles the script, and manages to achieve that sense of true dread referred to earlier; the story creeps the spine long after having been put aside.

Psycho 1974 Yearbook

Cover: Cover Gallery
Frontispiece: Paul Pueyo
"The Saga of the Frankenstein Monster: The Brides of Frankenstein"—Alan Hewetson, Zesar (Lopez)
"Slime World"—Charles McNaughton, Ralph Reese (*Nightmare* no. 5)
"The Man Who Stole Eternity"—Gardner Fox, Bill Everett (*Psycho* no. 3)
"Beware Small Evils"—Jack Katz, Katz/Frank Giacoia (*Nightmare* no. 3)
"The Inner Man"—Tom Sutton, Sutton/Dan Adkins (*Nightmare* no. 3)
"The Deadly Mark of the Beast"—Len Wein, Syd Shores/Tom Palmer (*Nightmare* no. 1)

Although well into the "Horror-Mood" phase by this time, Skywald still manages to emulate Warren on a couple of counts with this yearbook, but in positive ways. Most of Warren's yearbooks or annuals were all-reprint affairs except, for some reason, *Vampirella*, which always contained a new Vampi story among the old. Skywald does the same with a new Horror-Mood Frankenstein Monster story that leads off the parade of pre–Horror Mood gems. The other Warren influence was the look of the book itself—Warren had decorated previous specials and yearbooks with Cover Galleries of the best of the best covers from that particular line in groups of anywhere from four to twelve, sometimes placing a painted figure in the center of the composition. This made for some really memorable, eye-grabbing covers (see *Vampirella* no. 19 for more on the other covers of this kind). Skywald does the same here, either as an homage to or a stab at Warren (probably the latter), but it works anyway, as Warren's did. The six covers selected included the Boris cover for *Psycho* no. 3, which features the Frankenstein Monster (resembling his cover for *Monsters Unleashed* more than just a little); *Psycho* no. 8 and no. 9, which followed up the Hammer tribute with one to Conrad Veidt and *The Man Who Laughs*; and the cover of the very first issue, which featured (literally) brain-popping art that recalled the best moments and approach of the legendary "Mars Attacks" bubblegum card series.

The Frankenstein tale is pretty grim, but it's actually outdone by two early classics, which anticipate the Horror-Mood more than just a little. These were the infamous "Slime World," which really was, due to some vividly atmospheric Ralph Reese art and a dose of palpable helplessness against an all-consuming curse; and Kothar-creator Gardner Fox's "The Man who Stole Eternity," with some truly cosmic and mind-bending Bill Everett art. Again, the contents, if not the concept, resemble Marvel more than Warren, with yet more Marvel vets represented, including a terrific Len Wein/Syd Shores/Tom Palmer short-short, "The Deadly Mark of the Beast." To Skywald's credit, not only did it put the effort into a new story for this issue, but went the extra mile and further in future specials and yearbooks, which also contained all-new material. For more on Skywald, see the following chapter for its unique variations on the legend of the vampire.

ATLAS

Weird Tales of the Macabre

What's really weird about *Weird Tales of the Macabre* is that while Skywald's early stuff actually looked more like Marvel publications than Warren publications, *Weird Tales of the Macabre*, which was conceived, in theory, to look as much like a Marvel or Warren mag as possible, actually comes off looking more like the Skywald mags (particularly no. 2). But, like every other Atlas/Seaboard title, it never got the chance to develop any sort of distinctive identity. A right-on horror host or hostess always went a long way in this department, but like Skywald and Marvel, Atlas eschewed the use of such characters. This was perhaps a tacit admission by all that there was no point in trying to match Uncle Creepy, Cousin Eerie and Vampirella, who'd already achieved the seemingly impossible task of becoming as iconic as the beloved EC trio.

Weird Tales of the Macabre no. 1 (1974)

Cover: Jeff Jones
"The Demon Is Dying"—Pat Boyette
"Time Lapse"—Augustine Funnell, Leo Duranona
"The Many Horrors of Dan Curtis"—Gary Gerani (Text/photo feature)
"A Second Life"—Ramon Torrents
"The Cheese Is for the Rats"—Villanova
"Tour de Force"—Martin Pasko, Leo Summers
"Speed Demon"—Ernie Colon

Weird Tales of the Macabre certainly got off to a great start cover-wise, with a superior Jeff Jones piece that would have been right at home in the series of pieces he did for Zebra Books' Robert E. Howard paperbacks of the mid–'70s. "The Many Horrors of Dan Curtis" was an article about the man who produced so many TV horror classics, including *The Night Stalker* (movie and series) and the Jack Palance-starring Dracula. Augustine Funnell takes time off from Skywald to pen "Time Lapse," and Ramon Torrents sneaked away from Warren long enough to write and draw the best-looking story in the book, "A Second Life." Enough Warren talent is on hand to make it look like a left-handed *Creepy*, but like a great deal of the other Atlas product, that was the main problem — good work, but most of it too imitative to leave a lasting impression.

Weird Tales of the Macabre no. 2 (1974)

Cover: Boris Vallejo
"The Bog Beast"—Gabe Levy, Badia Romero
"Dr. Mercurio's Secret"—Al Moniz, Xirinius
"Carrion of the Gods"—Pat Boyette
"The Films of Edgar Allan Poe"—Carl Macek (Text/photo feature)
"Who Toys with Terror!"—George Kashdan, John Severin
"The Staff of Death"—Leo Summers

Have we got the Boris cover to make it look like Marvel? Check. Are the Skywald people here? Check. Is there someone to remind us of Warren or EC? John Severin's here, so check that off, too. Nothing here that establishes our own identity? Check. Some good stuff though, especially that witch-burnin' bondage cover by Señor Vallejo.

• THREE •

Invasion of the Vampires, or Bat's Entertainment!

Vampires need no introduction. The legends are as old as time itself, and Bram Stoker's take on the legend in *Dracula* saw the vampire sink its fangs into the public consciousness and never let go. The reasons for this popularity are as varied as the legends and permutations of those legends — sexual, psychological, religious, political — topics that have been dissected many, many times. Those aspects of the vampire will not be addressed in this chapter, except in relation to a particular story. Suffice it to say that there have been more vampire stories (and movies and comics and what have you) than there have been about any other kind of monster. All of the above themes (especially the sexual) have been dealt with more and more frankly as time goes by, but one of the most interesting changes has been in the image of the vampire itself. The male vampire, it seems, has gone from one extreme to the other. For years, the standard vampire attire was suavity at its utmost: formal wear no matter what the occasion, impeccable grooming and manners (at least until the point his bloodlust was revealed). In recent times, the acceptable stereotype is somewhat like that of a dead rock star: flowing locks to complement the fangs, bare chests and leather pants. The female vampire has, in a sense, returned to its roots. At first, the term was applied to sexually predatory females of the Theda Bara school, monstrous on a human level, but not actually supernatural. Then came Dracula's wives, Carroll Borland in *Mark of the Vampire*, and Gloria Holden in *Dracula's Daughter*. They had straight, flowing hair, with gowns to match. What sexuality was in the characters was implied more than demonstrated. In the '50s, and especially the '60s, this changed drastically. Movies from Mexico, Britain, France and Italy (as well as in Warren's pioneering *Vampirella* magazine discussed below) featured a new breed of female vampire, both bloodthirsty and buxom, their ever-increasing bust lines barely concealed (and sometimes not at all) in outfits so flimsy as to be useless for covering up anything anyway. Their sexual appetites increased as well, bringing a whole new old meaning to the term, and "vamp" is once again a predatory female. Now they have fangs as well as claws to sink into unsuspecting (and more often than not, willing) victims.

Warren

Warren did many, many vampires, in many forms, including Dracula, but any discussion of its vampiric output must inevitably begin, and perhaps even end, with Vampirella (see below), who, like Dracula, rose above her humble pulpy origins to become a certified pop culture icon. (Two *Vampirella* covers were directly inspired by pulps: no. 56 *Terror Tales*, vol. 12, no. 1, 1940, and no. 68 *Startling Stories*, vol. 20, no. 3, 1950). In some ways, Vampirella manages to evoke much more pathos than Dracula, because Dracula revels in his state of being as much as he is tormented by it.

Since Vampirella is a vampire who comes from a whole planet of vampires where the blood literally flows in rivers, she feels no shame in being a vampire, but when her planet dries up and she comes to Earth, she is tormented that she might have to harm innocents to get what she needs. If any vampire could ever have been said to be pure of heart, Vampirella would be that vampire. (The story is one of the few ever to successfully answer the question, If an alien vampire like The Thing lives on human blood, exactly how has it managed to sustain itself before finding a buffet on Earth?)

Warren Publishing

Vampirella

In 1968, Warren Publishing was in trouble. Despite being responsible for the seminal monster movie and horror titles, the company was in the red. To make matters worse, Archie Goodwin had just resigned as an editor, leaving the illustrated horror titles directionless. A good part of the original crack artistic staff disappeared in his wake. Warren personally took over editorship of *Creepy* and *Eerie*, which barely subsisted on a diet of reprints and mediocre talent. After a particularly stressful day slaving over hot monsters, Warren and Forry Ackerman went to the movies. The two old pals checked out a new hip sci-fi spoof that featured Jane Fonda as a smart and super-sexy siren from outer space. She becomes involved in all manner of tongue-in-cheek misadventures, each of which also just happens to divest her of most of the clothes she's not wearing at the time. The luscious and liberated lady's name, as well as the title of the movie, was *Barbarella*. Both Jim and Forry loved it, and even better, it gave Warren an idea. Armed with little more than an idea and a little help from some friends, they created Warren's most enduring, endearing, and recognizable original character–Vampirella.

The character of Vampirella (or "Vampi") as we all know and love her didn't have much direction until Archie Goodwin started working for Warren again and began writing her adventures with issue no. 8. Her first two adventures, written by Forry, are, by design, lightweight, pun-filled affairs that only hint at the potential of the character, but her impact as a visual icon was immediate, and that would carry the strip until she realized that potential. At her (and her stories') best, Vampi was fun and funny, sexy and scary, a combination of otherworldly innocence and smoldering beauty and sensuality that successfully utilized all the classic elements of the vampire story and gothic horror while remaining firmly rooted in the now. She was a strong female character, but unlike any seen in the comics field until this time. Wonder Woman and Sheena Queen of the Jungle were obviously strong women characters, but Vampi was no super-heroine. She might have been a vampire from outer space, but she couldn't leap tall buildings in a single bound, although she could certainly handle her own in most situations. And then there was her costume — what little of it there was. Designed by Trina Robbins, it was fetishistic yet cute, daring yet demure, exploitative, but so perfectly suited to her innocent yet unashamedly sexy manner. However, Vampirella came across as no mere sex object, but a genuinely independent woman who treated men or her own terms.

But the exploitation value of a beautiful, nearly nude woman has no value at all if the artist who renders the character doesn't know how to draw women. Most comic artists, especially modern ones, draw them either like men with breasts or so grossly overdeveloped that any erotic appeal is laughable. Ironically, the revitalized Vampirella was at the forefront of the "bad girl art" trend of the '90s — itself a cruelly ironic term. Sheena, the Phantom Lady, and Torchy — all these classic female characters were examples of "good girl art." That's merely pinups applied to comic panels, strips that are nothing but an excuse to showcase pretty girls. But since Vampi was a vampire, she was a "bad girl," and her revival in the '90s spawned an avalanche of comics that featured evil (or at least naughty) women with ridiculously huge breasts. They were not only bad — they really were drawn that way. Luckily, the original run of *Vampi*'s was blessed with a succession of artists who understood the nature and requirements of the character and had the talent to put that vision across. The premier name was that of Jose Gonzalez, who began drawing Vampi with issue no. 12, and was her most prolific and well-loved delineator.

Many long-time Vampi fans were aghast at the new version of the character, exploitative in the worst way, and the perpetrators actually had the gall to suggest, in one of their most recent story arcs, that all of Vampirella's previous adventures (the Warren years) are "false memories" (*Vampirella: Revelations*). That doesn't stop the artists from capitalizing on all those falsely-implanted recollections. Too often they use this as an inexpensive means to publicize the newer version. A hardcover edition of Vampi's "Horror Classics" included only one Warren story, and while a number of fine artists contribute their talents, the writers just don't seem to get it. Only time will tell if they do. At least the company seems committed to reprint the Warren series from beginning to end, and must be commended for that, and for helping bring Vampi back into the public eye, however well-intentioned but misplaced some of those efforts have been.

VAMPIRELLA no. 19 (September 1972) 1972 Yearbook

Cover: Jose Gonzalez
Frontispiece: "Everything you always wanted to know about Vampirella"
"Vampirella: Shadow of Dracula"—T. Casey Brennan, Jose Gonzalez
"To Kill a God"—Wallace Wood (no. 12)
"Two Silver Bullets"—Don Glut, Reed Crandall (no. 1)
"Fate's Cold Finger"—Doug Moench, Ken Barr (no. 9)
"Jack the Ripper Strikes Again!"—Chris Fellner, Jerry Grandenetti (no. 9)
"The Survivor"—Buddy Saunders, Ernie Colon (no. 7)
"The Soft, Sweet Lips of Hell"—Denny O'Neil/Steve Englehart, Neal Adams (no. 10)
"The Silver Thief and the Pharaoh's Daughter"—Dean Latimer, Jose Bea (no. 13)

This is not to be confused with the 1972 annual, a high-ticket collector's item that, quite frankly, isn't worth the money. Both contain mostly reprints, and characteristic of the Vampi yearbooks but none of the other Warren titles, an original story in each. True, the 1972 Annual features the painting that would have been used as the cover to *Vampirella* no. 1 had Warren not decided to go with Frazetta instead; but *Vampirella* no. 19 features the definitive Vampi painting, which stands as the character's ultimate realization even today. Everything about the piece is perfect: pose, proportion, color, and the look on Vampi's face are the monster magazine's equivalent to the Mona Lisa's smile. Its most famous and beloved utilization was a six-foot-tall poster that you could order from Captain Company. It's a cornerstone of any self-respecting monster fan's collection. (The 1972 Comic Art Convention Book, which also uses the painting, makes for interesting reading. Warren has placed an awards section which contains kudos for a few creators but mostly just takes swipes at everybody Warren didn't like.) The lineup in the year book is just as good, if not better than in the annual. Wallace Wood is represented in both, but his "To Kill a God" is not only superior to "The Curse" but also a towering graphic storytelling achievement as a whole. Plus, you get Dracula, Reed Crandall, Neal Adams, Ernie Colon, Doug Moench, Denny O'Neil — a "Super Special Issue!" indeed, and if you're looking for Vampi's "Best Issue Ever!" then look no further.

VAMPIRELLA no. 36 (September 1974)

Cover: Sanjulian
Frontispiece, inside back cover: Jose Gonzalez
"Vampirella — The Vampire of the Nile" — Flaxman Loew, Jose Ortiz
"A Wonderful Morning" — Fernando Fernandez
"The Tiara of the Dragon" — John Jacobson, Esteban Maroto
"Good to the Last Drop" — Martin Pasko, Ramon Torrents
"Swordplay" — Martin Pasko, Felix Mas
"Prey for Me" — Rich Margopolous, Auraleon
"Puppet Player" — Jose Bea
Back cover: Enrich

This was another key issue, for several reasons, most of which start with the cover. Sanjulian's Vampirella is almost as perfectly realized as Gonzalez's, and the pose became almost as iconic (and merchandised). But it's not just the painting; it's the design and composition itself — Vampi is actually on a huge playing card and billed as "The Blood Red Queen of Hearts!" A couple of years later, this would become the name of one of her greatest foes, but the term was first used for Vampi herself. It also references the lead story, which was a quite a revelation at the time. Turns out that Vampi was actually Cleopatra, who was vampirized by Ptolemy, in reality the vampire-king of the Nile. She stakes Ptolemy, but Amon-Ra cannot remove the evil from her soul, and so grants her a human death (Cleopatra's asp) so that she can be reincarnated on Drakulon. A nifty trick that, and one that manages to expand on her origin without denying or altering what came before it. Virtually every important Vampi artist is represented, save Frazetta, and the issue features the cream of Warren's Spanish crop.

VAMPIRELLA no. 67 (March 1978)

Cover photo: Barbara Leigh as Vampirella (Leigh was to have starred in the movie, which was never made.)
"Vampirella — The Glorious Return of Sweet Baby Theda" — DuBay, Gonzalez
"The Quest" — Budd Lewis, Ramon Torrents
"Fish Bait" — Nicola Cuti, Alex Nino
"Home Sweet Horologium" — Nicola Cuti, Paul Neary
"Choice Cuts" — Cary Bates, Russ Heath
"The Last Dragon King" — Roger McKenzie, Esteban Maroto

It's a shame that Hammer Films never got to put its distinctive stamp on a Vampi film, even though Barbara Leigh (although a beautiful woman) didn't really fit the bill as much as some other Hammer girls might have, like Valerie Leon or especially Caroline Munro. When a Vampirella movie finally was made, everything about it was fatally flawed, especially Roger Daltrey of The Who as Dracula. By this time, Vampi had been around for nearly ten years, and though the art remained stellar, her main scripter at this time, Bill DuBay, had begun to steer the series into the cheese/sleaze-cake direction it would follow until its demise, although the story does contain some amusing Hollywood satire. "Fish Bait" is in the grand EC tradition; Paul Neary shows the smooth sci-fi form that made his "Hunter" stories in *Eerie* so successful, and Cary Bates fills in what would seem to be Bruce Jones's usual shoes as he teams up with Russ Heath.

VAMPIRELLA no. 94 (March 1981)

Cover: Enrich, Frazetta, Sanjulian
Frontispiece: Jose Gonzalez
"Vampirella: Death Machine"—R. Margopolous, Rudy Nebres
"Cassandra St. Knight: Assault"—R. Margopolous, Auraleon
"Pantha: Druids of 54th St."—Margopolous, Jose Ortiz
"The Big Shot"—Michael Fleisher, Delando Nino
"The Last Gift"—Roger McKenzie, Esteban Maroto
"Gunplay"—Artifact

Vampirella had always been intended (or billed) as an illustrated magazine that centered its fantasy features on female characters, but it never really became that until just a couple of years before it bit the dust. By this time, the magazine was little more than soft-core porn (Vampi even started making appearances in the nude), and the secondary strips featured heroines who began with a weak premise. (Cassandra was a psychic, Pantha was Simone Simon of *Cat People* update.) Their appeal was limited to their limit of clothing. Of course, sex appeal was always one of the guiding ideas behind Vampi and her mag, but what was daring, fun and funny in the late '60s/early '70s turned, in the '80s, into simple pandering. The end was near.

VAMPIRELLA no. 103 (March 1982)

Cover: Enrich
Frontispiece: Jose Gonzalez
"Vampirella: The Last Prince"—R. Margopolous, J. Gonzalez
"Cassandra St. Knight: The Mephisto List"—Margopolous, Auraleon
"Pantha: A Night Full of Zombies Pt. 6"—Margopolous, Jose Ortiz
"The Fox: Terror in the Tomb"—Nicola Cuti, Luis Bermejo
"Pentesilea"—Timothy Moriarty, Esteban Maroto
"Lover"—Artifact

There would only be nine more issues of Vampirella and a year for Warren Publishing. The quality had become extremely uneven by this point, but Warren, in selected moments, showed its spirit had not gone completely, with covers like this one by Enrich, a simply beautiful painting of Vampi swimming barefoot underwater. The pose brought back memories of Maureen O'Sullivan in scenes from *Tarzan and His Mate*. Jose Gonzalez had come back, too. (Even when he wasn't doing the regular feature, he did one-page pencil drawings that were often used as frontispieces.) He was there with her at the end, which was only fitting. His last story for the series, "The Walker of Worlds," appeared in the last issue (no. 112). It was the first of two Vampi stories in the issue, but it really should have been the second, because Jose Gonzalez will always be the last word in Vampirella artists.

Dracula (*Warren Presents* no. 9) (September 1979)

Cover: Basil Gogos
Frontispiece: Bruce Pennington
"Pursuit of the Vampire!"—Archie Goodwin, Angelo Torres (*Creepy* no. 1)

This issue of *Warren Presents* took a break from trying to capitalize on science fiction by capitalizing on Dracula, who was undergoing a surge of popularity due to two recent films, *Dracula*, starring Frank Langella, and *Love at First Bite*, featuring Hollywood suntan king George Hamilton. Unlike most of the other issues of the title, this one relied mostly on reprints from *Famous Monsters*, with the always-welcome classic "Pursuit of the Vampire" from Creepy no. 1. It's puzzling that the issue wasn't released under the *FM* title. Even the cover is from an old *FM* (no. 105), though you can't argue with its greatness: a masterful portrait of Christopher Lee as the King of the Vampires by Basil Gogos, the King of the Monster Artists.

Strange Stories of Vampires Comix (*Warren Presents* no. 10) (October 1979)

Cover: Sanjulian
"Curse of the Vampire!"—Archie Goodwin, Neal Adams (*Creepy* no. 14)
"A Flash of Lightning"—Gerry Boudreau, John Severin (*Creepy* no. 76)
"Like Icarus, Quickly Falling"—Roger McKenzie, Leopoldo Sanchez (*Creepy* no. 85)
"A Game of Hide and Seek"—Roger McKenzie, Leo Duranona (*Vampirella* no. 65)
"Swamped!"—Archie Goodwin, Angelo Torres (*Creepy* no. 3)
"Day of the Vampire!"—Bill DuBay, Gonzalo Mayo (*Eerie* no. 73)

This was yet another Warren stew of old and new, with the emphasis on the new, showing just how much and how little concerning vampires had changed, because of or despite of magazines like Warren's. It's curious to note that for all his *Warren Presents* specials, the term "comix" was used, a term normally associated with the undergrounds. Even though Warren had defied the code, and had helped nurture the form, and certainly some of his comics had taken chances, they were still not close to the creative freedom of expression that the true undergrounds enjoyed. In terms of language and depictions of sexual and other taboo subject matter, even in their adult title, *1984/1994*, "comix" respected few boundaries. Thus *Warren Presents* disappointed those who were either looking for, or thought they were getting, "comix" comics.

MARVEL

Dracula Lives

Dracula was set to join the ranks of Marvel as early as 1971. With the anticipated success of *Savage Tales*, plans were made for another black-and-white magazine, to be called either *Tomb* or *House of Dracula*. But when the success of *Savage Tales* turned out to be only anticipated, the Dracula project was then announced as a "king-size" comic, which later got scaled back to a regular-size title. So after the color *Tomb of Dracula* became a hit, it was only logical that Marvel return to the concept for the re-launch of the magazine line. But *Dracula Lives* never caught on the way the color comic did, and it perished along with many of the other magazines in 1975.

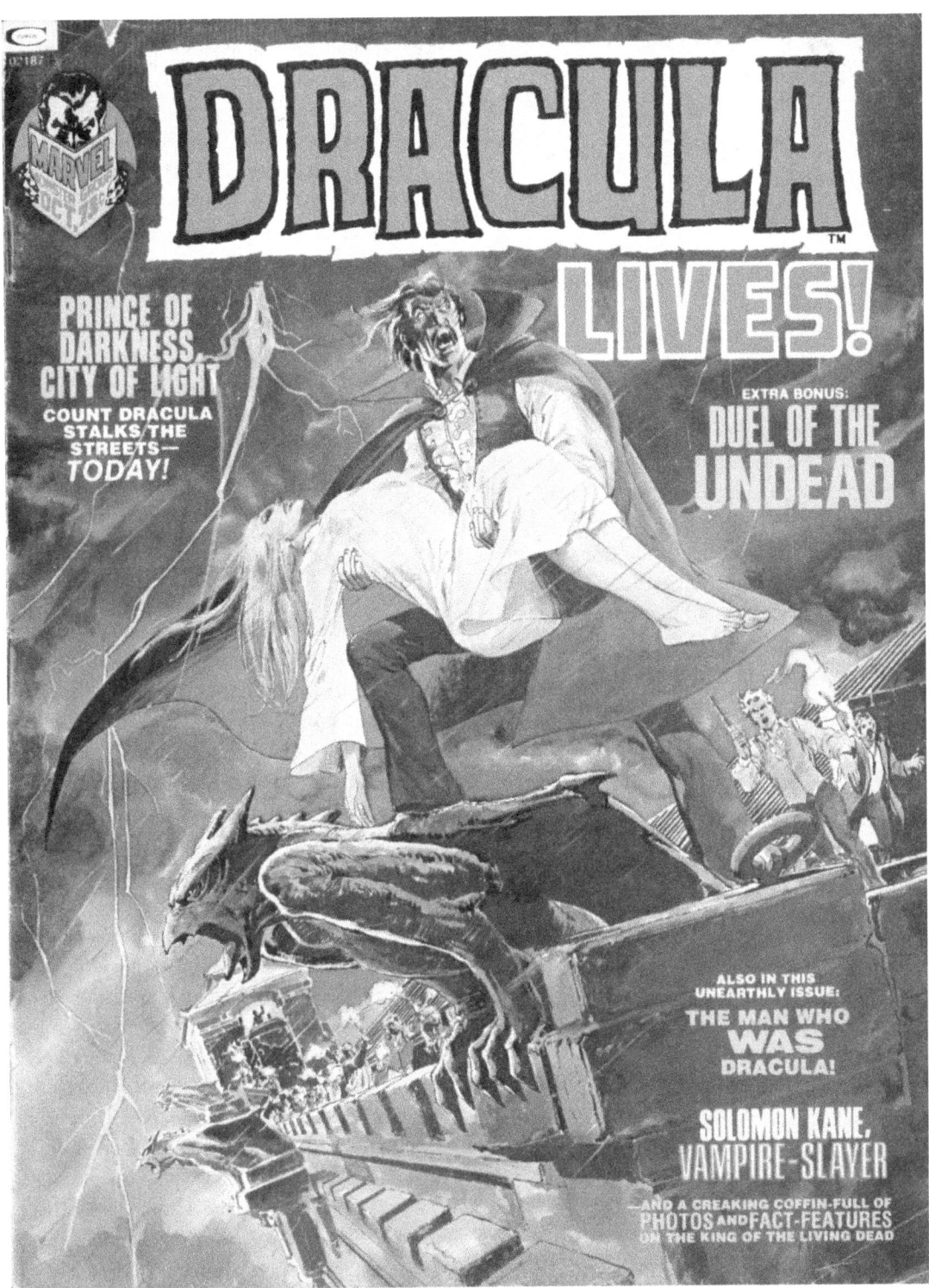

Dracula Lives no. 3 (Marvel) — Neal Adams not only drew many great strips for Marvel, he also contributed some memorable covers (courtesy Marvel Entertainment, Inc.).

Dracula Lives no. 1 (1973)

Cover: Boris Vallejo
"A Poison of the Blood"— Gerry Conway, Gene Colan/Tom Palmer
"Suffer Not a Witch"— Roy Thomas, Alan Weiss/Dick Giordano
"To Walk Again in Daylight"— Steve Gerber, Rich Buckler Sr./Pablo Marcos
"What Can You Say About a 500-Year-Old Vampire That Refuses to Die?"— Marv Wolfman (text feature)
"Fright"— Stan Lee, Russ Heath
"Ghost of a Chance"
"Zombie"— Tony DiPreta

Boris Vallejo's painting for the first issue's cover was a montage of various children of the night, and the central portrait of Dracula is neither like the Marvel conception nor the movies,' but more like the conception from the novel, where he is depicted in some scenes with flowing white hair and moustache. Colan and Palmer are a team, but they miss out on Marv Wolfman, who instead writes the Dracula introductory piece. "Zombie," of course, is out of place, but it's used for cross-promotional purposes, and is an Atlas reprint, although different from the Stan Lee/Bill Everett story. A strong debut, but better was yet to come.

Dracula Lives no. 2 (1973)

Cover: Jordi Penalva
"Dracula: That Dracula May Live Again!"— Marv Wolfman, Neal Adams
"Vampires Drink Deep!"— Stan Lee, Joe Sinnott
"Who Is Bram Stoker, and Why Is He Saying These Terrible Things About Me?"— Chris Claremont
"The Terror That Stalked Castle Dracula!"— Steve Gerber/Tony Isabella, Jim Starlin/Syd Shores
"One Corpse — One Vote!"— Stan Lee, Fred Kida
"Dracula: The Voodoo Queen of New Orleans"— Roy Thomas, Gene Colan/Dick Giordano

Boris Vallejo would only do one cover for *Dracula Lives*; Jordi Penalva, who would also go on to do several covers for Warren's bloodsucker-in-residence, Vampirella, handled the second. The action painted is one that would be repeated on nearly every cover afterwards, regardless of who painted it, that of Dracula menacing a flimsily clothed Virginal Maiden. The Flimsily Clothed Virginal Maiden differs from Conan's Half Naked Wench in only one sense, if you know what I mean. That said, it's an appropriately menacing cover, although Dracula looks a lot like Count Yorga (Robert Quarry).

The biggest reason for the success of the color *Tomb of Dracula* title was its creative team of Wolfman, Colan and Palmer, and it was a hard act to live up to. Marvel tried mightily to match the level of inspiration found in that strip, and in single cases succeeded, but, overall, the *TOD* team's handling of the character came to dominate the vision of the character, as the role of Dracula would seemingly come to dominate nearly every actor who played it. Oddly, Marvel didn't continue the tandem in *Dracula Lives*, although admittedly the black-and-white stories took place outside the continuity of the regular strip, much like the Frankenstein Monster, who inhabited Mary Shelley's time in his color title and the present day in *Monsters Unleashed*. Wolfman and Colan both work on this issue, however; Wolfman scripts Dracula's amazing origin, and Colan handles the pencils on a Roy Thomas-scripted story. "That Dracula May Live Again" is a cracking tale. Wolfman explores much the same territory that Coppola would (much less successfully) in *Bram Stoker's Dracula*. Neal Adams rises to the occasion with a superlative art job, his flair for innovative design and layout evident on every page — and Adams models Dracula on himself! The strategic placement of red color overlays on this and some of the other pages of the magazine, a novelty that didn't last long, heighten his special effects. While the lead story takes place in 1459, Colan and Thomas give us modern-day terror with "The Voodoo Queen of New Orleans." Colan is extremely well-served by Giordano's inks, and they get in a nice visual tribute on the splash page, where the fellow leading the tour of the cemetery looks exactly like Bela Lugosi.

"The Terror That Stalked Castle Dracula" is the other original story in the issue, and features smooth artwork by Syd Shores for a tale of those Nazi vampires, always good for a few laughs. Unfortunately, laughs are mostly what the reprints generate; despite competent artwork in both cases, they're sunk by obvious clever, EC-style endings. The text piece by Chris Claremont is also a little too clever for its own good. It's intended as a scary, serious warning to Van Helsing from the big D himself, but the tone is somewhat undercut by the cutesy-pie title — somewhat like the lead-ins to the stories. Once again, choice photos from choice vampire movies are spoiled by *Monster Madness*-type humor, and in terms of mood-setting, are extremely ineffective. Nothing's wrong with mixing humor and horror, but you can't just have bon mots roll out of the mouths of ghouls. It has to be done with a love and knowledge of the subject, and it has to be done well. Most of these weren't.

Neal Adams provides the best cover of the run with his powerful, windswept effort for no. 3. "Lord of Death... Lord of Hell" is a sequel to the previous "That Dracula May Live Again," but is drawn by the Buscema/Shores team rather than Adams. No doubt they got a big kick out of rendering a naked Dracula for the splash page, and Dracula, by the look on his face, evidently realizes that it's pretty darn tough to be scary when you're naked (although admittedly, some people are). The main event, of course, is Dracula versus Solomon Kane, naturally (and ably) written by Roy Thomas, aided by Alan Weiss and his crusty pals from the bunker. Kane finds his morals severely put to the test when one of Dracula's negligeed wives starts crawling all over him. He finds he can't kill Dracula because the vampire saved his life (even though he knows that by not killing him, he'll be responsible for thousands of deaths.) By the end, he's one pretty frustrated puritan — and stupid, too. Don Thompson's book review is for the paperback *Dracula Returns* by Robert Lory, the first of a (then) new series of adventures for the vampire king.

Dracula Lives no. 3 (October 1973)

Cover: Neal Adams
"Dracula: Lord of Death... Lord of Hell!" — Wolfman, Buscema/Shores
"The Vampire Man" — "Bela Lugosi: Dracula of Stage, Screen and Coffin" — Doug Moench (Text feature)
"Dracula and Solomon Kane: Castle of the Undead" — Roy Thomas, Alan Weiss/The Crusty Bunkers
"I Was Once a Gentle Man" — Chris Claremont (Fiction)
"Fire Burn and Cauldron Bubble" — C.A. Winter
"Shadow of the City of Light" - Gerry Conway, Alfonso Font
"*Dracula Lives* Feature Page" — (Stan Lee bio; book review)

Dracula Lives no. 4 (January 1974)

Cover: Earl Norem
"Dracula: Fear Stalker" — Marv Wolfman, Mike Ploog/Ernie Chua
"In Search of Dracula" — Chris Claremont (Text feature)
"When Calls the Vampire!" — Stan Lee, Joe Maneely
"Transylvania: Vacation Spot of Europe?" — Dwight R. Decker (Text)
"This Blood Is Mine!" — Gardner Fox, Dick Ayers
"Yes, Marv Wolfman Is His Real Name!" — *Dracula Lives* Feature Page
The Horror of Dracula — Gerry Boudreau (Film review)
"Of Royal Blood!" — Stan Lee, Tony Mortellaro
"Look Homeward Vampire!" — Gerry Conway, Vincente Alcazar

Earl Norem, Marvel's all-purpose cover artist, turns in his first effort for the series, and shows that he's just as adept at delineating monsters as barbarians or Nazis—it just all depended on who was menacing the damsel in distress. Norem's cover illustrates the lead story, "Fear Stalker," which takes Dracula to Hollywood for a variation on the tried-and-true "ham actor becomes consumed by horror roles and becomes deranged" plot. The story is entertaining enough, but is seriously let down by the art team of Ploog and Chua. It was really neither of their faults. Ploog is one of the top horror artists ever to lift a pencil, and Ernie Chua was an able and dependable inker, but their styles mesh about as well as milk and vinegar. Dracula gets two more turns in the issue. "This Blood is Mine!" details the Count's collaboration with real-life villainess Countess Elizabeth Bathory (seems that Dracula's blood supply is running low due to her bathing habits!) and "Look Homeward Vampire" pits the Lord of the Vampires against a werewolf priest. Novel idea, somewhat spoiled by Dracula's declaration, in the middle of the fight, that a wolf is something he can't turn into. Since when? The reprints are a little easier to take this time around, particularly "When Calls the Vampire," which features the artwork of the criminally overlooked Joe Maneely. "In Search of Dracula" and "The Horror of Dracula" are reviews of the book and film respectively, and in "Transylvania: Vacation Spot of Europe?" Dwight Decker expresses his horror at the prospect of the greedy claws of capitalism opening up Castle Dracula for tours to the paying general public. A historical landmark exploited for profit? Imagine that.

Dracula Lives no. 6 (May 1974)

Cover: Earl Norem
"Dracula: Death in the Chapel"—Steve Gerber, Gene Colan/Ernie Chua
"Yes, Virginia, There Is a Real Dracula (Undead and Well in Wallachia)"—Doug Moench (Text feature)
"The Mark of a Vampire"—Mac Pakula
"Blood Moon"—Marshall O'Rourke (Prose); Ernie Chua (Illustrations)
"Dracula: Shadow over Versailles"—Tony Isabella, J. Buscema/P. Marcos
"Marvel's Monster Movie Museum: *Dracula Has Risen from the Grave*"—Tony Isabella
"Dracula, Chapter Two: Into the Spider's Web" (adapted from Bram Stoker)—Roy Thomas/Dick Giordano

The sixth issue continues Marvel's fascination with the phrase "Yes, Virginia, there is a Santa Claus," and its endless re-workings of it, in this instance another feature on the historical Dracula. Gene Colan gets the lead Dracula strip, but Ernie Chua's style doesn't mesh with Colan's free-flowing compositions.

Dracula Lives no. 7 (July 1974)

Cover: Luis Dominguez
"Dracula: Here comes the Death-Man"—Gerry Conway, Vincente Alcazar
"Blood Moon" (Pt. 2)—Marshall O'Rourke (prose); Ernie Chua (Chan) (Illustrations)
"Dracula: Assault of the She-Pirate!"—Mike Friedrich, George Evans
Taste the Blood of Dracula—Tony Isabella (Photo/text movie feature)
"Dracula, Chapter Three: Female of the Species" (adapted from Bram Stoker)—Roy Thomas/Dick Giordano
"The Coffin Chronicles"—Carla Joseph (Media reviews)

Luis Dominguez takes over from Earl Norem as cover artist for a spell; the real treat of the issue is EC legend George Evans's art on the Dracula installment "Assault of the She-Pirate." And for the second straight issue, a Hammer classic is reviewed.

Dracula Lives no. 8 (September 1974)

Cover: Luis Dominguez
Frontispiece: Pablo Marcos
"Dracula: Last Walk on the Night Side"—Doug Moench, Tony DeZuniga

"Dracula: Black Hand, Black Death"—Len Wein, Gene Colan/Ernie Chua
"Dracula: Child of the Sun"—Chris Claremont (Prose); Pablo Marcos (Illustrations)
"The Coffin Chronicles"—Carla Joseph (media reviews)
"Dracula, Chapter Four: And in That Sleep..." (adapted from Bram Stoker)—Roy Thomas/Dick Giordano

Colan is once again teamed with Chua, and their styles still don't mesh, but the mood is different, as Len Wein, instead of Steve Gerber, handles the script. Pablo Marcos takes time out from his Zombie labors to provide a frontispiece and spot illustrations for the Dracula prose story, another effort from Chris Claremont, who wrote a whole bunch of prose for the monster magazines before becoming X-Men scripter supreme. Thomas and Giordano's Dracula adaptation advances faithfully on, somewhat at odds with the general house style of frantic action.

Dracula Lives no. 9 (November 1974)

Cover: Luis Dominguez
Frontispiece: "How to Ward Off Vampires"—Tony Isabella, Ernie Chua
"Dracula: The Lady Who Collected Dracula"—Doug Moench, Frank Robbins/Frank Springer
"Dracula: Scarlet in Glory!"—Moench, Paul Gulacy/Mike Esposito
Scars of Dracula—Gerry Boudreau (Movie review)
"Dracula: A Night in the Unlife"—Gerry Conway, Alfredo Alcala
"Dracula: Twice Dies the Vampire!"—Conway, Sonny Trinidad

The problems of any artist drawing Dracula for Marvel were twofold: he had to be able to do horror convincingly and he had to follow Gene Colan. Neither is an easy task. Frank Robbins and Frank Springer were good artists, and while perfectly suited to action/adventure strips, the Milton Caniff approach wasn't exactly right for Dracula.

Dracula Lives no. 10 (January 1975)

Cover: Luis Dominguez
"Dracula: The Pit of Death" (Pt. 1)—Doug Moench, Tony DeZuniga
"A Vampire Stalks Melrose Abbey"—Script/art: Winslow Mortimer
"Lilith: The Blood Book"—Steve Gerber, Bob Brown/F. Chiramonte/Pablo Marcos
Dracula A.D. 1972—Gary Gerani (Movie review)
"Dracula, Chapter Five: Ship of Death" (adapted from Bram Stoker)—Roy Thomas/Dick Giordano

After focusing on Dracula in the majority of the strips of the series' run, this issue gave a spot to Dracula's daughter Lilith. Obviously inspired by Vampirella, Marvel's Lilith was ensnared by a catch-22: not only was Lilith inspired by Vampi, she would inevitably be compared to that inspiration, a no-win situation. Add to this the fact that, like Robbins and Springer on Dracula, the artists chosen to illustrate Lilith's adventures were not exactly known for "good girl art," so even any exploitative potential the strip might have had was lost.

Dracula Lives no. 11 (March 1975)

Cover: Steve Fabian
Frontispiece: Hall
"Dracula: The Pit of Death (Pt. 2) Agent of Hell"—Doug Moench, Tony DeZuniga
"The Vampire of Mednegna"—Moench, Winslow Mortimer
"Dracula, Chapter Six: If Madness Be Thy Master" (adapted from Bram Stoker)—Roy Thomas/Dick Giordano
"Lilith: Nobody Anybody Knows"—Steve Gerber, Bob Brown/Frank Chiramonte/Pablo Marcos

Although there were two regular issues of the title left to go, the cliff of Roy Thomas and Dick Giordano's adaptation of the Stoker novel is left hanging, to be continued in other Marvel magazines (see *Legion of Monsters*). Steve Fabian's cover looks as much like Dominguez as his painting for *Savage Tales* no. 8 looks like Gil Kane, which may not be so much a question of his personal style as it was trying to conform to the "house style" for the title.

Dracula Lives no. 12 (May 1975)

Cover: Ken Bald
Frontispiece: Photo of Christopher "Dracula" Lee reading *Dracula Lives*
"Dracula: Parchment of the Damned"—Doug Moench, Sonny Trinidad (Pt. 1), Yong Montano (Pt. 2), Steve Gan (Pt. 3)
"Christopher Lee: Hammer's Hero of Horror"—Doug Moench
"Dracula: The Sins of the Fathers"—Gerry Conway, Tom Sutton

Dracula Lives no. 13 (July 1975)

Cover: Earl Norem
Frontispiece: Vincente Alcazar
"Dracula: Bounty for a Vampire"—Tony Isabella, Tony DeZuniga
"Dracula: Bloody Mary"—Rich Margopolous, George Tuska/Nestor Redondo
"The Toad"—Tom Sutton
"A Dracula Portfolio"—Russ Heath
"Dracula: Blood of My Blood"—Gerry Conway, Steve Gan

This provides a more fitting end to Marvel's series than the last issue of *Tales of the Zombie* was to its own; at least the title character was featured in the issue. It would have seemed fitting to have Wolfman, Colan and Palmer on hand for at least one of the stories, but this is compensated for by the great Earl Norem cover, his best for the series, and the stunning Russ Heath portfolio of Dracula art.

Dracula Lives Annual no. 1 (Summer 1975)

Cover: Gray Morrow
Frontispiece: "How to Ward Off Vampires"—Tony Isabella, Ernie Chua
"Dracula: That Dracula May Live Again!"—Marv Wolfman, Neal Adams
"Dracula: Lord of Death... Lord of Hell!"—Wolfman, Buscema/Shores
"Look Homeward Vampire!"—Gerry Conway, Vincente Alcazar
"Dracula and Solomon Kane: Castle of the Undead"—Roy Thomas, Alan Weiss/The Crusty Bunkers
"A Duel of Demons"—Gerry Conway, Frank Springer
"Dracula: Shadow over Versailles"—Tony Isabella, J. Buscema/P. Marcos

The *Dracula Lives* annual featured mostly his earlier, funnier stuff, including both of the epics from no. 3. All in all, much stronger than the Vampire Tales annual, except that the cover was somewhat below Gray Morrow's usual unerring standards. It does contain one nice in-joke: as Dracula is being burned at the stake in what looks like Times Square, a marquee in the background prominently showcases a poster for the Doc Savage movie, which coincidentally was not only in the theaters, but on the cover of Marvel's new Doc Savage black-and-white.

Tomb of Dracula

When the color title *Tomb of Dracula* was cancelled, Marvel tried to revive it as a black-and-white magazine, but although all of the talents that had made the regular comic such a success were on hand at one time or another, only once did the legendary team work on the same story, and the magazine failed to recreate the magic of its four-color predecessor. It lasted only half as long as *Dracula Lives*.

Tomb of Dracula no. 1 (October 1979)

Cover: Bob Larkin, plus Photos of Frank Langella and George Hamilton

Frontispiece: Gene Colan
"Dracula: Black Genesis"—Marv Wolfman, Gene Colan/Bob McLeod
"The Newest *Dracula*"—Jason Thomas (Text feature)
Love at First Bite—Tom Rogers (preview)
"Legend—According to the Movies" Tom Rogers (Text feature)

Is it a Dracula movie magazine with a comic strip, or is it a Dracula black-and-white magazine with movie features? The story is fine; two-thirds of the magic team are on for it, and Bob McLeod was a decent inker for Colan, although the fans wondered why Palmer wasn't on board. But the fact that the new films covered were mediocre to begin with made the magazine less impressive than a debut should be.

Tomb of Dracula no. 2 (December 1979)

Cover: Bob Larkin, plus photo of Klaus Kinski
Frontispiece: Tom Palmer
"Dracula: The Dimensional Man"—Marv Wolfman, Steve Ditko
"John Badham: The Making of *Dracula*" Steve Swires (Interview)
Nosferatu, the Vampyre—Tom Rogers (Review)
"Dracula: Court of the Undead"—Marv Wolfman, Frank Robbins/John Tartaglione

With the second issue, the world got to see what legendary mystery-master Steve Ditko would do with Dracula, but it wasn't a good look. Not that's there's anything wrong with the art, but a really substandard print job makes all of Ditko's washes, which added so much tone to the graphics, look completely washed out.

Tomb of Dracula no. 3 (February 1980)

Cover: Bob Larkin
Frontispiece: Jerry Bingham
"Dracula: And Out of Order Will Come Chaos!"—Marv Wolfman, Gene Colan/Tom Palmer
"Bloodline"—Peter Gillis (Fiction)
"Lilith: Metamorphosis of a Vampire"—Lynn Graeme, Frank Miller/Gene Colan
"One Curse, with Love"—Lora Byrne
"The Soul of an Artist"—Marv Wolfman, Gene Colan/Tom Palmer

Finally, the big three, and for two whole stories. And Colan is even on hand for Lilith, making Frank Miller look much better than he was at the time.

Tomb of Dracula no. 4 (April 1980)

Cover: Gene Colan/Tom Palmer
Frontispiece: "Freff"
"Dracula: Angelica"—Roger McKenzie, Gene Colan/Tom Palmer
"The Dark Beyond the Door"—Stephen King interview by "Freff"
"Dracula: Death Vow"—Roger McKenzie, John Buscema/Klaus Janson

Colan and Palmer team up not only for the story, but a knockout cover that would have made a wonderful print or movie poster. Roger McKenzie had plenty of experience with vampires at Warren, so he makes for an interesting couple of scripts, and the Buscema/Janson work on his second one in the issue puts it on a par with the first.

Tomb of Dracula no. 6

Cover: Howard Chaykin
Frontispiece: Haim Kano
"Dracula: A House Divided"—Jimmy Shooter, Gene Colan/Dave Simons
"Lilith: Violets for a Vampire"—Lynn Graeme/Ralph Macchio, Bill Sienkiewicz/Eric Von Krupp
"Vampires Around the World"—Tom Rogers (Text), Marie Severin (Illustrations)
"Chelsea Quinn Yarbro: An Alternative Reality"—Lora Byrne (Text), John Tartaglione (Illustrations)
"In a Literary Vein"—Gil Fitzgerald (Reviews)
"Shadow Shows"—Tom Rogers (Reviews)

The Dracula strip this time is entitled "A House Divided," which could just as well have been a comment on the state of internal affairs at Marvel under Shooter's editorial reign. You know it's the last issue because Dracula is also barely featured. Six issues compared to seventy — not exactly the way to live up to a highly respected namesake.

Vampire Tales

The obvious problem with vampires not named Dracula is that they don't have the marquee value, the name recognition, so they have to work that much harder to make an impact. Marvel did some fine stand-alone vampire stories in *Vampire Tales*, but hedged its bets by including its top bloodsucking series character, Morbius, augmented by various other "names" such as Satana, Lilith, and Blade. Morbius gave the mag staying power, but not enough to survive the Summer of Death in 1975.

Vampire Tales no. 2 (December 1973)

Cover: Jad
"Morbius: The Blood Sacrifice of Amanda Saint" — Don McGregor, Rich Buckler Sr./Pablo Marcos
"Witch Hunt" — Stan Lee, Manny Banks
"A Vampire by Any Other Name" — Doug Moench (Text feature)
"Five Claws to Tryphon" — Gardner Fox, Jesus Blasco/John Romita
"A Generation of Vampires" — Chris Claremont (Text)
"Satana, the Devil's Daughter" — Roy Thomas, John Romita
"At the Stroke of Midnight!" — James Steranko
"The Praying Mantis Principle" — McGregor, Buckler/Carlos Garzon/Janson
"*Vampire Tales* Feature Page" — Film reviews: Carla Joseph, Mark Evanier

Vampire Tales no. 3 (February 1974)

Cover: Luis Dominguez
"Satana, the Devil's Daughter: The Kiss of Death" — Gerry Conway, Esteban Maroto
"The Collection" — Russ Jones/Bhob Stewart, Paul Reinman
"Vampire Hunting for Fun and Profit: The Vampire — His Kith and Kin" — Chris Claremont (Text feature)
"Don't Try to Outsmart the Devil!" — Stan Lee, Carmine Infantino
"Everything You Always Wanted to Know About Satana, but Were Too Awestruck to Ask!" — Carla Joseph (Text); Esteban Maroto, John Romita (Illustrations)
"Bat's Belfry" — (adapted from August Derleth) — Don McGregor, Vincente Ibanez
"Vampires in Time and Space" — Tony Isabella, Pablo Marcos
"Morbius: Demon Fire" — McGregor, Rich Buckler Sr./Janson
"*Vampire Tales* Feature Page: Support Your Local Short Autobiographer" — Don McGregor

Satana underwent quite a makeover in this issue, and Esteban Maroto contributed some lyrical artwork, which saves the routine sex-and-Satan saga. No matter what her look, she could never make it to the next level.

Vampire Tales no. 4 (April 1974)

Cover: Boris Vallejo
"Morbius: Lighthouse of the Possessed" — Don McGregor, Tom Sutton
"Everything You Always Wanted to Know About Vampires but Were Afraid to Ask" — Chris Claremont (Text feature)
"Somewhere Waits the Vampire" — Stan Lee, Paul Reinman
"A Vampire's Home Is His Castle" — Doug Moench, Lombardia
"Hell House Is Dying" — Don McGregor (Film review)
"The Vampire's Coffin" — Stan Lee, Tony DiPreta
"The Drifting Snow" — (adapted from August Derleth) — Tony Isabella, Esteban Maroto

Three • Invasion of the Vampires, or Bat's Entertainment!

Vampire Tales no. 4 (Marvel) — Boris Vallejo again, with a sexy-yet-creepy cover illustration for the issue's classic adaptation of August Derleth's "The Drifting Snow" (courtesy Marvel Entertainment, Inc.).

"Lilith: The First Vampire"—(Inside back cover) Isabella, Ernie Chua

This was the high point of the run. Boris Vallejo's cover is outstanding—a spooky, sexy vampire woman—that is matched only by the story it illustrates, August Derleth's "The Drifting Snow," a crowning jewel in Marvel's illustrated horror output, an adaptation that ranks with anything else produced in the field of illustrated horror.

Vampire Tales no. 5 (June 1974)

Cover: Esteban Maroto
Frontispiece: "The Vampire Viscount of France"—Doug Moench, Winslow Mortimer
"Morbius: Blood Tide"—Don McGregor, Rich Buckler Sr./Chua (Chan)
"Count Yorga, Vampire of the Year"—Don Glut (Text/photo feature)
"The Living Dead" (adapted from Robert Bloch)—Roy Thomas, Alan Kupperberg/Dick Giordano
"The Devil's Den"—Carla Joseph (Movie previews)
"Morbius: The Way It Began!"—Thomas, Gil Kane/Frank Giacoia
"The Vampire Wants Blood"—Doug Moench, Val Mayerik

Vampire Tales no. 6 (August 1974)

Cover: Boris Vallejo

This issue is notable only for a cover that was not characteristic of Boris Vallejo's usually high standards. It looks as though it were dashed off in an hour or less. Come to think of it, so does the rest of the issue.

Vampire Tales no. 9 (February 1975)

Cover: Jad
Frontispiece: "The Vampire of the Inn"
"Blade: Blood Moon"—Marv Wolfman/Chris Claremont, Tony DeZuniga
"Blood Lunge"—Doug Moench, Russ Heath
"The Bleeding Time"—Gerry/Carla Conway, Nestor Redondo/Alfredo Alcala/Tony DeZuniga
"Blood Stalker"—Larry Leiber/Jesus Blasco
"Shards of a Crystal Rainbow"—Doug Moench, Tony DeZuniga

"Blood Death," "Blood Tide," "Blood Moon," "Blood Lunge," "Blood Stalker," "The Vampire Wants Blood," "The Bleeding Time"... Bloody hell!

Vampire Tales Annual no. 1 (Summer 1975)

Cover: Bob Larkin
"Vampires in Time and Space"—Tony Isabella, Pablo Marcos
"Morbius: Lighthouse of the Possessed"—Don McGregor, Tom Sutton
"Blood Death"—Doug Moench, Alfredo Alcala
"The Praying Mantis Principle"—Don McGregor, Rich Buckler, Sr.
"Satana, the Devil's Daughter: The Kiss of Death"—Gerry Conway, Esteban Maroto
"Blood Lunge"—Doug Moench, Russ Heath
"The Vampire Wants Blood"—Doug Moench, Val Mayerik
"Morbius: Blood Tide"—Don McGregor, Rich Buckler, Sr./Chua (Chan)

Why on earth was "The Drifting Snow" left out? Admittedly, the magazine hadn't been around that long, but editors could have included a little more early stuff.

SKYWALD

Skywald never put out a vampire magazine per se, but it featured plenty of them in its pages, including Dracula, and of course gave them the distinctive Skywald sheen — for instance, Skywald cornered the market on Nazi vampires. Skywald's Dracula stories weren't a series, and appeared in all three of its horror-mood titles.

Nightmare no. 17 (February 1974)

Cover: Sebastia Boada
"The End of all Vampires" — "Howard Anderson" (Alan Hewetson), Suso
"The Night in the Horror Hotel" — "Edward Farthing" (Alan Hewetson), Ricardo Villamonte
"An Exclusive Interview with Christopher 'Dracula' Lee" — Alan Hewetson
"The Psycho" — Alan Hewetson, Ruben Sosa
"The Inquisition" — Joe Dentyn, Lombardia
"The Autobiography of a Vampire" — Alan Hewetson, Ricardo Villamonte
"The Lunatic Creations of Edgar Allan Poe" — Back cover

A terrific sexy-girl-and-monster cover by Boada kicks off this almost all-vampire issue of *Nightmare*. "The Autobiography of a Vampire" was a mini-series that also had chapters in *Scream* no. 5 (see below) and *Nightmare* no. 19.

Scream no. 5 (April 1974)

Cover: Fernando
"Autobiography of a Vampire: I, Vampire" — A. Hewetson, R. Villamonte
"Darkkos Manse: Get Up and Die Again" — "Howie Anderson" (Alan Hewetson), Al Font
"A Cask of Amontillado" (adapted from Edgar A. Poe) — Hewetson, Maro Nava
"The Black Orchids and the Tale of Anne" — "Stuart Williams" (Alan Hewetson), Jose Cardona
"The Conqueror Worm and the Haunted Palace" (adapted from Poe) — Hewetson, Domingo Gomez
"Are You Dead Yet?" — A. Hewetson, R. Villamonte
"Shift — Vampire" — Augustine Funnell, Emilio Bernardo
"The Picture of Dorian Grey" (adapted from Oscar Wilde) — Hewetson, Zesar (Lopez)

A classic zombie cover kicks off this truly archaic issue of *Scream*, with both Poe and Oscar Wilde represented. Everybody adapted Poe, but Skywald was the only one that really captured the decay, in both the physical and moral sense, that the works of Poe embody.

Scream no. 10 (October 1974)

Cover: Sebastia Boada
"My Flesh Crawls" — Alan Hewetson, "Roberto Martinez" (Bob Martin)
"A Fragment in the Life of Dracula — Creatures in the Night" — Hewetson, Jose Cardona
"The Murders in the Rue Morgue" (adapted from Edgar A. Poe) — Hewetson, Zesar (Lopez)
"The Art of Killing Human Monsters" — Hewetson (Text/photo feature)
"The Stranger Is the Vampire" — Hewetson, Paul Pueyo
"Tales Out of Hell: In His Master's Blood" — "Howie Anderson" (Alan Hewetson), J. Duran

This was another vampire-oriented issue of Scream, including the king himself, with another great cover by Boada, a classic vampire and female victim pose that is quite accomplished, and conspicuously lacking the usual Skywald cover histrionics.

Scream no. 10 (Skywald) — Another Skywald exercise in elegant bloodletting (courtesy Gary Brodsky).

STANLEY PUBLICATIONS

Stanley Morse had been in the comics game for a while, and had extensive experience with horror comics, having published *Mister Mystery, Weird Chills, Weird Mysteries* and *Weird Tales of the Future.* For the reprints used in his black-and-white magazines, Morse had an inventory of stories to draw from of not only his own titles, but those of the American Comics Group as well, like *Adventures into the Unknown, Forbidden Worlds, Clutching Hand* and *Skeleton Hand.*

At least Morse had the good taste and sense to reprint (especially) work by Bernard Bailey, best remembered as being the primary artist for National's "The Spectre." Bailey is a criminally underrated comic artist, and, while his early style is admittedly stiff, he developed into one of the true originals of comics' golden age. His covers for the horror comics of the '50s (and thereby Morse) not only achieve the delicate balance of horror delineated with skill, coupled with an incredible eye for composition, but are in some cases truly horrifying, like the visions of a true deranged mind, and remain unsettling long after first viewing. Oddly, although Morse wouldn't mess with the reprinted stories (more or less; see below), he would sometimes chop Bailey's cover work up in strange ways or give it bizarre coloration.

Much has been made of the gory covers of the second-raters like the Morse and Eerie publications, but this offers a chance to examine an interesting parallel — Morse was reprinting the original works that had gotten horror kicked off the newsstands in the first place, and the Eerie publications had new, sick, twisted covers, very badly rendered. Is it all in how it's drawn? Does having horror drawn by Bernard Bailey or Graham Ingels or Jack Davis somehow make it more acceptable? Well, in most cases, yes. It's not so much a question of taste, which is subjective, but of skill. Case in point: DC's "Lobo," a sort of Atomic Biker from Hell, was an extremely popular character in the '80s and '90s, and his adventures were hilarious exercises in over-the-top gore which made the films of Herschell Gordon Lewis seem tame in comparison. The first few (and best) were rendered by Simon Bisley, an artist of prodigious talent, who took the gory side of Frazetta to its logical blood-spattered conclusion. Like Ingels and Davis and Bailey before him, he removed some of the inherent disgust through exquisite rendering. The same could be said for the "classical" artists illustrating battle scenes or Bible stories. The Eerie Publications like *Terror Tales* and *Witches Tales* and *Horror Tales,* conversely, had covers that were maybe not even as gory in concept as war stories, Bible stories or the competition, but seemed that much more horrible because of poor execution.

Stanley published more reprint comics in *Ghoul Tales. Horror Stories, Adventures in Horror, Stark Terror,* and *Gothic Secrets* featured text stories accompanied by lurid photos. None of the publications lasted more than six issues.

Shock

Shock (Chilling Tales of Horror and Suspense) no. 1 (May 1969)

Cover: Bernard Bailey (*Weird Tales of the Future* no. 7 May/June 1953)

Of all the stories contained in this issue, "The Gossips" has such an unbelievably gruesome climax that it's hard to believe it was done in the '50s. I had to check for verification that it hadn't been "gored up" for modern audiences.

Shock (Chilling Tales of Horror and Suspense) no. 6 (March 1970)

"Evil Returns"
"The Buried Curse"—Frank Simienski (*Forbidden Worlds* no. 18 June 1953) "Ghostly Destroyer"—Charlie Sultan (*Adventures into the Unknown* no. 17 March 1951)
"The Land of Living Myths"—Art Gates (*Skeleton Hand* no. 6 August 1953) "Death at the Carnival!"—Harry Lazarus (*The Clutching Hand* no. 1 August 1954)
"Fangs of the Fiend"—Art Gates (*Forbidden Worlds* no. 8 August 1952) "Mirror of Doom"—King Ward (*Skeleton Hand* no. 4 April 1953)
"Werewolves of the Rockies"—Leo Morey (*Forbidden Worlds* no. 17 May 1953)

EERIE PUBLICATIONS

And now it's time for a nod to the notorious Eerie Publications, and since that's as good as a wink to a blind man, then the nod will be little more than a slight shake of the head. That's because the notoriety Eerie achieved (indeed, its legacy to the genre) is based entirely on its magazine covers, which were some of the most ridiculously gory, sadistic and misogynistic (and sometimes just plain ridiculous) ever to be found on newsstand magazines up to that time. A bloody, nearly nude vampire girl in bondage is bloodily staked by a bloody mummy while she has her arms bloodily ripped from their sockets by bloody vampires and bloody werewolves, or (shades of *Robot Monster*) a man (not bloody) is attacked by a creature with the body of a gorilla and the head of a styracosaurus. Nobody was outraged by the contents. Well, actually, they had been, twenty years before, because Eerie Publications, like Morse, published mostly obscure pre–Code reprints. And in comparing the two, it's interesting to note how much and how little had changed in a generation. But then again, whereas Morse had simply reprinted the stories as they had originally appeared (except in a couple of cases involving Basil Wolverton), Eerie Pubs was not above the occasional retouching or even adding panels of gore to stories it felt were lacking in punch. Actually, the most interesting thing about Eerie Publications covers was that there only seemed to be about ten or twelve, total. The covers were literally interchangeable, each piece of art appearing on different covers of every title. Eerie also published *Witches' Tales, Weird, Horror Tales, Tales of Voodoo, Tales of Terror* and *Terror Tales* (the title of which was also used for a pulp magazine published by Popular Publications).

Tales from the Crypt (vol. no. 10—no. 1—1968)

"A Skeleton in the Closet"—(from *Strange Fantasy* no. 7 August 1953) "Experiment in Terror"
"Blood and Old Bones"—(from *Strange Mysteries* no. 14 November 1953) "Forever Dead"
"Thief of Souls"
"The Beautiful and the Dumb!"
"Horror Harbor"

Jim Warren wanted to emulate the style and spirit of EC. When Jim Warren found out that a competitor wanted to publish an imitation of *Creepy* called *Eerie*, he had his staff put together a magazine literally overnight

Weird Vampire Tales (Eerie) — Eerie Publications led the pack in gore on its covers, but looked strictly back to the 1950s for its content.

in order to secure a copyright on that title. Jim Warren may have trumped Eerie Publications for a magazine title, but Eerie Publications pulled off an even more audacious move; the company just ripped off EC, period. Eerie lifted the title *Tales from the Crypt* lock, stock, and barrel, and actually published a magazine with that title, cover-dated July 1968. Only one, since, obviously, Bill Gaines wasn't having any of that nonsense. To add insult to thievery, Eerie even lifted the host lock and stock, falling short of the barrel by calling her "The Old Crone." In a field littered with cynical hackwork and cheap knockoffs, this was surely one of the boldest moves ever. Edited by the legendary creator of the golden age Human Torch, Carl Burgos, who apparently needed the work, this magazine also naturally contains reprints from more pre-code horror comics (but no actual EC stories).

Weird Vampire Tales Vol. 5 no. 2 (August 1981)

"Vampire"—Art: Dick Ayers
"Satan's Warlock"—Art: Marchionne
"Vampire's Bride"
"Pool of Horror"
"The Vampire Flies"—Art: Oscar Fraga
"Give Me Back My Brain!"
"Cats of Doom"—Art: Kato

One can look at the Morse and Eerie publications in one of two ways — either as valuable sources of pre-code horror, or no-cost moneymakers geared to the lowest common denominator in exploitation. They're both, although more the latter: they would be a valuable source if more of the stories didn't deserve to be obscure. Oh, sure, each issue has one or two genuinely twisted tales, like "Corpses... Coast to Coast," "The Mummy's Evil Eyes," "Yeech" and "Give Me Back My Brain," but overall, the stories are too often faceless, as were the mags themselves.

• FOUR •

Conan the Franchise: Monsters, Muscles and Maidens

Robert Ervin Howard was born in 1906, in Peaster, Texas, and took his own life just thirty years later. He wrote and sold pulp fiction for fifteen of those years. In the span of that tragically short career, Howard wrote some amazing fiction and created some memorable characters; among them was one who would become a certifiable pop culture icon: Conan the Barbarian of Cimmeria, all of whose original adventures were published in the legendary *Weird Tales*. On the genesis of his legacy, Howard wrote: "He is simply the combination of a number of men I have known, and I think that's why the character seemed to step full-grown into my consciousness ... some mechanism ... took all the dominant characteristics of various prize-fighters, gunmen, bootleggers, oilfield bullies and honest workmen I have come in contact with, and, combining them all, produced the amalgamation I call Conan the Cimmerian." He neglected to mention his father, to whom the barbarian bears a striking physical resemblance, or himself, the archetypal bookish, sickly kid who transforms himself into a burly he-man. And coming right after the turn of the century, this transformation took place in a climate that still retained many frontier elements, an atmosphere which easily translated into tall tales of adventure and monsters. He wrote his fiction as if the world were going to explode in the next three minutes, and perhaps nowhere else in his Conan saga is the intense, bloody, passionate, white heat/purple splendor of his writing and the indomitable will of Conan (and by extension, himself) better exemplified than in this scene from "A Witch Shall Be Born," maybe the most famous single episode in the entire series, certainly the one moment most fans remember above all others. Conan has been crucified in the middle of nowhere, and the vultures have begun to circle:

> In his dulled ears sounded the louder beat of wings. Lifting his head he watched with the burning glare of a wolf the shadows wheeling above him. He knew that his shouts would frighten them away no longer. One dipped—dipped—lower and lower. Conan drew his head back as far as he could, waiting with terrible patience. The vulture swept in with a swift roar of wings. Its beak flashed down, ripping the skin on Conan's chin as he jerked his head aside; then before the bird could flash away, Conan's head lunged forward on his mighty neck muscles, and his teeth, snapping like those of a wolf, locked on the bare wattled neck.
> Instantly the vulture exploded into a squawking, flapping hysteria. Its thrashing wings blinded the man, and its talons ripped his chest. But grimly, he hung on, the muscles

starting out in lumps on his jaws. And the scavenger's neck bones snapped between those powerful teeth. With a spasmodic flutter, the bird hung limp. Conan let go, spat blood from his mouth....

    Ferocious triumph surged through Conan's numbed brain. Life beat savagely and strongly in those veins. He could still deal death; he still lived. Every twinge of sensation, even of agony, was a negation of death.

And then after all that, having been partially set free by Zuagir tribesmen, he proceeds to pull the nails out of his own feet! Conan may seem invincible, but, like Will Eisner's Spirit, he bleeds enormous amounts, feels equally enormous amounts of pain, and even if we know he will overcome, we also know that he will surmount the insurmountable to do so. Conan does what he does because that's what he is. He is more of an elemental force than Tarzan, but another famous scene shows that Conan, for all his berserker furies, is no mere engine of destruction — he wouldn't be the stuff of legend if he were. Witness this philosophical discourse between Conan and Belit, the titular monarch of "Queen of the Black Coast," another all-time Conan classic:

> "Do you fear the gods, Conan?"
> "I would not tread on their shadow."
> "What do you believe, then?"
> He shrugged his shoulders. "I have known many gods. He who denies them is as blind as he who trusts them too deeply. I seek not beyond death. It may be the blackness averred by the Nemedian skeptics, or Crom's realm of ice and cloud, or the snowy plains and the vaulted halls of the Nordheimer's Valhalla. I know not, nor do I care. Let me live deep while I live; let me know the rich juices of red meat and stinging wine on my palate, the hot embrace of white arms, the mad exultation of battle when the blue blades flame and crimson, and I am content. Let teachers and priests and philosophers brood over questions of reality and illusion. I know this: if life is illusion, then I am no less an illusion, and being thus, the illusion is real to me. I live, I burn with life, I love, I slay, and I am content."

Pretty existentialist stuff from a guy who kills vultures with his bare teeth, but that's part of what makes Conan such an unforgettable creation. Unlike most of the other sword-wielding savages who followed in his wake, he's a fleshed-out, complex character, whose personality evolved as the series progressed, although the stories themselves were not related in chronological fashion.

Conan was *Weird Tales'* most popular character during its original run, but perhaps Robert E. Howard had only dared dream of the life that the barbarian would take on beyond *Weird Tales*. The Cimmerian would become a certifiable pop-culture icon. That this was never realized in Howard's lifetime is certainly lamentable, but it took a number of incarnations above and beyond the original time frame to lead to this iconic status. Gradually, the character and canon of Conan became expanded far beyond the original core of Howard stories, so there evolved two types of fans: Conan fans, who may or may not enjoy the original stories, and simply like the character, regardless of who writes the stories, and Robert E. Howard Conan fans. Obviously, the two factions have to intersect at various points, but both the purists and the more general fans have insured that the legacy will live on, just like all good legends.

Before 1970, there was little separating the two groups. As stated previously, all of Robert E. Howard's original Conan stories that were published during his lifetime are to be found in the pages of *Weird Tales*. After the last of these had appeared, the character was out of the public eye until the mid–'50s, when Martin Greenberg's Gnome Press re-introduced him to the general reading public via a series of well-received hardcover editions, now prized collector's items. There were no interior illustrations, but the entire series featured striking dust jacket art by a combination of top-flight pulp and comic book artists, like Frank Kelly Freas (*The Coming of Conan*) and our old friend Wallace Wood (*The Return of*

Conan). Some of the renditions like Emshwiller's for *Conan the Barbarian* still leaned on the Roman gladiator-type image that had been favored by the pulps, but Freas and Wood gave fans an altogether more savage portrayal, one that would inspire and pave the way for the modern-day image of Conan.

It was in the Gnome Press editions that the expansion beyond the original core of stories began. Conan was proving just as popular as in his *Weird Tales* days, but there were only 21 stories by Howard, and the readers wanted more. The expansion of the canon was very controlled at first, even tentative. Possibly concerned that non–Howard stories about Conan might not fly, Greenberg had hard science fiction writer L. Sprague DeCamp, who had worked as an editor on Gnome's *Conan the Conqueror* volume, refashion four of Howard's non–Conan stories into Cimmerian sagas, which in turn made up the Gnome edition *Tales of Conan*. They did fly, although some purists' hackles were already raised, and so, with the next pastiche, Greenberg really took a flyer — all the way to Sweden. The aforementioned *The Return of Conan* was a novel-length sequel to *Conan the Conqueror* (or *The Hour of the Dragon*, its original title) written by fan Bjorn Nyberg, and because English was not his native tongue, re-written a bit and edited by DeCamp. According to Roy Thomas in *Savage Tales* no. 5, the whole thing "reads ... like the result of a freeway collision between Robert E. Howard and Edgar Rice Burroughs, but Nyberg's sheer enthusiasm ... comes fairly close to pulling the whole thing off." So in terms of its first non–Howard Conan story, Gnome scored on the first try. But any further expansion of the Conan mythos would have to be put on hold — Gnome Press did announce another Conan title to follow *Return*, but its contents will forever remain a mystery, as it went belly-up soon after *Return*'s publication.

But the fact that non–Howard stories could be accepted by fans was a green light for more posthumous collaborations and continuations, which began again once DeCamp worked out a backhanded deal with Lancer Books to publish Conan in paperback (undercutting Greenberg, who was trying to do the same deal with Bantam Books). Which brings us to new Conan stories, both in paperback, and more importantly for this study, in comics. As for the paperbacks, the idea of new Conan stories was not new — Greenberg had it ten years before, and enlisted DeCamp's aid in the effort. DeCamp merely took the idea and ran with it, much like he did with the series as a whole when he took it to Lancer. Some of the pastiches, like the Gnome *Tales of Conan*, were obscure or unpublished Howard stories that were re-written into Conan stories. Some were fleshed out from Howard's outlines, some were entirely new, but all share one quality — they are uniformly bad. Fortunately, Lancer closed up shop before it could perpetrate many of these transgressions, and by the time that Ace Books picked up the series and finally published *Aquilonia*, both men were close to death. (Carter passed away in 1988 and DeCamp died eight years later, which limited their involvement in the series.)

Marvel Comics sat up and took notice of Conan's ten-million-plus sales, and licensed the character in 1970. (The title of the comic, *Conan the Barbarian*, was inspired by the Gnome Press edition of the same name.) Marvel had great timing; not only was there a ready-made audience because of the paperbacks, but the relaxation of the Comics Code rules on violence and horror meant that the sex-, gore-, and monster-drenched Conan stories could be published in an atmosphere which had not existed just a few short years before. The editor and writer of the series, for many years, was Roy Thomas. Thomas was Stan Lee's right hand, and a longtime, extremely knowledgeable and respectful fan of Robert E. Howard and Conan, not only keeping his scripts directly based on Howard stories as close to the originals as possible, but infusing his own originals with what can be described as "the spirit of Howard." If, as Howard claimed, Conan was standing at his shoulder, relating the tales to him, then surely, at times, Howard was standing by Roy Thomas. Thomas was also keen to pay tribute to Gnome Press whenever possible, using the Gnome book title, and the title of the first story in that book, which was entitled "The Coming of Conan."

But, like the paperbacks, the art in the comics also had a lot to do with Conan's success, because he is such a visual character. Part of Howard's genius was his ability to paint indelible, vivid images with words, although the Conan art is more than simply drawing what Howard wrote. It takes a truly talented artist, paired with the correct muse, to translate Howard's words into successful illustrations or panel-to-panel continuity. Conan is more than just a superhero without the long johns. Fortunately, Marvel realized this, and made sure, for a long time at least, that it placed the art chores in the hands of artists who understood this. The first was Barry Smith, a young Briton who adored Jack Kirby, was just beginning to make a name for himself in comics, and would go on to prove that Frazetta wasn't the only artist that Conan could turn into a superstar. Smith was still imitating Kirby when he started the strip, but as the series progressed, so did Barry's style, into a thing of beauty that was not afraid to show his art nouveau influence. It was almost as if Aubrey Beardsley had drawn Conan. Unfortunately, the time that it took him to produce graphic beauty and style was not quite in sync with the monthly production schedule ("I'm terribly slow," he once said). In addition, other issues caused him not only to leave *Conan*, but comics altogether for a time (see *Epic Illustrated* no. 7, Chapter 7). John Buscema (who,

in time, would turn out more Conan comic stories than any other artist) and Gil Kane followed, both using their distinctive styles to visualize a muscular, brooding, gritty and dynamic barbarian, which proved quite a contrast to Smith's ornate approach. All were brilliant, and any question the Marvel strip's "definitive" artist comes down to which style you prefer. Marvel tried for years, in vain, to get Frazetta to do a *Savage Sword of Conan* cover, but he always refused, citing Marvel's work-for-hire system and its refusal to grant creator's rights or return original artwork. They obviously worked out some sort of deal, as he eventually did do one cover for them; unfortunately, it was not for the magazine of the character he helped to make famous, it was for Marvel's version of *Heavy Metal*, *Epic Illustrated* (no. 1, see the last chapter).

The comics, like the paperbacks, were a smash hit, and hardly a year went by in the '70s when *Conan the Barbarian* and its creators were not nominated for or win the prestigious Eisner award, the comic industry's highest honor. If anything, the comics reached an even wider audience than the paperbacks, counting similar sales, in the millions. *Conan the Barbarian* became one of Marvel's flagship titles, with an eventual run of over 250 issues. It spun off several companion titles (not to mention titles or series for every other Howard hero), including the one that makes up the bulk of this chapter, *The Savage Sword of Conan the Barbarian*, which lasted nearly as long as the regular four-color title. While Marvel didn't have an *original* black-and-white series character to equal Vampirella, *Savage Sword of Conan* ran for 235 issues, perhaps the longest run for any series character in an American black-and-white illustrated magazine. His reign actually began in *Savage Tales*, but he was too big not to have his own book. Without King Conan (a Gnome Press title which actually became one of the spin-off titles); to support the hallowed name, it disappeared along with rest of the black-and-white's in the Great American Comic Book Cutback of the mid-'70s. See Chapter Four for more on Marvel's groundbreaking black-and-white title, and the Conan stories contained therein.

Obviously, with such hefty runs of all the Conan titles, plus a slew of specials, annuals, and graphic novels ad infinitum, there would once again (and much more quickly) arise the question of new material. Once Marvel ran out of the 21 original Howard stories, the company was on its own. This is not to imply, though, that Marvel adapted all of Howard's originals and then went from there. From the beginning, Thomas mixed adaptations of Howard stories, with his own, some based on suggestions from "A Probable Outline of Conan's Career" and others simply from his own fertile imagination. He also turned barbarian stories by other authors, like Gardner Fox's Kothar series, into Conan stories. At first, although he had to negotiate with Marvel and grant the company the license, DeCamp, with his usual grace, refused to let Marvel adapt any of his or Lin Carter's Conan stories. He relented a few years later when he saw that it would put money in his pocket. Even more than the paperbacks' Conan, the Marvel Conan set the template for graphic continuity of the character for a long time to come, and, unwittingly and ironically, contributed to the division between the purist Howard fans and general Conan fans. *Conan the Barbarian* and *The Savage Sword of Conan the Barbarian* maintained a high level of quality and continuity for a long time, perhaps a longer time than anybody had a right to expect, and maybe it was inevitable that Conan would turn into the Mighty Thor in a loincloth. But this was not entirely Marvel's fault — there was one other huge outside influence on the popularity and image of the Conan character. It stemmed from the popularity of Frazetta and in turn Marvel, and influenced the way Marvel would present the character until the end, which was the movies.

The first film to feature Robert E. Howard's greatest creation, like the comic book, was titled *Conan the Barbarian*. It was released in 1982, and was directed by John Milius. Milius has called Frazetta "The High Priest of Conan" (in *Cinefantastique*, vol. 12, no.'s 2 and 3, 1982). "We were aware of this all the time we were shooting the film. He certainly was an influence on me. Frazetta's Conan illustrations were more important to me than the books were." If this is true, then why did he make such an uninspired movie? Arnold Schwarzenegger possesses absolutely none of the qualities that Frazetta gave the character visually or Howard gave the character conceptually, and Milius's ponderous, pretentious, leaden pacing suggests none of the epic sweep or action of a Frazetta painting. Visually, Schwarzenegger has a lot of muscles, but they are different muscles than someone like Conan would have had. They are a bodybuilder's muscles — muscles for show, not for action. Schwarzenegger is a bodybuilder, and this is reflected both in his performance and the ridiculous poses that he strikes, which suggest none of the lithe, panther qualities that Howard ascribed to the character. Schwarzenegger's Conan is an oaf. The movie Conan is more like Li'l Abner, and the situation is not helped by his much-parodied accent.

But the bottom line is that despite past and present (and certainly future) critical reservations, the movies were enormous hits. Unfortunately, this version of Conan became the model for pretty much anything concerning the character for a long, long, time, even the comics and other books that had made it possible. Conan became just another muscle-bound nitwit. Howard's Conan may have been a savage, but he was nobody's fool. However the characterization fostered by the movies, along with a decline in the talent of the creative teams assigned to the book (except in rare cases), saw the title and the character lose most of what had made him unique to begin with. He became just another cog in Marvel's production machine. Which is a real shame, because, at their best, Marvel's various Conan titles offered some of the finest examples of graphic storytelling ever seen in the field of horror and fantasy.

As for other publishers' contributions to the sword and sorcery genre in the black-and-white magazines, as Howard invented the genre and laid out the ground rules so ably, all other attempts at this type of fiction and character must be considered as imitations, although that in itself does not condemn an idea. The creative artistry lies in using those conventions inventively. Unfortunately for the genre, few have been able to rise above the pack, either in the literary field or in its bastard offspring, the comics, and this continues to hold true today. Many publications tried to jump on the bandwagon, mostly of the four-color variety, to varying degrees of success, but ultimately, the original was the one with the staying power. Even Marvel's versions of Howard's other heroes (which are covered in the following chapter) ran a parallel course to their original sources—with some very unique characters, and some very fine stories. But none were a match for Cimmeria's No. 1 son.

The Savage Sword of Conan the Barbarian no. 1 (August 1974)

Cover: Boris Vallejo
Frontispiece: Esteban Maroto
"Conan: Curse of the Undead Man"—Roy Thomas, John Buscema/Pablo Marcos
"Red Sonja"—Roy Thomas, Maroto/Neal Adams/ Ernie Chua
"Conan's Women Warriors"—Fred Blosser (Text); Maroto, Steve Gan, Roy G. Krenkel, Hugh Rankin (Illustrations)
"Blackmark" (Chapter 1)—Gil Kane
"An Atlantean in Aquilonia"—Glenn Lord (Text); John Severin, Ross Andru (Illustrations)
"Conan: The Frost Giant's Daughter" (adapted from R.E. Howard)—Roy Thomas, Barry Smith

The first pulse-pounding issue of *Savage Sword of Conan* was indeed an impressive debut. It set a high standard which the magazine maintained for a number of years to come, and, in terms of artistic quality, was as good as anything Warren or any other published had on the stands at the time. The cover was the first for the magazine by the early mainstay of the black-and-white line, Boris Vallejo, who had started his career at Tower Comics (*Fight the Enemy*), and had previously done covers for Warren and Skywald. Since Marvel couldn't get Frazetta, it got the next best thing. Vallejo, who simply signed his paintings "Boris," would become almost as closely associated with Conan as Frazetta, and would come to occupy a position in the fantasy art field nearly equal to his inspiration. Unfortunately, this meant that he would soon price himself out of Marvel's range, but, during his tenure at Marvel, he gave his magazine covers a high-class, paperback look, and turned in the finest group of cover paintings that any of Marvel's artists did for its black-and-white line. Although his technique is technically incomparable in its nearly photographic realism, his work, for the most part, lacks two things that separate all artists from Frazetta—the tangible sense of fantasy and imagination that enable complete suspension of disbelief and an epic sweep and unique eye for composition. The explanation may be that Boris Vallejo is a weightlifter, and his figures often reflect the stiff poses of muscleman competitions. However, Vallejo continued to improve, and his efforts for *The Savage Sword of Conan the Barbarian* led directly to a job illustrating the covers of Ace paperback reissues of the Lancer series–the ones not done by Frazetta. When Ace got the rights to Conan, it used Frazetta's paintings on books that had them originally, but replaced those painted by John Druillo. Vallejo would go on to do several more covers for the character, when Ace farmed the writing out to authors such as John Maddox Roberts, Leonard Carpenter, and the ubiquitous Robert Jordan, who, like John Jakes, would use a barbarian as a springboard to mainstream success. Vallejo's cover for the first issue features Conan and Red Sonja in those stiff poses battling living (or is it undead?) skeletons, recalling the films of Ray Harryhausen. Isn't it a shame that Harryhausen never turned his talents to a Conan feature film?

But Boris Vallejo was not the only thing that made the first issue impressive. Esteban Maroto, who had made a very large name for himself among American audiences with his work for Warren, managed to sneak in a few assignments for Marvel (see also *Vampire Tales*). He must not have gotten a copy of Jim Warren's infamous "loyalty oath" letter, or else he just didn't care. He turns in some particularly elegant work in this issue, from his frontispiece to his dream teaming with Roy Thomas and Neal Adams for the Red Sonja story. Maroto is the man towards whom all red-blooded males can direct their thanks for designing Red Sonja's chain-mail bikini! The first Conan story in the issue, "Curse of the Undead Man," is a Thomas original, and was ably rendered by John Buscema, although Pablo Marcos, a fine artist in his own right, was not the best inker for Big John; actually, neither was Ernie Chua, also on hand. Conan is better served by his second feature, reprint though it may be. "The Frost Giant's Daughter" actually gains something by losing its color. In those days, printing techniques for four-color comics were not as sophisticated, and quite often, an artist's sensitive linework could be obscured with blobs of color that looked as though they had been spooned on. This showed the full range of Barry Smith's detailed stylistic flourishes. The Red Sonja story is top shelf, and the accompanying feature "Conan's Women Warriors" was made to shine as well, with illustrations by Maroto, Howard and Burroughs veteran Roy G. Krenkel, and Hugh Rankin from the pages of the pulps. Its author, Fred Blosser, was a long-time Robert E. Howard scholar and contributed a great deal to fan publications. Much has been made of Warren's discoveries and utilizations from the ranks of fandom, but they found a strong outlet at Marvel as well, particularly in *The Savage Sword of Conan*. Gil Kane is represented by the first chapter of "Blackmark," which he both wrote and drew. The all-star art lineup was completed by John Severin and Ross Andru, who provided the stunning illustrations for a piece by Glenn Lord, the literary agent for the Howard estate. John Severin, of course, had done the four-color *Kull the Conqueror*, and would become as identified with that character as Barry Smith or John Buscema would be with Conan. When Marvel put the effort into it, it could really put out a great magazine. This one would not only outlive all of Marvel's other magazine titles, including future ones, but it would outlive the black-and-white magazine field itself.

The Savage Sword of Conan the Barbarian no. 2 (October 1974)

Cover: Neal Adams
Frontispiece: Mike Zeck
"Conan: Black Colossus" (Robert E. Howard) — Roy Thomas, Buscema/Alfredo Alcala
"Chronicles of the Sword: An Informal History of Sword and Sorcery Fiction" (Part 1) — Lin Carter (Text feature)
"Blackmark" (Chapter 2) — Gil Kane
"Kull: The Beast from the Abyss" (adapted from Howard/Carter) — Steve Englehart, Howard Chaykin/The Crusty Bunkers

Neal Adams's cover for issue two is easily the equal of his effort for *Savage Tales* no. 4, and for once, the color doesn't obscure his fine line work. Actually, the reproduction on his Marvel magazine covers was superior to that on his Tarzan paperback covers, which featured some superlative work marred by muddy reproduction. Adams also has a hand in the Kull story, as a member of the informal "Crusty Bunkers" crack inking squad, which included Adams, Alan Weiss, and whoever else happened to be hanging around Adams's studio at the time. For "The Beast from the Abyss," they applied their brushes to the pencils of Howard Chaykin, who would go on to delineate most of Robert E. Howard's other heroes in one form or another for Marvel, as well as the delightful barbarian duo "Fafhrd and the Grey Mouser," created by Fritz Lieber for the four-color DC comic *Swords of Sorcery*. Gil Kane returned with the second chapter of his Blackmark saga. Like Wallace Wood, his artistic skills outstripped his literary ones most of the time, but their stories were usually at least as good as those by writers who couldn't draw, period, or the stories that had good scripts and mediocre art. The ultimate triumph, though, came with the Conan story, an adaptation of Howard's "Black Colossus." Of course, Roy Thomas's script was strong, and faithful to the letter, but the art — well, it was just a revelation. Big John Buscema was an old hand at Conan by this time, having penciled a fair number of stories for the color Conan title after supplanting Barry Smith as the regular artist, but he had never been inked by Filipino artist Alfredo Alcala, and the pairing proved to be inspired. Alcala's feathered, supple, intricate linework melded with Buscema's muscular, gritty style to create an artistic vision that looked as though it had been carved in iron. Many think it is the definitive look for the character in comics. The only real weak spot in the issue was the text piece by Lin Carter. Carter was a modestly talented science fiction hack who was moderately adept at aping other writers' styles, a skill that landed him the plum role of L. Sprague DeCamp's collaborator on the unfinished and new Conan sagas. The ever-tactful DeCamp later admitted this "may have been the wrong thing to do." Carter was a better editor than creative writer.

The Savage Sword of Conan the Barbarian no. 3 (December 1974)

Cover: Mike Kaluta
Frontispiece: Alfredo Alcala
"Conan: At the Mountain of the Moon God" — Roy Thomas, John Buscema/Pablo Marcos
"The First Barbarian" — Lin Carter (Text); John Severin (Illustrations)
"Kull of Atlantis" — Robert E. Howard (Story quotations), Barry Smith
"Conan: Demons of the Summit" (Bjorn Nyberg) — Roy Thomas, Tony DeZuniga

The third issue of *Savage Sword of Conan* was actually not as titanic as the first two, but it certainly was no wreck on an iceberg. Mike Kaluta handled the cover this time around. Kaluta is as fine a painter as he is a penciler, and his covers are extremely pulpy, but sometimes they're a little too busy. This piece doesn't have that problem. A strong, central, dynamic figure of Conan leaps to the aid of a half-naked wench in the hands of fanged monsters, against a solid black background. Kaluta achieved his greatest comics fame with just six issues of another pulp legend, the Shadow, done for DC at around this time.

Alfredo Alcala contributes a dynamic frontispiece, but his presence is missed on the Conan stories — they're not bad at all, but we had been spoiled by the previous issue's epic. The first, another Thomas original, again featured the team of Buscema and Marcos; the second, an adaptation by Thomas of the Bjorn Nyberg short story, was done solo by Tony DeZuniga. DeZuniga was a suitably gritty replacement for Buscema, but lacked Big John's gift for composition. At this time, DeCamp was still not letting Marvel do his stories, but, of course, he was more than happy to collect the fees for the use of Nyberg's! Bjorn Nyberg is familiar as the man who wrote the sequel to *Conan the Conqueror* for Gnome Press, *The Return of Conan* (re-titled *Conan the Avenger* in paperback form). He fares even better in this story, and it's a shame that he wasn't the one (if such a thing had to be done) to either finish Howard's outlines or write more new stories, because, unlike seemingly everyone else connected with the project with the exception of Glenn Lord, he had a genuine love for the character and Howard's writing.

Gil Kane returns with Chapter Three of his Blackmark serial, as does Barry Smith, who illustrates quotes from Howard's short story "Exiles of Atlantis." Kull looks more than a little like Smith's Conan, the only difference being the helmet, but enjoy it anyway. It's Barry Smith! It's Robert E. Howard! It's delicious! It more than makes up for the text of the Lin Carter piece, which is more of his phony-sounding material, but the John Severin illustrations are to die for.

The Savage Sword of Conan the Barbarian no. 4 (February 1975)

Cover: Boris Vallejo
Frontispiece: Richard Corben
"Conan: Iron Shadows in the Moon" (adapted from Robert E. Howard) — Thomas, Buscema/Alcala
"The Corben Conan Collection" — Richard Corben (Illustrations)
"Blackmark Triumphant" — Gil Kane

The frantic fourth issue of *Savage Sword of Conan* avoids the somewhat piecemeal feel of the previous issue by featuring a heaping helping of the title character, in the longest-yet (at least until the next issue) Robert E. Howard Conan adaptation in comic book form. The only non–Conan in the whole magazine is the concluding chapter of Gil Kane's space barbarian, Blackmark, and a rousing conclusion it is. Boris Vallejo returns as cover artist, and contributes a fine piece that recalls a similar Frazetta painting for a different scene (the cover of the *Conan* paperback which contains "Rogues in the House"). No stiffness this time around; his Conan is snarling, pantherish, and lithe, and is just a taste of even more superb work yet to come. The frontispiece, by Richard Corben, recalled yet another Frazetta piece (illustrating the same scene), his cover for *Conan the Usurper*, as the dark-maned barbarian takes on a huge serpent. Corben's art was possessed of a uniquely exaggerated reality that was honed in the undergrounds, and flowered at Warren; at Warren he also personally developed the most advanced coloring techniques of the time, applying them to stories that he didn't even draw. Corben and Howard would cross paths again years later when Corben illustrated the short Howard novel *Bloodstar* for Fantagraphics.

But the centerpiece of the issue, of course, is the 45-page adaptation of the Robert E. Howard story "Shadows in the Moonlight," here going under its original title of "Iron Shadows in the Moon." The epic format really allowed Roy Thomas to stretch his writing muscles, and is one of those instances when Howard seems to be standing at his shoulder. Even better, "Iron Shadows in the Moon" features the return of the Buscema/Alcala art team, and they turn in one of their most striking tandem jobs ever. For example, see page nine for the truly crazed look on Conan's face as he squares off against Shah Amurath, or the last panel of that page, as Conan stands over the body he has just literally hacked to pieces — you can practically feel the sweat dripping from his brow, and hear his gasping for breath. Or take page 15, where Conan seems to be rowing a boat through the cosmos — which, oddly enough, calls to mind a similar scene involving two children from the Charles Laughton-directed *Night of the Hunter*. Other great examples include the scene where the giant iron statues come to life, or the frenzied battle with the ape-creature, particularly the panel in which Conan has sliced off one of the hairy horror's arms, and the bugger has Conan by the hair with the other hand. Whoever had the idea to bring these two artists together deserves a special place in comic book Valhalla, and, fortunately, there was much more to come.

The Savage Sword of Conan the Barbarian no. 5 (April 1975)

Cover: Boris Vallejo
Frontispiece: Jeff Jones
"Conan: A Witch Shall Be Born"—(adapted from Robert E. Howard)—Thomas, Buscema/The Tribe
"Caravans and Kingdoms"—Robert L. Yaple (Text feature)
"The Kline Conan"—Robert Kline (Illustrations)

After many promises and even more delays, the frantic fifth number featured the longest self-contained, single-serving story ever to appear in *The Savage Sword of Conan*, the epic take on one of Robert E. Howard's most justifiably famous Conan stories, the one that was quoted early in the chapter, "A Witch shall be Born." Thomas, naturally, handled the script, and Big John Buscema was inked by "The Tribe," another crew of inkers who, like the Crusty Bunkers, employed some regular hands like Tony DeZuniga and whoever brought lunch. The tone is markedly different than that of Buscema and Alcala; grittier, and perfectly suited to the desert surroundings. Buscema's compositional skills perfectly delineate the crucifixion/vulture scene, as visually intense as Howard's own words. And, speaking of intense, let's not forget the great Boris Vallejo cover: Conan nailed to that cross (and just imagine the indignation it caused), death's head looming large in the background, with our fine feathered fiend licking his chops in the foreground. There wasn't much room left for anything else in the issue, but they managed to slip in "The Kline Portfolio" by semi-pro artist Robert Kline (not the comedian), and another of Robert L. Yaple's textual examinations of the minutiae of the Hyperborean mythos, "Caravans and Kingdoms." Yaple's articles were always well-researched, and are instructional readings for those wishing to learn all they can about Conan and his background, and the backgrounds against which his tales take place. Kline, however, was pretty much a Jeff Jones clone, and since the magazine already had a frontispiece by the original, it's hard to see why the editors would run this in the same issue, where it had to stand in direct competition with his inspiration, when such comparisons would inevitably favor the source.

The Savage Sword of Conan the Barbarian no. 6 (June 1975)

Cover: Alfredo Alcala/Frank Magsino
Frontispiece: Don Newton
"Conan: The Sleeper Beneath the Sands"—Roy Thomas, Sonny Trinidad
"The Gods of the Hyborian Age"—Robert L. Yaple (Text feature)
"Can Anything Good Come Out of Cimmeria?"—Lin Carter (Text feature)
"Conan: People of the Dark" (adapted from Robert E. Howard)—Roy Thomas, Alex Nino

Even great bands can put out weak songs so it stands to reason that a great magazine can have a relatively weak issue here and there, for example, *The Savage Sword of Conan* no. 6. Instead of the book-length epics readers had started to expect from the previous two issues, they once again got two shorter Conan stories, one original from Roy Thomas and one from Robert E. Howard—except that the Howard story was not originally a Conan story. But writers had been turning non–Conan stories into Cimmerian tales ever since the Gnome Press days (it helped in this instance that the hero of the story had already been named Conan, although a different Conan). This time it works, not only because Roy Thomas was more adept at adaptation than was L. S. DeCamp, but also because of the artistic interpretation by Alex Nino, whose highly-stylized, flamboyantly decorative brushwork really brings out the sorcery in Howard's sword. The original, though, *The Sleeper Beneath the Sands*, was sunk by the lackluster art of Sonny Trinidad, whose style was as plain as Nino's was ornate. Nino also handled the cover, along with Frank Magsino, and Don Newton handled the frontispiece; Newton was, like Robert Kline, a Jeff Jones clone. Robert L. Yaple and Lin Carter again contribute the text pieces. Yaple's focuses on various deities of the Hyborian Age, while Carter's was entitled "Can Anything Good Come Out of Cimmeria?"

The Savage Sword of Conan the Barbarian no. 7 (August 1975)

Cover: Boris Vallejo
Frontispiece: Vincente Alcazar
"Conan: The Citadel at the Center of Time"— Thomas, Buscema/Alcala
"Crom and Mitra: The Gods of Conan"— Robert L. Yaple (Text feature)
"The King Is Dead"— Lin Carter (Text feature)
"Lines Written in the Realization That I Must Die"— Robert E. Howard; Barry Smith (Illustrations)
"The Hyborian Age" (Ch. 1)— Robert E. Howard (Serialization), Walt Simonson (Illustrations)

Now this was more like it! *The Savage Sword of Conan*, in its early years, featured much in the way of Robert E. Howard, but occasionally would come up with a story of its own that seemed to have been ripped from the pages of Howard's own notebook. "The Citadel at the Center of Time" is one such tale. Thomas employs every convention associated with Conan without making them seem conventional, and John Buscema and Alfredo Alcala's artwork is simply breathtaking in its sweep. Conan meets the obligatory half-naked wench. They then meet a wizard who likes to dip his mystical bucket into the well of time and see what he brings up. On his last trip to the well, he brings back a Terrible Lizard, which does plenty of terrible things to the local populace before Conan terribles it right back. Conan and Half-Naked Wench ride off into the sunset, while the town butcher figures out how much he can get a pound for prime rib of T. Rex. A great little scene has the selfsame fat little butcher complaining to Conan (in disguise) how much his trade has fallen off since "that devil Conan and his freebooters began their raids," and may Ishtar grant him that "this devil will come within easy reach of my cleaver." "May Ishtar grant," the hooded Cimmerian says with a smile.

More great art followed, with Barry Smith providing some haunting illustrations for the equally haunting lines of Howard's poem, "Lines Written in the Realization that I Must Die," and Walt Simonson for the first chapter of "The Hyborian Age." Simonson was a contemporary and colleague of Chaykin, Wrightson and Kaluta, and like those already formidable professionals, remembered his roots. He still found the time to contribute to fan publications. Another spectacular Howard job he did around this time was a batch of illustrations for a digest-sized, chapbook edition of Howard's *The Grey God Passes*, published by Chuck Miller. Actually, he did them nine months after he drew "The Hyborian Age," because Simonson always dated his work. *The Grey God Passes* is of interest to those who would know more of Conan's roots — the hero of the story is named "Conn" and swears by Crom. (This made it even simpler to turn into a Conan story for a comic book, in *Conan the Barbarian* no. 3, as "The Twilight of the Grim Grey God"). Howard's "The People of the Dark" also featured a hero named Conan, although it was a different Conan, and Leigh Brackett's "Lorelei of the Red Mist" features still another Conan. Robert L. Yaple continues his examination of Hyborian Age Pies-in-the-Sky, but focuses more specifically on the deities continually invoked by Conan, Crom and Mitra.

The Savage Sword of Conan the Barbarian no. 8 (October 1975)

Cover: Frank Brunner/Bob Larkin
Frontispiece: Tony DeZuniga
"Conan: The Forever Phial"—Roy Thomas, Tim Conrad
"The Elder Gods"—Robert L. Yaple (Text feature)
"The Death Song of Conan the Cimmerian"—Lin Carter, Jess Jodloman
"The Hyborian Age" (Ch. 2 "The Rise of the Hyborians")—Robert E. Howard, Walt Simonson (Illustrations)
"Corsairs Against Stygia" (Howard)—Thomas, Gil Kane/Yong Montano

Conan, in his black-and-white incarnation, was really better served by the format of the long single story. Generally, the issues that featured two titanic tales meant that one might not be as good as the other, and this holds true for *The Savage Sword of Conan* no. 8. In this case it is the first story, "The Forever Phial," an original by Roy Thomas, drawn by Tim Conrad. As Paul Gulacy was to James Steranko, so is Conrad to Barry Windsor-Smith—but not as Smith was to Jack Kirby. Some artists idolize other artists, and get their start by incorporating elements of their idols' style into their own (or even aping it completely), but then use it as a guide to finding their own voice. Who could predict from Barry Smith's early stuff, such as the Ka-Zar cover he did for *Marvel Superheroes* no. 19, that his style would develop how it did? Other artists are "style vampires," like Gulacy and Conrad, who appropriate their idols' style lock, stock, and barrel, and any artistic progression becomes merely a question of just how close they can get to that style. They never quite get it right, lacking the imagination and compositional skill of the inspiration. They're capable of some solid work, but even at their best, they just make you want to go back and check out the original.

The "good" story is unsettling, in that it was a single chapter in an adaptation that Marvel had yet to finish, with no indication of when or in which title the conclusion would appear. Marvel began the thing, an epic adaptation of Howard's equally epic, single Conan novel, *The Hour of the Dragon* in the four-color *Giant-Size Conan* comic. (It was retitled *Conan the Conqueror* when it was finally published in book form. For some reason, Marvel did not finish it in the same title, and it took some time to reach its conclusion in these pages, so there was no rhythm to the appearance of the chapters. The other unsettling element was that Gil Kane couldn't stick around to finish what he had started, and the use of many different inkers to aid him in finishing the task only added to the feeling of inconsistency, despite Kane's overall brilliant job. This chapter starts off totally penciled by Kane and inked by Montano, but after a few pages, Montano shoulders most of the load, while Kane supplies some main figures and breakdowns. By the end, Kane has disappeared. It's unfortunate he couldn't complete the job (see the entry on *The Savage Sword of Conan* for more details). Taken as a whole, it turned out to be a faithful and worthy adaptation. The second chapter of "The Hyborian Age" is sharp, as is Tony DeZuniga's frontispiece. Lin Carter writes a comic book story. Both story and art are mediocre.

The Savage Sword of Conan the Barbarian no. 9 (December 1975)

Cover: Boris Vallejo
Frontispiece: Tim Conrad
"Conan: Curse of the Cat Goddess" — Roy Thomas, Pablo Marcos
"Things from Beyond" — Robert L. Yaple (Text feature)
"The Hyborian Age: A Map" — Tim Conrad (Illustration)
"A Fabian Portfolio of Conan" — Steve Fabian (Illustrations)
"Kull: When a Tiger Returns to Atlantis" — Doug Moench, Sonny Trinidad
"The Conjurer from Cross Plains" — Fred Blosser (Book review), Steve Fabian, Roy G. Krenkel (Illustrations)

This was another mixed bag of an issue, but it starts well with one of Boris Vallejo's best covers for the series, one that bears a distinct compositional resemblance to his later cover for the Ace paperback edition of *Conan the Freebooter*. It was originally intended to accompany "The Abode of the Damned," but that story didn't arrive on schedule, and Marvel used the cover anyway (that story would finally see print two issues later). The frontispiece is Tim Conrad's, and highlights what's wrong with all of his Conan illustrations — the Cimmerian looks constipated. Barry Smith always did wonderfully expressive faces, another aspect of his style that Conrad couldn't master. Conrad also re-draws the map of the countries of the Hyborian Age that originally appeared in the Gnome Press books.

Usually, if an issue didn't feature one long Conan story, it at least featured two shorter ones, more or less of equal length. No. 9 featured only one Conan story, and it was shorter by half than the Kull story! The lead character not even getting the longest story in his own magazine. Pretty embarrassing. Nothing against Kull, but while it was longer than the Conan story, it wasn't as good, and Doug Moench's decent script was torpedoed by more lackluster Sonny Trinidad art. The Conan story was an original by Thomas. A real bonus is a portfolio of Conan/Howard art by Steven Fabian, another very talented artist who had come up through the fan ranks. Fabian's lush stipple-work made him the spiritual and stylistic heir to Virgil Finlay, one of the all-time great pulp artists. Like Barry Smith, he used his inspiration to cultivate a distinctive style that he could truly call his own. "The Conjurer from Cross Plains" is a review of *The Miscast Barbarian*, a fan-published biography of Howard by DeCamp, who used mostly previously published fanzine articles to piece together this somewhat less-than-sympathetic biography.

The Savage Sword of Conan the Barbarian no. 10 (February 1976)

Cover: Boris Vallejo
Frontispiece: Tim Conrad
"Conan the Conqueror" (Robert E. Howard) — Roy Thomas, J. Buscema/the Tribe
"Conan the Cannibal" — Fred Blosser (Text feature)
"Portrait of the Cimmerian as a Middle-aged King" — Thomas (Text feature)

The truly terrific tenth issue featured the long-awaited final chapter of Marvel's adaptation of *Conan the Conqueror*, the longest Conan story ever published in *The Savage Sword of Conan*, beating out the epic "A Witch Shall be Born" by three pages (although "Witch" is still the longest self-contained story).

The whole issue, in fact, is a celebration of Howard's lone Conan novel — not only the 58-page story, but the incidental articles as well. Fred Blosser contributes the insightful and cheekily titled "Conan the Cannibal," which examines the various ways that Howard recycled concepts, characters and even whole scenes from earlier Conan stories to create the novel. This was not wholly conscious on Howard's

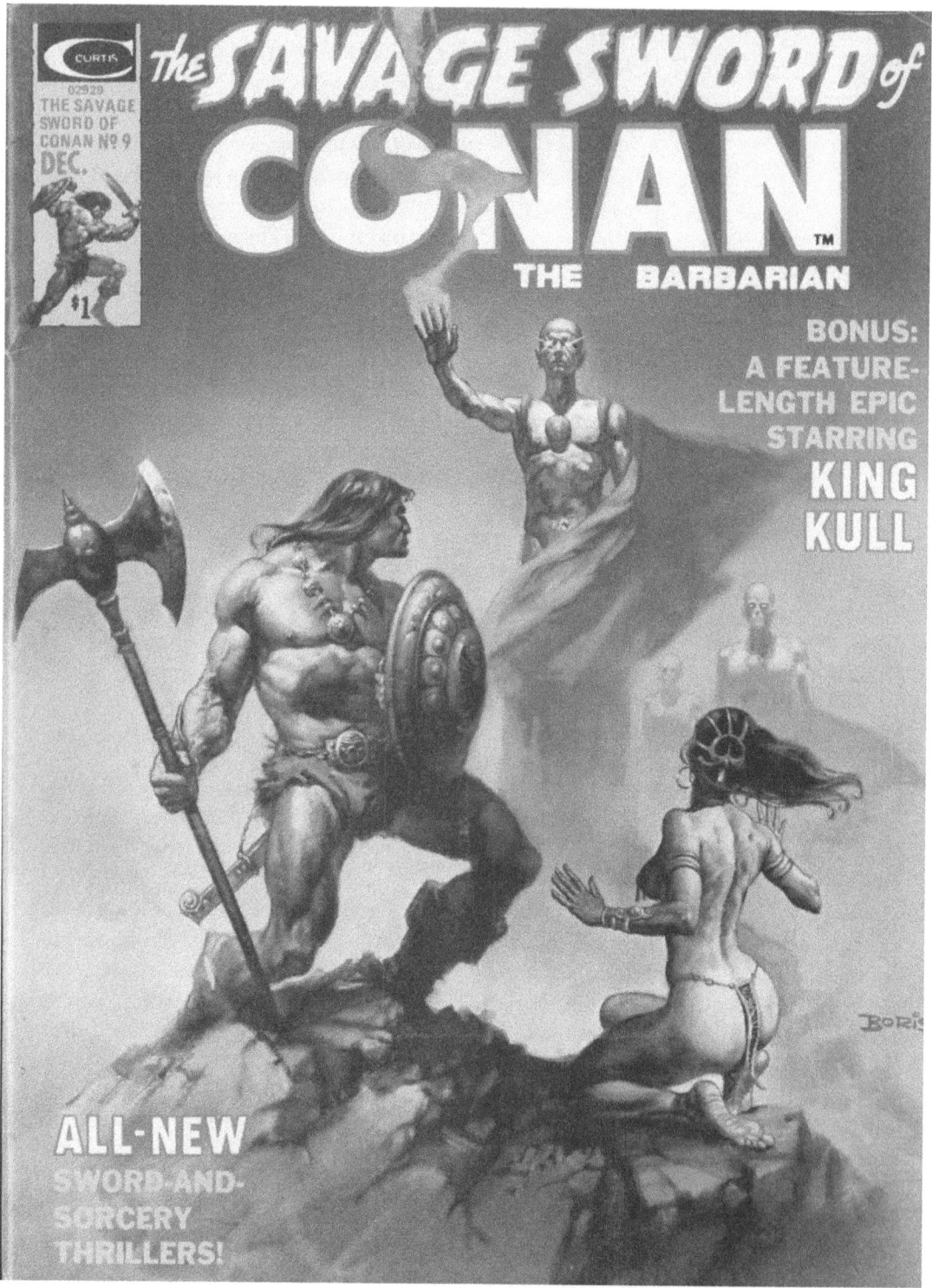

Savage Sword of Conan no. 9 (Marvel) — One of Boris Vallejo's greatest *Savage Sword of Conan* covers, which led to his doing paintings for the Conan paperbacks (©2008 Conan Properties International, LLC. All rights reserved).

part, and even when it was, it was not laziness. Howard longed to see Conan in proper book form, between hard covers. He could find no American publisher, but struck a deal with a British one. Howard, perhaps aware that the time he had left was short, turned on the steam and, using self-plagiarizing techniques coupled with his usual white-hot imagination, hammered out the novel and sent it off across the pond. But once again, he hit a brick wall, as the publisher went under before it could publish *The Hour of the Dragon*. The novel would appear posthumously in *Weird Tales*, which was a bittersweet break for publisher Farnsworth Wright. He didn't have to pay Howard for this story, or any of the others for which he still owed Howard money. Roy Thomas's article is quite informative and graphically attractive, an overview of the various artistic interpretations of *The Hour of the Dragon/Conan the Conqueror* from the pulps to the present, including a couple of rarely-seen Japanese editions. *Savage Sword of* Conan no. 10 was another landmark issue, and a worthy overall tribute to Howard.

The Savage Sword of Conan the Barbarian no. 11 (April 1976)

Cover: Ken Barr
Frontispiece: Boris Vallejo
"Conan: The Abode of the Damned!" (adapted from Robert E. Howard) — Roy Thomas, John Buscema/Yong Montano
"El Borak the Barbarian" — Fred Blosser (Text feature)
"The Scribes of Hyboria" — Fred Blosser (Text feature)
"Conan and the Tower of Vinyl" — Ed Summer (Record review)

The frontispiece is by Boris Vallejo, a black-and-white, pen-and-ink version of his cover for *Savage Sword of Conan* no. 9, which was to accompany the story "The Abode of the Damned" in that issue. The story didn't run, but the cover art did. "Abode of the Damned" appears in this issue, with essentially the same piece of art on the inside of the front cover. The front cover is by Ken Barr, and has nothing to do with the story inside. Nevertheless, "Abode" is a solid tale, well worth waiting for, and a welcome return to the novel-length format. Fred Blosser gives us a double shot, the more interesting of which deals with the adventures of Howard's "Lawrence of Arabia," El Borak. Ed Summer's record review is for an album entitled "The Tower of the Elephant." The jacket art is by Tim Conrad, and the radio-style performances apt and enjoyable. The stories on this album are "The Tower of the Elephant" (the voice of Conan is Paul Falzone and the narrator is Owen McGee), and "The Frost Giant's Daughter." Another Conan album came out in 1976, from Moondance Productions, and featured L. Sprague DeCamp reading "The Bloodstained God" and "The Curse of the Monolith." It's a rare record, with only 1,500 copies, but it's not worth what you'll bid for it on online auction sites.

The Savage Sword of Conan the Barbarian no. 12 (June 1976)

Cover: Boris Vallejo
Frontispiece: Tim Conrad
"Conan: The Haunters of Castle Crimson" (adapted from Robert E. Howard) — Roy Thomas, John Buscema/Alfredo Alcala
"Chivalry Is Alive and Well and Living in Berkeley" — Sam Maronie (Text)
"The Hyborian Age" (Ch. 3 "The Hyborian Kingdoms") — Robert E. Howard, Walt Simonson

With "The Haunters of Castle Crimson," Roy Thomas used the L.S. DeCamp ploy of taking almost any non–Conan Howard story and changing the name of the lead character and the time period to create an instant Conan tale. As we've seen elsewhere, sometimes this works, and sometimes it doesn't. This time it

Savage Sword of Conan no. 12 (Marvel) — Boris Vallejo's interpretation of Conan became nearly as popular with some fans as Frazetta's (©2008 Conan Properties International, LLC. All rights reserved).

worked overtime, providing the fans with one of Marvel's most satisfying Conan stories ever in the black-and-white medium. The task is not nearly as simple as one would assume. It's really more than just making substitutions, as DeCamp often did, as well as making arbitrary changes because he thought that Howard missed a few things. Thomas avoids this pitfall; he takes care that the story actually becomes a Conan story. His transposal of Howard's narrative about a beautiful young girl who may be a kidnapped princess to the Conan mythos makes you wish it were part of the official Conan canon. Exceptional care is taken with all of the supporting characters. Conan is not the only figure in the story with a personality, and their individuality is accentuated in vivid strokes by art team extraordinaire Buscema and Alcala. The art is moody when it needs to be, sexy when it needs to be (Buscema is a much-underrated delineator of the female form), epic, thrilling, and horrifying all in the right places, especially in the frantic finale, which has Conan and pals again facing off against an army of skeletal warriors, bringing to mind cinematic equivalents such as Harryhausen's *The 7th Voyage of Sinbad* or *Jason and the Argonauts*.

The effort is fully complemented by what may be Boris Vallejo's best cover for the series (and, unfortunately, his next-to-last). Gone is the stiffness of the first cover, and the skeleton army that advances toward the brawny, supple Cimmerian and Half-Naked Wench from under the baleful gaze of a red-eyed wraith manages to catch a whiff of the tangible sense of the fantastic which is the backbone of Frazetta's style. Like no. 9, it also bears a very strong resemblance to his later cover for the Ace paperback edition of *Conan the Freebooter*. This adaptation was another novel-length thriller, not leaving much room for backup, but at least the third chapter of "The Hyborian Age" finally saw print, still illustrated by Simonson and still stunning. The only other feature is a text/photo feature about The Society for Creative Anachronisms, an organization of people who like to pretend that they live in the Middle Ages.

The Savage Sword of Conan the Barbarian no. 14 (October 1976)

Cover: Earl Norem
Frontispiece: Frank Brunner/Steve Leialoha
"Shadows in Zamboula" (Robert E. Howard)— Roy Thomas, Neal Adams/the Tribe
"The Worms Return"— David Anthony Kraft (Book review)
"A Kull Glossary"— Fred Blosser (Text feature)
"Solomon Kane: The Silver Beast of Torkertown"— Doug Moench, Mike Zeck

One thing you could always count on with *Savage Sword of Conan* was that if a story (especially one with a guest star creative team) was announced for the next issue, chances were the next issue would feature an explanation and apology in the letter or editorial page as to why it wasn't in that issue. This was proved true again with the lead story of issue no. 14, the much-announced and long-anticipated Marvel version of Howard's "Shadows in Zamboula," written, naturally, by Roy Thomas, with main pencils by Neal Adams, inked by the Tribe. It had been delayed so that Adams could devote his full artistic attention to it, but when it was finally delivered, he had done only the main action, the splash pages, and the central figures, so Tony DeZuniga and crew stepped up to the plate and completed the story. The difference in styles can sometimes be a bit jarring, but enough of Adams remains so that it doesn't upset the flow of the tale, which proved well worth waiting for. It's a long story, but not as long as some of the other novel-length Conan stories. There was still room left to squeeze in a few more goodies, the best of which was an original Doug Moench/Mike Zeck tale of Howard's dour Puritan swordsman Solomon Kane, "The Silver

Beast of Torkertown," in which the adventurer dispatches a werewolf. Moench was already established at Marvel, and within a few years, Zeck would become a household name when he illustrated the first Punisher mini-series, "Circle of Blood." David Anthony Kraft's "The Worms Return" is a review of the hardcover edition of *Worms of the Earth*, and Fred Blosser's Kull Glossary is useful for sorting through Howard's admitted tendencies towards similar-sounding names of both people and places.

The Savage Sword of Conan the Barbarian no. 15 (December 1976)

Cover: Boris Vallejo
Frontispiece: Mike Zeck
"Conan: The Devil in Iron" (Robert E. Howard) — Roy Thomas, John Buscema/Alcala
"Arms and the Manner" — Sam Maronie (Text feature)
"A Portfolio of Robert E. Howard" — Howard Chaykin, John Buscema, Tim Conrad, John Byrne, John and Marie Severin (Illustrations)
"Conan in the City of Blood" — Fred Blosser (Book review)
"An Interview with Conan Artist John Buscema" — John Collier, John Wren
"The Hyborian Age" (Ch. 4 "The Beginning of the End") — Robert E. Howard, Walt Simonson

In a way, *Savage Sword of Conan* no. 15 was like the end of an era — it was Boris Vallejo's last cover for the series, and one of his last for Marvel; like Frazetta, he was now getting much higher-paying commissions for paperback covers and movie poster art, among other things. He certainly gets a proper sendoff, as the issue features an all-star lineup of artists of a number and quality not seen since the first issue. Mike Zeck's frontispiece showed just how fast and far he was progressing, and Roy Thomas once again teamed with John Buscema and Alfredo Alcala in presenting a top-notch Howard adaptation, "The Devil in Iron." The story (the original as well as the adaptation) bears a passing resemblance to "Iron Shadows in the Moon" in more than title, but is none the less for it.

The art portfolio centers not on one artist, but an immensely satisfying variety of top and regular talents, with six full-page illustrations of six different Howard heroes and heroines: Howard Chaykin gets Solomon Kane; John Buscema, of course, handles Conan; John Byrne renders Red Sonja; and the Severin siblings, John and Marie, naturally do Kull. Tim Conrad gets two pages that are shapes of things to come. His Bran Mak Morn in a scene from "Worms of the Earth" is a foreshadowing of the very next issue, and his depiction of the outer-space warrior Esu Cairn (from Howard's only science-fiction novel, *Almuric*) portended an adaptation of the story he would draw five years later for Marvel's *Epic Illustrated* (see the last chapter). And speaking of top talent, Walt Simonson is back with another chapter of "The Hyborian Age," and John Buscema is also featured in a short but informative interview. "Conan in the City of Blood" is a review of the Donald Grant-published hardcover edition of "Red Nails," another quite legendary Conan saga. The Grant editions of Conan were indeed well produced with quality materials, but failed to satisfy in artistic terms, as none of the artists enlisted for the jobs had the ability to render Conan as dynamically as, not just Frazetta, but Boris Vallejo and many of the Marvel artists. Barry Smith had already shown what could be done with "Red Nails" when given the chance, coupled with the talent, and it's unfortunate Grant couldn't match it.

The Savage Sword of Conan the Barbarian no. 16 (February 1977)

Cover: Earl Norem
Frontispiece: Mike Zeck

"Conan: The People of the Black Circle (Pt. 1)" (adapted from Robert E. Howard)—Roy Thomas, John Buscema/Alfredo Alcala
"A Probable Outline of Conan's Career"—P. Schuyler Miller, John D. Clark
"A Portfolio of Robert E. Howard"—Frank Giacoia, Gene Day, John Buscema and Tim Conrad, John Allison, Virgil Finlay, Richard Corben, Roy G. Krenkel (Illustrations)
"Bran Mak Morn: Worms of the Earth (Pt. 1)" (adapted from Robert E. Howard)—Roy Thomas, Barry Smith/Tim Conrad
"The Hyborian Age" (Ch. 5 "Fire and Slaughter")—Robert E. Howard, Walt Simonson

The Boris Vallejo Era ended with the previous issue, and the Earl Norem Era officially began with this one. Earl Norem was a veteran painter, and had done literally hundreds of cover paintings for the men's sweat mags, with titles like *True Men, True Adventure, True Danger, Real Men, Real Adventurous Men, True Danger Women,* and *Nut-Bustin' Danger*. He did more covers for the series than any other artist, eclipsing Vallejo in sheer volume if not adoration. Norem's association with *The Savage Sword of Conan* was somewhat ironic. When *Savage Tales* no. 1 (featuring Conan) hit the stands, it missed its target audience by being grouped in with the very men's mags for which Norem was painting covers. Norem had actually already done one *Savage Sword* cover, no. 14, but it failed to make an impression, not only due to weak composition, but because many of the covers were printed with the colors out of registration. His piece for this issue, however, is right on the money: a strong central figure of the mighty Cimmerian hacking his way through a horde of foes.

Like the previous issue, the sanguinary sixteenth issue featured an all-star lineup. Mike Zeck contributes another fine frontispiece, and the venerable Thomas/Buscema/Alcala team begin their epic adaptation of Howard's novelette "The People of the Black Circle." The art portfolio again offered an astounding variety of talent both past and present, with the best efforts being turned in by a couple of the masters, Virgil Finlay and Roy G. Krenkel. Walt Simonson is on hand with another chapter of the (drawn-out but still worth waiting for) Hyborian Age serialization, and Roy Thomas, Barry Smith and Tim Conrad finally treat fans to the first chapter of Marvel's adaptation of Howard's novel "Worms of the Earth." Conrad wasn't the inker; when Smith failed to meet even the extended deadline (he had only finished seven pages), the project was turned over to his clone, who could not only meet the deadline, but also lend continuity stylistically. Given Conrad's built-in limitations, he does an admirable job, almost matching Smith's gift for composition and mood in a panel or three. The only text piece in the issue is "A Probable Outline of Conan's Career," reprinted from *Savage Tales* no. 2 for the benefit of those who might have missed it the first time around.

The Savage Sword of Conan the Barbarian no. 17 (April 1977)

Cover: Earl Norem/Ernie Chan (Chua)
Frontispiece: John Buscema
"Conan: The People of the Black Circle (Pt. 2)" (Robert E. Howard*)—Roy Thomas, John Buscema/Alfredo Alcala
"Of Buccaneers and Barachans"—Fred Blosser (Text feature)
"Bran Mak Morn: Worms of the Earth (Pt. 2)" (Robert E. Howard)—Roy Thomas, Tim Conrad
"The Hyborian Age" (Ch. 6 "The Darkness and the Dawn")—Robert E. Howard, Walt Simonson

In the words of Yogi Berra, *Savage Sword of Conan* no. 17 was "Déjà vu all over again!" It was composed entirely of chapters of stories continued from the previous issue, but given the quality of the stories, this was not a bad thing. "The People of the Black Circle" is a great Conan story, and it was well-served by the fact that Buscema and Alcala were able to

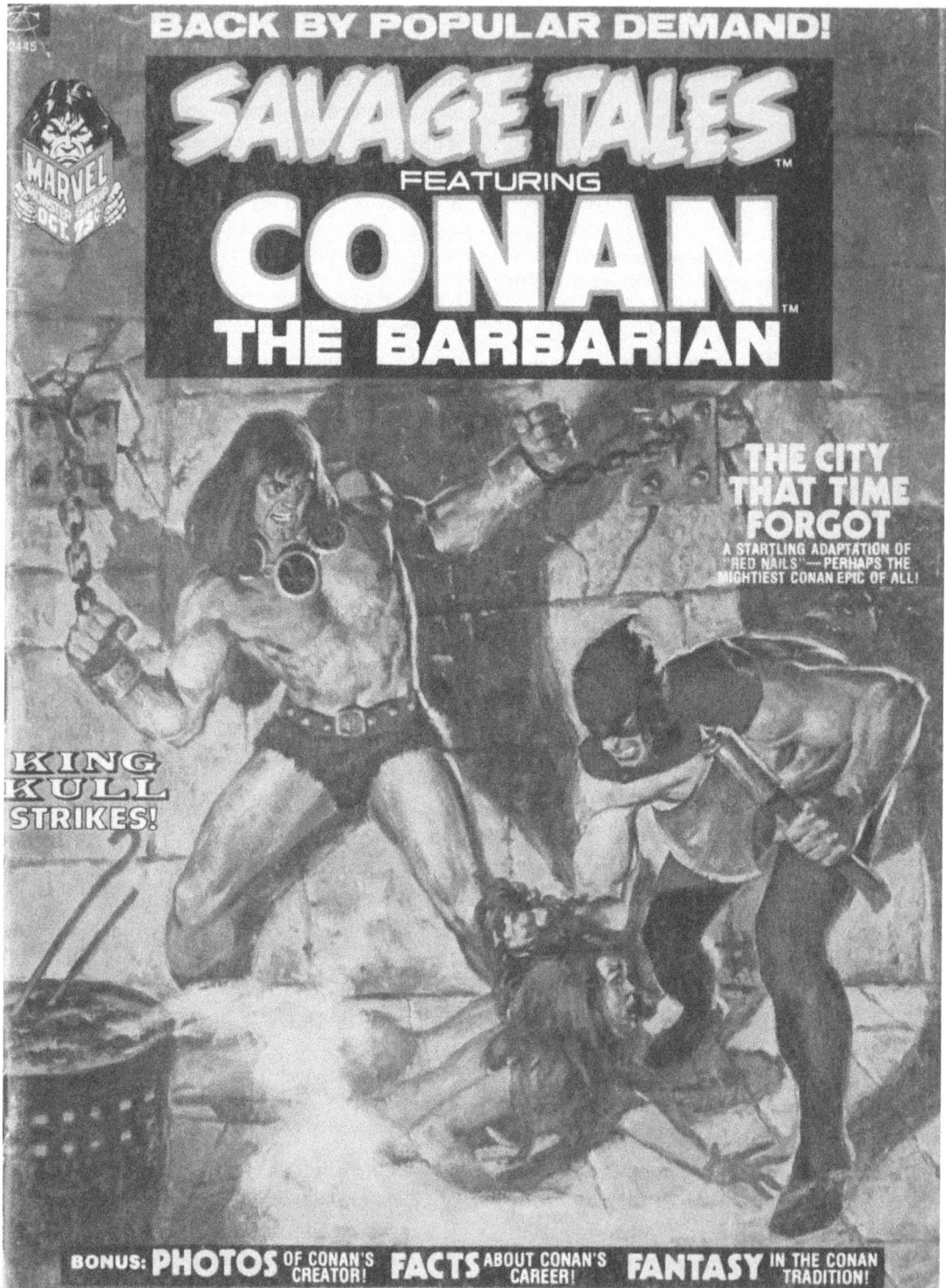

Savage Tales no. 2 (Marvel) — John Buscema's cover painting for *Savage Tales* no. 2 could have graced the front of any pulp magazine with distinction (©2008 Conan Properties International, LLC. All rights reserved).

do the complete adaptation, and have it presented consecutively, unlike the piecemeal treatment afforded to *The Hour of the Dragon*. The Thomas, Smith and Conrad *Worms of the Earth* would be collected in 2000 in a deluxe trade paperback. Computer coloring was added along with a magnificent cover by Mark Schultz, the creator of the acclaimed *Cadillacs and Dinosaurs* and the stylistic and spiritual heir to Frazetta, Williamson and Wood. Schultz is another of those artists who have taken the inspiration of their idols and built upon it to create a distinctive style of their own. He would return to Howard again a couple of years later with a cover and numerous illustrations for *The Coming of Conan the Cimmerian*. Not to be confused with the Gnome Press version of nearly the same name, this volume was the first in an ongoing reissue of the Robert E. Howard Conan stories in a deluxe, unedited format, which present the stories as Howard intended, without editorial interference from other parties.

The Savage Sword of Conan the Barbarian no. 18 (June 1977)

Cover: Dan Adkins
Frontispiece: Tim Conrad
"Conan: The People of the Black Circle (Pt. 3)" (Robert E. Howard) — Roy Thomas, John Buscema/Alfredo Alcala
"A Handbook Shall Be Born" — Fred Blosser (Text feature)
"Crimson Blades of Dark Vendhya" — Fred Blosser (Book review)
"Solomon Kane: A Rattle of Bones" (Robert E. Howard) — Roy Thomas, Howard Chaykin

Even the unbelievably fast Earl Norem needed a break once in a while, so Dan Adkins provided the cover for this issue. It's a good composition, but the rendering is flat. It's not nearly as accomplished as some of the covers he did for Warren's magazines, such as his King Kong vs. the Pterodactyl for *Famous Monsters* no. 44, or his Lon Chaney Jr. Mummy for *Eerie* no. 12. The longest Thomas/Buscema/Alcala adaptation ever was brought to its stunning conclusion, and "People of the Black Circle" must rank high in any discussion of the team's work. Also notable was the Solomon Kane story, which continued Howard Chaykin's association with the character (solidified by further stories in four colors) and showed that his style, although not yet at its stylized peak, was rapidly approaching it.

The Savage Sword of Conan the Barbarian no. 24 (June 1978)

Cover: Earl Norem
Frontispiece: Vincente Alcazar
"Conan: The Tower of the Elephant" (Robert E. Howard) — Roy Thomas, John Buscema/Alfredo Alcala
"Swackles, Thuds, and Blunders" — Don/Maggie Thompson (Text)
"Fionn McCumhal Day in Eastmere" — Michael Mahaney (Text)
"Cimmeria" — Robert E. Howard, Barry Smith/Tim Conrad

Black-and-white films are often remade in color. Marvel did the reverse in this case, and remade the Eisner-nominated "Tower of the Elephant," the memorable Robert E. Howard short that had originally been done in the color Conan title by Thomas and Barry Smith. One cannot choose between the two. Both are incredible achievements. Roy Thomas outdoes himself, really makes the most of the longer format, and injects even more pathos into this than in the original comics version, which can still bring tears to the eyes (as the story can, period). Add to this the immaculate art job turned in by John Buscema and Alfredo Alcala, in one of their last tandem efforts, and you have a transcendent moment in the field of illustrated fantasy. Very rarely has an author's vision been so well realized by another hand. Earl Norem's cover complements the epic perfectly.

Barry Smith was on hand for a different sort of reprint. Redoing "Tower of the Elephant" meant a different medium and different artistic interpretation. "Cimmeria" was just another *Savage Tales* no. 2 reprint, with Tim Conrad adding new inks and tones to a work that didn't need them. The effects were so lightly applied you have to wonder why it was done at all. Overall, though, when added to the average text pieces, this was not enough to distract from the towering achievement of the lead story.

The Savage Sword of Conan the Barbarian no. 31 (August 1979)

Cover: Howard Chaykin
Frontispiece: Carl Potts/Pablo Marcos
"Conan: The Flame Knife" (Robert E. Howard) — Thomas, Buscema/DeZuniga
"A Gazetteer of the Hyborian World of Conan" — Lee Falconer (Text)

Five years after the first issue, and long after the disappearance of Marvel's black-and-white line, *The Savage Sword of Conan* was still going strong, a testament to the popularity of the character, as opposed to the general disdain for non-color product. By this time, the magazine had settled into a comfortably solid, dependable workhorse — if not as flamboyantly spectacular as the first couple of years, it could usually be counted on to deliver the goods. Roy Thomas was still scripting and John Buscema was still pushing the pencils, although the selection of inkers was not always as sympathetic as one would like, and his titanic team-ups with Alfredo Alcala were almost a thing of the past. Speaking of past glories, the team of Thomas/Buscema/DeZuniga invokes memories of their epic turn on "A Witch Shall be Born" with their take on "The Country of the Knife," made possible by a new legal agreement which allowed Marvel to adapt stories by Howard that DeCamp had a hand in; previously they had only been permitted to adapt pure Howard work.

Earl Norem was spelled on cover work by Howard Chaykin, who contributes a piece which is certainly fine, but a little too busy, with equal definition given to every character in the fore-, back-, and middle ground. Chaykin knew better — look at his cover for the Atlas (Seaboard) color comic *The Scorpion* no. 1 for a textbook illustration on the strategic use of simple strong design elements. The cover is not helped by muddy coloring, or the weird cover blurb, which bills the story inside as "The Friends of the Flame Knife!" This sounds like Conan will be doing battle with Cub Scouts or something — perhaps "fiends" would have been more appropriate.

The Savage Sword of Conan the Barbarian no. 47 (April 1982)

Cover: Earl Norem
Frontispiece: Tony DeZuniga
"Conan: The Treasure of Tranicos" (Robert E. Howard) — Roy Thomas, Gil Kane, John Buscema
"The Secret of the Black Stranger" — Fred Blosser (Text feature)

The Savage Sword of Conan no. 47 is a landmark of sorts; the end of an era or two, and not just for the magazine itself. In 1982, the venerable Warren Publishing would abruptly close up shop, truly signaling the end of not only an era but also an aesthetic, leaving *Savage Sword of Conan* the lone keeper of the black-and-white faith, sticking out like a sore pulp thumb amongst all the color slicks. Interestingly, the cover was a tribute to the paperbacks that had started the sword rolling: Earl Norem's pastiche of Frazetta's masterpiece for *Conan the Adventurer*, heralding the end of the Earl Era. It wasn't his last, but he didn't do many more, and none as good as this. The comic fans wanted fresh faces and stronger stuff, and Norem's sturdy, pulpy men's magazine style was becoming, to the newer fans, old hat.

No. 47 also marked the last of any of Robert E. Howard's stories to be adapted by the magazine, be they his or finished by De-Camp, which this one was. Roy Thomas wouldn't stick around much longer either, and the magazine's stories were placed in the hands of writers who could never quite get the feel for the character that Thomas had. John Buscema had the same problem. He finished the art on this story begun by Gil Kane — shades of *Conan the Conqueror*! Unlike that scattered epic, however, this story was contained all in one issue. Fred Blosser was also on the way out — now that the influence of the Conan movies was making itself felt, a lot of fans were not much interested in Robert E. Howard, his history, or his other characters — they just wanted more muscles, monsters, and maidens. *The Savage Sword of Conan* would continue to give them that for some time, although soon the magazine lost its plot entirely.

The Savage Sword of Conan the Barbarian no. 134

Cover: Joe Jusko
Frontispiece: Vincent Waller
"Conan: Cursers of the Light"— Chuck Dixon, Gary Kwapisz/Ernie Chan
"Kull the Conqueror: Keeper of Laws"— Chuck Dixon, Kwapisz/Chan

As noted, by this time *The Savage Sword of Conan* had fallen into a rut, and not even Charles Dixon or the return of Ernie Chua (Chan) to the inking duties could pull the magazine out of it. Gary Kwapisz is a mediocre artist. His anatomy is atrocious; his faces, male or female, all look the same; his compositional skills are practically non-existent (even the least of the Spanish artists at Warren could tell a story and illustrate it better), and there is nothing even remotely original or endearingly quirky about his style. His style consists mostly of medium-shots and crowded panels, with no spotting of blacks, or any apparent understanding of basic drawing or storytelling techniques. Chan fared much better in his stints on both the Conan and Kull color comics. In fact, the team handles both the Conan and Kull stories in the issue, and the result is something like the serial *Flash Gordon Conquers the Universe*, wherein all the leading males (except for Flash, of course) have a moustache, making it hard to tell them apart. So it goes with half-naked barbarians. The best thing about the issue is the top-notch cover by Joe Jusko, who offers up his own take on the Conan/Ape Monster scene from "Rogues in the House." Jusko developed his own dynamically realistic style that served him well as he followed in the footsteps of Frazetta, Boris Vallejo and Neal Adams by not only delineating Conan but Tarzan as well for a new generation of fans. He also did some stunning covers for the Punisher as well, both for the character's various color titles and the magazine that reprinted them as well. That said, Jusko does tend to suffer the same faults as Boris Vallejo. At his worst, or at least when not particularly inspired, his figures look like steroid junkies in search of a fix or a pose. He has come under fire from hardcore Burroughs fans in particular, who complain that Tarzan's bulk suggests little of the lithe hero that Burroughs envisioned — much like the argument of Howard-Conan fans against Arnold Schwarze-negger's "reel"-life portrayal of Conan.

The Savage Sword of Conan the Barbarian no. 200

Cover: Joe Jusko
"Conan: Barbarians of the Border"— Roy Thomas, John Buscema/E. Chan

"A Short History of Conan"—Roy Thomas (Text feature)
"The Father of Conan"—Glenn Lord (Text feature)

In 1968, about a year before his death, Boris Karloff made an acknowledged masterpiece of a film called *Targets*. It was not the last movie of his career. He would appear in four Mexican horror films before he died, but artistically, it was the last one. Likewise, *The Savage Sword of Conan the Barbarian* no. 200 was not the last issue of the title, but, considering what came after, it might as well have been (and perhaps should have been). It had been around for nearly twenty years, and would limp along for a few more, but this special anniversary issue recalled the glory days of the publication to such an extent that it seemed pointless to continue. Joe Jusko really rose to the occasion with his final and finest *Savage Sword* cover ever, a savage and extremely intense piece of art that can even be mentioned in the same breath as those by Frazetta or Boris Vallejo. Even better, Roy Thomas and John Buscema return, and, aided by yet another vet, Ernie Chua, give the readers an original story whose like had not been seen in the magazine for some time, proving once again that when it came to Conan, nobody did it better. Thomas also contributes a text feature, as does Glenn Lord, making a truly special anniversary issue, a potent reminder of how truly powerful the character could be when molded by the right hands.

WARREN

If there was anything that rankled James Warren, it was an imitator—not so much a competitor, although he despised them in a professional and sometimes personal way as well—but an imitator. Warren had virtually created the monster movie magazine genre, and he felt that any publication that followed was an imitation of *Famous Monsters*. He felt the same way about all of the illustrated horror magazines that came after *Creepy*. So imagine his consternation when he found himself in the role of having to play catch-up, or at least having to jump on the bandwagon, rather than building it, when *Conan the Barbarian* became such a monster hit. Warren had, of course, published sword and sorcery strips well before Conan came back into the comic picture, and some very good ones, but nothing of a continuing nature. So, eyeing Marvel's success, Warren scrambled and ordered his staff members to give him a Conan, which is easier commanded than done. As it turned out, not only could they not come up with the equal of Conan or his mighty sales, they couldn't even come up with their own idea.

"Dax the Warrior" (a.k.a. Dax "the Damned"), written and drawn by Esteban Maroto, the most popular, and perhaps the best, of all of Warren's Spanish artists, was a translated import. It was published in Europe under its original title of "Manly." Maroto did another Conan knock-off called "Wolff" for the Spanish *Dracula* magazine, which was also collected in a volume by Warren. Although they were, as was everything he did, beautifully drawn, alas, the pieces regurgitate every tried-and-true cliché of the sword and sorcery genre. It wasn't bad stuff at all, but the all-important element of character that made Conan what he was is sadly missing from both. "El Cid" was the same, only different and somewhat less. It had incredible, elaborate artwork by Gonzalo Mayo, but a hero who was more refined than barbaric, and whose constant prattling on about the glories of God really got to be quite tiresome after a while. Perhaps Warren's most blatant Howard pastiche was a story that originally appeared in *Vampirella* no. 10, "The War of the Wizards." Written and illustrated by Wallace

Wood, its barbarian protagonist, Torin, is Conan in every way except name. Once again, all of the classic genre tricks are checklisted, almost defiantly. But as in the case of Dax or Wolff, Torin can be enjoyable simply because of the exquisite artwork, this time courtesy of Wallace Wood, who even has the cheek to give his hero exactly the same outfit he gave Conan for the dust jacket of *The Return of Conan*! There's also a twist in the tale, which, while nothing earth shattering, certainly gives it an EC-like flavor. And speaking of the Wood/EC connection, Conan also puts in a one-panel cameo as "Conman the Conqueror" in the delightful (and delightfully naughty) Wood-written/Ralph Reese-drawn "Warmonger of Mars," published in *Creepy* no. 87. It was a wonderful *Mad*-style parody of Burroughs's John Carter as only Wood could and would know how to do it. The next-to-last-page, in true *Mad* style, goes all out, and features an invasion of loony takeoffs on popular comic heroes popping up en masse to do exaggerated battle with one another — "Conman," "Flashy" Gordon, Dr. "Barkoff" and "Mung" the Merciless; "Fongor," "Fanthar," "S. F. Wryter," and "The Pulp Men of *Planet Stories*!" There's even a cameo by Alfred E. Neumann, if you squint hard enough. He's sitting on the wing of "Junk" Carter's "Futuristic Martian Flyer," which, naturally, resembles the Wright brothers' first airplane.

Creepy no. 27 (June 1969)

Cover: Frank Frazetta
"Creepy's Loathsome Lore" — Forrest J Ackerman, Tony Tallarico
"Collector's Edition!" — Archie Goodwin, Steve Ditko
"Make Up Your Mind" — Bill Parente, Tony Tallarico
"The Coffin of Dracula (Part Two)" — Archie Goodwin, Reed Crandall
"Barbarian of Fear" — Bill Parente, Tom Sutton
"Brain Trust" — Archie Goodwin, Angelo Torres
"Surprise Package" — Bill Parente, Ernie Colon

Published while Conan was a paperback success, but before Marvel began either of its versions, this issue of *Creepy* capitalized on the burgeoning heroic fantasy craze by featuring one of Frazetta's most fondly remembered barbarian pieces, which was, as always, great, and another one-off sword and sorcery tale, "Barbarian of Fear," which wasn't. Tom Sutton was an artist with an enjoyable, original, and idiosyncratic style that worked for some subject matter ("Grub," which appeared in the following issue, or "Masque of the Red Death," for instance), and didn't for others (Vampirella, this story). On the whole, though, a satisfying issue, even if the two best things on the inside are reprints — "Collector's Edition!" and the second chapter of "The Coffin of Dracula."

Eerie no. 59 (August 1974)

Cover: Ken Kelly
Frontispiece: Sanjulian/Bernie Wrightson
"Dax the Damned" — Esteban Maroto
"Dax: The Paradise Tree" — Esteban Maroto
"Dax: Chess" — Esteban Maroto
"Dax: Let the Evil One Sleep" — Esteban Maroto
"Dax: The Golden Lake" — Esteban Maroto
"Dax: The Witch" — Esteban Maroto
"Dax: Cyclops" — Esteban Maroto
"Dax: Starlight" — Esteban Maroto
"Dax: The Lord's Prayer" — Esteban Maroto
"Dax: Death Rides This Night!" — Esteban Maroto

This was another Warren special all-reprint issue, but at least with a purpose. By this time, both the four color Conan and *The Savage Sword of Conan* had taken the candy stores by storm, and since Warren didn't have a specific sword and sorcery title, it would occasionally turn *Creepy* or *Eerie* into theme-issue collections of the series that ran in those titles. The artistic talent on display is impressive, and the story is entertaining, but the character himself failed to generate the kind of response that would make it a profitable ongoing venture.

Creepy no. 27 (Warren) — One of Frank Frazetta's signature barbarian pieces, this time for Warren's flagship illustrated horror magazine.

Eerie no. 66 (June 1975)

Cover: Sanjulian
Frontispiece: Bernie Wrightson
"El Cid: The 7 Trials (Part 1)"—Bill DuBay/ Budd Lewis, Gonzalo Mayo
"El Cid: The 7 Trials (Part 2)"—Bill DuBay/ Budd Lewis, Gonzalo Mayo
"El Cid and the Vision"—Gerry Boudreau/Budd Lewis, Gonzalo Mayo
"El Cid: The Lady and the Lie"—Gerry Boudreau/Budd Lewis, Mayo
"El Cid: The Emir of Aragon"—Jeff Rovin/ Budd Lewis, Gonzalo Mayo

This was another all-reprint, all-imported, all-translated compilation, with a less-compelling hero than either Dax or Wolff, although El Cid's epic-style adventures contain enough monsters and maidens to make them diverting at least, and, of course, the graphics are beyond reproach. The biggest problem with El Cid was his Catholic dogma, which, while not as irksome as Solomon Kane's "God told me to" pronouncements from his Puritan pulpit, is nonetheless just as irksome to hear. He prattles on about the glories of God while running through a brigand or a monster. Sanjulian's cover would have sat well on any Conan paperback, and Gonzalo Mayo contributes the kind of illustrations that made him the second most prolific and second most popular Vampirella artist.

Sword and Sorcery Comix (*Warren Presents* no. 13) October 1981

Cover: Sanjulian
"A Scream in the Forest"—Greg Potter, Esteban Maroto
"Spotlight on 'Dragonslayer'"—(Text/photo feature)
"The Kingmaker"—Budd Lewis, Esteban Maroto
"Goddess in a Kingdom of Trolls"—Gerry Boudreau/Esteban Maroto
"Scheherazade"—Esteban Maroto
"The Sleeping Beauty"—Bill DuBay/Esteban Maroto

Near Warren's bitter end, employees didn't just fill issues of *Famous Monsters, Creepy, Eerie,* and *Vampirella* with reprints, they created entirely new titles and filled them with reprints. Such was the case with *Warren Presents*, a catchall title with a different theme from issue to issue. The theme for this issue is obvious—a compilation of some of the better one-off sword and sorcery stories they'd published, all featuring art by Maroto, with an *FM* reprint thrown in for good measure. That reprint quibble aside, it's a wonderful collection of stories and art, from the whimsical ("Goddess in a Kingdom of Trolls," *Creepy* no. 92) to the classical ("Scheherazade," *Vampirella* no. 72; "The Sleeping Beauty" *Vampirella* no. 58).

Ring of the Warlords (*Warren Presents* no. 5) (January 1979)

Cover: Sanjulian
"The Curse"—Wallace Wood
"The Last Dragon King"—Roger McKenzie, Esteban Maroto
"Jackie and the Leprechaun King"—Bill DuBay, Esteban Maroto
"Prelude to Armageddon"—Nicola Cuti/Wallace Wood
"Merlin"—Budd Lewis, Gonzalo Mayo
"Dax: Chess"—Esteban Maroto

• FIVE •

Thrilling Savage Adventure Tales: The Bloody Pulps

The pulps, or pulp magazines, were so known because of the cheap, grainy pulpwood paper they were printed on. The bridge between dime novels and comic books, they afforded millions their only taste of literature, and in turn afforded many authors the exposure that would someday turn their names into household ones, and their creations into pop culture icons. Robert E. Howard and Conan (along with all his other series heroes, who will be covered in this chapter), sprang from the pulps. So did Edgar Rice Burroughs, with his tales of Tarzan, John Carter of Mars, David Innes and Abner Perry at the Earth's core, and Carson Napier on Venus. Dashiell Hammett (*The Maltese Falcon*, *The Thin Man*), Raymond Chandler (*Farewell, My Lovely*, *The Big Sleep*), Erle Stanley Gardner (Perry Mason), Louis L'Amour (westerns), and L. Ron Hubbard (Scientology) all earned their wings in "The Bloody Pulps," so nicknamed because of the amount of the stuff spilled within those cheap pages. Packaged under oftentimes beautifully painted covers were novels, novelettes, short stories, serials, and columns devoted to every type of subject imaginable. Many of the artists would find fame as well, and as the authors came to define pulp fiction, so names like J. Allen St. John, Edd Cartier, Virgil Finlay,

Margaret Brundage, Hannes Bok, and Norman Saunders would come to define the look of fantasy art and influence generations to come.

Of course, being a pulp wordsmith or artist was not the fast track to fortune and glory. Ironically, some of the most prolific and widely published authors of the century were hidden behind company pen names for years, their legions of adoring fans having absolutely no idea who their favorite writer actually was, or who was actually relating the current adventure of their favorite character. One such man, Ryerson "Johnny" Johnson, who ghosted three Doc Savage novels for the series' primary author, Lester Dent, told me what it was like trying to make it as a freelance writer during the dark days of the Depression. "Well, there in the big city, they had these machines called an automat that you could go up and put in a nickel or a dime and get a sandwich or soup or something. Hot water, for tea and such, was free. There were many times we couldn't even afford the dime for the soup or sandwich, so we would get a cup of hot water and fill it up with ketchup and presto, instant tomato soup! Sometimes we had tomato soup four or five times a day."

But the real-life horror of the Great Depression seemed almost trivial when compared to some of the horrors and monsters unleashed by the bloody pulps — every conceivable and inconceivable or unpronounceable creature, creep or crackpot slithered, oozed, hacked and slimed its way out of the pulps, most notably in the legendary *Weird Tales*, which was the first magazine devoted exclusively to weird fiction. Although never as financially successful as its aesthetic standing would indicate, *Weird Tales* nonetheless showcased an honor roll of some of the most respected names in horror literature — Clark Ashton Smith, Seabury Quinn, C. L. Moore, August Derleth, Fritz Leiber, and Ray Bradbury. H. P. Lovecraft and his tales of creeping unutterable horror and even more unpronounceable dark monster gods found a home there, as did the man who would one day write "Psycho," Robert Bloch. Robert E. Howard wrote stories other than bloodletting tales of barbarians. He wrote stories about bloodletting supernatural horrors such as "Skull-Face," the villain of which is named Kathulos in tribute to his pen pal Lovecraft, and *Weird Tales* published those, too. The magazine was even able to add Mary Shelley to the list by serializing *Frankenstein*. But not all of the horror pulps tried to be so respectable — for every issue of *Weird Tales* that featured a tastefully-done nude by Margaret Brundage on its front cover, there was an issue of a pulp like *Horror, Terror,* or *Dime Mystery* that went hammer-and-tongs for the most lurid subject matter available, both inside and out. Whereas the Brundage cover would feature a demure lass, rendered in gentle pastels, perhaps erotically intertwined with an idol or menaced by a snake or something, the typical *Dime Mystery* cover would be rendered in obscenely colorful oils. The nude or nearly-nude girl in peril was usually in some sort of bondage, pawed over by salivating hunchbacks and leering mad scientists, hypo in hand, with caged hell-monster just waiting to break loose. Another pulp, *Strange Tales*, was conceived as a competitor with *Weird Tales* on its own terms, using authors like Howard. It only lasted seven issues, but the title would live on courtesy of Atlas/Marvel, first in the '50s as a weird title like its pulp forebear. It switched to superheroes in the '60s, although admittedly at least one of the superheroes was supernatural, the venerable Dr. Strange. Remembered for his alliterative mystical oaths like "By the hoary hosts of Hoggoth!" and some of the most cosmic art ever to appear in comics, courtesy of legends like Steve Ditko and Gene Colan. *Strange Tales* was a clone of *Weird Tales* in every aspect except one: it actually paid its authors on time. *Marvel Tales* was another title Marvel would adopt as its own, and although it used the pulp name, the content was not fantastic in nature; it was just a catchall title for superhero reprints, mostly of Spider-Man.

During the late '30s and early '40s, concerned parents and civic groups, as always in a state of denial as to their responsibilities to children, ever searching for someone or something to blame other than themselves, protested against the rising trend of gore in the horror pulps. But unlike their four-color offspring, the pulps endured no governmental scrutiny or senate subcommittees. The government had a few more important things to worry about, like another World War, a series of real-life horrors that more or less killed the taste for that kind of stuff anyway — at least for a few years. The big difference between the horrors perpetrated in the pulps as opposed to the comics was that you actually had to be able to read to discover the horrors awaiting in a pulp magazine, whereas the comics, literally laid it out before your eyes.

The pulps gave us whole new genres. Science fiction found its name and voice in the pulps, and there was almost as much variety in that field as in the rest of the pulps. They held everything from the space operas of intergalactic adventurers like Burroughs's John Carter and E.E. "Doc" Smith's Gray Lensman, to reprints of the scientific romances of H.G.

Wells and Jules Verne, to good, old-fashioned paranoid weirdness like Richard Shaver's "Dero Mysteries" in *Amazing Stories*. That magazine was the dean of science fiction pulps that also gave birth to another pop icon, Buck Rogers. Likewise, detective fiction had been pretty polite stuff until the advent of *Black Mask*, which invented the hardboiled detective, a new breed of cynical, hooch-swillin', tough-talkin', gun-totin', dame-slappin' anti-hero. *Adventure* might have been a generic title, but it was also the title of one of the most respected and successful pulps, which managed to survive the death of the pulps by morphing into a "men's sweat" magazine. Westerns were huge, the century just having turned along with a generation not that far removed from the wild west itself. The previously mentioned Louis L'Amour and Max Brand were but the two most famous names of literally hundreds of writers who turned out oaters for pulps like Street and Smith's *Wild West Weekly* just as fast as the technology was changing. Movies from the '30s and '40s will show a quick glance at a character reading a pulp every now and again, in a horror film or a Thin Man movie. (In *The Thin Man Goes Home*, William Powell is shown lying in his hammock reading an issue of *Nick Carter, Detective*.) *Spicy Western Stories* helps move the plot along in *The Grapes of Wrath*. The popularity of westerns in the dime novels, pulps and movies not only provided work for a whole parcel of ranch-hands, both real and imaginary, but also was an unfortunate influence on American attitudes and foreign policy for decades to come. These are simply the most popular genres. It seemed that in the early half of the twentieth century there was not an invention, occupation, social activity or world event that did not have at least one pulp magazine devoted to it: *Fire Fighters, Speakeasy Stories, Racketeer Stories, Speed Stories, Oriental Stories, Prison Stories, Railroad Magazine, Fifth Column Stories*— even *Zeppelin Stories*.

Truly, the pulps offered something for everyone. By 1950 the great pulp dinosaurs were mostly extinct, supplanted by comic books, which were easier and quicker to read, and paperbacks, which were sturdier and more compact, more portable in accordance with the mood of the times and more like real books. The pulps that survived, like the dinosaurs, became smaller and speedier creatures called digests, which were actually just smaller, trimmed pulps. The difference between them and paperbacks was purely cosmetic, as much a question of size and cover stock as anything else. The digests became a haven for science fiction, and, with the genre's advancing pretentiousness, also became adopted by the bearded, pipe-smoking, patches-on-the-jacket-elbows crowd. They considered themselves the keepers of the key to the riddle of life, the only earthlings capable of discerning the true cosmic secrets contained in the sacred writings of their favorite authors. It's a good thing *Star Wars* came along when it did, bringing a sense of fun back to a genre that had grown seriously introspective. *Star Wars* bred its own horrors, however.

The concept of the costumed adventurer did not originate with the red-and-blue-costumed Superman, nor did the concept of do-gooders with more-than-human abilities. The concept didn't originate in the pulps either, but there the form was refined and perfected. Superheroes truly began with the pulps. In fact, very few comic book superheroes are not inspired by pulp superheroes. Batman, for instance. Creator Bob Kane readily admits the inspiration of The Shadow — and for more than just the character of Batman. Kane and ghostwriter Bill Finger not only borrowed a Shadow story ("Partners in Peril") to use as the basis for the first Batman story in *Detective Comics* no. 27, but also borrowed the concept of Batman's 'batarang' from a Shadow story, "Lingo." Kane also cites Johnston McCulley's Zorro, Lee Falk's Phantom, and the movie *The*

Bat, but what he fails to mention is that Batman's costume is a nearly exact copy of one worn by the pulp hero the Black Bat. Marvel Comics' version of Daredevil would also be inspired by the Black Bat, with the hero's blind lawyer alter-ego. And Marvel's number-one son, Spiderman, was directly inspired in name by the pulps' Spider. Superman will be dealt with shortly. The point is that the pulps had almost as many heroes as monsters. And they had a lot of monsters.

The Shadow was the pulps' preeminent and penultimate dark avenger, appearing in more novels (325) than any other pulp character; in fact, more than any single character in pop literature. It only seems like there are that many Executioner novels. The Shadow first found fame on the radio as the host of *Street and Smith's Detective Story Hour*, which featured readings from that week's issue of Street and Smith's pulp of the same name (minus the hour). At first, he was just the guy who read the stories, but Street and Smith, wisely deciding that a bit more flash was needed, re-named him the Shadow, and he soon became quite the personality in his own right. He quickly took to laughing in a hollow, sinister voice and asked the listener "Who knows what evil lurks in the hearts of men?" Suddenly, Street and Smith had a hot new character, and the character nudged out the magazine readings in favor of original Shadow adventures. The longest-serving radio Shadow was Bret Morrison, but his contribution is often eclipsed by that of Orson Welles, who is as linked to the character in the public mind as he is to "The War of the Worlds." Welles's Mercury Theatre cohort Agnes Moorehead played Margo Lane to both men's Lamont Cranston. The Shadow's success was soon consolidated in print, the character beginning his record run in 1931. At the height of his print popularity, the magazine was coming out twice a month. The big difference between the radio and pulp Shadow was that the radio version had "the power to cloud men's minds so that he appeared invisible to them." The pulp hero rather resembled the popular stereotype of the anarchists of the day, with black slouch hat and cloak, hawk nose, and twin .45 automatics that he wasn't afraid to use. This vision provided the basis for some of the finest pulp cover art ever, done primarily by the Rozen brothers, Jerome and George. The Shadow's foes were as much creatures of the night as he was, except they had given over to the darkness: "The Hydra," "The Golden Vulture," "The Blue Sphinx," "The Black Falcon," "The Voodoo Master," "The Murder Master," "The Robot Master," "The Ghost Makers," "The Cobra," "The Salamanders," "The Devil Monsters," and "Charg Monster." Also a star of golden-age comics and the serial screen, the Shadow died when the majority of the other pulps did, but would find new life again in the very same comics and paperbacks that helped knock off the pulps in the first place. The very best version was the mid–'70s DC run by Denny O'Neil and Mike Kaluta, still a high water mark in the medium, and the worst was the 1964 Radio Comics series, which, like the long underwear versions of Dracula and Frankenstein, turned a creature of the night into a gimmicky, brightly-costumed superhero.

With the runaway success of the Shadow, hero pulps took off. Some of them literally took off— the aviation hero was quite the salable commodity in the days when airplanes were still relatively new, and getting more sophisticated all the time. The most popular of the aviator heroes, though, was one with exploits set in the then-recent World War I — *G-8 and His Battle Aces*. It was a war that no veteran would have recognized, for the skies over Europe were not only patrolled by the Hun in their Fokkers, but by "The Bat Staffel," the "Squadron of Corpses," "The Spider Staffel," "The X-Ray Eye," "The Cave-Man Patrol," "The Headless Staffel," and the all-encompassing "Staffel of Beasts" and "The Death Monsters." *Dusty Ayres and His Battle Birds* (not to be confused with *Terence X. O'Leary's War Birds*) fought a war in the future, while Bill Barnes was set squarely in the present, albeit in planes that were not only on the cutting edge of technology, but often a step or three ahead of it. The aforementioned Spider began his career as a Shadow clone, but soon developed his own unique persona, throwing himself in the way of "Death's Crimson Juggernaut." He fed justice to "The City That Dared Not Eat," filed the "Claws of the Golden Dragon," and put a stake in "The Death Reign of the Vampire King." *Operator no. 5* was, in civvies, Christopher, James Christopher. Jimmy to his friends and the American James Bond of the Depression, staving off an even more horrifying horde than S.P.E.C.T.R.E, "The Purple Invasion" of America in a truly epic thirteen-issue storyline. *The Avenger*'s adventures were allegedly (but not actually) written by "The famous creator of Doc Savage, Kenneth Robeson," whose third novel, *The Sky Walker*, was another inspiration for you-know-what. But the one who (literally) stood head-and-shoulders above the rest of the competition (and, some whispered, even above the Shadow himself), and whose number of adventures (181) was second only to the alter ego of Lamont Cranston, was the direct inspiration for the comic book Superman, Dr. Clark Savage, Jr., better known to the world at large as Doc Savage, the invincible Man of Bronze!

Doc Savage

"But he would never be mistaken for another, this Herculean figure ... his skin, remarkably fine of texture, had been turned a rich bronze hue by countless tropical suns, and his hair ... was of a bronze color only slightly darker.

"The most striking feature, however, was his eyes. They were slightly weird, like pools of flake-gold stirred continually by tiny whirlwinds. They held an almost hypnotic quality, a compelling power" ("Death in Silver").

Doc Savage was a mental and physical marvel that had been raised from the cradle by the top men in every field of endeavor to become, literally, a superman (and a lasting pop culture icon on the level of Conan or Tarzan). In fact, that very term, "superman," was applied to the character in an early ad for the magazine. Jerry Siegel and Joe Schuster, the creators of the comics' Superman, were admitted, avid pulp fans, so it's no coincidence that the term was used in the first place, that both supermen are named Clark, that both are "men of metal," or that both periodically retire to a Fortress of Solitude. Both had a familiar supporting cast of characters, but whereas Lois Lane and Jimmy Olsen were often more of a hindrance than a help to the alien Superman, Doc was aided in his relentless battle against evil by a hand-picked team, "The Amazing Five," all former members of Doc's World War I outfit, and each the top in his field (second only to Doc, of course). The most popular with fans of Doc's aides was "Monk," or, more properly, Lt. Col. Andrew Blodgett Mayfair, whose sophisticated-sounding name, rank, and abilities as a chemist were totally at odds with his brutish appearance and strength. He had a pet pig, Habeas Corpus, so named in order to irritate his dearest friend and constant foil, Col. Theodore Marley "Ham" Brooks, a "fastidious fashion plate" and "high-flying legal eagle."

Ham received his nickname in the Great War after being framed by Monk for stealing a truckload of hams. In retaliation for Habeas Corpus, Ham adopted a pet ape he christened "Chemistry." Col. John "Renny" Renwick was a civil engineer with huge hands that he just loved to punch through heavily paneled doors, whose dour, "Puritan-like" face and disposition was merely a mask for the joy he felt in fighting crime. "Long Tom" (the nickname of a cannon used in World War I), was an electrical wizard who looked as sickly as Doc did healthy, and William Harper "Johnny" Littlejohn was a rail-thin, eminent archaeologist who loved to confound his comrades with the most intricate examples of the English language he could find. Doc's cousin Patricia Savage, who was as beautiful, naturally, as Doc was handsome, and almost as tough to handle, also aided Doc occasionally:

> "Want to help me, Pat?" Doc asked.
> "Help *you*?" Pat said cheerfully. "Do I want to fly the Atlantic? Do I want to stand up and get shot at? Do I want to go in for parachute jumping? All those are safer than helping you."
> "Do you want to help?" Doc repeated.
> "Sure," Pat laughed. "Who's trying to kill you now?" ["Death in Silver"].

Doc Savage Magazine benefited from one of the most talented pulp fictioneers of all time, Missouri's Lester Dent, who penned most of the stories, and two of the most gifted pulp artists of all time, Walter Baumhofer and Robert G. Harris. Together, they brought the Man of Bronze to vivid life. The inside spot illustrations were mostly done by the solid Paul Orban. He bowed out late in the game and was ably replaced by Edd Cartier, among others, although he did return for the final three issues. Doc Savage spent his whole pulp cover career depicted as a rugged Clark Gable lookalike (hence the inspiration for Doc's first name) with a spit-curl from hell (Superman even stole his hairstyle). But with the paperback revival of the '60s, his look changed into an even sterner visage, with a helmet-like skullcap of hair that formed a widow's peak from hell. Any resemblance to former television Flash Gordon Steve Holland was not coincidental, as Holland was primary cover artist James Bama's model. They all illustrated the words of a man who certainly had a way with them — Lester Dent brought a screwball, sardonic wit and a newspaper reporter's directness to the proceedings which, when coupled with his incredibly vivid imagination and gift for headlong action, gave the Doc Savage adventures a style like no other:

> Paine L. Winthrop was dead. No doubt of that, as it was necessary for the ambulance surgeons to assemble the scattered parts of his body on a stretcher before it could be carried away ["Death in Silver"].
>
> Doc Savage flashed downward. One arm whipped out. The man went down without a sound. His companion turned, squeezed the trigger of his gun. There was a streak of bronze as Doc's fingers went forward, lightning fast. One finger caught between the trigger and the trigger guard, preventing the ambusher from firing ["The Golden Peril"].

Besides possessing abilities far beyond those of normal mortal men, Doc Savage has tricks up his sleeve that go above and beyond even a normal superhero, as cheekily demonstrated by this passage from "The Devil Genghis":

> Doc Savage, on the stage, did not look nearly as ill at ease as he felt. He had been trained to conceal his emotions. And certainly the skill with which he played his classical number on the violin left no suspicion that he was not perfectly at home. The quickest and loudest applause had come from the members of the audience who really knew music.
>
> Now the bronze man played the clarinet number with the swing orchestra. The result was a joyful uproar. No one had to have an advanced education in classical music to know here was a number well done. In the vernacular of swing, the boys "sent gate," "slapped jive on the dog house," "busted hide" and "gripped that git box." They really went to town. The "jitterbugs" in the audience got up and danced in the aisles.

Doc Savage was a globetrotter who found trouble in the most exotic locations on the earth (not to mention over, under and inside of it), with plotlines and villains as exotic and as monstrous as the locations: "The Land of Terror" (a lost world/dinosaur thriller that ranks favorably with the Edgar Rice Burroughs Pellucidar series novel of the same name), "The Brand of the Werewolf," "The Dagger in the Sky," "The Monsters," "The Phantom City," "The Red Skull" (Captain America took notes), "The Land of Always-Night," "The Living Fire Menace" (Carl Burgos was also in class; the spot illustrations for this story depict flaming men that uncannily anticipate the look of the Human Torch), "The Thousand-Headed Man," "The Fortress of Solitude," "The Sargasso Ogre," "The Mystic Mullah," "The Czar of Fear," "Hex," "The Crimson Serpent." Month after month, Doc and his band of brothers fought ceaselessly against the onslaught of evil, until at last, in his final story, "Up from Earth's Center," he faced off against the very source of that evil and the minions of Hell itself.

The larger-than-life adventures of Doc Savage and his fabulous crew ended in the pulps in 1949, but enjoyed a massive revival via the paperback in the pop culture-crazy '60s. Defined by the incredible James Bama covers as the Conan series was by Frank Frazetta, Doc Savage developed a whole new generation of fans, an audience that maintained itself long enough to merit the reprinting of the entire series all over again. Bama did most of the first seventy covers; Fred Pfeiffer took over for a couple of years, whereupon two former Marvel men, Boris Vallejo and Bob Larkin, assumed the mantle. And speaking of Marvel, as in the case of Conan, that new paperback audience was large enough for Marvel to take notice and act accordingly.

By the '70s, Doc Savage had already seen duty in the comics. In the golden age, the success of the pulp did not translate to its four-color counterpart, and *Doc Savage Comics* only lasted twenty issues, with further stories appearing as back-up features in the more successful *Shadow Comics*. Doc had been usurped on the newsstands and in the candy stores by the bunch that had stolen his act, both in terms of fantastic powers and haberdashery. So Street and Smith felt compelled to fix what wasn't broken — they gave Doc a sort of monk's hood with a ruby on it that gave him the power to cloud men's minds. Yes, you've read it before, and, no, it didn't work. Spurred by the success of the paperbacks, Gold Key had a go at Doc Savage in 1966, but the magazine surprisingly lasted only one issue. It was an adaptation of *The Thousand-Headed Man* from the novel of the same name, which reprinted the astounding James Bama paperback cover. (Gold Key also tried to cash in on the pulp revival with an equally well-done G-8 and his Battle Aces, but that, too, lasted only one issue.) It was Marvel's turn the third time around, in the early '70s, but it was no charm — the series lasted only eight issues, plus a "Giant-Size Annual" that reprinted the first two. The stories were adapted from pulp originals: *The Man of Bronze, Death in Silver, The Monsters,* and *Brand of the Werewolf* were all done faithfully, with solid scripting and artwork, plus some truly striking covers by Gil Kane and Jim Steranko, but failed to catch on. Doc even guest-starred with Spider-Man in *Marvel Team-Up,* but his style was rooted too deeply in pulp tradition to mix well with his mutated offspring.

With the release of the 1975 film *Doc Savage: The Man of Bronze,* directed by George Pal (*War of the Worlds, Destination: Moon, The Time Machine*), and starring former television Tarzan Ron Ely as Doc, Marvel decided that it would try Doc again, this time as part of the Marvel Magazine Group (more on the film shortly). This would seem to be the ideal format for the venerable pulp icon. It offered the opportunity for painted covers like the paperbacks and longer stories, and served the character well, with all-new single-issue epics, but once again, it only lasted eight issues. This was as much to do with Marvel's dismantling of its magazine line as with the quality, which was without question above average. Somewhat fittingly, like its pulp forefather, the last few issues of Marvel's black-and-white *Doc Savage* came out quarterly.

Doc Savage, the Man of Bronze no. 1 (August 1975)

Cover: Roger Kastel
Frontispiece: Photo of Ron Ely as Doc Savage
"Doom on Thunder Island"—Doug Moench, John Buscema/DeZuniga
"The Man Who Shot Doc Savage"—Chris Claremont/Jim Harmon (Text feature/interview)

The cover of the first issue of Marvel's magazine *Doc Savage, The Man of Bronze* sported spiffy, upscale-looking bronze ink (in the days before such things became almost an afterthought) and artwork featuring a full-figure pose of Ron Ely as Doc taken from the movie poster (hence the unfamiliar name Kastel, Roger Kastel in the cover credits). The movie was hyped greatly in the Mighty Marvel Manner from cover to cover, but was a box-office dud, quashing any hopes of pulling in a new audience. The movie is really not a total washout, despite its reputation and admitted (sometimes huge) faults, but it had the potential to be so much more.

To somebody's credit, the movie is a period piece, but it's that awful "1930s as filtered through the horrible fashion sense of the 1970s" period look that made even movies like *Chinatown*, great as it is, ring slightly inauthentic. In other words, there are pinstripe suits, but with '70s, interstate-wide lapels, and flappers with Farrah Fawcett-style blow-dried hair. Ron Ely's performance is as sincere as the script allows, although the perennially boyish-faced actor looked a bit young in the role and not quite big enough. Many fans would have preferred the original choice for the proposed Doc Savage television series, Chuck Connors (who looked almost as much like a Doc Savage paperback cover as Steve Holland did), or another former television cowboy star, Clint Walker, who looks as though he stepped right out of a Walter Baumhofer painting. Still, some thought went into the casting, which is more than can be said for the Fabulous Five, some of whom resemble their pulp counterparts a little more than the others. Unfortunately, the key role of Monk went to an actor who was not intimidating and brutish, just fat. Darrell Zwerling, who also appeared in *Chinatown*, portrays Ham, but he's more like an angry canary than a high-flying legal eagle. William Lucking, as Renny, comes off the best, and even though he doesn't get to punch through any doors, he does get in a good "Holy Cow!" or three. Paul Gleason and Eldon Quick are Long Tom and Johnny, respectively, and both come off fairly well in their limited roles, although Gleason, as Tom, looks a bit too healthy, and is somewhat incompetent.

Now, it only stands to reason that if you want your hero to seem really heroic, he has to face up to a villain of equal or arguably even greater stature. Holmes had his Moriarty. Bond has his Blofeld (and Doctor No and Goldfinger et al.). In the pulps, for Doc Savage, it was John Sunlight, the only villain in the series to appear twice. Unfortunately, the main villain in *Doc Savage, the Man of Bronze*, is not John Sunlight, nor is he taken directly from any of the other pulps, and he is unfortunately the biggest disappointment in the film—Captain Seas, played by Paul Wexler. Wexler had been a serviceable Christopher Lee look-alike zombie henchman in *The Four Skulls of Jonathan Drake*, and had a commanding voice as well as physical presence, but played his role for comedy, undercutting any sense of menace to the hero. His part was cobbled together from several Dent villains, as was the script. The "brains heavy" is drawn more directly from the pulps. "The Deadly Dwarf" from *Repel*, Cadwiller Olin, is three feet high, drinks martinis from a toy martini glass in a crib, and likes to have lots of big strong half-naked men around, making him one of Dent's most twisted and colorful villains. He's not so named in the movie, but he was clearly the inspiration, and he's not silly, merely foolish, and is even less threatening than Captain Seas. They also throw in "The Valley of the Vanished" and its inhabitants from the pulps, including the princess who is in love with Doc, but understands that he feels his life is too dangerous to share with anyone. To this sentiment Ely responds with the immortal line: "Monja, you're a brick" (which, to be fair, is not only a quote from the first novel, and Doc's response to another princess in another story, but the context in which it's used and the delivery, then as now, draws guffaws).

Actually, for the first twenty minutes or so, the movie is a straightforward, faithful, and fairly well done adaptation of the first Doc novel, "The Man of Bronze." But everything falls apart at the moment that Doc and crew make ready to fly to Hidalgo. Doc stands on the steps leading up to the plane and gives an oral recitation of "The Doc Savage Code" (something along the lines of the Boy Scout Oath, only a little more global in outlook), with march music of John Philip Sousa swelling up in the background. His aides listen enraptured and then break out in a brisk round of applause. The plane then takes off in the direction of Camp-Land, and never comes back. It has become a guilty cult pleasure for fans who regret that Doc has never been given a second celluloid chance.

So it's entirely possible that people passed up the magazine because of the quality of the movie. It was a big mistake if they did, because the story that was done on paper was a lot better than the million-dollar screen gem. "The Doom on Thunder Isle" is not an adaptation of a pulp tale, but you wouldn't know it. The splash page declared it "a return to greatness!" and for once, that wasn't hype. It succeeded where the movie failed, capturing the characters and feel of the pulps as well as the boys over at *Savage Sword of Conan* were doing. Doug Moench's script shows that he did his homework well and retains an amazing amount of fidelity to Dent and his style, his patterns of speech and so forth, and the artwork by John Buscema and Tony DeZuniga is the equal of anything they ever did in tandem for *Savage Sword of Conan*. "The Man Who Shot Doc Savage" is not the tale of an assassin, it's a history of Doc Savage and an interview with George Pal, although after seeing the film, many fans were inclined to believe that Pal really did murder Doc Savage.

Doc Savage, the Man of Bronze no. 2 (October 1975)

Cover: Ken Barr
"Doc Savage: The Hell Reapers"—Doug Moench, Tony DeZuniga
"Ron Ely: The Man of Bronze"—John Warner (Interview); Michele Wolfman (Photos)

Doc Savage, the Man of Bronze no. 3 (January 1976)

Cover: Ken Barr
Frontispiece: Rich Buckler/Klaus Janson
"The Inferno Scheme"—Doug Moench, John Buscema/DeZuniga
"A Most Singular Writ of Habeas Corpus"—Doug Moench, Rico Rival

The Doc Savage movie may not have caught on, but the Marvel magazine did (for a short time, anyway), and each of the eight issues has something to recommend it. No. 3's lead story is particularly fine, one of the best, if not the best, in that short run. For once, the story centers not around Doc, but Renny, and the big engineer is actually given a personality, and creates a great deal of pathos. The master villain is called Inferno, and he not only has a — shall we say savage — menagerie of deadly mechanical lions, tigers, and bears, but that favorite device of '30s pulpsters, a death ray. The long story format provides the space needed for the epic tale, which sounds and reads like a genuine pulp novel. Monk, always a fan favorite, gets a solo filler story. It's a diverting piece of fluff, and Rico Rival maintains the Buscema/DeZuniga style for a nice overall look of continuity. The cover art was by Ken Barr, who does a reasonable enough imitation of Bama, although there are so many veins bulging on Doc's chest and forehead, he looks like he's about to turn into Swamp Thing. The problem with trying to follow or work in the style of Bama was common, as with the many who tried to mimic Frazetta's style — in only focusing on photo-like realism, they actually drew too much, and missed the point. Bama's genius wasn't that his paintings looked like photos, but that fantastic subject matter was rendered with photographic realism. Merely trying to make the figure look as realistic as possible wasn't the whole point of the painting. Oddly, Bob Larkin, who worked for Marvel and later went on to do Doc Savage paperback covers, never did a cover for Marvel's Doc Savage. Of his work for the Doc paperback covers, Larkin was later to remark: "I brought the Marvel style of action and color to Doc Savage" (*Comics Scene Yearbook* no. 2, 1993). It's a shame he never brought it to Doc while he was actually at Marvel.

Doc Savage, the Man of Bronze no. 4 (April 1976)

Cover: Ken Barr
"Ghost Pirates from the Beyond"—Moench, DeZuniga/M. Severin

This was another superlative issue. Ken Barr contributes his best, most paperback-like effort yet, although Doc still has too many veins, and, an unfortunate relic of the movie incarnation, a belt buckle adorned with Bantam Books' Doc Savage logo, a none too subtle product identification ploy that was totally out of character. That being said, though, it's an excellent issue from beginning to end. Once again, Doug Moench simulates Dent's style and rhythm wonderfully, and manages to include all the little touches, like Doc's two-hour physical and mental exercise routine. Art-wise, it's basically all Tony DeZuniga's show, although he gets some penciling help from Marie Severin for the first eight pages, plus the splash page, which is reminiscent of, and compares favorably to, some of the Edd Cartier-designed title pages from the pulps.

Doc Savage, the Man of Bronze no. 5 (July 1976)

Cover: Ken Barr
Frontispiece: Neal Adams
"Doc Savage: The Earth Wreckers"—Doug Moench, Tony DeZuniga
"The Pulp Doc Savage"—Robert Sampson (Text); Marshall Rodgers (Illustration)
"An Interview with Mrs. Lester Dent"—David Anthony Kraft

Finally, in this issue, fans get to see a Neal Adams Doc, and Doug Moench's epic tale recalls such similar planet-threatening Doc tales as "The Man Who Shook the Earth" and "He Could Stop the World." Robert Sampson was one of the leading experts in the pulp fan field, and Mrs. Dent, of course, was the wife of Lester, and was just one of the nicest people you would ever want to meet. She really did say things like "How's the weather up there?" and was always gracious with her time, and for the adulation Mr. Dent received for Doc from new generations due to the paperbacks. Sadly, he would never be aware of those future generations' discovery of his work, having passed away in 1959.

Doc Savage, the Man of Bronze no. 6 (1976)

Cover: Ken Barr
"Doc Savage: The Sky Stealers" — Doug Moench, Tony DeZuniga

The cover to this issue is pretty weak. The composition and the color (not to mention the epic story) are just fine, but the look on Doc's face, which is already too aged, makes it looks like he's constipated. Good are the text feature on Renny, the pinups, and the stratospheric story.

Doc Savage, the Man of Bronze no. 7 (1977)

Cover: Ken Barr
"The Mayan Mutations" — Doug Moench, Tony DeZuniga

Unfortunately, the series had only one issue to go after this action-packed horror-adventure, with Doc returning to the Valley of the Vanished and fighting always-creepy giant insects. The magazine was now quarterly, although Marvel didn't bother to announce that. This issue simply came out four months after the last one, and it would be four months until the next, and last.

Doc Savage, the Man of Bronze no. 8 (1977)

Cover: Ken Barr
Frontispiece: Tom Sutton
"The Crimson Plague" — Doug Moench, Ernie Chan (Chua)
"Doc Savage Art Portfolio" — Ed Davis, Bob Layton/Dick Giordano

The series ends on a somewhat flat note. The cover and art portfolio are just fine, and Doug Moench's script is as inventive as always, but is let down by Ernie Chan's solo artwork, which was much more suited for sword and sorcery. Chua had also worked on the first couple of issues of Marvel's color Doc Savage title, but there he was paired up with Ross Andru, who did a whale of a job on that series as a whole.

WARREN

Screen Thrills Illustrated

Screen Thrills Illustrated was Warren's action film magazine. The emphasis was on the serials, but it also covered westerns, war movies, even comedies — in short, anything with action. With such a diverse range of topics, the contents of the mag often read like the contents page of a pulp magazine like *Adventure*, and many of the pulp heroes who were featured in serials were covered in these pages.

Screen Thrills Illustrated no. 4 (April 1963)

Cover: Photos of "The Crimson Ghost" and Linda Stirling, Batman (Lewis Wilson), Bowery Boys (Huntz Hall and Leo Gorcey), Kermit Maynard
Frontispiece: Photo from *Batman and Robin* (1943)
"From Tarzan to Lion-Man"
"Batman and Robin: From Comic Strip to Movie Screen"
"Fists on Film"
"D-Days"
"Behind the Shadow's Mask"

"Hollywood: Life or Death?"
"Western Hall of Fame"
"Siren of the Serials"
"Private Screening"
"Flashbacks"

The first two issues of *STI* featured the standard full-page cover painting, but with the third issue, they took to showcasing their variety of features right up front, featuring photos of all the major attractions of that issue. The serials get the bulk of attention this issue, with features on both Batman chapter plays, Buster Crabbe ("From Tarzan to Lion-Man") and Linda Stirling ("The Siren of the Serials"), and the pulps are right in there with a feature on the Shadow films of Kane Richmond.

Screen Thrills Illustrated no. 8 (May 1964)

Cover: Photos of "The Spider," The Marx Brothers, and Sabu

Frontispiece: Photo from *The Spider's Web*
"The Spider — Nemesis of the Underworld"
"The Harp, the Piano, and the Moustache"
"TV Honors Six-Gun Heroes"
The Scarlet Letter
"Sabu: A Hero of Modern Arabian Nights"
"Flashbacks: Tom London"
"Jimmy Stewart — Hits That Never Miss"
"Western Hall of Fame"
"Private Screening"

The Spider was a competitor of the Shadow in the pulps, and although he lasted for a long time, the number of novels published about the character came nowhere close to the Shadow. But in the serial arena, however, the Spider emerged the victor, in both the number of serials (two to one), and the quality, particularly of the first, *The Spider's Web*. Both the pulp and the serials receive some welcome and informative coverage in this issue, even Jimmy Stewart. Don't forget he starred in some of Hitchcock's greatest films.

THE ROOK

The Rook was a time-traveling adventurer with a robot sidekick, whose gimmick was meeting up with real-life "masters of time" like H.G. Wells and Jules Verne. He first appeared in Eerie no. 82, and was a series fixture there for a number of years as well as in 14 issues of his own magazine, which folded about a year before Warren did.

The Rook no. 3 (June 1980)

Cover: Bob Larkin
"The Rook: The Original Master of Time" — Will Richardson, Lee Elias
"Bravo for Adventure!" — Alex Toth
"Voltar: Comes the End Time" — Will Richardson, Alfredo Alcala

The cover, by Bob Larkin, is Doc Savage (right down to the pose) with a different hairstyle, and Voltar is Conan by any other name. Both are beautifully rendered, but the class of the issue is "Bravo for Adventure," the pulpiest strip Warren ever published, by the brilliant Alex Toth. The Rook series was mildly diverting pulp fiction, but how he ever stuck around for so many appearances is as much a mystery as the Master of Time himself.

Savage Tales

Savage Tales, a pulp title if there ever was one (but it was never the title of a pulp

The Rook no. 3 (Warren) — Change the shirt and hair and — presto! Instant Doc Savage cover from the man who would paint the final round of Doc paperback covers, Bob Larkin.

magazine), is often thought of as the first Marvel black-and-white magazine, but it was actually the second. A few years earlier, in 1968, Marvel had attempted to expand Spider-Man's domination of the comic book spinner racks to the magazine portion of the newsstand with *The Spectacular Spider-Man*. The first issue was black-and-white, but Spidey didn't seem to have the same appeal in that format, so the second issue went to color — but neither format captured enough of an audience to survive. Plus, there was the problem of both size and subject matter, roughly the same problem that Warren had faced trying to get *Famous Monsters* or *Creepy* placed on the newsstands when they first appeared. Spider-Man was a comic book character, but this wasn't a comic book, it was a magazine. It couldn't be placed with the magazines because it was a comic book. More than this, though, the magazine essentially offered the same kind of stories Marvel was already telling in the comics, not utilizing the magazine format to take a more mature approach, so it seemed that the fans preferred Spidey in his familiar, cheaper format.

So Marvel tried again with *Savage Tales*, but ran into the same problem. This magazine contained characters that had originally appeared in four-color comics (although they weren't superheroes), but with the first issue's cover featuring Conan the triumphant, holding aloft the bloody severed head of his recently-deceased foe and a More-Than-Half-Naked Wench, there was no way it was going to be confused (or mixed in) with the comic books. And so, when it was distributed at all, it was placed with the men's sweat magazines and completely missed its target audience. (This has always been the accepted explanation, although you wonder why it wouldn't have simply been placed next to the already-established Warren magazines.) The magazine wasn't really all that savage, although it must have seemed so when it first appeared. Although the characters are all handled in a more adult manner for the time, the passage of time has rendered the fare quite tame, especially in light of the level of violence acceptable in mainstream comics of the present. This definitely disappointed any men's sweat aficionados looking for their particular brand of thrills (although "The Femizons" strip in that first issue may have helped in that direction). Besides those "Femizons," who made such an overpowering impact that they never appeared again (at least in another original story; their amazing origin was reprinted a scant three years later in *Savage Tales* no. 3), *Savage Tales* no. 1 featured Conan, plus the Man-Thing and Ka-Zar. Conan and the Man-Thing have already been discussed in previous chapters, so let's take a look at the history of the Lord of the Hidden Jungle.

Ka-Zar has a history almost as long as the history of Marvel itself. *Ka-Zar* no. 1 was published in 1936, only four years after Goodman began publishing, and was his first continuous pulp series character. Unfortunately, *Ka-Zar* was not what you would call a smash success. In fact, you couldn't call it a success at all, because it only lasted three issues. All you could call it was all it has ever been, one of but dozens of jungle heroes cranked out by hundreds of writers and publishers trying to jump on the coattails of Edgar Rice Burroughs' Tarzan. There was Sangroo, who was the lord of the jungle until Tarzan copyrighted the phrase; Kwa, the Son of the Sun; Kroom, the Tarzan of the South Seas; Kioga, the Hawk of the Wilderness (and the subject of a particularly fine Republic serial of the same name); Ki—Gor, who appeared in Fiction House's *Jungle Stories*, and had the longest shelf-life of any of the imitation Greystokes; and probably the most distinctive of them all, Bomba, the Jungle Boy, simply because his name didn't begin with the letter "K." Bomba also enjoyed a B-movie career, in a series of films featuring Tarzan's ex–"Boy," Johnny Sheffield. Joining the dozens in 1936 was Ka-Zar "The Great" (a title which made him sound rather like a magician), by Bob Byrd, who did little to distinguish his hero from the other noble savages, including beginning his name with the letter "K," which for some reason had become the accepted letter to start an imitation Tarzan's name. The story is the usual: Upper-class twit John Rand and his wife Constance, along with their infant son David, crash in the heart of the Congo. Constance soon dies, John goes nuts and then gets it himself from evil trappers. Lions find the orphaned infant — and you know the rest. The lions eat him. No, not really, but just substitute the lions for apes, and you really do know the story. It doesn't take much space to index Ka-Zar's Karbon Kopy adventures: the amazing origin tale was "King of Fang and Claw," which would unfortunately inspire Ted Nugent. "The Lost Empire" was Ka-Zar's "Opar," and "Roar of the Jungle" was the third strike, and it's a good thing the jungle was roaring, because the crowd certainly wasn't. Ka-Zar was also among the long line of superheroes that appeared in *Marvel Mystery Comics*.

In comics, no idea is ever bad enough to stay truly dead and buried, so Ka-Zar joined the long 1960s line of Mighty Marvel Makeovers of heroes both famous, like Captain America, and not-so-famous, like Ka-Zar. Marvel kept the character's name and blonde hair, but his alter-ego was now Lord Kevin Plunder, a fitting name, as Marvel ransacked not only one Burroughs creation (Tarzan), but two others, the "Pellucidar" series and the "Land That Time Forgot" trilogy. Marvel moved his jungle locale from the Congo to deep in the heart of Antarctica and added dinosaurs and gnarled gnazghouls. Both versions of the character had Big Cat sidekicks — a lion named Zar for the first, and a more savage saber-toothed tiger named Zabu for the Marvel incarnation (shades of the human star of the first *Jungle Book*, Sabu). Perennially a second-stringer, whether in his pulp or comic identities, Ka-Zar hovers about the Marvel Universe, dropping in when a book needs a little dinosaur action, or in various and sundry solo stints which never succeed on a long-term basis. Why Marvel thought this qualified him to be a lead feature in a magazine is open to conjecture, although he really can't be blamed for the downfall of *Savage Tales*, since practically the whole black-and-white line went extinct at the same time. Still, as far as derivative jungle lords go, Ka-Zar can at least entertain when the work is in the right hands and the reader is in the right mood.

And while we're on recycling, let's talk about Marvel's other jungle star, who also made her first appearance in a four-color comic and then graduated to *Savage Tales*, Shanna the She-Devil. Shanna, obviously, was inspired by Sheena, Queen of the Jungle, who was herself an imitation Tarzan. Sheena was a comic book legend, and had even dipped her shapely foot into the pulps for a single issue, but didn't make it there for the simple reason that the comics offered a lot more opportunities to showcase that "good girl art." Her status as a pop culture icon was cemented by her television series of the 1950s, in which the Jungle Queen was portrayed by the now equally-legendary beauty Irish McCalla, who filled out Sheena's leopard-skin bikini in a way that still thrills boys both young and old. Shanna had no such impact, and performed the same function for Marvel as Ka-Zar. In fact, Shanna may have the better chance of surviving in the long run, because savages come and savages go, but beautiful jungle goddesses in leopard-skin bikinis never go out of style. And maybe the name *Savage Tales* never will either, the term having become linked to Robert E. Howard over the succeeding generations. In 2005, a collection of the adventures of Howard's "dour-faced puritan adventurer" appeared, entitled *The Savage Tales of Solomon Kane*, and a couple of years later, the title would be appropriated again for a comic book (not produced by Marvel) featuring yet another incarnation of Red Sonja.

Savage Tales Featuring Conan the Barbarian no. 2 (October 1973)

Cover: John Buscema
"Conan: Red Nails (Pt. 1)" (Robert E. Howard*) — Roy Thomas, Barry Smith
"Robert E. Howard: Lone Star Fictioneer" — Glenn Lord/Roy Thomas (Text feature)
"Dark Tomorrow" — Gray Morrow
"Cimmeria" — Robert E. Howard, Barry Smith
"The Crusader" — Joe Maneely
"A Probable Outline of Conan's Career" — P. Schuyler Miller, John D. Clark
"King Kull: The Skull of Silence" (Robert E. Howard) — Thomas, Bernie Wrightson

As noted in the previous chapter, Marvel would often announce stories or titles that didn't appear on schedule, and so it was with *Savage Tales*, except that the delay between issues one and two was just a wee bit longer than the usual couple of months. It was two and a half years, in fact. The time was used to create another magazine line to provide a support group of titles, and to give the magazine itself a bit more focus. The first issue had been a grab bag of characters and ideas. With a whole line, Marvel could afford to specialize. Man-Thing soon found a home in sister title *Monsters Unleashed*, and the Femizons never had another story. At the time of the first issue, Conan had been a popular character, but only for a short time. By 1973, he'd become a true heavyweight, and the chances of success with the title this time around were pretty much a sure thing. Ironically, the character was so popular that he would soon need his own title to meet the demand for more Conan per issue, and that title ended up outlasting all the others.

Marvel was ready to put out the second issue, as some of the material was already at hand. The holdup wasn't, as some wags have suggested, that Barry Smith took so long to finish "Red Nails," although Roy Thomas claimed on the editorial page that "Barry labored for several months to make each page — nay, each panel — a veritable masterpiece." Even if that did cause the delay, the story is a masterpiece, and would have been worth waiting for no matter how long it took to produce. Smith's style had progressed tremendously by this time, and he brings every skill to bear in what the cover calls "perhaps the mightiest Conan epic of all!" That wasn't far off the mark. Smith was also supposed to handle the cover, but — surprise! — he couldn't meet the deadline, so, in an echo of the regular comic, the job was turned over to John Buscema. Big John wasn't caught with his knickers down. He had already painted a cover for the second issue that was to have come out a couple of years before. With a few new brush strokes, boom — it was ready to roll. The painting is really quite grand, the essence of pulp, and makes you regret that he spent so much time chained to the drawing board instead of turning out pieces like this one. The story "Dark Tomorrow," written and drawn by Gray Morrow, was planned for the original second issue of *Savage Tales*, so it was complete too. "The Crusader" wasn't planned for that original No. 2, but was a reprint from the 1950s. It had more swords than sorcery, but it had art by Joe Maneely, which is always enough to make up for any other flaws a story might contain. The other outright reprint was "The Skull of Silence," a Kull story by Thomas and (then-newcomer) Wrightson, from *Creatures on the Loose* no. 10. It was very welcome. Not only did the fans get to see the previously-unpublished Wrightson cover for that book (which had originally been *Tower of Shadows*), but they also got to see Wrightson's intricately inked artwork, as clear as an unmuddied lake. Wrightson is one artist in particular whose work the ham-handed printing and coloring processes of the 1970s obscured. The same goes for Smith, whose art for Howard's haunting "Cimmeria" was done completely in pencil, and produced some superb textures. As for the text articles, "A Probable Outline of Conan's Career" was technically a reprint, but since it hadn't seen print since appearing in an early fanzine, *The Hyborian Age*, in 1938, it was fresh to the newer generations. "Robert E. Howard: Lone Star Fictioneer" was a biography of Howard by Glenn Lord, and at about the same time became the title of a short-lived but very high-quality fanzine.

Savage Tales Featuring Conan the Barbarian no. 3 (1974)

Cover: Pablo Marcos/John Romita, Sr.
"Conan: The Lurker in the Catacombs" ("Red Nails" Pt. 2, Robert E. Howard) — Roy Thomas, Barry Smith
"Red Sonja: She-Devil of the Turanian Steppes" — Roy Thomas (Text), Esteban Maroto (Illustrations)
"The Crimson Bell" — Ray Capella (Fiction), Al Williamson, Frank Brunner (Illustrations)
"The Fury of the Femizons" — Stan Lee, John Romita (*Savage Tales* no. 1)
"Red Nails in the Sunset" — Roy Thomas (Text); Margaret Brundage, Hugh Rankin (Illustrations)
"The Once and Future Talon" — Jim Steranko
"*Savage Tales* Feature Pages" — Roy Thomas and Barry Smith biographies
"Conan: He Comes from the Dark" ("Red Nails" Pt. 3 Robert E. Howard) — Roy Thomas, Barry Smith

Savage Tales no. 1 is discussed in terms of impact, but the contents aren't listed because everything (except for the cover) showed up again. In this issue we find The Femizons. Otherwise, though, the mag shines. The epic "Red Nails" is concluded, Esteban Maroto contributes more wonderful illustrations to the Thomas article on Red Sonja, and Thomas also gets in a history of the artists who illustrated "Red Nails" for the pulps. In the bio pages, we find out that Barry Smith loves The Beatles!

Savage Tales Featuring Conan the Barbarian no. 4 (May 1974)

Cover: Neal Adams
Inside front and back cover: Craig Russell
"Conan: Night of the Dark God" (Robert E. Howard) — Roy Thomas, Gil Kane, Adams, Diverse Hands
"Jason and His Electric Argonauts" — Erwin Stevenson (Film review)
"The Crusader" — Joe Maneely (not a reprint)
"The Hour of the Gnome" — Roy Thomas (Text feature)
"Conan: The Dweller in the Dark" — Thomas, Barry Smith

"Night of the Dark God" was a much-anticipated story, and it more than lived up to expectations. Thomas turns a non–Conan tale, an adaptation of "The Dark Man," into one of the Cimmerian's greatest adventures, deftly mixing action and emotion, and Kane and Adams and everybody else who worked on the story make it a pictorial delight from start to finish. "Jason and His Electric Argonauts" is simply a review of *Jason and the Argonauts*. How they got to be electric is a mystery. "The Hour of the Gnome" is the first part of a very knowledgeable two-part history of Gnome Press by, of course, Roy Thomas.

Savage Tales Featuring Conan the Barbarian & Ka-Zar no. 5 (July 1974)

Cover: Neal Adams
Frontispiece: Steve Gan
"Conan: The Secret of Skull River" — Roy Thomas, Jim Starlin/Al Milgrom
"The Hour of the Gnome" (Part 2), "The Legacy of Greenberg" — Roy Thomas (Text feature)
"Brak the Barbarian: Spell of the Dragon" — John Jakes, Dan Adkins/Val Mayerik/Joe Sinnott
"Ka-Zar, Lord of the Hidden Jungle: The Legend of the Lizard Men" — Stan Lee, John Buscema

Conan passes the Savage Torch to Ka-Zar in this co-billed issue, in which two of the three stories are reprints, including the Ka-Zar tale, which is still a great story, and pulpy as all get out. They're featured together on the cover, with accomplished Neal Adams portraits of each character.

Savage Tales Featuring Ka-Zar, Lord of the Hidden Jungle no. 6 (Sept. 1974)

Cover: Neal Adams
"Ka-Zar: The Damnation Plague"—Gerry Conway, Buscema/DeZuniga
"The Sword and the Road: The Saga of Brak the Barbarian"—Fred Blosser (Text feature)
"Jan with One N: A Review of Otis Adelbert Kline's Jungle Hero"—Fred Blosser (Text feature)
"Jann of the Jungle"—Al Williamson/Ralph Mayo
"Dragon Seed"—Len Wein, Steve Gan
"Ka-Zar, Lord of the Hidden Jungle: The Night of the Looter"—Stan Lee, John Buscema

Ka-Zar gets his first solo cover, again courtesy of Neal Adams, an action-filled piece that finds Lord Plunder in the midst of a dinosaur stampede. One of the Ka-Zar stories is again a reprint, and the Buscema/DeZuniga team on the new one makes it look an awful lot like a Conan story. Jan with one "N" was another pulp Tarzan copy who was even more derivative than Ka-Zar, but who enjoyed a longer career. Jann with two "Ns" was a Sheena knock-off with some nice good girl art.

Savage Tales Featuring Ka-Zar, Lord of the Hidden Jungle no. 7 (Nov. 1974)

Cover: Boris Vallejo
Frontispiece: Alfredo Alcala
"Ka-Zar: Stalker in a Savage Land"—Gerry Conway, Buscema/DeZuniga
"Brak: The Unspeakable Shrine (Part 1)"—John Jakes/Doug Moench, Steve Gan
"Creating a Fantasy Hero"—Lin Carter (Text feature)
"Ka-Zar: The Dream Temple of Kandu Ra"—Gerry Conway, Buscema/the Crusty Bunkers

Boris Vallejo weighs in with a great cover that really flows, with Ka-Zar attacking a monster that looks like a combination of a ceratosaurus and an iguana; the colors are vivid and subtle at the same time, and the surrounding atmosphere is sparse yet evocative. Alcala follows that up with an equally fine pen-and-ink effort. Ka-Zar gets two new stories, both illustrated by Buscema, and Lin Carter writes about creating a fantasy hero, something he was never able to do successfully on his own.

Savage Tales Featuring Ka-Zar, Lord of the Hidden Jungle no. 8 (Jan. 1975)

Cover: Steve Fabian
"Ka-Zar: The Billion Year War"—Gerry Conway, Buscema/DeZuniga
"Brak: The Unspeakable Shrine (Part 2)"—Doug Moench, Steve Gan
"Ka-Zar of the Pulps"—Robert Weinberg (Text feature)
"Jann of the Jungle: The Drum Beats at Midnight"—Al Williamson/Ralph Mayo

Steve Fabian's cover looks more than a little influenced by Gil Kane (which in turn may have been influenced by editorial decision), but his painting style would soon find its own voice. Robert Weinberg is an author and lifelong pulp fan and expert; his contributions to the genre are plentiful and essential, and some of his more noteworthy works were *The Man Behind Doc Savage*, the Shadow history *Gangland's Doom*, and *The Annotated Guide to Robert E. Howard's Sword and Sorcery*.

Savage Tales Featuring Ka-Zar, Lord of the Hidden Jungle no. 9 (Mar. 1975)

Cover: Mike Kaluta
Frontispiece: Mike Zeck

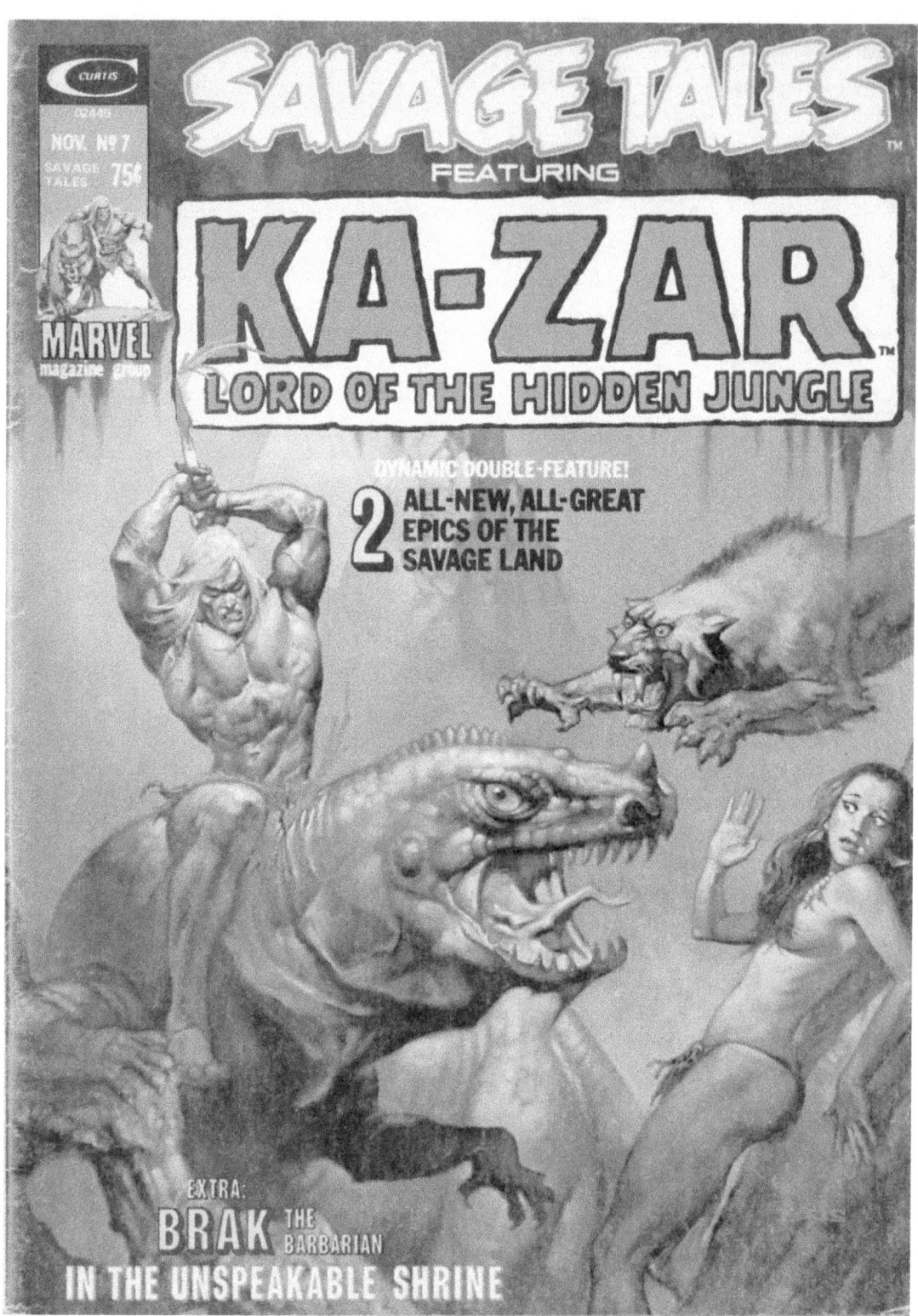

Savage Tales no. 7 (Marvel)—The star of the magazine might have changed, but the muscles remain the same. Ka-Zar rides the bucking dino, courtesy of Boris Vallejo (courtesy Marvel Entertainment, Inc.).

"Ka-Zar: Dark Island of Doom"— Doug Moench, Steve Gan
"Shanna the She-Devil: The Golden Blood Beast of Daka-Jur" Carla/Gerry Conway, the Tribe

When a character didn't make it in their own regular comic book, you could almost be certain they would turn up again in the black-and-whites. Such was the case with our lovely jungle goddess Shanna, who managed a couple of sexy savage tales before the magazine folded (again). It's actually the best thing about the issue. Even Mike Kaluta's cover was a victim of weak composition.

Savage Tales Featuring Ka-Zar, Lord of the Hidden Jungle no. 10 (May 1975)

Cover: Boris Vallejo
Frontispiece: Richard Bryant
"Ka-Zar: Requiem for a Haunted Man"— Gerry Conway, Russ Heath/The Crusty Bunkers
"The Running of Ladyhound"— John Jakes (Fiction)
"Shanna the She-Devil: Blood Purge" Carla Conway, Ross Andru/Vince Colletta

Ka-Zar might have been Tarzan Lite, but he somehow almost always seemed to draw top artists. For this story he got not only Russ Heath, who would've done just fine by himself, but the Bunkers, too, and their tandem work gives the story a quality that is ... well, haunted. Boris Vallejo contributes his last cover of the series, another beauty in which Ka-Zar fights what is apparently the same tribe of man-apes that menaced Conan on the cover of *Savage Sword* no. 7.

Savage Tales Featuring Ka-Zar, Lord of the Hidden Jungle no. 11 (July 1975)

Cover: Michael Whelan
Frontispiece: Sandy Plunkett
"Ka-Zar: Marauder in a Cage of Time"— Doug Moench, Steve Gan/Rico Rival
"Intruder"— Archie Goodwin, Russ Heath

This was the last issue of *Savage Tales* to feature new material. The cover is by Michael Whelan, and doesn't look like it began as a Conan painting. Russ Heath returns, although not on the Ka-Zar story. The Ka-Zar story, although of novel length, was no epic, mostly due to the art.

Savage Tales Featuring Ka-Zar, Lord of the Hidden Jungle Annual no. 1 (1975) (listed as *Savage Tales* no. 12 in contents.)

Cover: Ken Barr
Frontispiece: Steve Gan
"Ka-Zar: A Day of Tigers"— Roy Thomas, Gil Kane/Frank Giacoia
"Dragon Seed"— Len Wein, Steve Gan
"Ka-Zar: Back to the Savage Land"— Gerry Conway, Barry Smith/Sam Grainger
"Ka-Zar: The Sun God"— Conway, Smith/Grainger
"Ka-Zar: Rampage"— Conway, Smith/Giacoia
"Dark Tomorrow"— Conway, Gray Morrow

This was either the last issue of *Savage Tales* or the first *Savage Tales* annual — the issue itself can't seem to make up its mind — but either way, it was the end of the line, at least for the time being. Whereas the other black-and-white annuals comprised material that had actually appeared in those magazines, this included Ka-Zar reprints from the comics, more from Barry Smith in his Jack Kirby phase.

Kull and the Barbarians

With the runaway success of *Savage Sword of Conan*, Marvel hoped that a magazine devoted (mostly) to Robert E. Howard's other sword-and-sorcery heroes would find the same sort of success. Unfortunately, Marvel hoped in vain. *Kull and the Barbarians* lasted only three issues, despite being loaded with some of the best talent Marvel had to offer. Perhaps it was the title, which sounded like the name of a bad rock band. But none of Howard's other series heroes had ever caught the public fancy the way Conan had. Kull came before Conan, both in real time and fictional time, and while the seeds of the Cimmerian can be seen in the Kull stories (indeed, the first published Conan story was a rewrite of a Kull story that had failed to sell), the differences in the personalities of the characters and their interaction with others certainly make it possible to read the Kull stories without mentally substituting Conan. Kull's character and stories lack Conan's polish, but that is because they came earlier. Howard dropped Kull when he began writing the Conan stories.

He also dropped Solomon Kane. Kane was no Conan or Kull (or Bran Mak Morn or Black Turlough); no barbarian savage was he. Solomon Kane was a "dour Puritan adventurer," and there lies the rub. Like the Kull stories, the Kane chronicles came before the Conan stories, so they too lack polish, but crackle with the vitality that characterized all of Howard's work. It's not the stories that are a problem, it's the character of Solomon Kane himself. Because a synonym for Puritan is religious fanatic, and religious fanatics of any stripe don't go over well any more, except with religious fanatics of the same persuasion. If your cup of tea is sword and sorcery with a heaping helping of righteous indignation, and lopping heads off or shooting someone in the name of God, you will surely get your collection plate's worth with this Puritan. Although the action and the monsters are great, and the character is a fine swashbuckler in the strictest sense, you have the feeling that if he weren't out fighting those monsters he'd be out burning witches. One man's Solomon Kane is another's Matthew Hopkins, the Witchfinder General.

For years, there was a prevailing belief in monster fandom that in the Ed Wood film *Bride of the Monster*, Bela Lugosi said "Don't be afraid of Lobo, he's as gentle as kitchen." This is a patronizing perfidy perpetuated by people who like to make fun of Lugosi. (The actual line is, "Don't be afraid of Lobo, he's as gentle as a kitten.") Likewise, it's become a prevailing belief in fantasy fandom that Red Sonja — like Kull, Kane and Conan — was created by Robert E. Howard. She wasn't — except tangentially. In a story entitled "Shadow of the Vulture," he introduces a character named Red Sonya (note the difference in spelling), a sixteenth-century hellcat. After getting a letter from a fan that suggested that she might pair well with Conan, Roy Thomas set her back in time and tweaked her name. Esteban Maroto designed her chain-mail bikini, and the new heroine was a hit. Not pure Howard, but sometimes not bad at all. Like girls in leopard-skin bikinis, girls in chain-mail bikinis never go out of style.

Bran Mak Morn is one of Howard's lesser-known characters, but one of his most compelling. His hatred of the Romans is palpable, and the few stories that Howard wrote featuring the King of the Picts contain some of his most passionate writing. The crucifixion scene in "Worms of the Earth," where Bran Mak Morn must stand by and watch one of his countrymen die at the hands of the gloating Legionnaires is riveting as is the story itself.

Both Kull and Red Sonja eventually would get their own feature films. One each, although most fans are inclined to believe that this is one too many in both cases. Red Sonja was played by Brigitte Nielsen, which rather says it all. *Kull the Conqueror* was made in 1997, many years too late to capitalize on Arnold's Conan movies — but not too late to capitalize on the success of the then-current television series starring Kevin Sorbo as

Hercules, who unfortunately plays Howard's barbarian king. The Sorbo Hercules series was sort of like the *Moulin Rouge* of heroic fantasy. *Moulin Rouge* was a period musical that featured modern rock and pop songs. Sorbo's Hercules was a Greek man-god who spoke nauseatingly modern English, and his Kull is played the same way. Take the tagline — "Kull reigns. Kull rules. Kull ROCKS!" The movie did nothing to entertain, much less create any kind of new audience for Howard or the character, and sank without a trace, although, regretfully, it survives to this day via the miracles of videotape and DVD.

Kull and the Barbarians no. 1 (May 1975)

Cover: Michael Whelan
Frontispiece: John Severin
"Hail the Barbarians"— Roy Thomas (Text), Neal Adams (Illustrations)
"Kull: A King Comes Riding"— Thomas, Ross Andru/Wallace Wood (reprinted from *Kull the Conqueror* no. 1)
"Kull: The Shadow Kingdom" (Robert E. Howard)— Thomas, Marie/John Severin (reprinted from *Kull the Conqueror* no. 2)
"The Valley of the Worm" (Robert E. Howard)— Thomas/G. Conway, Gil Kane/Chua (reprinted from *Supernatural Thrillers* no. 3)
"King Kull"— Fred Blosser (Book review); Roy G. Krenkel (Illustrations)

The premiere issue of *Kull and the Barbarians* was a welcome addition to the fold. It featured superlative art and stories throughout and gave no indication that the title would only last three issues, although perhaps the number of reprints suggested that bets were being hedged and costs were being cut from the beginning. Even the cover was already on hand. It was intended for *Savage Sword of Conan*, but when Marvel decided to do a Kull magazine, the artist, Michael Whelan, added a scar and headband to the finished piece and presto — instant Kull! That was pretty much the only thing that distinguished one from the other, except Kull, being King, had a better tailor from time to time. Whatever the circumstances, it's a fine painting, Kull standing victorious over a hideous giant ant-beast (although he doesn't meet the creature in the issue).

The frontispiece artist, John Severin, became almost as identified with Kull as Frazetta or Barry Smith or John Buscema are with Conan. The Hal Foster influence that has always been a strong feature of his work was never more in evidence, particularly in the color *Kull the Conqueror* (later changed to *Kull the Destroyer*, which made him sound like a battleship). Severin portrayed both battle and throne room with equal aplomb, and makes you wish he had done *Prince Valiant*. Despite the superior work, the series failed in both color and black-and-white, and subsequent attempts to revive the character in color failed to capture either the talent level or even the number of issues of the original run. "Hail the Barbarians" (one of only two new features in the whole magazine) was basically the editorial page, introducing Howard's other barbarian heroes to those who might be familiar only with Conan. But this was taken far beyond the level of the usual editor's whys and wherefores by some superlative Neal Adams interpretations of the subject matter. In fact, the drawing he did of Red Sonja was used (like the Maroto Sonja piece from *Savage Sword of Conan* no. 1) as a special limited edition "variant" cover when the character was revived midway through the 2000s. The art and writing are superior throughout the issue. Thomas takes as much care with the Kull stories as he did with Conan, and really tries to give the characters distinct personalities despite their similar attire. And with greats like Ross Andru, Wallace Wood, and the Severin siblings to illustrate those words, what we have is simply more superior sword-and-sorcery from the company that put it on the comics map. Who cares if they were reprints? It's hard to argue with this much talent in one place. Besides, you couldn't pick better introductory stories.

One of Howard's greatest sword-and-sorcery stories that did not feature Conan was entitled "The Valley of the Worm," and was first seen in the third issue of the four-color title *Supernatural Thrillers*. It's a superlative adaptation, Howard's feverish tale of racial memory and reincarnation grippingly written and drawn by Gil Kane at his most dynamic and savage. Perseus, Beowulf, St. George, Siegfried — many have been the names of James Allison, who, in his dying throes, now lives the saga of Niord, the Worm's Bane. It's reprinted here only two years after its original appearance, but was certainly an appropriate (not to mention cost-effective) inclusion.

Kull and the Barbarians no. 2 (July 1975)

Cover: Michael Whelan
Frontispiece: Bernie Wrightson
"Kull the Destroyer: The Teeth of the Dragon" — Gerry Conway, Jess Jodloman
"Solomon Kane: The Hills of the Dead" (Robert E. Howard) — Roy Thomas, Alan Weiss/Neal Adams
"Red Sonja: She-Devil with a Sword" — Roy Thomas, Howard Chaykin
"Blackmark Versus the Mind Demons" — Gil Kane

The supporting cast steals the show in this issue. The Kull story is only average, but is more than made up for by Gil Kane, Chaykin, and part one of the adaptation of "Hills of the Dead," one of Howard's best Solomon Kane stories, by Thomas, Weiss and Neal Adams. We only get a taste, though of Kane's Blackmark story, "The Mind Demons." See *Marvel Preview* no. 17 for the entire story.

Kull and the Barbarians no. 3 (September 1975)

Cover: Michael Whelan
Frontispiece: Howard Chaykin
"Kull: Omen in the Skull" — Doug Moench, Vincente Alcazar
"An Informal History of Solomon Kane" — F. Blosser/G. Lord (Text feature)
"Red Sonja: The Day of the Sword" — Moench, Howard Chaykin
"Out of the Silent City" (Robert E. Howard) — Roy Thomas, Alan Weiss/Pablo Marcos

Kull is cut down in the prime of his magazine life. Chaykin contributes not only more Red Sonja art, but a cracking frontispiece as well. The conclusion of "Hills of the Dead" is exciting, but not as graphically so as the first installment. Neal Adams was a great inker for someone whom he had trained, who naturally drew like him, but Pablo Marcos didn't mesh as well with Weiss.

ATLAS/SEABOARD

Thrilling Adventure Stories

Thrilling Adventure Stories was another pulp title if there ever was one. Oh, wait, actually there was, or one pretty close to it, *Thrilling Adventures* (1930's). That publication continued the tradition of great pulps like *Adventure* that did not specialize in one genre, but offered all types of tales, from the Foreign Legion to fantasy, all under one cover. The magazine even employed the Marvel tactic of throwing one of its four-color heroes in the mix for the first

Five • *Thrilling Savage Adventure Tales*

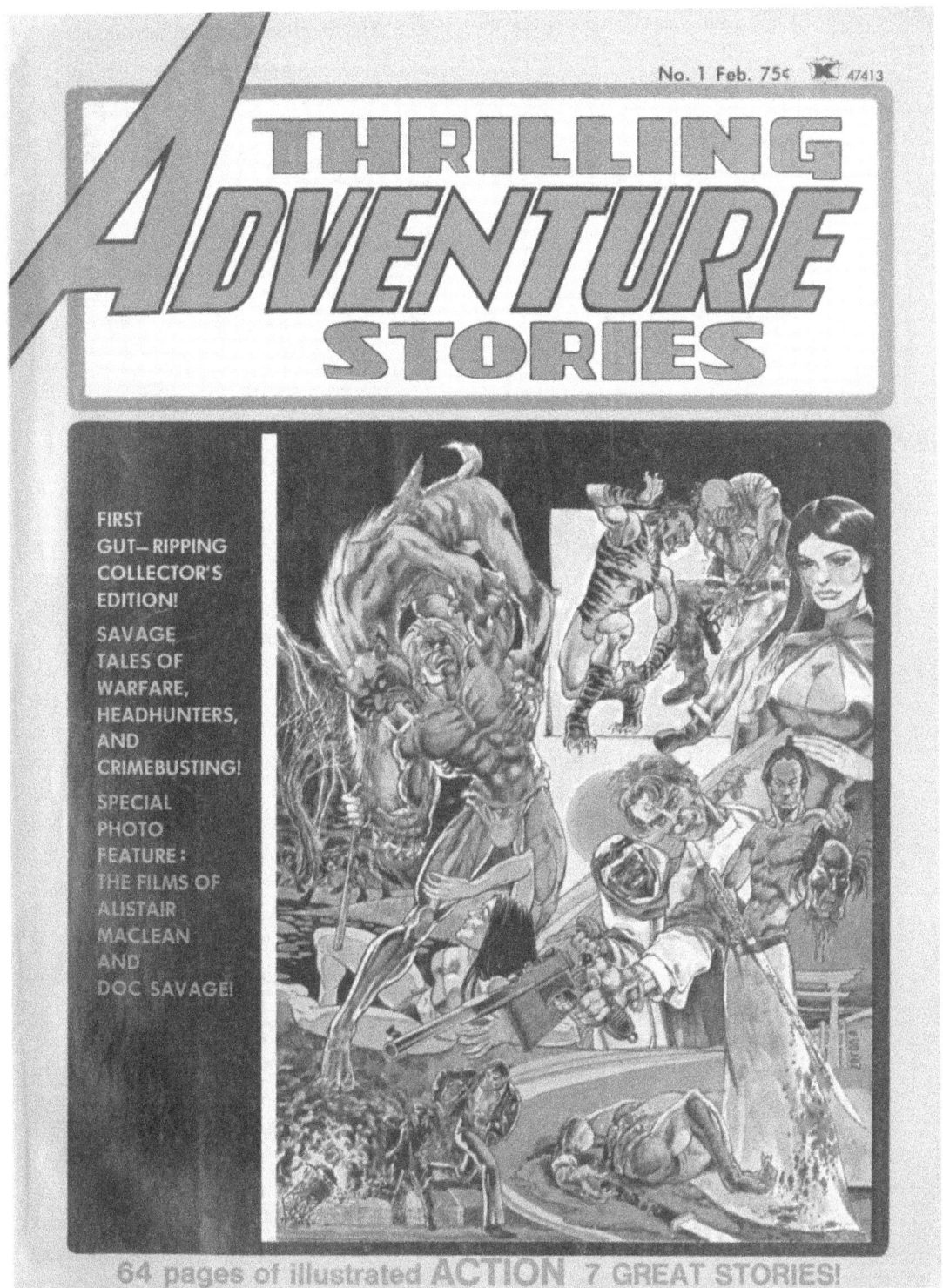

Thrilling Adventure Stories no. 1 (Atlas/Seaboard)—Ernie Colon did a collage for the cover of Atlas/Seaboard's pulp-like anthology magazine, *Thrilling Adventure Stories*, a pulp title if there ever was one.

issue, but Tiger-Man wasn't even popular in his own comic, so he was ditched in the second issue. Like some of the other Atlas magazines and comics, it's a shame that *Thrilling Adventure Stories* had to end so soon. The talent on both issues was first-rate, and gave readers a taste of what great pulp anthology titles were like.

Thrilling Adventure Stories no. 1 (February 1975)

Cover: Ernie Colon
"Tiger-Man: The Flesh Peddlers"—John Albano, Ernie Colon
"Sting of Death"—John Albano, Leo Summers
"Kromag the Killer"—Jack Sparling/Gabe Levy, Jack Sparling
"The Films of Alistair Maclean"—Ric Meyers (Text feature)
"Lawrence of Arabia"—Jeff Rovin, Frank Thorne
Doc Savage—Photo feature
"Escape from Nine by One"—Russ Heath

Ernie Colon had come up through the ranks at Warren, and had developed a crisp, clean style that adapted itself well to many types of stories. His cover was a collage of the inside features, one of which he also drew, the silly Tiger-Man. He was made a tad more daring by raising the level of violence and language, but was still silly, despite good art. In fact, the art on the whole issue was solid. Russ Heath in particular shines with one of his patented war tales which he both wrote and drew, seemingly inspired by *Stalag 17* and almost as entertaining. The issue, like its pulp inspirations, had a little of everything: war, jungle adventure, dinosaurs and cavemen, even desert adventure in the person of the real-life Lawrence of Arabia, a cracking tale expertly done by Jeff Rovin and Frank Thorne. The photo features are informative and well stocked with illustrations, and fit the tone perfectly. Doc Savage and his ilk were the inspiration for the magazine and MacLean's action novels foreshadowed the next generation of pulp.

Thrilling Adventure Stories no. 2 (April 1975)

Cover: Neal Adams
"Temple of the Spider"—Archie Goodwin, Walt Simonson
"Kromag: The Kromag Saga Part 2"—Gabe Levy, Jack Sparling
"Tough Cop"—John Albano, Russ Heath
The Towering Inferno—Carl Macek (Text/photo feature)
"Town Tamer"—Steve Mitchell, John Severin
"A Job Well Done"—Ric Meyers/Alex Toth

The first issue of *Thrilling Adventure Stories* had been pretty darned good, much better than you would've had hoped to expect. But no. 2 was so good it increases the disappointment at the magazine's demise. As at some of the classic Warren and Marvel mags, the art lineup was a virtual all-star team. Some would say that it was one of the most satisfying mags of the whole black-and-white era. Neal Adams contributes a dynamite cover of Kromag the Killer and a lithesome cave girl facing off against some particularly ferocious cave bears. Kromag is the only holdover from the first issue, and as before, mines familiar Burroughs territory. At least it was better than Tiger-Man.

The gem of the issue is an Archie Goodwin/Walt Simonson piece, "Temple of the Spider." Done around the same period as their award-winning "Manhunter" series that appeared in *Detective Comics*, it is every bit that series' equal, if not anything either did at Warren. Not only does it employ two genres in one story, samurai and horror, but it does it with a skill and poetry seen rarely in comics. The Kromag saga was hardly epic, but at least it had good art and prehistoric monsters. Cops, soldiers and detectives are the subjects of some great art by Heath, Severin and a very welcome guest shot by Alex Toth. You almost had to keep flipping back to the cover to make sure it wasn't a Warren magazine.

• Six •

Crazy Kung Fu Apes Fight Space Wars; or, Jump on In, the Bandwagon's Fine

In some ways, every subject covered in this book is a trend; indeed, the same could be said for the history of popular fiction. The tricks seem to be in either creating the bandwagon, or jumping on it firmly enough to share in the ride. The first is obviously the more difficult in the beginning, but the second may be harder in the long run, because it requires enough similarity to be recognized as part of the genre, but enough variation to make an additional contribution. This chapter deals with trends in the more popularly accepted use of the term, aspects of pop culture that have grabbed hold of the public fancy in a big way for a short, intense period of time. Some of the subjects survived beyond their initial periods of hysteria to become actual ways of life or thriving genres, but all are indicative of their eras, and all either exerted an influence on or benefited from the existence of monster magazines.

ROCK AND ROLL

Rock and roll and monster movies/horror magazines are two trends that have turned into ways of life, and the two have been linked from the beginning of both. From the outset, rock was referred to as "The Devil's Music." Early rock-and-rollers like Screamin' Jay Hawkins and appeared out of a coffin, on a stage decorated with skulls, and sang "I Put a Spell on You." Many of the early horror hosts were also crazy rock and roll disc jockeys, and their hep talk, their patter, became part of their host persona (the first shock jocks?) The link was solidified forever in 1957 with the release of *I Was a Teenage Werewolf*, the first monster movie to feature the music, lifestyles and the members of the burgeoning youth subculture. Soon, the screen was awash with hapless teenagers confronting or cavorting with monsters: the other two parts of the *Teenage* trilogy, *I Was a Teenage Frankenstein* and *How to Make a Monster*; *The Ghost of Dragstrip Hollow*, *The Giant Gila Monster* and maybe the last word in rock and roll/monster movies, *The Horror of Party Beach*. In a classic episode of *The Munsters* entitled "Far-Out Munsters," the Munsters play host to The Standells ("Dirty Water"), and host a wild party with Herman reciting unforgettable beat poetry — "Umm... Ibbity Bibbity Bab...." Many stories in the original *Vampirella* magazine are titled after rock songs. Twenty years later, the children of those Monsterkids turned the imagery back on itself with the advent of punk, and showed that the real horrors of the world were not on a screen, but right outside your door. The Damned (*Plan 9 Channel 7*), and The Misfits (see below) cemented the link between reel and real horror, and soon horror-punk became one of the staples of the form. It is still being practiced today, and gave birth to goth and much of heavy metal, from Black Sabbath (inspired by the Karloff film) on down. In turn, many of the punks became involved in the genre to such an extent they began to exert as great an influence over it as it had them. Some became authors or filmmakers. Mike Vraney, the absolute peach of a guy who heads up Something Weird Video, was also the manager for The Dead Kennedys.

How's this for a legacy? Everybody knows about young *FM* fans like George Lucas, Steven Spielberg, Stephen King and award-winning makeup man Rick Baker, but not so many may be aware of a punk band from Lodi, New Jersey, who, when its members were little, were big *FM* fans, too. They channeled their love for *FM* and monster movies and horror comics back into their music and image, and grew up to be The Misfits. The band also reintroduced the image of "The Crimson Ghost" (from the Republic serial of the same name) to mass consciousness and claimed it. Now, when people see the image, they think of the band, not the serial. The band's logo was in the same lettering style as the word "Monsters" in *Famous Monsters*, and their style was hard and fast — The Ramones meet Frankenstein, as it were. Their song titles were like flipping through a monster movie encyclopedia: *Vampira*; *Astro Zombies*; *Return of the Fly*; *Dr. Phibes Rises Again*; *Night of the Living Dead*; *Halloween*; *Halloween II*; *Die, Die My Darling*; *Horror Hotel*; *Mephisto Waltz*; *She*; *Green Hell*; *Blood Feast*; *The Haunting*; *The Hunger*; *Devil Doll*; *Fiend Without a Face*; *Die Monster Die*; *Kong at the Gates*; *Rat Fink*; and *1,000,000 Years* B.C. The original lineup, featuring vocalist Glenn Danzig, broke up in 1983, but when a re-formed roster released its first record under the band name in 14 years, 1997's "American Psycho," who should the cover artist be but the venerable Basil Gogos, who graced the album sleeve with a magnificent portrait of the Crimson Ghost that looked as it if might be a great lost *FM* cover. For their next album, the new Misfits not only retained the services of Gogos again, but went right to the heart of the matter with the title: *Famous Monsters*. In fact, The Misfits filmed three episodes of an aborted cable TV or direct to DVD project, where they played horror host to classic B monster movies, and had interview segments for each show. Along with Ben "Creature from the Black Lagoon" Chapman and Roger Corman, Basil Gogos was interviewed (and rightfully fawned over) by band members Jerry Only and Doyle Von Frankenstein (actually brothers), who took the opportunity to show off their favorite issues of their favorite magazine with their favorite cover artist. "Now, the circle is complete."

In fact, Gogos has a whole new generation of fans, and by virtue of his CD covers for bands formed by *FM* fans like The Misfits, Electric Frankenstein and Rob Zombie, he remains in demand, and has not lost an ounce of ability. His cover for Rob's trillion-selling *Hellbilly Deluxe* is particularly striking, creating another exquisitely horrible portrait that would not look out of place on a cover for *FM*. After being mistaken by Basil for a member of The Misfits at a Monster Bash Convention, I got a chance to chat with Gogos, and asked him, among other things, with whom he preferred to work, The Misfits or Rob Zombie. Gogos broke into one of his patented broad grins and laughed as he replied: "I love them both — but Rob Zombie pays me more!" When Rob Zombie broke up White Zombie, his former bass player, Sean Yseault, (as "Devil Doll"), along with Brigitte West ("Vampire Girl") and Carol Cutshall ("She-Zilla"), formed a great, frenetic horror/punk/surf band of her own. The name of the band: "Famous Monsters."

From the very beginning to what seems, fortunately, to be no end, their names and songs are truly legion: Bobby "Boris" Pickett ("The Monster Mash"), The Zombies, The Count Five (who dressed in Dracula capes and aped The Yardbirds with *Psychotic Reaction*), Black Sabbath (*Iron Man, Black Sabbath, Children of the Grave, Sabbath Bloody Sabbath*), White Zombie and Rob Zombie solo ("Dragula," "Living Dead Girl," "How to Make a Monster," "The Beginning of the End"), The Groovy Ghoulies, Famous Monsters ("Vampire Cosmonaut," "F Is for Fiend," "International Monster Presentation"), Electric Frankenstein, 45 Grave ("Surf Bat"), Alice Cooper ("Ballad of Dwight Frye," "I Love the Dead," "Feed My Frankenstein"), The Cramps ("Creature from the Black Leather Lagoon," "I Was a Teenage Werewolf"), Talking Heads ("Psycho Killer"), Alien Sex Fiend, A.F.I., Tiger Army, The Dead Boys, Monster Magnet, Sepultura, The Phantom Creeps, The Crimson Ghosts, Gein & the Grave Robbers, Psycho, Doomwatch, The Hillbilly Werewolf, Screaming Lord Sutch ("Jack the Ripper," "Monster Rock," "Rock and Horror," "Murder in the Graveyard," "Scream and Scream"), legendary outlaw DJ Wolfman Jack, ? & the Mysterians, Them, UFO, Scream, Destroy All Monsters, The Undead, Samhain, Man ... or Astroman? and The Five Blobs ("The Blob"). "Monster Mag" songs included "Psycho," "The Witch" (The Sonics); "Werewolves of London" (Warren Zevon); "Frankenstein" (The Edgar Winter Group); "Texas Chainsaw Massacre," "Teenage Lobotomy," "Pinhead," "I Don't Wanna Go Down in the Basement" (The Ramones); "Flying Saucer Rock & Roll," "Bela Lugosi's Dead" (Bauhaus); "Scary Monsters (and Super Creeps)," "The Lodger" (David Bowie); "Creature from the Black Lagoon" (Dave Edmunds); "Nosferatu," "Godzilla," "Don't Fear the Reaper" (Blue Oyster Cult); "King Kong" (Bow Wow Wow); "Invisible Man" (Generation X); "Swamp Thing" (The Chameleons); "I Walked with a Zombie" (Roky Ericsson & the 13th Floor Elevators); "Monster's Holiday" (Buck Owens); "The Green Slime," "Haunted House," "Planet of the Apes," "Metropolis" (Motorhead); "Mothra" (Anvil); "I, Robot" (The Alan Parsons Project); "Night Creatures," "Islands of the Dead," "Futurama" (Be Bop Deluxe); "Boris the Spider" (The Who); "Makin' Monsters for my Friends" (Dee Dee Ramone); "The Creature Stole my Surfboard" (The Dead Elvi); "When I See Mommy, I Feel Like a Mummy," "Big-Eyed Beans from Venus" (Captain Beefheart); "Jack the Ripper" (Link Wray); "It Ain't Easy Bein' Green" (The Incredible Hulk); "Brains and Eggs" (Los Straightjackets); "Jason and the Argonauts" (XTC); and "The One-Eyed One-Horned Giant Purple People Eater." On *Another Saturday Night*, Sam Cooke is hooked up with a date that has a "face like Frankenstein." Record sleeves featured some imaginative uses of horror and sci-fi film imagery whether they had anything to do with any of the songs or not. Ex-Beatle Ringo Starr particularly liked the stuff. The cover of his *Goodnight Vienna* LP featured the classic shot from *Day the Earth Stood Still* with Ringo's face taking the place of Michael Rennie's, and the picture sleeve and the promo film for *Back Off Boogaloo* featured the Frankenstein Monster. The video also featured King Kong and Fay Wray. Stills from *Metropolis* adorned the front and back of *Live in the Air Age* by Be Bop Deluxe, and the bat/rat/crab/spider from *Angry Red Planet* menaced The Misfits on *Misfits Walk Among Us*. The Crimson Ghost made the covers of *Legacy of Brutality* and *Misfits Collection 1* and *2*. They weren't rock and roll artists, but Ferrante and Teicher decorated the front cover of their exotica classic *Soundproof* LP with a still from *Forbidden Planet*. And let's not forget the greatest monster album of all time, *Famous Monsters Speak*, which isn't rock or exotica, it's former Bowery Boy and *Corner Bar* owner Gabe Dell doing the voices of Dracula and the Frankenstein Monster, and has a wonderful painted cover, which features not only Drac and Frankie, but the Wolfman, the Mummy, and the Creature as well. Some of the poses of the monsters are based on James Bama's Aurora model kit box paintings.

In an amusing sidelight, Johnny and Edgar Winter were the subjects of a hilarious scene from a *Simpsons Tree House of Horror* episode, in which Homer runs down the albino twin brothers with his car, thinking that they're zombies. "I'll get you, you pasty-faced jerks!"

"GIRLY" MAGAZINES

Certainly, "girly" or "cheesecake" or "pinup" magazines are a long-standing institution, but we're going to consider the trend created by *Playboy*, which was not just a showcase for attractive women, but an advocate of a certain type of male lifestyle. The trend wasn't all about nude or semi-nude models, it was about conspicuous consumption and pseudo-sophistication. Many publishers tried to emulate Hugh Hefner's bombshell, but few succeeded — and James Warren was among the also-rans. Although girly-magazine pictorials of sexy, semi-clad women being menaced by monsters are innumerable, they don't really concern us here, nor do the innumerable *Playboy* bandwagon-jumpers, except Warren, because there lay the germ for the monster movie magazine genre, which created the climate for the return of horror comics. Girly magazines are what you start buying after monster magazines, which intensifies your attraction to the opposite sex, which gets you married, which starts you collecting monster magazines again.

After Hours

Although later quite scornful of imitators of his line of magazines, Warren founded the line on a magazine that itself was an imitation. It's well done in the style of the time, but like so many others, simply couldn't compete with *Playboy*. *After Hours* lasted only four issues, but that pivotal fourth issue contained a "Science Fiction Folio," overseen by and book-ended with two articles by Forry Ackerman. The response to them was so enthusiastic that Warren decided to do a whole magazine like it — and the rest is history.

After Hours no. 4 (1957)

Cover: Photo of Anita Eckberg
Frontispiece: Photo of Lori Nelson and a monster/ *The Day the World Ended*
"After Hours with Eve Meyer"—(Pictorial)
"Confessions of a Science Fiction Addict"—Forrest J Ackerman (Text)
"I Meet My Love Again"—Arthur Porges (Science fiction)

"The Cartoonists Look at Scientific Fiction" — (Portfolio)
"Scream-o-Scope Is Here!" — Forrest J Ackerman (Text/photo feature)
"The Great Male Robbery" — Weaver Wright (Science fiction fantasy)
"Out of This World Girl" — (Pictorial–Madeline Castle)
"Those Hilarious TV Bloopers" — George Glazer (Text)
"The Camera and the Woman" — (Pictorial)
"*After Hours* Limericks" — (Verse)
"The Sensational Swede" — (Pictorial–Anita Eckberg)
"The One, The Only, The Magnificent Bettie Page" — (Pictorial)
"Artists Have a Ball" — (Photo/text feature)

This was not only of enormous importance by containing the seeds of Warren's future success, but the issue also features a generous layout of legendary pinup queen Bettie Page before she disappeared from the scene.

(On the Scene Presents:) Super Heroes

Cover: Photos of Captain Marvel (Tom Tyler), Flash Gordon (Buster Crabbe), The Phantom (Tom Tyler), Captain America (Dick Purcell), Superman (Kirk Alyn), Batman and Robin (Adam West and Burt Ward)
Frontispiece: Superhero photo collage
"Batman and Robin: From Comic Strip to Movie Screen"
"The Phantom"
"The Saga of Superman"
"The Ace of Space"
"Return of Captain America"
"Shazam!"
"Exclusive — The New Batman Movie"

The long-underwear boys were bigger than big in the mid–'60s, what with your Marvel Comics and Batmania — and since Warren didn't publish color or superhero comics, he jumped on the bandwagon the best way he knew how: by publishing an issue of reprints. Well, to be fair, not all the articles were reprints. The centerpiece of the issue is coverage of the new Batman movie, and as usual, the photos are big and plentiful. The other articles are all reprints from *Screen Thrills Illustrated*, true, but it's nice to have them all collected in one book. The cover, featuring photos of all of the above-named icons in blazing color on a fire engine red background with the title in bold yellow letters is especially eye grabbing, and one of the best Warren photo covers ever. The article titles are all pretty self-explanatory, except for "The Ace of Space," which is about the Flash Gordon serials. All of the other articles (except for the "new Batman" article) concern the serials of those respective heroes. This magazine is a dream come true for comic book movie fans and serial fans.

MARVEL

The Deadly Hands of Kung Fu

"There was never a trend we wouldn't jump on," said Len Wein, a former Marvel editor. Kung Fu was an ancient martial art that became one of the biggest trends of the 1970s. Kung Fu and its filmic equivalent might have remained an Asian phenomenon, but for the charisma and athletic ability of Bruce Lee, whose most notable role until that time was Kato, the Green Hornet's sidekick. That series, which had been created to capitalize on the Batman trend of the '60s, featured Van Williams as The Green Hornet. A personable sort who was convincing as the Hornet, Williams was totally shown up by Lee, who stole the show with his high-flying kicks and smart-ass attitude. His screen persona found its ultimate expression in *Enter the Dragon*, which became an unexpected smash, and rocketed Lee to superstardom overnight in an industry in which he had been toiling literally since he was a child. His unexpected mysterious death a short time later has only added to his iconic stature, and has fuelled as many conspiracy theories as the equally mysterious demise of George "Superman" Reeves. *Enter the Dragon* was huge, launching a craze that weaseled its way not only into the Top 40 music charts (the classic "Kung Fu Fighting" by Carl Douglas), but onto television as well. Ironically, *Kung Fu* was created as a starring vehicle for Bruce Lee, but the studio heads set about to re-cast the lead because they felt that the mainstream American public wouldn't accept a Chinese in a lead role. The pivotal role of Kwai Chang Caine went to David Carradine (son of John Carradine), who lent his own unique presence to the show. Carradine is in no way Chinese, but fortunately he did not attempt to play the part in a stereotypical manner, underplaying his lines as much as his father sometimes overplayed his. He had a truly wonderful supporting cast of Chinese actors, like former Charlie Chan "sons" Keye Luke and Benson Fong. David Carradine would go on to create his own unique legend.

Warren didn't have much truck with the Kung Fu trend, nor did Skywald, except in limited doses (see *Hell-Rider*). In fact, it wasn't that much of a presence in the black-and-white illustrated magazine field, other than in single story efforts—kung fu fans went in more for how-to magazines and endless rehashings of Bruce Lee's life and mysterious death. Many comic publishers were elbowing for space on the bandwagon, but their efforts were directed primarily towards the color field. Marvel had its share of these titles too, and naturally, they crossed over to the magazine line. Shang Chi was not only "The Master of Kung Fu," but also the son of Fu Manchu, which allowed for the ongoing presence of his father. Iron Fist, "The Living Weapon," had an origin not unlike that of Kwai Chang Caine, and had a cool yellow and green costume. The four-color title had a lot of really keen covers by Gil Kane. The worst of the bunch were The Sons of the Tiger, a blatant rip-off of *Enter the Dragon* with its multi-racial team of heroes (white, black, Asian). Like the movie, this would have been a breakthrough, except that, even moreso than the movie, all three are embarrassing caricatures of their respective races. Guess which member is responsible for each of the following lines: "Heads up, guys!" "I would advise trying not to breathe." "Right on! Look, man, we dig what you dudes been goin' thru...." Fortunately, when the magazine line went under, so did they. Unlike Shang Chi and Iron Fist, they were never revived. Which is not to say that Shang-Chi or Iron Fist were any great shakes either, but at least their original adventures contain the element of period charm, unlike their rather belabored second incarnations.

The Deadly Hands of Kung Fu no. 4 (August 1974)

Cover: Neal Adams
Frontispiece: Al Milgrom
"Shang Chi, Master of Kung Fu: Circle of Serpent's Blood"—Doug Moench, Mike Vosburg/Al Milgrom
"The Dragon Has Entered"—Text/photo feature
"*Kung Fu* Revisited"—Text/photo feature
"Sons of the Tiger: Night of the Death Dream"—Gerry Conway, Don Perlin/Dan Adkins

The three cardinal rules for *The Deadly Hands of Kung Fu* seem to be as follows: Bruce Lee whenever possible; the *Kung Fu* TV show whenever possible, and Neal Adams covers whenever possible, at least for the first seventeen issues, of which he did eight. This issue follows all those rules to the letter. Adams's effort for this issue is a great David Carradine-in-action piece, Kwai Chang Caine spinning to face the reader as a fat cowboy is in mid-reel from one of Caine's deadly strikes. There's an accompanying feature, which has a nice balance of photos and illustrations. The *Enter the Dragon* piece might be obligatory, but it's still more interesting than either of the strips. When Paul Gulacy did *Master of Kung Fu*, the look might have been taken from Steranko, but at least the strip had its own look and mood, and while Vosburg and Milgrom were certainly very competent artists, they don't quite achieve that mood. The Sons of the Tiger isn't even good exploitation for a genre whose middle name is exploitation.

The Deadly Hands of Kung Fu no. 17 (October 1975)

Cover: Neal Adams
Frontispiece: Keith Giffen/Bob McLeod
"Shang Chi, Master of Kung Fu: The Key to the Dragon's Heart!" — Doug Moench, Rudy Nebres
"Robert Clouse: In Search of a Legend" — Walter Cichy (Interview)
"The Oriental World of Aaron Banks" — Roberto Fuentes (Text feature)
"Sons of the Tiger: The Politics of Death!" — Bill Mantlo, George Perez/Jack Abel

Here are three great trends that taste great together: a Neal Adams, Bruce Lee, *Enter the Dragon* front cover (the film's director is interviewed as well), a dynamically realistic depiction of the film's climactic kung fu duel in the house of mirrors (the scene itself was inspired by Orson Welles' *Lady from Shanghai*). Aaron Banks was a real-life martial arts expert in the mold of Chuck Norris.

Marvel Preview

Marvel Preview was intended as a launching pad, a tryout book to see if a character or strip would fly, or for stories that didn't really fit in the other titles. This was an idea that either catered to trends or attempted to create them (which it only did once, but that was enough — see *Marvel Preview* no. 2 below). After a mixed bag of 24 issues, the title was changed to *Bizarre Adventures,* but they weren't bizarre enough for the fans, and the title as a black-and-white magazine finally expired with no. 35. Other horror-themed issues besides the ones listed below include *Marvel Preview* no. 3, which had a cover by Gray Morrow and featured Blade the Vampire Slayer. Issue 8 was another one-shot for The Legion of Monsters and had great Mike Ploog art, and no. 12 was yet another stab at The Haunt of Horror, with Mike Kaluta and Gene Colan on hand for an anthology that was well done but failed to generate significant interest.

Marvel Preview (Featuring Man-Gods from Beyond the Stars) no. 1 (February 1975)

Cover: Neal Adams
Frontispiece: Easter Island statue photo
"Man-Gods from Beyond the Stars" — Doug Moench, Alex Nino
"Erich von Daniken: The Man Behind a Phenomenon" — Ed Summer (Text)
"The Chariots of Erich von Daniken" — Ed Summer (Text)
"The Books of the Gods" — Ed Summer (Book reviews)
"Good Lord!" — Marv Wolfman, Dave Cockrum/the Crusty Bunkers

Erich von Däniken was the first popular expositor of the theory that all of our notions of God are based on visitations from aliens, which was not a new theory, but one whose

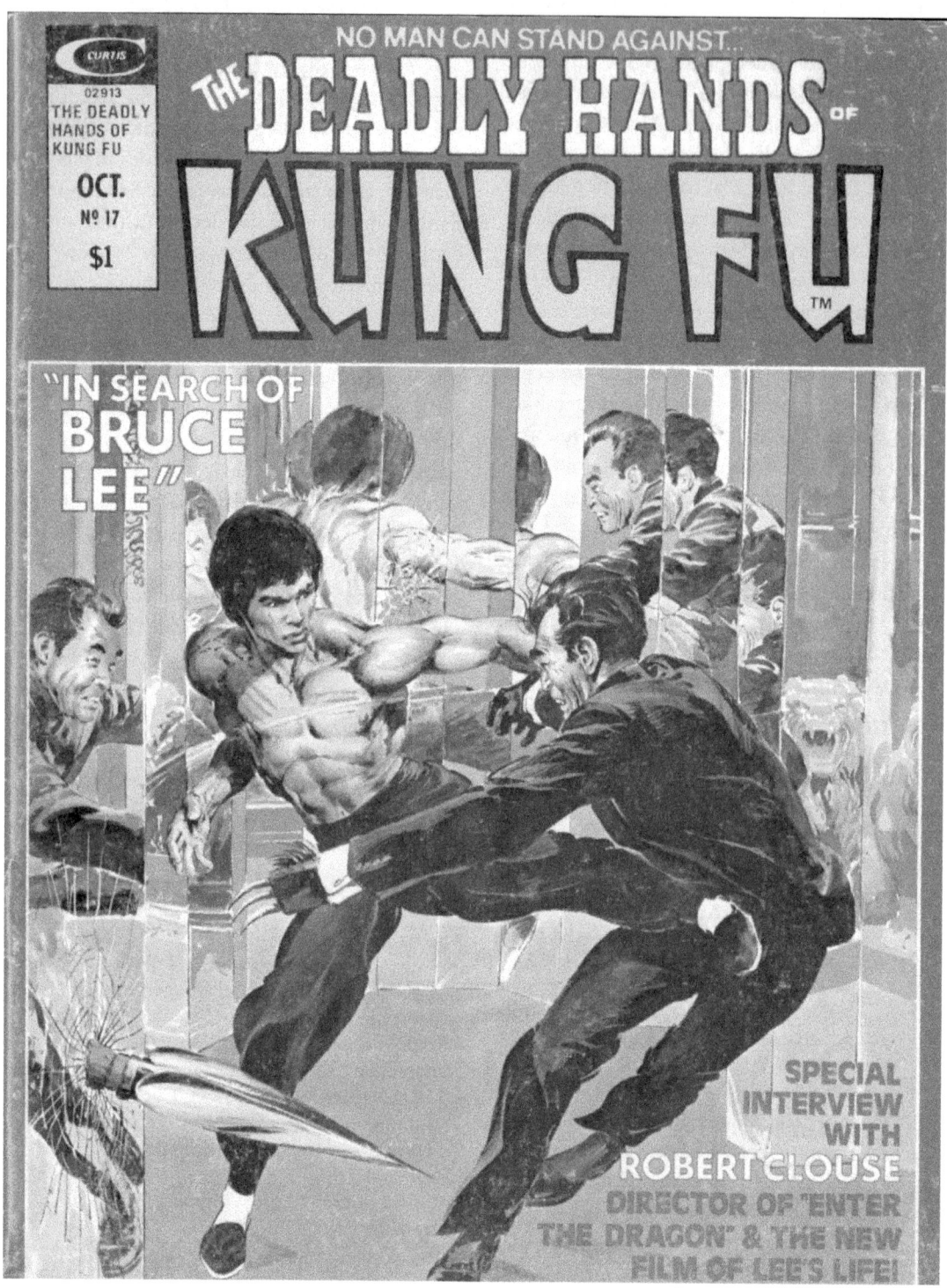

Deadly Hands of Kung Fu no. 17 (Marvel) — Three great trends that taste great together: Neal Adams, Bruce Lee, and Kung Fu (courtesy Marvel Entertainment, Inc.).

time of consideration would not happen until the cynical '70s. The lead story is an entertaining variation on that theme, made even more so by the usual mind-expanding artwork of Alex Nino. But the most enjoyable piece is the affectionate EC tribute, "Good Lord!"

Marvel Preview (Featuring the Punisher) no. 2 (April 1975)

Cover: Gray Morrow
Frontispiece: Howard Chaykin
"The Punisher: Death Sentence" — Gerry Conway, Tony DeZuniga
"Interview with *The Executioner*'s Don Pendleton" — David Anthony Kraft
"Dominic Fortune: The Power-Broker Resolution" — Len Wein, Howard Chaykin

Marvel Preview no. 2 has nothing to do with monsters, but this issue rates a mention simply because it presented the origin of a character who would become one of the most popular characters in the Marvel Universe of the '80s and '90s, the Punisher. Originally conceived as a long underwear knock-off of the very trendy "Mack Bolan — The Executioner" paperbacks, and Clint Eastwood's *Dirty Harry* and Charles Bronson's *Death Wish* movies, the character took a little time to build momentum, but later the Punisher became so popular that he carried three regular color titles, numerous specials, limited series, and one-shots, finally coming full circle and headlining a black-and-white title. The sixteen-issue run featured some dynamite painted covers, but the insides were merely reprints from the regular comics titles, with no new stories. Dominic Fortune is Chaykin's Scorpion character from Atlas Comics — everything but the name is exactly the same.

Marvel Preview (Featuring Satana) no. 7

Cover: Bob Larkin
Frontispiece: Vincente Alcazar
"Satana: The Damnation Waltz" — Chris Claremont, Vincente Alcazar
"From the Devil, a Daughter" — Chris Claremont (text); Mike Nasser, Esteban Maroto (Illustrations)
"Just a Little Over a Year Ago–Today" — Bill Mantlo (Text); Austin (Illustration)
"Witchworld" — Bill Mantlo, Keith Giffen

Satana was another Vampirella wannabe (see *Vampire Tales*) who couldn't make the grade, and although the art on both the strip and the accompanying text feature is pretty sweet, Alcazar is still no Maroto. Bill Mantlo also gets a text feature and a strip, and both are as derivative as most of his other work, although Keith Giffen, still searching for a style, does well on the second feature.

Marvel Preview (Featuring Masters of Terror) no. 16 (Fall 1978)

Cover: Tom Palmer, Gene Colan
Frontispiece: John Buscema
"The Hero Killer Principle" — Richard Marschall, Gene Colan/Tony DeZuniga
"Voices" — Marv Wolfman, Gene Colan/Tom Palmer
"The Rise of the Private Eye" — Ron Goulart (Text)
"Lilith: Death by Disco" — Steve Gerber, Gene Colan/Tony DeZuniga

The Masters of Terror concept had undergone somewhat of a re-definition. Whereas the two previous issues of the title had been devoted to adaptations by classic authors, not a classic is in sight here, although the Lilith story does have a certain amount of period kitsch appeal.

Marvel Preview (Featuring Blackmark) no. 17 (Winter 1979)

Cover: Romas
"Blackmark: The Mind Demons" — Gil Kane

The Winter 1979 issue carried a new book-length Blackmark saga by Gil Kane, a cause for celebration. But the question remains: Of the thousands of covers he executed for Marvel in the '70s, why couldn't he do one for the magazine which was devoted to his character? A grand tale, though — as always, Kane's art is impeccable, and having gotten the amazing origin of Blackmark out of the way, he was able to develop a little more character for the character.

Marvel Preview (Featuring Kull) no. 19 (Summer 1979)

Cover: Bob Larkin
Frontispiece: Ernie Chan (Chua)

"Kull: Riders beyond the Sunrise" (adapted from Robert E. Howard and Lin Carter) — Roy Thomas, Sal Buscema/Tony DeZuniga
"Tiger of Atlantis" — Jim Neal (Text feature)
"A Kull Portfolio" — John/Marie Severin (Illustrations)
"Solomon Kane: The Footfalls Within" (Robert E. Howard) — Don Glut, Will Meuginot/Steve Gan

This is the great lost fourth issue of *Kull and the Barbarians*, if you will. It reads like it, for sure, right down to the Kull text feature and John and Marie Severin's beautiful Kull portfolio. Roy Thomas is at the helm of the lead story, and Howard is at the root of both.

SCIENCE FICTION

Science fiction was born to be a trend, rising and falling in popularity in accordance with the technological advances of the times in which it is written. Although the form itself can take many directions (satirical, speculative, adventurous), science fiction at its core is one of two things — either a celebration or condemnation of those technological advances. At first, it was all celebration, an enthrallment with all of the ever-expanding technological advances of the early twentieth century, and much of the science fiction was of a predictive nature (television, men on the moon, etc.). In the year 2000, people would be flying to work with their own personal rocket packs, or could shuttle the family around in the family rocket ship. Adventure and romance soon joined the mix, which begat the space opera strain of science fiction, the most popular exponent being Edgar Rice Burroughs in the immortal John Carter of Mars series. Soon science fiction abounded with epics on a cosmic scale, including battles between exotic people, monsters and machines (and sometimes combinations of both), stretching across galaxies and planets both known and unknown. Throughout the '30s and '40s, this strain of the genre dominated the newsstands. Orson Welles scared the nation with the Mercury Theatre's dramatization of *War of the Worlds*. The hard science material was always there for those who knew where to look for it, but how was hard science supposed to compete with sexy girls being menaced by bug-eyed monsters? Everybody saw things a little differently, though, after Hiroshima.

Death rays and exotic weaponry had long been a part of science fiction, but the atom bomb was a real, deadly result of mad, weird science, and all of a sudden, all the horrible implications were no longer exotic. The genre became more cautionary than ever, spurred on by the now very realistic threat of man's self-annihilation, or the prospect of our lives being ruled by computers. There were still monsters, but now they were atomic mutations, or came from other worlds in flying saucers bent on conquering the earth, thinly disguised euphemisms for the communist threat. Hideous aliens (commies) would make us all faceless slaves, robbed of our free will. What a frightening prospect for the newly affluent post-war generation. As Ursula Le Guin so insightfully pointed out in her essay "Science Fiction Chauvinism" (*Ariel* no. 2, 1977):

> The only change presented by most Science Fiction literature has been towards authoritarianism, the domination of ignorant masses by a powerful elite — sometimes presented as a warning, but often quite complacently. Socialism is never considered as an alternative, and democracy is quite forgotten. Military values are taken as ethical ones. Wealth is assumed to be a righteous goal and a personal virtue. Competitive free-enterprise capitalism is the economic destiny of the entire Galaxy. In general, American Science Fiction has assumed a permanent hierarchy of superiors and inferiors, with the rich, ambitious, aggressive ... at the top ... and then at the bottom, the poor, the uneducated, the faceless masses....

Thirty years later, the only wording she would have had to change was the substitution of Society for Science Fiction, and it would no longer be speculation.

At the time of her essay, it was the fun that was in short supply. The space junk was there if you knew where to look for it, but the fun had gone out of it. Science fiction, like life itself, got to be pretty grim; faith was being lost in ideals and institutions faster than burglars could break into the Watergate. We found our government was capable of doing things we thought only other governments did. Science fiction had become science fact; technology was now inevitable, not a question of if but a question of when. The exploration of other worlds was now a reality as well. Man had landed on the moon, and now thoughts of exploration turned to thoughts of escape, in case humankind was stupid enough to blow itself up, a possibility which becomes more and more real as each day of the new millennium passes. The year 2000 came and went, and nobody was flying to work with a rocket pack, but more people than ever were fleeing from insane governments, crushing social inequality and the politics of fear. *Star Wars* brought back fun and space opera, but the fun was now accompanied by a very real sense of desperation, increasingly unstable world conditions making it seem as if each day might really be the last of society as we know it.

But this panic has not resulted in a rejection of the machines or the weapons. Instead, humanity has plugged itself in. We speak in electrical language. Science fiction has not only become science fact, it has become mainstream, an embrace of the technology, still with the grim undertones, but with the faint hope that if we do embrace the machines, they will save us instead of destroy us. To paraphrase Lester Bangs: Science fiction from the beginning was a genre born from those machines and electronic appendages, as much as from human hearts and minds. As a genre, it is more popular than ever, but also increasingly irrelevant. Science fiction has become the foremost victim of a cybernetic revolution spawned by itself, and technology once again closes the gap between frustration and profit.

WARREN SCIENCE FICTION

Spacemen

In the early 1960s, before humankind had landed on the moon, the space race was big news. If America didn't conquer the stars (and make the galaxy safe for that free-enterprise capitalism that Le Guin talked about), then the godless commies would, and either turn us all into zombies of the stratosphere or start peppering us with A-bombs. In such a context, astronauts were seen as the new heroes, the gallant scouts of the new frontier. It was only natural that Warren should exploit that fascination. The first companion magazine to *Famous Monsters* wasn't *Monster World*, it was *Spacemen*, and it enabled Forry to focus on his real love, science fiction. The magazine certainly bears his stamp, but it was no carbon copy of *Famous Monsters*, and perhaps therein laid the rub. The articles are a cross between his infectiously enthusiastic reminiscences and the dry, fact-filled style of *Screen Thrills Illustrated*, which didn't last much longer. Nevertheless, like *Famous Monsters*, it is a treasure trove of information and stills, with a couple of truly classic issues. The 1965 *Spacemen Yearbook* features the ultimate visualization of the "space age bachelor pad" concept, by Russ Jones and Wallace Wood. A pipe-smoking astronaut reclines on futuristic furniture, attended by a bevy of alien beauties. Perhaps Warren might have succeeded if there were more articles about John Glenn.

Spacemen no. 2 (September 1961)

Cover: Bruce Minney
"The Space Film Tele-scoop"—(Previews)
"The Phantom of the Space Opera"
"O'Henry's Comet"—Donald A. Wollheim (Fiction)
"How Mars Attacked the World"
"Wings of Tomorrow"
"How Do You Say Hello to a Martian?"—William F. Temple (Instructional)
"Jules Verne's Lost World"

The second issue finds the magazine still trying to appeal to the real-life space race fans with a straightforward (and just a little boring) astronaut cover by Bruce Minney, with blurbs like "Will there be war in space?" and silly filler like the "How Do You Say Hello to a Martian" feature, just in case the race got us there faster than we wanted. The problem with (*The Shape of*) *Things to Come* is that while it's imaginatively ambitious and visually extravagant, it's also ultimately a very boring film, a fact that must have disappointed those who had their hopes built up by all those great photos in *Spacemen*.

Spacemen no. 6 (January 1963)

Cover: Basil Gogos
"Time for Space"—(News and reviews)
Radar Men from the Moon—(Filmbook)
Buck Rogers—Sam Sherman (Filmbook)
"Through Time and Space with Donovan's Brain"—Forrest J Ackerman
"Spacemen of Distinction"—(Photo feature)
Metropolis—Forrest J Ackerman (Filmbook)
"The Monster Maker"—Leonard Spaulding (Fiction)
"Super Space"—Photo feature
Flying Disc Man from Mars—(Filmbook)
Journey to the 7th Planet—(Photo feature)

Spacemen no. 6 is the ultimate issue of the title, highly prized and desired among fans and collectors alike, and it's easy to understand why. The cover by Gogos features an iconic pose of that most iconic of serial heroes, and the inspiration for Dave Stevens's "Rocketeer," Commando Cody (or "Rocket Man," or even "Larry

Martin," if you will). The contents are a treat for serial lovers as well. No less than three classic chapter plays—*Radar Men from the Moon* (featuring Commando Cody), *Buck Rogers* (starring Buster "Flash Gordon" Crabbe), and *Flying Disc Man from Mars*—get the patented filmbook treatment, featuring many rare stills and movie graphics. Forry Ackerman contributes two articles: "Through Time and Space with Donovan's Brain" is a personal memory of that book's author, Curt Siodmak, who contributed mightily to the Universal Horror mythos as well, and he does a filmbook for his favorite movie, *Metropolis*. From cover to cover, the whole magazine is an informative and visual treat, one of the key issues of the golden age of monster magazines, and an essential building block in any self-respecting monster magazine collection.

Movie Aliens Illustrated (*Warren Presents* no. 8) (October 1979)

Cover: Space monster photo collage
Frontispiece: Basil Gogos
Alien
Journey to the 7th Planet
Night of the Blood Beast
The Green Slime
"The Movies Look at Other Worlds and Other Aliens"
"The Fun-tastic Adventures of Dr. Who"
Invasion of the Saucer Men

This was another collection of articles previously published in *Famous Monsters* and *Spacemen*. It's aimed at the new generation with Darth Vader on the cover, the *Alien* story, a reprint of Basil Gogos's "Tusken Raider" cover in black-and-white on the inside, and a *Dr. Who* story. It's also a nice introduction to some older classics for those newer fans. James Arness as the original *Thing (from Another World)*, the Saucer Men, and the creature from *Destination: Inner Space* make up the balance of the collage by John Stone on the cover. While many fans consider *Alien* to be the last word in "monster loose on a spaceship" movies, some fans still prefer two of its admitted inspirations—*It, the Terror from Beyond Space* (unfortunately not included in this issue) and *The Green Slime*, which fortunately is. *Slime* certainly has it all over *Alien* with that totally rockin' theme song, available on a 45, and needless to say, also a highly-prized relic of pop culture.

UFO and Alien Comix (*Warren Presents* no. 1) (1977)

Cover: James Warren/Kim McQuaite
"U.F.O."—Joseph Toutain, Ramon Torrents (*Vampirella* no. 62)
"The Pie: Daddy and the Pie"—Bill DuBay, Alex Toth (*Eerie* no. 64)
"The Pie: The Pie and I"—Budd Lewis, Luis Bermejo (*Eerie* no. 72)
"Companions to the Sun"—Bruce Jones, Leo Sanchez (*Vampirella* no. 61)
"The Generations of Noah"—R. McKenzie, Leo Duranona (*Creepy* no. 92)
"Visitation at Pliny Marsh"—Gerry Boudreau, Martin Salvador (*Creepy* no. 79)
"The Stars My Salvation"—Doug Moench, John Severin (*Creepy* no. 68)

Future World Comix (*Warren Presents* no. 2) (September 1978)

Cover: Larry Todd
"Starvisions"—Larry Todd (*Eerie* no. 72)
"Mates"—Doug Moench, Esteban Maroto (*Creepy* no. 64)
"Incident in the Beyond!"—Archie Goodwin, Gray Morrow (*Creepy* no. 3)
"Behold the Cybernite!"—Rich Margopolous, Tom Sutton (*Creepy* no. 46)
"The Taking of Queen Bovine"—Gerry Boudreau, Ramon Torrents (*Eerie* no. 81)
"Hunter 3"—Jim Stenstrum, Alex Nino (*Eerie* no. 87)
"Within You … Without You"—Bruce Jones, Richard Corben (*Eerie* no. 77)
"The Argo Standing By!"—Paul Neary (*Creepy* no. 73)

Starquest Comix
(*Warren Presents* no. 3)
(October 1978)

Cover: Ken Kelly
"Last Light of the Universe"— Budd Lewis, Esteban Maroto (*Creepy* no. 73)
"Epilogue"— Bill DuBay, Jose Ortiz (*Creepy* no. 73)
"Star Wars Revisited"— Kris Stulken, Deb Thompson, Ann Wilson (text)
"The Last Hero"— Steve Skeates, Ramon Torrents (*Creepy* no. 52)
"Unprovoked Attack on a Hilton Hotel"— Jim Stenstrum, Richard Corben (*Creepy* no. 73)
"Judas"— Rich Margopolous, Richard Corben (*Creepy* no. 62)
"War"— Roger McKenzie, Paul Neary (*Creepy* no. 81)

Galactic War Comix
(*Warren Presents* no. 4)
(December 1978)

Cover: Patrick Woodroffe
"Killer Hawk"— Bill DuBay, Wallace Wood (*Eerie* no. 61)
"Battlestar Galactica"— Terri Pinckard (Text)
"Star Slaughter"— Rich Margopolous, Ramon Torrents (*Creepy* no. 51)
"Star-Bright Lantern 909"— Gerry Boudreau, Jose Ortiz (*Vampirella* no. 48)
"The Time Eater!"— Jack Butterworth, Paul Neary (*Vampirella* no. 40)
"Mother Knows Best"— Bruce Jones, Al Williamson (*Creepy* no. 86)
"Now You See It...."— Bruce Jones, Al Williamson (*Creepy* no. 83)

Alien Invasions Comix
(*Warren Presents* no. 7)
(August 1979)

Cover: Kim McQuaite
"The Beast Is Yet to Come"— Nicola Cuti, Carmine Infantino/Alex Nino (*Vampirella* no. 59)
"It!"— Archie Goodwin, Dan Adkins (*Eerie* no. 7)
"The Mound"— Tom Sutton (*Eerie* no. 45)
"Alien"— Forrest J Ackerman (Text)
"The Man-Hunters"— Gerry Boudreau, Wallace Wood (*Eerie* no. 60)
"The Star Saga of Sirius Sam"— Nicola Cuti, John Severin (*Creepy* no. 95)
"Tibor Miko's Christmas"— Alex Toth (*Creepy* no. 77)

Empire Encounters Comix
(*Warren Presents* no. 12)
(November 1980)

Cover: Jim Laurier
"The Rubicon"— Budd Lewis, Pepe Moreno (*Creepy* no. 107)
"The Empire Strikes Gold"—(Text/photo feature)
"Gotterdammerung!" (Pt. 1)— Budd Lewis, Isidro Mones (*Eerie* no. 100)
"Gotterdammerung!" (Pt. 2)— Budd Lewis, Isidro Mones (*Eerie* no. 101)
"The Green"— Bruce Jones, Luis Bermejo (*Creepy* no. 96)
"Gravity Field"— Bob Toomey, Pepe Moreno (*Vampirella* no. 76)

Common threads that run through the preceding Warren collections are titles that are oh-so-close to a familiar movie title or term to capitalize on the current trend (*Alien, Star Wars, Battlestar Galactica*), and the fact that most of them are newer in vintage. There's some classic stuff all the way around for sure, but instead of half-a-dozen reprint mags, just one of new material would have sufficed, especially as it was the second or third time around for some of the stories.

Six • Crazy Kung Fu Apes Fight Space Wars

Famous Monsters no. 147 (Warren) — By this issue, even *Famous Monsters* had surrendered to not only one of the biggest trends of the '70s, but of all time. Can you guess what that is?

MARVEL

Unknown Worlds of Science Fiction

Unknown Worlds of Science Fiction was part of the second wave of Marvel monster mags that appeared just before the demise of the original line. It managed to survive the ax, although it, too, like the others that survived, would soon feel the sting of the blade.

Unknown Worlds of Science Fiction no. 1 (January 1975)

Cover: Frank Kelly Freas/John Romita Sr.
Frontispiece: Esteban Maroto
"Slow Glass (Prologue)" (based on concepts by Bob Shaw) — Tony Isabella, Gene Colan
"The Day of the Triffids (Pt. 1)" (adapted from John Wyndham) — Gerry Conway, Ross Andru/Ernie Chua (Chan)
"A View from Without" — Neal Adams
"The Bradbury Chronicles" — Shel Dorf (Interview)
"Smash Gordon" — Frank Brunner
"Savage World" — Wallace Wood/Al Williamson
"Frank Kelly Freas: Past and Present Master" — G. Conway (interview)
"Hey Buddy, Can You Lend Me a...." — Mike Kaluta
"Slow Glass: Epilogue — Light of Other Days" — Isabella, Colan/Esposito

Marvel surely could put together a great first issue. Yet again Marvel assembled an all-star team, and proved it could play at Warren's level if it really tried. Thoughtful science fiction might have been in vogue, but nothing sells like sex or monsters, so Freas and Romita's cover has the young, hip '70s couple menaced by a classic bug-eyed monster. The magazine probably would have been more successful had it been launched a couple of years later, but the black-and-white line was on its last legs by this time, so it's not only surprising the magazine came out, but that Marvel took this much care with it. It's not all great — unfortunately, the featured story, an adaptation of *Day of the Triffids*, doesn't come off that well. Nor does "Smash Gordon," which was done funnier elsewhere.

Unknown Worlds of Science Fiction no. 2 (March 1975)

Cover: Mike Kaluta
Frontispiece: Alex Nino
"Slow Glass: Epilogue — Through a Glass Slowly" — Tony Isabella, Frank Brunner/Klaus Janson
"War Toy" — Isabella, George Perez
"Alfred Bester: There Are No Yesterdays" — Denny O'Neil (Interview)
"Adam and Eve" (adapted from Alfred Bester) — Denny O'Neil, Frank Robbins
"The Hunter and the Hunted" — Mike Kaluta
"Science Fiction, Fans, and the Hugo" — Don Thompson (Text)
"Specimen" — Bruce Jones
"The Day of the Triffids (Pt. 2)" (adapted from John Wyndham) — Gerry Conway, Rico Rival

Unknown Worlds of Science Fiction no. 3 (May 1975)

Cover: Michael Whelan
Frontispiece: Gray Morrow
"Slow Glass: The Star-Magi" — Tony Isabella, Gene Colan
"Occupation Force" (adapted from Frank Herbert) — Gerry Conway, George Perez
"Not Long Before the End" (adapted from Larry Niven) — Doug Moench, Vincente Alcazar
"Frank Herbert: Sandworms and Saviors" — Ed Leimbacher (Interview)
"Gestation" — Bruce Jones
"S.F.W.A. — The Thing That Spawned Nebulas" — Don Thompson (Text)

"'Repent, Harlequin,' said the Ticktockman"—(adapted from Harlan Ellison) Roy Thomas, Alex Nino

The Ellison story is one of his best, and it gets a fittingly fine adaptation in this issue courtesy of Roy Thomas and Alex Nino. Bruce Jones, a giant in the genre, contributes another of his patented twisted tales. He was one of the few talents whose work always provided the joyful dilemma of "is he a better writer or artist?"

Unknown Worlds of Science Fiction no. 4 (July 1975)

Cover: Frank Brunner
Frontispiece: Robert L. Kline
"Slow Glass: The Trial of Mr. Tyme"—Tony Isabella, Don Heck
"Enchanted Village" (adapted from A.E. Van Vogt)—Don/Maggie Thompson, Dick Giordano
"A.E. Van Vogt: The Dreaming Kind"—Alan Brennert (Interview)
"A Vision of Venus" (adapted from Otis A. Kline)—David Anthony Kraft (Introduction), Tim Conrad
"FANtastic Worlds"—Don/Maggie Thompson (text), Robert Kline (Illustrations)
"Good News from the Vatican" (Silverberg)—Gerry Conway, Ading Gonzales
"Encounter at War"—Jan Strnad, Richard Corben
"Kick the Can"—Bruce Jones

Thoughtful science fiction may have been in vogue, but if you want to sell a magazine, put a monster on the cover. Frank Brunner responds with a classic bug-eyed monster. The last two tales have a distinct Warren flavor, as they are handled by longtime Warren contributors Jan Strnad, Richard Corben and Bruce Jones. Otis Adelbert Kline was an Edgar Rice Burroughs imitator whom Burroughs in turn imitated with his Carson of Venus stories.

Unknown Worlds of Science Fiction no. 5 (September 1975)

Cover: Puigdomenech
Frontispiece: Howie Chaykin
"Slow Glass Revisited"—Roy Thomas, Gene Colan
"Paradise Found"—Bruce Jones, Gray Morrow
"The Many, Many Worlds of Larry Niven"—Alan Brennert (Interview)
"All the Myriad Ways" (Niven)—Howie Chaykin
"FANtastic Worlds"—Don/Maggie Thompson (Text), Mike Kaluta (Illustrations)
"Addict"—Don Glut, Nestor Redondo
"Half-Life"—John Allison
"Slow Glass: Epilogue"—Thomas, Colan/Chiaramonte

Howard Chaykin hates to be called "Howie," but Howie is how he's listed. He did a nice job on the frontispiece and with Niven's "All the Myriad Ways," the best stuff in a good issue. The cover features an awfully Vampirella-looking sexy space chick carrying an astronaut's head in a bag—the other good way to sell a magazine.

Unknown Worlds of Science Fiction no. 6 (December 1975)

Cover: Frank Brunner
Frontispiece: Pat Broderick
"Slow Glass: One Giant Leap for Mankind"—Roy Thomas, Gene Colan
"Behold the Man" (adapted from Michael Moorcock)—Doug Moench, Alex Nino
"Through a Glass Slowly"—Bob Shaw (Text), Gary Brodsky, Brian Moore (Illustrations)
"Old Soldier"—Bruce Jones
"Mind Games"—John Allison
"Visitation"—Don Glut, Rueben Yandoc

By now, you're probably wondering just what all of this "Slow Glass" stuff is about. In short, it's a convoluted time-space continuum theory that is a load of bollocks, but it conveniently makes your stories work out the way you want them to. Better to delve into the adaptation of "Behold the Man," which features superior scripting and art, and is the subject of an excellent Frank Brunner crucifixion cover.

Unknown Worlds of Science Fiction Special no. 1 (1976)

Cover: Don Newton
Frontispiece: Rick Bryant
"A Martian Odyssey" (adapted from Stanley Weinbaum) — Don Glut, Yandoc
"Journey's End" — Bruce Jones, Alex Nino
"The Forest for the Trees" — Bruce Jones, Vincente Alcazar
"Fantastic Worlds" — Don/Maggie Thompson (Text); Kaluta (Illustration)
"Clete" — Bruce Jones (Story/art)
"Preservation of the Species" — Bruce Jones, Nestor Redondo
"Sinner" — Archie Goodwin (Story/art)
"Arena" (adapted from Frederic Brown) — Gerry Conway, John Buscema/Dick Giordano
"Threads" — Mat Warrick, Gonzales

Unknown Worlds of Science Fiction survived the Summer of Death, but not for long. This was actually an inventory issue, sized like an annual, but with all-new material. The covers came full circle with Don Newton's giant bug-eyed monster. Bruce Jones was all over the place, writing four of the stories, and even finding time to illustrate one of them himself. His best teamwork is with Alex Nino on "Journey's End." An added bonus is a story written and drawn by Archie Goodwin, whose writing talents have always received the praise that they richly deserve, but whose art has often been overlooked. Possessed of an idiosyncratic style that's actually quite underground and an instinctive understanding of graphic storytelling, his story "Sinner," although not artistically as slick as the mag's other offerings, was easily the best thing in the issue.

Planet of the Apes

Until the release of *Star Wars* and its succeeding sequels, the most popular and successful science fiction movie series of all time was the *Planet of the Apes* series. The original, starring Charlton Heston, was a box-office smash that not only spawned four follow-up films, but a television series. Naturally (although the amount pales in comparison to the number of modern movie tie-ins), every variety of merchandise that could be conceived — models, toys, Halloween outfits, trading cards — went ape. The Statue of Liberty scene is an unforgettable, indelible moment of cinema. The much-loved series, which combined realistic ape makeup and wild sci-fi action with witty dialogue and sometimes accurate, sometimes heavy-handed social commentary and satire, survived beyond the trend phase and achieved pop culture icon status, a status only slightly dimmed by the lackluster Tim Burton remake.

Planet of the Apes no. 1 (August 1974)

Cover: Bob Larkin
"Terror on the Planet of the Apes" — Gerry Conway/Doug Moench, Mike Ploog
"Escape from the Battle for the Conquest Beneath the Planet of the Apes: An Overview of the *Apes* series" — Gary Gerani (Text/photo feature)
"Rod Serling Recalls" — David Johnson (Interview)
"The Face of the Apes" — Ed Lawrence (Text/photo feature)
"Planet of the Apes" (Pt. 1, adapted from the 20th Century–Fox film) — Moench, George Tuska/Mike Esposito

Surprisingly, Marvel was slow to exploit the *Apes* phenomenon. By the time the first issue of the magazine appeared, all of the movies of the motion picture series had already been made, although their popularity had not yet abated, and the TV show was

Movie Monsters no. 2 (Atlas/Seaboard) — *The Planet of the Apes* was everywhere in the early '70s, including this cover of Atlas/Seaboard's short-lived but solid *Movie Monsters* (portrait of the sly simian Dr. Zaius by Greg Theakston).

just getting off the ground. Marvel made up for lost time by making *Planet of the Apes* no. 1 a real treat for *Apes* fans — all *Apes*, all new (no silly '50s reprints about killer gorillas), all the time. Bob Larkin provides yet another dynamite, photo-realistic cover painting, working in more muted tones than usual that perfectly capture the look of the films. Mike Ploog and the Tuska/Esposito team, who work on the original story and the film adaptation respectively, also capture that feel and look in different ways.

Planet of the Apes no. 2 (October 1974)

Cover: Bob Larkin
Frontispiece: Art/photo montage
"Terror on the Planet of the Apes: The Forbidden Zone of Forgotten Terror" — Doug Moench, Mike Ploog
"The City of the Apes" — Ed Lawrence (Text/photo feature)
"Simian Genesis" — Gary Gerani (Review)
"Michael Wilson: The 'Other' *Apes* Writer" — David Johnson (Interview)
"Planet of the Apes, Pt. 2: World of Captive Humans" (adapted from the 20th Century–Fox film) — Doug Moench, George Tuska/Mike Esposito

Like the movie series itself, this was an issue of sequels. Doug Moench and Mike Ploog (far and away the perfect artist for the strip) continue their original epic, "Terror on the Planet of the Apes," which certainly would have made a better movie than the Burton remake. Moench is also pretty faithful in his movie adaptation, although he still had to "Marvel it up" here and there. Lines like "Take your hands off me, you damn dirty ape" are still there, although not quite as effective as they would be if the character was drawn to look like Heston.

Planet of the Apes no. 3 (December 1974)

Cover: Bob Larkin
Frontispiece: Photo from *Planet of the Apes*
"Terror on the Planet of the Apes: Spawn of the Mutant Pit" — Doug Moench, Mike Ploog/Frank Chiaramonte
"Journey to the Planet of the Apes" — Chris Claremont (Review)
"McDowall: The Man Behind the Mask" — Sam Maronie (Interview)
"Planet of the Apes, Pt. 3: Manhunt" (adapted from the 20th Century–Fox film) — Moench, George Tuska/Mike Esposito

Frank Chiaramonte is added to the art team for the monster-filled conclusion of "Terror on the Planet of the Apes." He was a great inker for Ploog because, like Tom Sutton, he didn't try to walk all over his style — like any good inker, he complemented it. Sam Maronie conducts an amusing interview with Roddy McDowall, the real face of the Apes series, who didn't seem to mind at all that he would be primarily remembered for that more than his Oscar-winning role as a child actor in *How Green Was My Valley*.

Planet of the Apes no. 4 (January 1975)

Cover: Bob Larkin
Frontispiece: Photo from *Planet of the Apes*
"A Riverboat Named Simian" — Doug Moench, Mike Ploog/Frank Chiaramonte
"A Half-hour with Harper" — Chris Claremont (interview)
"*Planet of the Apes* Fashions" — Ed Lawrence
"Planet of the Apes, Pt. 4: The Trial" (adapted from the 20th Century–Fox film) — Moench, George Tuska/Mike Esposito

Planet of the Apes no. 5 (February 1975)

Cover: Bob Larkin
Frontispiece: Photo from *Planet of the Apes*

"Evolution's Nightmare"—Doug Moench, Ed Hannigan/Jim Mooney
"An Interview with Dan Streipke"—Sam Maronie
"The Man Who Sold *The Planet of the Apes*"—Gary Gerani
"Planet of the Apes, Pt. 5: Into the Forbidden Zone" (adapted from the 20th Century–Fox film)—Doug Moench, George Tuska/Mike Esposito

Planet of the Apes no. 6 (March 1975)

Cover: Bob Larkin
Frontispiece: Photo from *Planet of the Apes*
"Malaguena in a Zone Forbidden"—Doug Moench, Mike Ploog
"Mark Lenard: Urko Unleashed" Chris Claremont (Interview)
"Ape for a Day"—Sam Maronie (Text)
"Planet of the Apes, Pt. 6: The Secret" (adapted from the 20th Century–Fox film)—Doug Moench, George Tuska/Mike Esposito

Planet of the Apes no. 11 (August 1975)

Cover: Gray Morrow
Frontispiece: Photo from *Planet of the Apes*
"When the Lawgiver Returns"—Doug Moench, Mike Ploog
"Outlines of Tomorrow"—Jim Whitmore (Text)
"Holocaust of Hell"—Doug Moench, Alfredo Alcala

A year later, and the book was still going strong—Moench was still chronicling both Apes adventures, and Alfredo Alcala was on board, soon to become a regular.

Planet of the Apes no. 14 (November 1975)

Cover: Michael McN
Frontispiece: Photo from *Planet of the Apes*
"Up the Nose Tube to Monkey Trash"—Doug Moench, Mike Ploog
"Shaping a Simian World"—Sam Maronie (Text)
"Escape from the Planet of the Apes, Pt. 3: Trouble in Paradise Lost" (adapted from the 20th Century–Fox film)—Doug Moench, Rico Rival

Breaking away from the Bob Larkin tradition was this eye-catching, luridly-colored cover by "Michael McN," who couldn't seem to find himself. On his next effort, he's billed simply as "McN," and for his next, "Malcolm McN."

Planet of the Apes no. 15 (December 1975)

Cover: Bob Larkin
Frontispiece: Photo from *Planet of the Apes*
"Dreamer in Emerald Silence"—Doug Moench, Tom Sutton
"Escape from the Planet of the Apes, Pt. 4: In the Cradle of a Father's Sins" (adapted from the 20th Century–Fox film)—Doug Moench, Rico Rival

Planet of the Apes no. 19 (April 1976)

Cover: Bob Larkin
Frontispiece: Photo from *Planet of the Apes*
"Terror on the Planet of the Apes, Phase Two: Demons of the Psyche Drome"—Doug Moench, Mike Ploog/Tom Sutton
"Simian Visions"—Jim Whitmore (Text)
"Conquest of the Planet of the Apes, Pt. 4: The Savage Is King!" (adapted from the 20th Century–Fox film)—Doug Moench, Alfredo Alcala

The previous adaptation of an Apes film, *Escape from the Planet of the Apes*, had been somewhat of a letdown, but the adaptations fall right back into line here with Alcala taking over the art chores for *Conquest*. Mike Ploog was back for the sequel to "Terror on the Planet of the Apes," but didn't stick around to finish it, although Tom Sutton was certainly the man for the job, and he was there until the end.

Planet of the Apes no. 20 (May 1976)

Cover: McN
"Terror on the Planet of the Apes, Phase Two: Secrets of the Psyche Drome"—Doug Moench, Tom Sutton
"SPFX on the Planet of the Apes"—James Glenn (Text)
"Conquest of the Planet of the Apes, Pt. 5: Army of Slaves" (adapted from the 20th Century–Fox film)—Doug Moench, Alfredo Alcala

Planet of the Apes no. 22 (July 1976)

Cover: Earl Norem
Frontispiece: Photo from *Escape from the Planet of the Apes*
"Quest for the Planet of the Apes, Pt. 1: Seeds of Future Deaths"—Doug Moench, Rico Rival
"Thirteen Decades of Ape"—Jim Whitmore (Text)
"Maurice Evans: From Shakespeare to Simian"- Robert Cleveland (Text)
"Quest for the Planet of the Apes, Pt. 2: Keepers of Future Deaths"—Doug Moench, Alfredo Alcala

Planet of the Apes no. 29 (February 1977)

Cover: Malcolm McN
Frontispiece: Pat Broderick
"Future History Chronicles V: To Race the Death Winds"—Doug Moench, Tom Sutton
"The 10th Anniversary of *Planet of the Apes*"—Sam Maronie (Text)
"Kim Hunter: The Woman Behind the Ape"—Sam Maronie (Text)
"From Simians to Sharks"—Sam Maronie (Text)

Give *Planet of the Apes* credit—it hung around a couple of years after the last movie and the TV series had become memories, not to mention most of the other Marvel magazine group, so it had something. Unfortunately, this, the last issue, leaves us with not much of that something. There's only one comic strip in the whole magazine; three rather dry articles by Sam "Bony" Maronie take up the rest. At least Doug Moench was still around. He'd been there from the start, and Tom Sutton had worked with Ploog on this and other strips, and their styles complemented each other so perfectly that Sutton was the logical artist to follow Ploog.

*Star*Reach*

"A new genre ... the unique synthesis of underground and overground comics ... Ground Level Comics" was the self-description of *Star*Reach* in an ad in issue no. 6, and at the time, that was right. The format was unique, too—it was larger than a regular comic, but not as big as a magazine; it had color covers, but was printed in black-and-white. As the editorial from issue no. 1 states in its "declaration of principles":

> Followers of the straight "overground" comics have probably noticed that some comics have become more sophisticated in their art and storytelling. The reason has been an influx of younger artists and writers ... who wanted to push the readership levels beyond the strictly juvenile strata into which comics had always appeared petrified. However, straight comics are geared as clockwork production efforts. They are "periodicals" and as such have schedules and deadlines. They are also operating a one-time, up-front, we-keep-all-the-rights-payment system.
>
> Until recently, the straight artists and writers had only two alternatives: submit to the hampering system, or get out of the field. However, out here on the west coast, undergrounders like Crumb, Corben, Shelton, Metzger, Holmes and all the others have shown them that they can do the comics material they want to do, worry about their own heads rather than the Sioux Falls ten-year old, and be paid on a royalty or percentage basis. If they make the work good enough to please even half the people they do with their straight work, they come out financially ahead. And their concepts, characters and artwork remain

theirs ... and so they work that much harder to make them better.

Not only did *Star*Reach* have a big influence on the creators' rights movement, but on the style of story that would become "overground" in another generation. It was considerably more daring than the normal black-and-white mag, but never adopted the vulgarity-for-its-own-sake tactics that characterized some of the undergrounds. The other difference was that whereas most of the people mentioned (except Corben) were staunch undergrounders, *Star*Reach* had some of the best young "overground" talent working for Marvel or Warren or the other black-and-white straight periodicals, names that would be more recognizable to the audience the magazine was trying to enlighten. Issue 2 featured *Stephanie Starr*, a sort of Modesty Blaise meets the aliens with many evolutions and consciousness changes by Dick Giordano, accompanied by a Neal Adams cover. No. 3 starred Dragonus, a barbarian by Frank Brunner that had appeared in the overground Monsters Unleashed. Not to give anything away, but let's just say the ending is a bad idea for creating a successful character that could make you a lot of scratch. *Star*Reach* 6 has a great Jeff Jones cover featuring Elric of Melnibone, and again is as good as anything he did for the Zebra Robert E. Howard books. Ray Bradbury and Alex Nino are also teamed, the latter illustrating the former's ruminations on the Mars landing of Viking One. No. 7 has a cover with Barry Smith at his most art nouveau.

*Star*Reach* no. 1 (1974)

Cover: Howard Chaykin
Back cover: Jim Starlin
"The Birth of Death!" — Jim Starlin
"Death Building" — Jim Starlin
"Fish Myths" — Steve Skeates
"Suburban Fish" — Steve Skeates
"A Tale of Sword and Sorcery" — Ed Hicks, Walt Simonson
"Cody Starbuck" — Howard Chaykin
"The Origin of God!" — Jim Starlin

The ambitious first issue of *Star*Reach* had acid-crazed Jim Starlin speculating on the amazing "Origin of God," while Walt Simonson gets to parody all the sword-and-sorcery work he'd been doing. Howard Chaykin is on hand with still another version of his Scorpion/Dominic Fortune character, this time situated in outer space and renamed Cody Starbuck, but don't let the name fool you. There's a lot more sex and cussing than coffee on this rogue's menu.

CHARLTON

Having failed with its forays into monster movie magazine territory, Charlton added a few black-and-white comics magazines to its publishing line in the '70s, based on popular TV shows. The magazines all employed solid talent, and featured some well-done adaptations and/or extrapolations, but only lasted as long as the interest in the shows did, which wasn't long.

The Six Million Dollar Man

In 1976, the U.S. had its bicentennial. The country was getting all patriotic and misty-eyed, and after having been burned by Nixon and Watergate, was searching for a hero, someone who could restore its faith in secret government agencies and misuse of taxpayers' dollars. *The Six Million Dollar Man* was not a series about an overpaid professional athlete; rather, it was based on the novel *Cyborg*, written by Martin Caidin, and was the story of Steve Austin, an astronaut who had been fatally mangled in a high-speed test flight. "We can rebuild him ... make him better ... faster ... stronger" went the opening narration, thereby setting the stage across the world for kids to imitate the slow-motion feats of super-strength and phased sound effects that were the show's trademark. The show starred Lee Majors, whose biggest small-screen success to that date had been *The Big Valley*, which had also starred Barbara Stanwyck, Linda Evans, Richard Long and Peter Breck. Among an ensemble cast of accomplished actors, Majors was able to blend in. But forced to shoulder the load in his own series, his earnest-but-wooden acting style was not enough. Richard Dean Anderson (*Forbidden Planet*) provided able support, and the series even had a spin-off, *The Bionic Woman*, which turned out to be more popular than the original, perhaps because Lindsay Wagner was prettier than Lee Majors and a better actress. Repetitious plots and special effects ultimately did in both series, and the Cyborg law-enforcement officer concept was much more successfully explored (and darkly parodied) a decade later in the movie *Robocop*.

The Six Million Dollar Man no. 1 (July 1976)

Cover: Neal Adams
"Lee Majors: The Six Million Dollar Man"—(Text/photo biography feature)
"The Cyborg Is Born"—Joe Gill, Continuity Associates
"An Eye for Details"—Joe Gill, Continuity Associates
"Lindsay Wagner: The Bionic Woman"—(Text/photo biography feature)
"The Deadly Raven"—Nicola Cuti, Continuity Associates

"Richard Anderson: He 'Owns' the Six Million Dollar Man!"—(Text/photo biography feature)
"Escape from Shark Island"—Mike Pellowski, Continuity Associates
"Your Day on the Set of The *Six Million Dollar Man*"—(Text/photo feature)

Continuity Associates was (and is) the name of Neal Adams's art studio; the credits list the members of the organization at that time, but no individual art credits are given on any of the stories, which would be impossible as different artists contributed bits and pieces to all of the strips. The members of Continuity Associates who were on staff or worked on the first issue of *The Six Million Dollar Man* are as follows: Neal Adams, Steve Austin, Terry Austin, Joe Barney, Joe Brozowski, Rick Bryant, Karin Daugherty, Dick Giordano, Klaus Janson, Bruce Patterson, Carl Potts, Mark Rice, Josef Rubenstein.

Artistically, the first issue of the run is above reproach; Neal Adams's staff had some crackerjack talent, and the whole book bears his influence, even in panels he didn't draw. The writing doesn't come off as well, but that's mostly due to the character's built-in limitations. His personality actually came off better in print than it did on screen, mostly because of Majors's built-in limitations as an actor.

The Six Million Dollar Man no. 7 (November 1977)

Cover: Earl Norem
Writers: Joe Gill, Mike Pellowski
Art: The Jack Sparling studio
"Steve Austin's Photo Scrapbook"—(Photo feature)
"Deadlier Than the Male"
"Nothing Can 'Bar' the Six-Million Dollar Man"—(Photo feature)
"The Ten-Minute Time Limit"
"An Alien Charm"

The ubiquitous Earl Norem supplies the cover for what would be the last issue; the TV

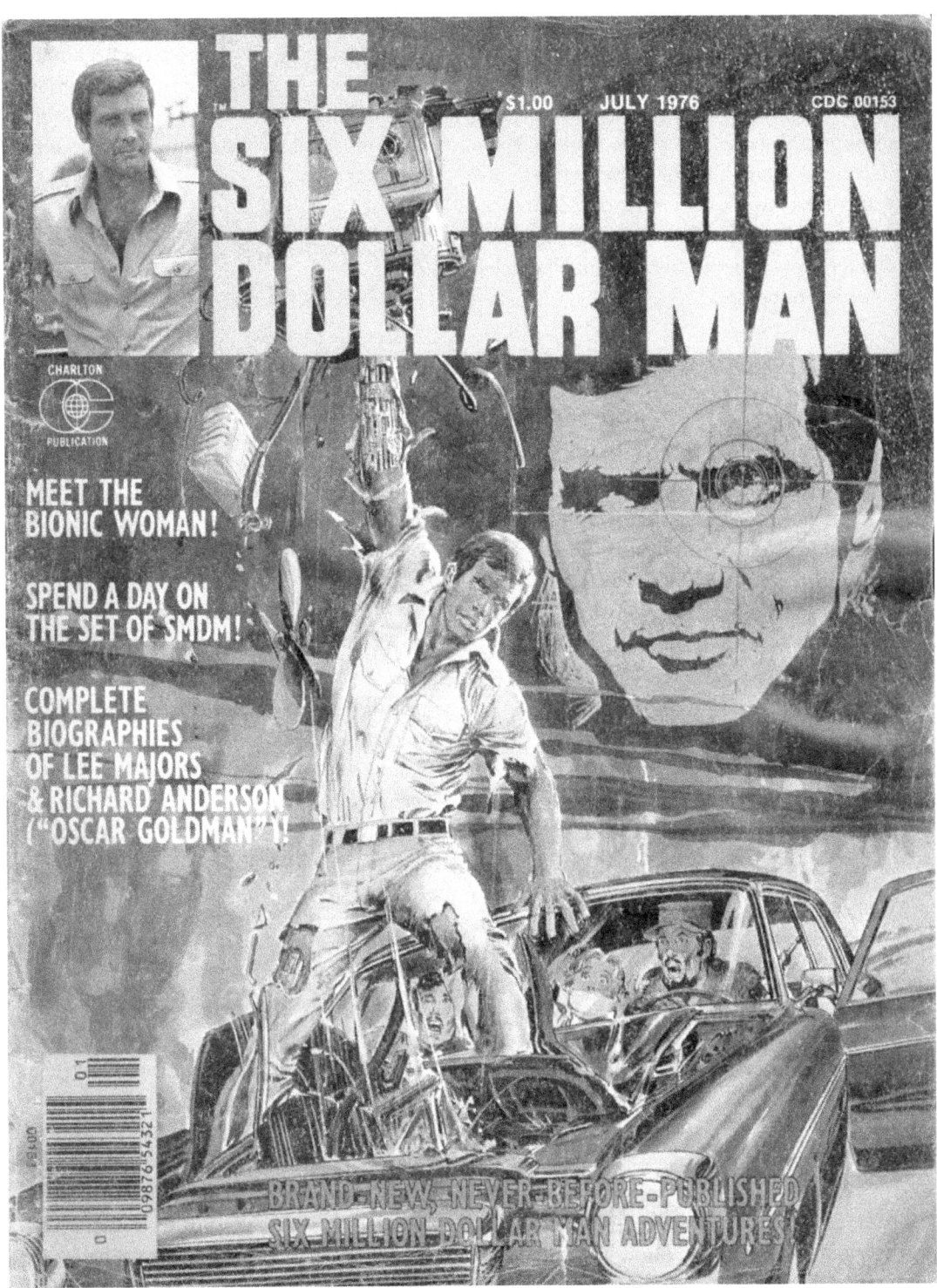

Six Million Dollar Man no. 1 (Charlton)—"We can make him better, faster, stronger...." The mantra for the *Six Million Dollar Man* didn't quite translate to the magazine of the same name, but it featured a mighty Neal Adams cover.

series had run its popularity course. The art was now being handled by the Jack Sparling studio. In the first issue, although Adams's style is dominant, the others' styles show through; this issue basically looks like Sparling did it all himself. The gritty style is in direct contrast to the slick work of Continuity, but works just as well for the character, first and foremost an action hero, despite the technological trappings.

Space: 1999

Space: 1999 was a popular British import of the '70s; it had engaging and talented actors in the leads (The *Mission: Impossible* husband-and-wife-team of Martin Landau and Barbara Bain), with the emphasis on thoughtful and cerebral science fiction rather than the sex-and-action antics of Captain Kirk. The show lasted longer than *The Six Million Dollar Man*, but the magazine lasted only about a year.

Space: 1999 no. 1 (November 1975)

Cover: Gray Morrow
Writers: Joe Gill, Nicola Cuti
Art editor: Gray Morrow
"How *Space: 1999* Was Born"—(Photo/text feature)
"The Last Moonrise"
"Seeds of Doubt"
"Finding a Home"—(Photo/text feature)
"Cornucopia"
"Visiting the Stars"—(Photo/text feature)
"Endgame"

Launched simultaneously with a color comic of the same name, both ended a year later, but the magazine published one more issue in that space of time. The magazine had the same format as *The Six Million Dollar Man*; strips mixed with photo features on the show and its actors and such, but was more interesting because it had better source material to work with. Gray Morrow is the art editor, but like the Sparling studio work on Six Million Dollar Man no. 7, it looks like he did pretty much all of it himself; it is as accomplished as usual.

Space: 1999 no. 8 (October 1976)

Cover: Gray Morrow
Writers: Joe Gill, Nicola Cuti, Mike Pellowski
Art editor: Gray Morrow
"Catherine Schell: A New Star in Our Galaxy"—(Photo/text bio feature)
"The Metamorph"
"Man-Made Moons"—Mike Pellowski (Text)
"The Primary Life Form"
"Scanning the Solar System"—Mike Pellowski (Text)

Gray Morrow is still the art editor, and contributes an absolutely stunning cover; Charlton maintained high standards from start to finish. Perhaps because it was the last issue, there is only one feature article connected with the actual show. "Man-Made Moons" and "Scanning the Solar System" are hard science articles that were unusual for a magazine of this type.

Man, Myth & Magic

In the 1970s a television show called *In Search of...* was hosted by Leonard Nimoy. The title ended with an ellipsis because each week featured a different subject, real-life monsters, legends and mysteries, such as Bigfoot, The Loch Ness Monster, Stonehenge, or the statues on Easter Island. The theories and investigations were given further credibility by Mr. Spock himself—after all, who better to explain the mysteries of the universe than one who had traveled it, or was at least willing to capitalize on that notion? *Man, Myth, and Magic* was a magazine version of the show. Not literally, but it dealt with explaining and exploring facts. Originally published in the U.K, it was released through Marshall Cavendish USA Ltd, and was literally encyclopedic in scope—112 weekly issues, starting with "A" and ending with "Z."

Man, Myth, and Magic

Cover: Photo of Christopher Lee as Dracula
"Films"
"Fingers"
"Finland"

A representative issue of the run, included here because of its snazzy cover featuring Christopher Lee's Dracula riding the red-eye express. The "Film" chapter is rather dry and perfunctory, but the entry for Finland is subtitled "The Struggle of Light and Darkness" and is rather interesting.

True-Weird

The odd and sometimes twisted little dollops of information that Robert Ripley doled out for years have become an American institution. The four-color comic book bearing his name had a long run, despite initial confusion as to what exactly to call the book. It began life in June 1965 as *Ripley's Believe It or Not! True Ghost Stories* and retained that title for two issues, when it became *Ripley's Believe It or Not! True War Stories*, an experiment that lasted one. Then it became simply *Ripley's Believe It or Not!* but still carried *True Ghost Stories* as a subtitle. This was the title that it carried unto its grave in 1980. An attempt to cash in on the success of *Creepy* was far less successful. *(Ripley's Believe It or Not) True Weird* lasted for only two issues, and is included in the "Trends" chapter for that reason. It's tough to place this one—it's black-and-white, and it certainly illustrates some weird things, but it's not really a continuity-type comic, except for an awful strip ("The $120,000,000 Dream Ghost") by someone who was rightly too embarrassed to sign his work. Ripley was a highly technically proficient artist, whose illustrations never got as weird as some of the incidents described, but this magazine certainly tried to make things appear as gruesome as possible to the prospective customer. The two covers featured a mad mummy and a shrunken head, and only the most horrible titles were spotlighted. But it was not weird enough for the target audience, and too weird for Ripley's normal fan base, which obviously preferred the Code-approved safety of the four-color comic.

(Ripley's Believe It or Not) True-Weird no. 2 (August 1966)

Cover: Photo of shrunken head
Frontispiece: "Ripley's Believe It or Not"
"Beware the Man with the Flaming Scar!"
"The Living Carpet"
"Executed Four Times"
"Iron Maiden"
"*True-Weird* Treasury of Horror, Pt. 2 — Heads of State: Strange Tales"
"Death Rang for the Bell-Maker's Daughter"
"Othello's Tower"
"Ripley's Supernatural Oddities"
"The $120,000,000 Dream Ghost"— Story/art unaccredited
"Escaped with Socks!"
"Death Vigil"
"The Devil's Castle"
"The Best of Ripley's Cartoons"
"Strong Neck"

It was not really that weird, but still had some nutty stuff, like the following tidbit: "The Living Carpet"—"Mohammed's birthday is celebrated in Cairo by the Grand Sheriff riding to church over the bodies of his parishioners—Anyone who is hurt is considered a sinner." Perhaps the weirdest thing about *True-Weird* is that there are eight pages of James Bond ads—which may not seem so strange, given that Bond was a bit trendy at the time, too, but they're the only ads in the magazine, almost leading one to suspect that the magazine was produced by Saltzman and Broccoli, the Bond movies' first producers. The catalog of products almost makes for an article in itself, and is actually an instructive time capsule as to the width and breadth of Bond merchandise — as well as a new list of things to look for on eBay forty years later.

Skywald

Hell-Rider

This character was allegedly an inspiration for Marvel's Ghost Rider, but this was more like a case of comic dealers making a vague connection to increase values of back issues. Both characters were written by Gary Friedrich and both rode motorcycles, but despite his moniker, the Hell-Rider was less supernatural and more in the style of the ultra-violent biker and kung-fu exploitation movies of the time.

Hell-Rider no. 1 (August 1971)
Cover: Harry Rosenbaum
"How... Why... Hell-Rider/About Andru and Esposito" — Gary Friedrich (Text), Ross Andru and Mike Esposito (Illustrations)
"Introducing ... The Hell-Rider!" — Gary Friedrich, Ross Andru/Mike Esposito
"The Butterfly" — Friedrich, Rich Buckler Sr.
"Introducing ... the Wild Bunch!" — Gary Friedrich, Dick Ayers
"Hell Rider: The Final Chapter" — Friedrich, Ross Andru/Mike Esposito
"Curly's Cycle Corner" — (Text feature)

Hell-Rider no. 2 (October 1971)
Cover: Harry Rosenbaum
"Hell-Rider: Night of the Ripper" — Gary Friedrich, Ross Andru/Mike Esposito
"The Wild Bunch: Blood on Their Spokes" — Gary Friedrich, Syd Shores/ Mike Esposito
"Curly's Cycle Corner" — (Text feature)
"The Butterfly: Against the Brothers of the Crimson Cross" — Buckler, Sr./Friedrich, Rich Buckler, Sr.
"Hell-Rider: Shanghai — '70s Style!" — Gary Friedrich, Ross Andru/Mike Esposito

Humor

Of course, humor isn't a trend, but an attitude that began with the publication of *Mad* made it possible for people like Jim Warren to follow suit and circumvent the code, and provided an atmosphere for the undergrounds, that could have cared less about it. The most important contribution of *Mad* was that it told members of society that things were almost never as they seemed. It promoted questioning of authority in every segment of society, not just political authority, but the authority of media, capitalism, and pre-conceived notions of normality. Some of the kids that grew up reading it became artists and cartoonists themselves, many gravitating towards Harvey Kurtzman when he started *Help* for Warren.

Harvey Kurtzman's *Help! (for Tired Minds)* is the all-important historical link between the inspiration of *Mad* and the actualization of the true underground comics movement of the '60s. *Mad*, of course, had been Kurtzman's crowning achievement, and a whole generation of artists and writers had been influenced by his inimitable style. Now they were working for him. But the best of the bunch even found this format too restrictive — remember, the Warren magazines and *Mad* might not have had to bear the code seal, but they were still mainstream publications. The underground artists answered to no one but themselves, and they not only circumvented the code, they created their own distribution system through head shops and record stores. At their best providing an even more damning view of societal hypocrisy than *Mad*, the undergrounds pushed the limits of decency to such an extent that the hypocrisy crumbled under its own weight, and in turn, this lead to previously unseen levels of freedom as to what could be published in the mainstream.

Mad

"What, me worry?"

Mad no. 89 (September 1964)

Cover: Norman Mingo
Contributing artists and writers: "The Usual Gang of Idiots"
"When the Cigarette Industry Fights Back"— Don Reilly, Jack Rickard
"The *Mad* Academy Awards for Parents"— Stan Hart, Mort Drucker
"The *Mad* Drive-In Movie Primer"— Larry Siegel, George Woodbridge
"World's Fair Pavilions We'd Like to See"— Stan Hart, Joe Orlando
"Comic Strips They'd Really Like to Do"— Charles M. Schulz, Walt Kelly, Ken Ernst/Allen Saunders, Mort Walker, Mell Lazarus/Milton Caniff
"The Phewgitive"— Stan Hart, Mort Drucker
Inside back cover: "Mad Fold-In"— Al Jaffee

One of *Mad*'s gifts was its uncanny ability to get right to the heart of any subject it chose to parody. There are countless examples contained within its many pages, but the cover of this issue is especially near and dear to the hearts of monster fans. If one piece of art has ever captured the spirit and moment of the monster boom, then this issue's cover is it, and it's not even on a monster magazine. Brilliantly executed by Norman Mingo (who would become to Alfred E. Neuman what James Bama became to Doc Savage), the painting features a spot-on Karloffian Frankenstein Monster (complete with fur vest) excitedly gluing together a plastic Alfred E. Neuman model kit! And it's not just the connection to the iconic Aurora models (that also featured Bama art), or the validation given to the subject merely by *Mad* taking notice of it, it's the fact that Mingo gets all of the little details right — the model box is the famed Aurora 'long box,' and, just like the accessories to the Aurora models, the Alfred E. Neuman kit comes complete with a "What, Me Worry?" headstone. But the icing on the cake is the way Mingo manages to create a look of anxious anticipation on Frankie's face, the same as we had putting the Aurora kits together. To a monster fan, the cover of *Mad* no. 89 says it all.

Of course, one of Mad's trademarks was its parodies of well-known comic strips and their styles; another of its popular continuing blackout features was "Scenes We'd Like to See," which, like everything else in the magazine, turned stereotypical moments completely on their head. For example, the swashbuckling Errol Flynn-type hero cuts a swath through an army of foes to get to the princess in distress, only to be run through in the last panel. A wonderful feature in this issue, of special interest to comic strip fans, combines those two ideas, with the bonus being that it's actually famous cartoonists making fun of themselves and each other's styles. It's an incredible collection of talent: Charles M. Schulz (*Peanuts*), Walt Kelly (*Pogo*), Ken Ernst and Allen Saunders (*Mary Worth*), Mort Walker (*Beetle Bailey*) and Mell Lazarus (*Miss Peach*), all let their hair down to hilarious effect. There's no other monster material per se in the mag, although the "The *Mad* Drive-In Movie Primer" will also recall many monstrous memories.

Mad no. 204 (January 1979)

Cover: Jack Rickard
Contributing artists and writers: "The Usual Gang of Idiots"
"Jaw'd, Too"—Dick DeBartolo, Mort Drucker
"New and Improved Products That Really Are New and Improved"—Al Jaffee
"Clones of the Future/Clones of the Past"—Paul Peter Porges
"Novelty Items for Practical-Joker Jocks"—Porges, Jack Davis
"This Year's 'Gimmick' Christmas Gifts"—Tom Koch, Bob Clarke
"The Incredible Bulk"—Lou Silverstone, Angelo Torres
Inside back cover: "Mad Fold-In"—Al Jaffee
Back cover: "One Rainy Afternoon in the Black Forest"—Don Martin

By now, *Mad* had become an institution—long gone were the days when it had created a furor by designing a cover to look like one of those old-school composition notebooks so that it could be read furtively during class. By now, although you might not be able to read it during class or borrow it from your teacher, it was entirely conceivable that your teacher might have been a subscriber as well. Even though *Mad* had ceased to be dangerous, it could still be pretty darned funny, and still featured top-drawer talent. Monster fans got (or will get, if you haven't read them) a kick out of the two fantasy-themed parodies in this issue. The longtime team of Stan Hart and Mort Drucker skewers Jaws II. Drucker is not only a master straight comics artist, but one of the most gifted caricaturists that has ever lived. *The Incredible Hulk* is similarly lambasted by Lou Silverstone and Angelo Torres, keeping the spirit of EC alive in more ways than one.

Help!

Help! no. 22 (January 1965)

Cover: Photo of the Beatles
"*Help*'s Public Gallery"—Jay Lynch, Skip Williamson, Paul Merta, Larry Walker, Ken Schneider, Peter Brock, Frank Marquez, Dennis Ellefson, Ardy Struwer
"Fritz the Cat"—Robert Crumb
"Station Break"—(Fumetti)
"Wonder Warthog Meets the Merangers"—Gilbert Shelton
"Harlem"—Robert Crumb

This magazine is fascinating not only for its collection of legendary underground creators like Lynch, Skip Williamson, Shelton and Crumb before they went X-rated (this was the first appearance of Crumb's character "Fritz the Cat"), but also for its cutting depiction of The Beatles (they're bald). Although the passage of time has seen them, like Elvis Presley, become god-like figures of pop culture, such was not always the case. At the climax of one memorable early *Mad* strip, the "monster" is revealed to be Elvis, and in 1965, everybody still wasn't sold on John, Paul, George and Ringo, either. Witness James Bond's quote from *Goldfinger*, released that same year: "My dear, there are some things which just aren't done, like drinking Dom Perignon '53 at room temperature ... It's like listening to The Beatles without earmuffs." How ironic, then, when former Beatle Paul McCartney and his post–Beatle band Wings wrote and performed the title song for the Bond film *Live and Let Die*.

Comix Book

Underground comics were obviously pretty hip and trendy in the seventies, but on a whole different level, and to a whole different crowd, and it was either utter genius or utter insanity for Stan Lee to think that he could actually harness them for general consumption. But he couldn't harness the best talents the field had to offer, because a lot of them refused to work for Marvel, and what he got from the rest was not a real representation of the true vitality of the undergrounds. Ironically, in the company's eagerness to acquiesce in terms of creators' rights for the underground artists, it made its own bullpen artists aware of rights that they weren't getting. So while the experiment was a failure in terms of sales, it was actually a success in terms of a much larger issue.

Comix Book no. 3

Cover: Denis Kitchen
Frontispiece: "The Rise and Fall and Rise and Fall and Rise and Fall of the American Revolution"—Joel Beck
"Dr. Future"—Peter Poplaski
"Panthea"—Trina Robbins
"Ozzie and Lotta"—Bob Armstrong
"The Fickle Freak"—Kim Deitch
"Barefootz"—Howard Cruse
"The Abduction of Dot Darling"—Leslie Cabarga
"On the Job"—Skip Williamson
"Junkie in a Grey Flannel Suit"—Joel Beck
"Profiles: Kim Deitch Rising"—Dave Schriener
"Waldo: Penny Pinchers from Outer Space"—Kim Deitch
"Tomorrow on Parade"—Steve Stiles
"The Bottle Shop"—Lee Marrs
"Two Fools"—Willy Murphy/Ted Richards
"Barefootz"—Howard Cruse
"The Star Sapphire"—Sharon Rudahl
"The Wide World of *Comix*: At a Comic Book Convention"—R. Meltzer
"Flip the Bird: Bad Karma"—John M. Pound
"We Fellow Travelers"—Justin Green
Back cover: "Claude Funston"—Bill Griffith

Crazy

The black-and-white descendant of the four-color Atlas comic *This Magazine Is ... CRAZY! Crazy* showed not only the obvious influence of *Mad* (which it parodied), but *National Lampoon* and the undergrounds as well. As was standard practice at Marvel, the first issue featured an all-star cast, including Basil Wolverton, whose detailed, twisted unearthly style has been seen as a prime influence on the underground movement, and one of the star pupils of that movement, Vaughn Bode.

Crazy no. 1 (October 1973)

Cover: Frank Kelly Freas
Frontispiece: "Virginia Slim Chances"—Stu Schwartzberg, Marie Severin
"Kung Fooey"—Schwartzberg, Mike Ploog
"The Future—Breaking and Entering Pandora's Box"—Harlan Ellison (Text), Basil Wolverton (Illustration)
"The Daily Survivor"—Tony Isabella, Carla Joseph, Gerry Conway, Steve Skeates (Text)
"Articles We'd Be Crazy to Print: The Lighter Side of Racial Violence; Foto Funkies (Pt. 1); Shush-Ups; Foto Funkies (Pt. 2)"
"The Great American Dream"—Fumetti featuring Neal Adams, Gayle Landers, Dick Giordano, Mary McPherran, Tony Isabella, Alex Simmons
"An Independent Survey Today Announced...."—Jean Shepherd (Text), Herb Trimpe (Illustrations)
"The Upseidown Adventure"—Len Wein, Ross Andru/Vic Martin
"Evolution and History of Moosekind"—Bob Foster
Back Cover: "Junkwaffel: Sole Survivor"—Vaughn Bode

The first issue of *Crazy* actually had some pretty fair stuff in it, including parodies of most of the other humor magazines' staple features that look as though those strips' regular creators were moonlighting.

• SEVEN •

The New Breed: Illustrated Horror, Science Fiction and Fantasy

The line of demarcation between the rise of the new slick fantasy movies and magazines and the fall of the old school is not clearly marked; it's not as simple as "everything was in black-and-white until everything was color." The shift in formats and aesthetics took a few years. *Star Wars* was the turning point in more ways than one. It not only shaped a new (and succeeding) generation's view of fantasy and science fiction in an entertainment medium, but perhaps more importantly, it shaped a generation's feelings about the effects of technology. The *Planet of the Apes* series was a lot of fun, but in the final analysis, like so much of the science fiction of the time, it boils down to a cautionary tale, a grim scenario for technology gone astray. *Star Wars* made out-of-bounds technology not only seem fun, but desirable. The succeeding generations took this to heart, paving the way for the roles that technology, particularly computer technology, increasingly plays in our lives, and indeed, shapes the way we view ourselves and the world and its events. The year 1984 happened a long time ago, both literally and figuratively; now the technology is in place to back up the literary scenario. The battle scenes in *Star Wars* can be seen as templates for the video game generation in the way they're filmed and the way they're acted. Luke, Han and the gang use their computer guidance systems to seek and destroy the empire's spaceships, thereby removing themselves personally from the act of killing, watching the ships explode on a screen just like a television. Vietnam was TV's first reality war, and though the horrors of war and its aftermath were broadcast daily, they still presented the events as taking place at a safe distance. *Star Wars* magnified and refined this distance — it was quick and "clean," no filthy hand-to-hand combat, no muss, no fuss, just program a computer, press a button and watch another piece of hardware blow up. It was perfect training for future generations of fighter pilots, and perfect desensitization for audiences at home and in the theaters, who seem to view each succeeding war as simply another, bigger video game.

Star Wars also heralded the resurgence of style over substance, not only in filmmaking and the related fields, but also in life itself. The story was certainly nothing new, but the (at the time) state-of-the-art technology made it seem so to a new generation. The paucity of real characterization was glossed over by the glitz and flash of the special effects, a trend that has only escalated in the ensuing years. Now many fantasy, horror and science fiction films are nothing more than vehicles for the latest computer-generated special effects. Thirty-second television commercials have more elaborate special effects than whole batches of classics put together, and what seems terribly innovative one moment is quickly rendered obsolete the next. What was once fantastic and special is now routine. It's the same with music videos and many other manifestations of pop culture — it doesn't matter what you're doing, just as long as you make a good show of it and look good while doing it. Unsurprisingly, having created the beast, the *Star Wars* films themselves increasingly fell victim to it, so that by the time of the second trilogy of films, any cohesive story is buried under an avalanche of special effects. We remember specific special effects moments in older films because they were the high points of those films. Now the barrage is so constant it becomes routine even in the space of one movie. There are no special moments to remember. They all pass by in a blur, each new effect seeking to top the one we've just seen.

It was the same with monster movie and black-and-white illustrated horror magazines. Black-and-white on newsprint was passé; flashy color on slick paper was the thing. Many classic art styles and stylists were shoved to the back burner in favor of new and outrageous techniques. Some real talent emerged, but so did a lot of flash for the sake of it. Monster movies would recover, but unfortunately, the black-and-white magazine as a medium for illustrated horror never did. There are still select instances of it, as there are of black-and-white filmmaking, but only as retro projects, nothing of a continuing nature. Even when *Creepy* and *Eerie* were briefly revived, it was as regulation-size four-color comic books, and Vampirella's current exploits, whether in magazine size or comic books, are in color as well. There's certainly no shortage of illustrated horror or fantasy now, but again, black-and-white magazines are a dead art form. With the advent of comics specialty shops, there were tons of black-and-white comic books and magazines, but most of these were done out of economical necessity rather than a devotion to that form, and very few survived.

But all of this is to dwell on the negative aspects of the phenomenon, even though there was a temporary dark lining in the silver cloud. The best thing about *Star Wars* was that it put fantasy squarely back in the mainstream, and the trickle-down effect enabled other areas of the genre to be fruitful and multiply. George Lucas and Steven Spielberg openly acknowledge their debt to serials, comic books, monster movies and monster magazines. As a result of their updating those themes and others, the classics and other neglected gems were once again brought to light, exposed to a whole new generation of fans. The downside was that a lot of newer fans preferred the newer movies to the older, or could only watch the older ones with a sense of camp, and this attitude, for a time, found its way into the monster magazines. "Well, sure, this was the inspiration, but everything is just so much more sophisticated now that what's new is obviously superior." For a time, it also killed many monster magazines. The public's relative lack of access to older films was probably a factor.

The second monster boom didn't really begin with *Star Wars*, it began with home video and grew with cable television, comic specialty shops, wider access to better printing technology, and the Internet. With the miracle of home video, fans no longer had to wait up until all hours of the night to watch a movie. They could own a copy, and at a fraction of the cost and weight of actual reels of film. And they no longer had to rely on somebody else's or their own faulty memories to judge any film, they simply had to rent or buy it and watch it. The video explosion, and the usual rush to fill the demand, unearthed movies that had gone unseen for decades, in much the same way such movies were now appearing on TV in the similar rush to fill cable programming. Got a question about a horror movie or actor? No need to write to Professor Gruebeard and wait for months hoping that he answers, just look it up online. We'll look more at the hopeless path mankind is on in a few pages, but first we'll take a look at what we are reading on the way there.

Heavy Metal

Heavy Metal, which takes its name from a strain of rock music, is the American version of the French *Metal Hurlant*. The first issue of "The Adult Illustrated Fantasy Magazine" was published in April 1977, and was "from the people who bring you *National Lampoon*." Besides featuring the work of old masters like Vallejo, Frazetta, Wrightson and Corben, it made stars of a whole new school. That included Simon Bisley, who pushed all of the implications of Frazetta's art to their apparent natural conclusion; Olivia, who showed all the boys that it took a woman to paint girls; Jean "Moebius" Girard, who brought an unquestionably organic feel to tales of intense technology; and Milo Manara. No more would fantasy magazines be poor pulpwood relations to real magazines. Here was a publication that was just as slick and colorful as the mag next to it, and featured almost as much advertising as that mag. For the first time, readers were treated to commercial breaks that featured more than just house ads or the company store, although the ads were necessary, as always, to get the message out, and that message was that art was still supposed to be about pushing boundaries. The European sensibilities imparted in its pages heralded a new day for illustrated fantasy, just as World War II had imparted European sensibilities to midwestern servicemen; fantasy magazines weren't in Kansas anymore. They've outlasted *Creepy*, *Eerie*, and even the magazine that brought them to us. Although still for adults only, the magazine doesn't seem quite so daring anymore, although its standards are still impeccable, and it continues to expand the frontiers of fantasy art.

Heavy Metal Vol. V, No. 1 (April 1981)

Cover: Esteban Maroto
"Art and the Nazis"—Brad Balfour
"Bloodstar" (Robert E. Howard)—John Jakes/John Pocsick, Richard Corben
"Tex Arcana"—John Findley
"Changes"—Matt Howarth
"The Heavy Metal Interview: Julio Ribera—Brad Balfour
"What Is Reality, Papa?"—Ribera, Godard
"Ambassador of the Shadows"—P. Christin, J.C. Mezieres
"Good-Bye, Soldier!"—Ricardo Barreiro, Juan Giminez
"Stories from London"—Harry North
"Dangerous Curve"—Caza
"Rock Opera"—Rod Kierkegaard, Jr.
Back cover: Les Edwards

Esteban Maroto's gorgeous cover for this issue might have borne the title of "Sybil," but it wasn't Sally Field, it was Red Sonja by another name, right down to the chain-mail bikini. This issue contained a chapter of "Bloodstar," a novel that was begun by Robert E. Howard, finished by John Jakes and John Pocsick, illustrated by Richard Corben and later released as a graphic novel, although shorn of the rich color that had added considerably to the pages in *Heavy Metal*. It's a good story, and the art is beyond reproach, but it is more than a little similar to "The Valley of the Worm." Perhaps Howard realized this, and that's why it was left unfinished.

The most intellectually stimulating piece in this issue isn't even illustrated—Brad Balfour's "Art and the Nazis" wasn't your father's typical illustrated fantasy magazine article. Witness these statements from Balfour's intro to the piece: "The Paris exhibit features certain Nazi painters ... some of their work, or at least the technique used, reminded me of certain science fiction art. Fascism appeals during economically troubled times and moments of personal trauma. When there is widespread desire for transcendental order that overcomes normal uncertainties, I see conditions amenable to fascist mentality. And I saw conditions favorable to fascism in some of these new painters' aesthetics. However strong this trend may be, it's forever a major issue to consider."

And it still is; the words, although written in the 1980s, unfortunately ring true even more so in 2007, and apply to a lot more than just art.

Metal Vol. XIV, No. V (November 1990)

Cover: Frank Frazetta
"Interview with Frank Frazetta"—Lou Stathis
"Dieter Lumpen: Enemies in Common"—Ruben and Zentner
"The Time Zuck Company"—Zeljko Pahek
"Semel Insanivimus Omnes AKA The Prisoner"—Angus McKie
"Bonnie and Clyde"—Rebecca Fletcher, Jim Fletcher
"Modern World"—Peter Kuper
"Behind the Cursed Curtain"—Rick Geary

1984/1994

Heavy Metal had stolen Warren's thunder, and Warren had to jump on the adult fantasy bandwagon fast. Of course, he had produced outstanding fantasy, horror and science fiction for years, and had even featured nudity. All that had to be done to make them adult was add some four-letter words and make the situations requiring nudity a bit more racy, and this Warren did. But under the editorial stewardship of Bill DuBay, the magazine took on a dark, misogynistic tone, and didn't seem so much about expanding concepts of illustrated fantasy and horror as it did about a grade school child's fascination with being able to get away with saying a four-letter word, or about mere exploitation. That's not to say there aren't some great moments. These include Jim Stenstrum's consistently inventive and hilarious writing, and "Ghita of Alizarr," who was Red Sonja in every way but name, even down to her chain-mail bikini and who had all the sex that Red Sonja didn't, by Frank Thorne. Richard Corben, Wallace Wood, Alex Nino, Alfredo Alcala—all contributed some extremely accomplished work, enough for the magazine to last six years and twenty-nine issues.

1994 no. 17 (February 1981)

Cover: Jim Stenstrum/Will Richardson
"Asshole of the Universe!"—Richardson (Bill DuBay), Alex Nino
"Mad Amy"—Richardson/Kevin Duane, Jose Ortiz
"Ghita of Alizarr"—Frank Thorne
"Kid Rust" (Color)—Jose Ortiz
"The Big Celebration"—Jim Stenstrum, Abel Laxamana
"Man Is God!"—John Ellis Sech, Alex Nino

The magazine *1984* became *1994* after Warren claimed to have encountered trouble with the estate of George Orwell; nothing changed except the title. The issue itself is the usual mixture of the good, the bad, and the ugly, but the cover is one of the best ever done for a Warren magazine—a wickedly funny parody of Frazetta's *Conan the Adventurer* cover painting. Featuring the title character from the "Mad Amy" story, the pencils of Jim Stenstrum and the colors of Bill DuBay depict a futuristic female barbarian, sledgehammer in hand, and a frightened man clinging to her shapely leg, atop a pile of robot "corpses." But these aren't just any robots,

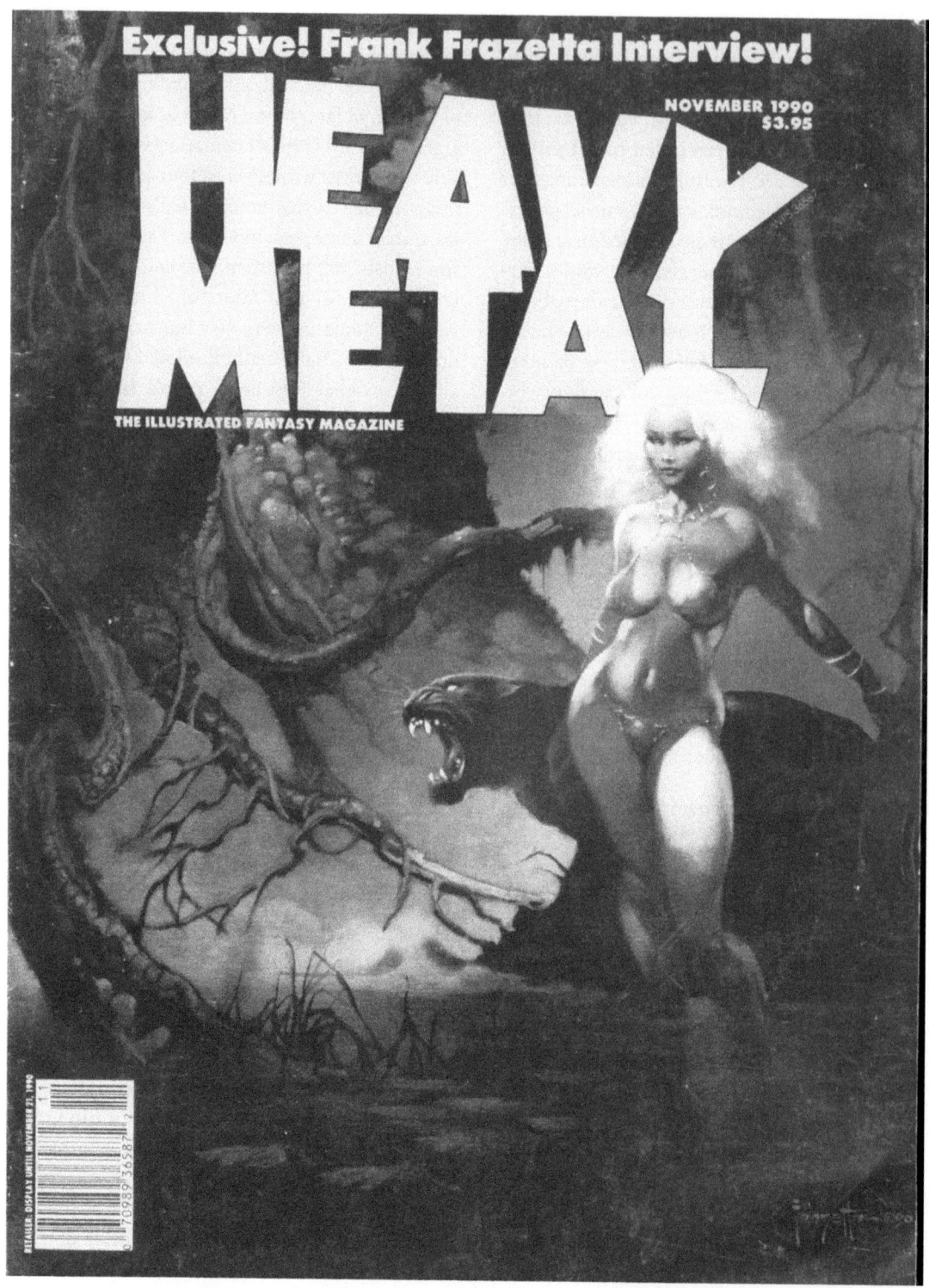

Heavy Metal vol. XIV no. V (HM)–Three, not two, things are certain in this crazy world: death, taxes, and that a Frank Frazetta cover painting can still sell any publication on the stands (courtesy Howard Jurofsky, *Heavy Metal*).

1994 no. 17 (Warren)–Jim Stenstrum's cover for *1994* no. 17, colored by Bill DuBay, is a joyous masterpiece of twisted inspiration.

they're Robby the Robot, Gort, R2D2, "Maria" from *Metropolis*, Yul Brynner's cowboy android from *Westworld*, and everybody's favorite, B9 from *Lost in Space*. The cover alone makes it essential.

Epic Illustrated

Marvel did *Heavy Metal* too. Marvel just waited a little longer to bring its title out, and although the life spans of *1984/1994* and *Epic Illustrated* were the same (six years), *Epic Illustrated* tallied seven more issues in that time. Unlike the Marvel magazines of only a few years previously, this was not the spearhead of a brand new magazine line, it was an extension of the Epic line of comics that published the offbeat stuff. Also unlike those books and like their inspiration, Marvel went to slick paper and full color. It employed the many of the same talents that had made the first magazine line great — Neal Adams, Boris Vallejo, Brunner, Buscema, Kaluta, Simonson, Starlin, Steranko, Reese, and Wrightson — as well as newer homegrown and international talent that really produced some quality graphic storytelling. If imitation is the sincerest form of flattery, then Marvel paid its respects to *Heavy Metal* in spades.

Epic Illustrated no. 4 (Winter 1980)

Cover: Michael William Kaluta
"Delloran Revisited" (Chapter 7 of "The Metamorphosis Odyssey") — James Starlin
"The Art of Shotaro Ishimori" — Art portfolio
"The Dreaming City" (Ch. 2) (adapted from Michael Moorcock) — Roy Thomas, P. Craig Russell
"Almuric" (Ch. 3) (Robert E. Howard) — Roy Thomas, Tim Conrad
"Elephant Grass" — Marc Hempel
"Retrospect" — B.K. Taylor, James Fox
"Survivors" — Paul Kirchner
"Solar Plexus" — Rick Veitch
"Sleeping Dogs" (adapted from Harlan Ellison) — Ken Steacy

Marvel made a good run at *Heavy Metal*, especially in the early going. Kaluta's cover art for "Almuric" was one of his most elegant, pulplike pieces, and the adaptation of the story by Roy Thomas and Tim Conrad made for a strong sense of déjà vu, as did the Thomas/Russell pairing on the adaptation of Michael Moorcock's "The Dreaming City." But it wasn't all a good old boys club; there were plenty of new faces (to Marvel) too, like Paul Kirchner, a Wallace Wood protégé who created "The Dope Rider," Rick Veitch, and Ken Steacy.

Epic Illustrated no. 7 (August 1981)

Cover: Barry Windsor-Smith
"Holocaust" — Neal Adams
"Mediaview" — Dennis O' Neil (Reviews)
"Epus" — Pepe Moreno
"Requiem" — (Chapter 10 of "The Metamorphosis Odyssey") — James Starlin
"Nightfire" — (Chapter 11 of "The Metamorphosis Odyssey") — James Starlin
"The Egg" — Tim Caldwell, Jeff Potter
"Gameview" — Steven Grant (Reviews)
"The Llehs" — Graham Marks/John Bolton, John Bolton
"Bookview" — Jo Duffy (Reviews)
"U.F.O." — Tim Conrad
"The Comedy" — Dean Motter

By 1981, Barry Smith had added a "Windsor" to his name so as to reinforce his Britishness, and his art style had continued its improvement. His barbarian cover for this issue is all the promise contained in his early Conan art realized — a composition simple yet exquisitely detailed, savage and beautiful. There are also some exquisite pieces accompanying the surprisingly frank interview, which is conducted by Archie Goodwin. Surprising, because Smith pulls no punches concerning his feelings on the Conan situation. "Things were so wrong in

Epic Illustrated no. 3 (Marvel) — The production techniques of this cover signaled the future, but the look was vintage Mike Kaluta (courtesy Marvel Entertainment, Inc.).

other corners, like Marvel keeping my artwork ... the closer I got to what I wanted with Conan the more I resented having to answer to anybody or explain myself every time ... They naturally assumed they owned me lock, stock, and barrel, and I was stupid enough to accept it." Obviously they resolved their differences to some extent, because Smith would again contribute significantly to Marvel, although very little in the way of Conan.

The legendary *Green Lantern/Green Arrow* team of Denny O'Neil and Neal Adams are on hand, although not in tandem. O'Neil is relegated to a couple of pages of reviews, while Adams handles both the scripting and art chores on "Holocaust," one of his most intense solo pieces, a stream-of-consciousness tale contrasting various levels and states of oppression and senseless death. Events culminate at a rock concert given by "Brother Able." Still, Adams has a powerful sense of social consciousness, which shows through in his own writing, not to mention the additional power given to his ideas through his ever-inventive page design and composition.

THE NEW MONSTER MOVIE MAGAZINES

Monster magazines are still around, and they fall more or less into two categories: slick products sold in mainstream bookstores and specialty shops, and slick products produced by fans and sold through other forms of distribution. The mainstream mags are technically descendants of *Famous Monsters*, but they carry very little of its spirit. The aesthetic is as different as the horror movies themselves are from the horror movies of *FM*'s heyday and before.

Monsterscene

Of the entire new crop of monster magazines, *Monsterscene* was the publication that tried the hardest to recapture the essence of *Famous Monsters*, right down to covers by Basil Gogos and a logo in the style of Warren's *Monster World*. Its tagline was, "Everything you loved about monster mags as a kid, but written for grown-ups!" Although you understand the spirit in which it was written, it still seems to rely on the old saw that all the old monster mags were strictly for the kiddies, which was and wasn't the case. Like the rest of its compatriots, *Monsterscene* was a mixed bag of contents that covered a lot of different areas of media, since there were now so many more kinds to cover. The magazine did it very well, maintaining the all-important balance of knowledge and enthusiasm that makes a great monster magazine great.

Monsterscene no. 3 (Fall 1994)

Cover: Basil Gogos
Frontispiece: *Inframan* movie poster art — Basil Gogos
"Not of This Earth–Anymore"— Richard Clemenson (Obituaries)
"Saturday Morning Monsters"— Scott Shaw
White Zombie— Mark D. Neel
"Hammer Horrors: The Dracula Films of Christopher Lee"— Mike Schneider
"Wolff and Byrd"— Batton Lash
"There Goes Tokyo!"— Frank Kurtz
"Artist Profile: Basil Gogos"
"Dead End Road Trip"— Steve Smith
"Living Legends: Bob Burns"— Steve Smith
"Sleep No More in the Video Vault"— Steve Smith, Frank Kurtz (Reviews)

"Preview: *Mary Shelley's Frankenstein*"
"Monster Television"—(Reviews)
"The Scary Library"—(Book reviews)
"The Monster Mall"—(Product reviews)
Inside back cover: Basil Gogos
Back cover: Photo from *Mary Shelley's Frankenstein*

This is a much-deserved tribute issue to Basil Gogos; his art graces three of the four covers, and he gets an article as well. One thing you notice about all of the new monster magazines is that half their pages are taken up by reviews, which is only fitting, as there is so much more stuff to review. "There Goes Tokyo!" was a regular feature on giant Japanese monsters, the title inspired by the Blue Oyster Cult song "Godzilla." The simply wonderful Bob Burns is in the running with Forry Ackerman for the title of Ultimate Fan, and his contributions to the genre could fill a book, and have (*It Came from Bob's Basement*, *Monsterkid Memories*). He's best remembered as "Kogar the Ape," who appeared in the original *Ghost Busters* TV series with Forrest Tucker and Larry Storch.

Monsterscene no. 8 (Summer 1996)

Cover: Basil Gogos
"A Star Is Unborn"—Forrest J Ackerman
"Carmilla: J. Sheridan LeFanu and Hammer's Karnstein Trilogy"—Steve Smith
"Universal's Master Makeup Artist"—Michael F. Blake
Vampirella—Steve Smith (Film preview)
The Frighteners—Steve Smith (Film preview)
"The Artomic Man"—(Profile)
"Cauldron of Culture and Class"—(Reviews)
"Sleep No More in the Video Vault"—Steve Smith, Frank Kurtz, William Harrison (Reviews)
"Music to Calm the Savage Beast"—(Reviews)
"The Scary Library"—(Book reviews)
"The Monster Mall"—(Product reviews)
Back cover: Photo from *The Vampire Lovers*

Ken Kelly did a very nice portrait of Ingrid Pitt for the cover of *Famous Monsters* no. 122. Gogos beats him fangs down with the intense and sexy Pitt art that graces the cover of this issue. Gogos hadn't used the color white like this since his first *FM* cover. Forry Ackerman regales us with a list of his film appearances, and Michael Blake contributes an article on Jack Pierce. Blake is the author of a couple of books on Lon Chaney Sr., and insists that Lon Chaney Sr. was not a horror star, and never made a horror movie.

Monsterscene no. 10 (Summer 1997)

Cover: Basil Gogos
"Pitt of Horror"—Ingrid Pitt
"The Curses of Dr. Phibes"—William Harrison (Film series overview)
"Grave Reservations: *Horror Hotel* Revisited"—William Burns
"That Little Monsterpiece"—Angus Scrimm
Halloween: The Happy Haunting of America—Steve Smith (Review)
"Welcome to the Hell Mouth!"—Steve Smith
"There Goes Tokyo!"—Frank Kurtz
"Sleep No More in the Video Vault"—Steve Smith, Frank Kurtz (Reviews)
"The Scary Library"—(Book reviews)
"The Monster Shindig!"—(Music reviews)
"The Monster Mall"—(Product reviews)
Back cover: Photo from *The Abominable Dr. Phibes*

The next-to-last issue features a fantastic Gogos portrait of Vincent Price as Dr. Phibes, adding yet another painting to the list he should have gotten to do for *Famous Monsters*, but never did. Of course, the Phibes films had been covered before, but William Harrison provides fresh insights as well as some all-important information concerning the unfilmed third Phibes movie.

Cinefantastique

"I learned a word in France during the War, but it might sound rather—suggestive."
"Most French words are."
—*Anatomy of a Murder*

Cinefantastique actually began its life in 1970, but did not settle on a regular publishing schedule or get wide distribution for a number of years. As is befitting the highfalutin' title, the magazine does indeed cover a broad range of horror films and related subjects, with noteworthy, lengthy pieces (nearly taking up the whole magazine) on *Forbidden Planet*, Ray Harryhausen, and Vincent Price, among others. Think of it as a classier *Fangoria*; although not published by the same company, they now bear a strong resemblance to each other in terms of both layout and articles that read more like press releases.

Cinefantastique v. 22 no. 1 (August 1991)

Cover: David Voigt
Mom and Dad Save the World— Steve Biodrowski (preview)
Radio Flyer— Sheldon Teitelbaum
Terminator 2: Judgment Day— Frederick S. Clarke
Child's Play 3— Todd French
Bill and Ted Go to Hell— Steve Biodrowski (Preview)
Bill and Ted's Excellent Adventure— Steve Biodrowski (Interview)
"The Making of *The Rocketeer*"— Daniel Schweiger
The Boneyard— Tim Vandehey (Preview)
"Michael Reeves–Horror's James Dean"— Bill Kelley
"Retrospect: *Witchfinder General*"— Bill Kelley
"Still Howling After All These Years"— John Thonen
Maniac Cop 2— Dan Scapperotti
Silence of the Lambs— Dan Persons

A typically diverse issue of *Cinefantastique* in that it showcases both old and new and demonstrates the effects of one upon the other. For instance, Dave Stevens' *Rocketeer* is covered, supplemented by pieces on the inspiration it took from comics and serials. For classic horror fans, there's also an insightful article on the tragic director Michael Reeves. *Bill and Ted Go to Hell*, which was actually probably a fervent wish on the part of many, was just the working title for the movie that would later become *Bill and Ted's Bogus Journey*.

Fangoria/Starlog

Fangoria, and its sister publication, *Starlog*, were the monster and fantasy magazines which carried on the newsstand tradition after the demise of *Famous Monsters*. *Fangoria*'s first cover featured Godzilla. Occasionally it would run articles by people like Johnny Legend on how wild it was to eat sherbet with Tor Johnson, but by and large, it was all about the gore, and soon became as faceless as the films it both covered and created a market for. When horror films began to rise out of their splatter for splatter's sake phase, so did *Fangoria*, although at times some of its articles still read more like extended promotional pieces for the films it covers, and any information seems to be limited to pre-digested sound bites that, like most hype, impart no information at all.

Fangoria no. 159 (January 1997)

Cover: Photo/*Mars Attacks*
"Monster Invasion"— Michael Gingold, Michael Rowe, Steve Puchalski (News, previews, etc.)
"I'm Dreaming of a *Black Christmas*"— Keith Bearden
"*Scream* with Fear, *Scream* with Laughter"— Chris Garcia
"Horrorcade"— Russ Ceccola (Video game reviews)
"The Video Eye of Dr. Cyclops"— Dr. Cyclops (Reviews)
"Duck for Cover When *Mars Attacks*"— Anthony C. Ferrante
"Beck's X-Files"— Dave Hughes
"Steve Johnson's Animal Kingdom"— Thomas Crow
"Laser Spotlight"— Michael Gingold, Tom Weaver (Reviews)
"The Many FX Chapters of *Necronomicon*"— Anthony C. Ferrante

"Terror on a Budget"—Thomas Crow
Christmas Evil—Keith Bearden
"Nightmare Library"—W.C. Stroby, Don Kaye, John Wooley (Book reviews)

Rue Morgue

Rue Morgue seems to be the first pro mag to be produced with a real punk/Goth sensibility; it's not just something to be into, it's a way of life, and in turn that way of life determines how we see the world or pop culture, which is in turn what we make of it. It looks like the product of offspring whose parents grew up on Skywald magazines and drive-horror. Not everybody who listened to the Sex Pistols or The Misfits OD'd or went straight and bought into the system. Many people created or discovered a lifestyle that became their own, and that's their legacy as well as a testament to the legacy of horror.

Rue Morgue no. 30 (Nov/Dec. 2002)

Cover: *Black Sunday* poster art
"Dreadlines"—Brad Abraham/Vulnavia Wrick, Mary Beth Hollyer
"Needful Things"—(Product reviews)
"Black Dreams: The Haunted Films of Mario Bava"—Chris Alexander
"Barbara Steele: The Maiden Behind the Mask"—Chris Alexander/David Del Valle (Interview)
"Lamberto Bava's Heritage of Horror"—Rod Gudino (Interview)
"The Misfits: 25 Years of Horror Business"—Aaron Lupton
"Dawn of the Living Dead Dolls"—Rod Gudino
"Playing with Pain"—Rod Gudino
"The Devil's Leitmotif"—John R. Bowen
"Cinemacabre"—(Reissue reviews)
"The Gore-Met"—(Gore Film reissue reviews)
"The Ninth Circle"—(Book reviews)
"Terror Has Big Eyes!"—(Anime reviews)
"Blood in Four Colours"—(Comic book reviews)
"Audio Drome"—(Music reviews)
"Play Dead"—(Video game reviews)
"Classic Cut"—*Weird Tales* history

Starburst

Starburst was a title actually started by Dez Skinn, former publisher of *House of Hammer*, but he only put out four issues before it was bought by Marvel, who left the production in the hands of the British. Stan Lee wanted a monster magazine, but he didn't actually want to do a monster magazine "after being bitten by the horror mags a few years earlier" (Dez Skinn, *From the Tomb* no. 10, June 2003). It succeeded where the others fell short, and is still going strong. But even with all those numbers under its belt, it has yet to achieve the kind of stature that *House of Hammer* achieved with far less ink, paper, and distribution.

Starburst no. 220 (December 1996)

Cover: Photo/*Mars Attacks*
"Things to Come"—(News, previews)
"Riker's Command"—Melissa Perenson (Interview)
"Designing the Final Frontier"—Pat Jankiewicz (Interview)
"Cybertech"—Gary Fenton (Video game reviews)
"Bookshelf"—(Book reviews)
"Reservoir Hogs"—Alan Jones (Interview)
"*Mars Attacks*/Mars Cards"—Pat Jankiewicz (Interview/article)
"Preview"—(Previews)
"A Good Tongue-Lashing"—Alan Jones (Interview)
"TV View"—John Peel (Reviews)
"Video File"—David Bassom (Reviews)
"Post-Cyberpunk and Skeletal Gothic"—Jeremy Clarke (Interview)
"It's Only a Movie"—John Brosnan

Chiller Theatre

The first monster magazine to take its title from one of the conventions that the original monster magazines and movies inspired, *Chiller*

Theatre is not, as one might suspect, merely an outlet with which to further publicize the convention. Some features are invariably tied to Chillers past or recent, but the quality of the magazine, from covers to contributors, displays the same enthusiasm and love of the genre that has made the convention so successful.

Chiller Theatre no. 3 (1995)

Cover: Keith Newton
"Tribute to Al Adamson"— Sam Sherman
"The Price of Fear"— Kevin Shinnick
"The Humorous Horrors of Vincent Price"— Terry Blass
"The Complete Films of Vincent Price"— Lucy Chase Williams
"The Vincent Price Quiz"— Les Williams
"P.J. Soles: *Rock & Roll High School* Alumni"— Dan Cziraky
"Gloria Talbott"— Scott Rhodes
"Reggie Bannister: For the Love of It"— Eddie Mika (Interview)
"Candace Hilligoss Interview"— Al Ryan/Dan Cziraky
"Haunted Hollywood"— Gregory Mank
"I Am Misfit"— Al Ryan
"Resin Rat Race: Misfit Models"— Al Ryan
"Why You Need a Laser Disc Player"— Jesse Obstraum
"Starting Your Laser Disc Collection"— Jesse Obstraum
"Laser Disc Reviews"— Ted Bohus
"Chiller Picks"— Robert Morgan
"Open at Own Risk"— Craig Goden
"Fright Frame/Saturday Shocker"—(Mystery photo)
"Ghoul's Gallery"— Cipriano (Illustration)
"Damn You All to Hell: Charlton Heston's Sci-Fi movies"— Richard Hilliard
Back Cover: Jurek (Misfits' Crimson Ghost)

The first few issues of *Chiller* were massive affairs, and stressed the rock and roll connection and sensibility with articles on The Misfits and an interview with P.J. Soles, who played Riff Randall in The Ramones' cult classic *Rock and Roll High School*. This issue was also a tribute to Vincent Price, the rock and roll generation's greatest horror icon.

Chiller Theatre no. 16 (2002)

Cover: Jeff Pittarelli
"Alex Gordon on *The Atomic Submarine*"— Tom Weaver (Interview)
"Beverly Washburn"— Tom Weaver (Interview)
"The Story of Aquanetta"— Bojak
The Tingler— Tom Weaver (Interview)
"Chiller People"—(Photo feature)
"George Romero's Pennsylvania: A Horror Fan's Travelogue"— Leon Marcelo
"David Carradine"— Louis Paul (Interview)
"John Saxon"— Louis Paul (Interview)
"Fright Frame"—(Mystery photo)

The magazine has lost a little of its heft in recent years, but has become slicker and more focused. *Chiller* is famous for its guest list, which in turn provides for some great interviews from names both high profile and obscure, resulting in some valuable information preserved from sometimes previously untapped sources. "Bojak" is actually fan-man supreme Richard Bojarski, who has done much himself in the way of preserving our horror heritage.

Cult Movies

The first issue was titled *Bela Lugosi: Then and Now*. The publishers were unabashed fans of psychotronica and trash as well as the classics and remained committed to Bela throughout the magazine's run. The magazine hooked up with Forrest J Ackerman to produce new issues of Forry's beloved *Spacemen* as the "flip side" to a couple of later issues of *Cult Movies*. Specializing in wildly offbeat, classic, psychotronic, and sometimes controversial material, *Cult Movies* was the first monster mag to realize that pornography is as much a staple of most horror fans' diets as Hammer or Universal. The magazine foundered and died after editor/heart-and-soul Buddy Barnett left.

Cult Movies no. 5 (1992)

Cover: Photo/*Frankenstein Meets the Space Monster*
Frontispiece: Photo/*Mothra*
"Video Reviews"—Unaccredited
"Fanzines in Review"—"Jason R. Gonauts"
"Rock and Roll Monsters"—Jerry Neeley
"Interview: Aaron Kincaid"—Jerry Neeley
"Party on the Beach"—Jeff Stevens
"John Andrews: A Personal Memory"—Edward G. Barnett
"Happy 20th Birthday *Deep Throat*"—Jean Lang
"Godzilla Scrapbook Pt. 2"—David Milner
"Freaks: Tod Browning's Original Film Reconstructed"—Buddy Barnett/Karl Theide
"Attack of the Chinese Hopping Vampires"—Lisa Feerick
King Kong Escapes—Michael Copner
Trader Horn—Ray Hall
"Jackie Gleason: The Great One Revisited"—Teri Wayne
"An Exclusive Interview with Lisa Mitchell"—Michael Copner
"*Horror of Dracula*: An Analysis of the Hammer Classic"—Ron Borst
Inside back cover: Photo/*Freaks*
Back cover: Ad art/*Ghidrah, the Three-Headed Monster*

Cult Movies no. 15 (1995)

Cover: Dave Stevens (Photo: Lon Chaney Sr./*London After Midnight*)
Frontispiece: Photo/*Vampirella*
"Video Reviews"—Michael Copner, Colette Olson, Bryan Senn, Tom Weaver, Spider Subke, Elliot Singer, Johanne L. Tournier
"Cult Movie Stuff"—(News)
"The Samurai Film: A Neglected Genre, Pt. 3"—Chris D.
"The Epic Saga of Kharis the Mummy"—Frank J. Dello Stritto
"Murderous Midgets and Crippled Thieves: Tod Browning, Hollywood and the Twenties"—David J. Skal/Elias Savada
"Dave Stevens: Take II"—Michael Copner (Interview)
"Backstage with Vincent Price"—Bob Madison (Interview)
Murders in the Rue Morgue—Bryan Senn
"Ray Dennis Steckler: Take II"—James Eliot Singer (Interview)
"Sleaze Cinema"—Todd Tjersland
"Gamera—Giant Monster Decisive Air Battle"—David Milner
"The Exploits of Nyoka"—John Marshall
Back cover: *The Curse of the Cat People* poster art

Scary Monsters

Taking its title from the song *Scary Monsters (and Super Creeps)* by David Bowie, Dennis Druktenis' long-running effort has grown from a thin fanzine reprinting mostly press book material to a thick newsstand publication with many notable contributors and the real "feel" of the old monster magazines, eschewing slick paper to both recall fond memories and be able to put that much more into each issue. *Scary Monsters* not only has its own host (Sam Scary), but even a black and white monster comic section. Unbelievably, the "Monster Memories" yearbooks have even more pages and features, being veritable books unto themselves. *Scary Monsters'* Basil Gogos is Terry Beatty, who took over the covers in the early going and has painted every one of them since, including all the yearbooks and special editions. Druktenis also revived *Castle of Frankenstein*, and produces that as well as *Scary Monsters*, although, like the original, subject to an irregular publishing schedule.

Scary Monsters no. 1 (October 1991)

Cover: Photo/*It Conquered the World*
Frontispiece: Photo/*Frankenstein*
Attack of the Crab Monsters
From Hell It Came
Horror of Dracula
Invasion of the Saucer Men
It Conquered the World
It! The Terror from Beyond Space
"Warren Publishing's First Year: *Eerie* Magazine"—Greg Chappell

"Plastic Monsters are Back!"
"Invasion of the Giant Saguaros"—Justin Humphreys
"Scary Movie View"—C.J. Winston

Scary Monsters no. 52 (September 2004)

Cover: Terry Beatty
Frontispiece: Photo/Monster Bash 2004
"Scary Secret Photo"
Gorgo—Allen A. Debus
"A Haunted Castle on Halloween"—Mark Mawston
"Clark Wilkinson: Wisconsin's Forry Ackerman"—Gary Dorst
"Tiny Tales of Terror"—Bob Statzer
"*Mad Monsters* Fiendish Filmbooks—*King Kong vs. Godzilla, The Deadly Mantis*"
"All Our October Memories"—Allen A. Debus
"Universal Monsters Kombat"—Dr. Griffin
"Make Your Mind Up on Halloween"—Kent R. Daluga
"Monster Bash 2004"—John Skerchock
"The Cosmic Drive-In: 1962"—Robert Freese
"The Women of Hammer/Peter Cushing Tribute"—Tim Troutman
"Dr. Swave's Monster Memories of that Crazy Cave Man Mask!"—Dave Piper (Dr. Swave)
"Scary Comics no. 34"—black-and-white horror comics
"Houses I Have Haunted"—Boris Karloff
"A Century of Fantasy and Fright Films, Pt. 11"—Joseph Winters
"Ferdie's Inferno!"—Dick Nitelinger
"Scare News"—Dr. Johnny Scareshock
"Scary DVD Headline Grues"—Ron Adams
Back cover: Terry Beatty

Midnight Marquee

Midnight Marquee is one of the longest-running monster publications around. It began life as a stapled-together fanzine called *Gore Creatures*, and is now as slick in both content and production values as any of the other monster publications. The husband-and-wife team of Gary and Susan Svehla were also responsible for the legendary, much-missed FanEx conventions. They have published their own line of books and have been unwavering in their devotion and commitment to the genre, which shows in every issue of their magazine.

Midnight Marquee no. 62

Cover: Photo of the Creature from the Black Lagoon
Frontispiece: Photo of the Creature from the Black Lagoon
"Mother Nature Fights Back"
"Science Goes Berserk"
"Alien Invasion and Saucer Threats"
"Gothic-a Go-Go"
"Robots on the Rampage"
"Female Monsters and Feminine Menaces"
"Glop Monsters and Slimy Critters"
"The Ultra-Ridiculous"
"That Old Black Magic"

This "Special All-Photo Issue" is atypical of *Midnight Marquee*, but stands out for that reason. The sheer variety of monsters represented demonstrates knowledge and is remarkable in its scope. The selection of photos is entertaining, with some old favorites and some rare treats, making this one of the best pure graphics monster mags ever done. Horror and horror films mean a lot of different things to a lot of different people, but one thing we can all agree on—monsters sure do look cool.

Monster Bash

Like *Chiller Theatre*, the *Monster Bash* magazine takes its name from the convention that inspired it. Like the conventions themselves, it keeps the spirit of fandom alive, and provides a place or a page for people to share their enthusiasm. Contributions from *Bash* staffers as well as various professionals (and some who are both) make it a worthy addition to the monster magazine family, and some wonderful covers make it one of the most attractive.

Monster Bash no. 2 (2004)

Cover: Kerry Gammill
Frontispiece: Photo from *Abbott and Costello meet Frankenstein*
"Drive-In Days"— Michael Legge, David Colton, Jerry Armellino, Charles Henson, Larry Underwood, Shawn H., Jeff Yeatter, Barb Heiss, Ron Adams
"An Evening with Sara Karloff"— Kevin Surnear (interview)
Chandu the Magician— Leonard J. Hohl
"The Lionel Atwill Filmography"— Kimball Jenkins
"Blobbed!"— Jeff Barnes
"Frankenstein's Retribution: The Ghost Stands Tall"— Bob Pellegrino
"The Gorilla Men and the Origin of an Apeman!"— Bob Burns
"Afraid of the Dark"— Charles Henson
"The Giant Gila Monster Mystery"— Dave Nelson
"The King of Monsters: The Creature from the Black Lagoon"— Sam Borowski
"Creepy Crossword"— Barb Heiss
"Mexican Creature Features"— Bobb Cotter
"Advertising Art History Dept."— Ad reproductions

Monster Bash no. 5 (2006)

Cover: Kerry Gammill
Frontispiece: Photo of Bill Edwards as Mr. Hyde
"Classic Monster Toys—The 1970s!"— Raymond Castile
"Deep Inside the Black Lagoon"— Kevin Surnear (Interview)
"*13 Ghosts*: An Inner-view with Charles Herbert"— Tom Weaver
"Gooey Slimy Blobs"— Jeff Barnes
"How to Make a Monster Movie" (Pt. 2)— Lawrence Fultz, Jr. (Interview)
"The Bride's Scrapbook"— Photo feature
"Favorite Robots"— Photo feature
"Herbert Rudley Takes *A Walk in the Sun* and a *Dark Valley* into *The Black Sleep*"— Lawrence Fultz, Jr. (interview)
"*El Mundo de Los Vampiros* ("The World of the Vampires")— Bobb Cotter
"The Critic's Notebook"— Joseph C. Romano
"Creepy Crossword: Ghostly Manors"
"Advertising Art History Dept."— Ad reproductions

Monsters from the Vault

At the forefront of the new breed of monster magazines is *Monsters from the Vault*, yet another labor of love that has grown in quality and stature with each issue. Most of the classic-oriented monster mags produced today are labors of love, as they must be, rarely achieving newsstand distribution, but kept alive by the fan network and alternative distribution systems. They openly proclaim their debt to *Famous Monsters*, and seek not only to emulate it, but also to continue the never-ending mission to extend the limits of horror film scholarship.

Monsters from the Vault no. 6 (Spring 1998)

Cover: Photo of Glenn Strange/ *The Mad Monster*
"Whom the Gods Would Destroy"— Steve Kronenberg
The Vampire's Ghost— Bryan Senn
"Zombies B.F. (Before Romero)"— John Stell
"Victory Vampires and Villains: Horror Films as Propaganda During World War II"— Brian Smith
"Enter My Dream: Cortlandt Hull's Witch's Dungeon"—(Photo feature)
"Films from the Vault"— John Stell (Reviews)
"Books from the Vault"— Steve Kronenberg (Reviews)
"Music from the Vault"— Vincent Dileonardi (Reviews)

This early issue gets five stars simply for because it's the first monster magazine ever to feature Glenn Strange as the hillbilly werewolf from *The Mad Monster* on its cover. There's much more, however, including an insightful piece on World War II–era monster films as propaganda, an angle seldom explored before. There's also a great article on the obscure *The Vampire's Ghost* by Bryan Senn, one of the most knowledgeable authors writing about horror films today.

Monsters from the Vault no. 23 (Spring 2007)

Cover: Sorko
"Don Dohler Tribute"—Don Leifert
"The Mummy of Red Rock Canyon: Locations of the Golden Age"—Richard J. Schmidt
"Personal Appearances of Karloff and Lugosi"—Gregory Mank
"An Interview with George R. Snell"—Gary Don Rhodes
"Treasures from a Monster Club"—Richard and Angie Olson
"Ape Fiends of the Silent Era" (Pt. 2)—Gary L. Prange
"George Barrows, Gorilla Guy!"—Bob Burns (as told to Tom Weaver)
"Films from the Vault"—Mark Clarke (Reviews)
"Books from the Vault"—David Colton, Gary Prange, Jim Nemeth, Bryan Senn

Computer technology has not only affected the production of monster magazines, it has even influenced art techniques and aesthetics. The embellishment and manipulation of photographs is becoming an art unto itself, as witnessed by this issue's cover, which is Lon Chaney Jr. as the Mummy, but touched up, and with a new and interesting background of hieroglyphics, all generated through the wonder of computer drawing programs. While very well done and incredibly striking, the practice makes one yearn for the brush-to-canvas approach of a Bama or a Gogos. There's certainly room for both approaches, although only time will tell if one form will replace another. As evidenced by the titles and content of the articles more information is unearthed every day. The monster magazine may be a much different beast in the new millennium, but it's in good hands.

Epilogue

It's easy to get caught up in the past. Very easy, because it's so seductive. The past is cloying; it's got a dangerous magnetic pull. Every generation gets nostalgic for what seemed the less complicated times of its youth. With the world's increasingly catastrophic problems, as more people begin to realize their lives are simply part of some political power play, it becomes ever more desirable to try and escape — and there are more ways to escape than ever. It helps the horror scene that the majority of the population ages 40 – 55 is in a state of arrested adolescence. Through technology, we now can involve or isolate ourselves completely; become part of the global village or construct our own little worlds. Both cottage industry and mega corporation practice specialization, and compartmentalization has made practically anything available in multiple forms of media. It's not a treat to find a model kit or a magazine or an action figure devoted to your favorite monster — it's expected. "Movie-by-committee" groups figure out the toy lines and fast-food giveaways before they even start shooting the film. There aren't just action figures of your favorite monsters or superheroes, there's a line from every film, TV show, and even single comic book stories. There's no longer any anxious anticipation of a movie, with curiosity fanned by a trailer or newspaper ad or magazine article. These days you can see practically a whole movie before it's even released. There's no need to wonder if your favorite monster mag will run an article on a movie; every movie now has its own magazine, not to mention its own website.

We are at this point entering into a phase of history where present and future generations will never know life before satellite television, cell phones, video games, instant information and entertainment, and the Internet. Our nation, indeed the world, is both connected and divided as never before. Impossible as it might be to imagine, at some point books, magazines, newspapers and comics may become environmentally unfeasible or socially undesirable. People can see anything they want online, or they may have chips installed in their heads so that entertainment or information can be directly piped in. Or perhaps the powers-that-be will once again decide that any type of horror (other than what they create) is just not good for us. They might decide that the original version of the Comics Code had something to it — after all, similar right-wing measures have been increasingly applied to other areas of society, media and entertainment ever since 2001, and who's to say that comics and monsters won't again suffer the same fate? If a government that can legally keep tabs on what you buy and listen to and read decides that what you're buying and listening to and reading is dangerous, then a movie like *Brazil* or a book like *Fahrenheit 451* doesn't seem so far-fetched after all. I once bought a copy of *The Satanic Rites of Dracula* on DVD for a buck. A few years later, the movie turned up in the same outlets again, with *Satanic* removed from the title, on the packaging graphics and a clumsily inserted new title card.

That's not to say the past was better, just different in some ways, and things will never be that way again, because they can't be. The past, the present, and the future are equally valid. Pop culture may be a shield or a window; it may be either an illuminating experience or an empty experience, but if it is the latter, to quote Woody Allen, "as empty experiences go, it's one of the best." The vintage monster magazines and black-and-white illustrated magazines made other futures possible, and they provided horror fans with a format that broadened, deepened, and expanded the artistic horizons of the genre.

Appendix: Publications by Category

I. Comic Books

A-1 Comics
Aces High
Adventures into Mystery
Adventures into Terror
Adventures into the Unknown
Adventures into Weird Worlds
Airboy Comics
Alarming Tales
Amazing Adventures
Amazing Adult Fantasy
Amazing Fantasy
Amazing Mysteries
The Amazing Spider-Man
Astonishing
Astonishing Tales
Avenging World
Baffling Mysteries
Beowulf
Best of the West
The Beverly Hillbillies
Bewitched
Black Cat Mystery
Black Magic
Black Phantom
Bobby Benson Comics
Boris Karloff Tales of Mystery/ Boris Karloff's Thriller
The Brute
Buck Rogers in the 25th Century
Captain America Comics
Captain America's Weird Tales
Casper, the Friendly Ghost
Chamber of Chills
Chamber of Darkness
Chilling Tales
Claw the Unconquered
Creatures on the Loose
Crime Does Not Pay
Crypt of Shadows
Daredevil
Dark Mysteries
Dead of Night
The Demon
Demon Hunter
Doc Savage (Gold Key)
Doc Savage (Marvel)
Doctor Solar, Man of the Atom
Doorway to Nightmare
Dracula
Eerie
The Fantastic Four
Fantasy Masterpieces
(Adventures into) Fear
Forbidden Tales of Dark Mansion
Forbidden Worlds
The Forever People
Frankenstein (Prize)
Frankenstein (Western)
Fright (Featuring Son of Dracula)
Frontline Combat
G-8 and His Battle Aces
Ghost Comics
Ghost Manor
The Ghost Rider (Superhero)
The Ghost Rider (Western)
Ghost Stories
Ghostly Haunts
Ghostly Tales
(Do You Believe in) Ghosts
Giant-Size Chillers
Giant-Size Dracula
Giant-Size Man Thing
Great Western
The Grim Ghost
The Haunt of Fear
Haunted (Baron Weirwulf's Haunted Library)
(This Magazine Is) Haunted
Haunted Love
Haunted Thrills
The Heap
Hot Stuff, the Little Devil
House of Mystery
House of Secrets
Incredible Science Fiction
Jimmy Olsen
John Carter, Warlord of Mars
Joker Comics
Journey into Mystery
Journey into Unknown Worlds
Kamandi, the Last Boy on Earth
Kona, Monarch of Monster Isle
(The Return of) Konga
Konga's Revenge
Korak, Son of Tarzan
Mad

Magnus — Robot Fighter
The Many Ghosts of Doctor Graves
Marvel Boy
Marvel Comics
Marvel Mystery Comics
Marvel Spotlight
Marvel Tales
Melvin Monster
Menace
Midnight Tales
Millie the Loveable Monster
Mister A
Mister Miracle
Mister Mystery
The Monkees
Monster Hunters
Monster of Frankenstein/The Frankenstein Monster
Monsters on the Prowl
Moorlock 2001
Motion Picture Funnies Weekly
Movie Classics
Movie Comics
Mysteries of Unexplored Worlds
Mysterious Adventures
Mystery in Space
Mystery Tales
Mystic
The New Gods
Nightmare
The Occult Files of Dr. Spektor
Out of the Night
Panic
The Phantom Stranger
Picture Stories from the Bible
Piracy
Planet Comics
Planet of Vampires
Prize Comics
Red Mask
Reptilicus/Reptisaurus
Scary Tales
The Scorpion
Secrets of Sinister House
Secrets of the Haunted House
Shazam!
Shock SuspenStories
The Sinister House of Secret Love
Space Squadron
Space Worlds
Speed Carter, Spaceman
Spellbound
The Spirit
Stalker
Startling Terror Tales
Strange Adventures
Strange Fantasy
Strange Stories of Suspense
Strange Tales
Strange Tales of the Unusual
Strange Worlds
Sub-Mariner Comics
Super Villain Team-Up
Supernatural Thrillers
Suspense
Swamp Thing
Sword of Sorcery
Tales from the Crypt (EC)
Tales from the Tomb
Tales of Evil
Tales of Ghost Castle
Tales of Horror
Tales of the Mysterious Traveler
Tales of the Unexpected
Tarzan (National)
Tarzan (Western)
Teen
The Thing
Thrills of Tomorrow
Tim Holt Comics
Time Warp
Tomb of Darkness
Tomb of Dracula
Tomb of Terror
Tower of Shadows
Two-Fisted Tales
Uncanny Tales
The Unexpected
Unknown Worlds
Unusual Tales
Valor
Vault of Evil
The Vault of Terror
Venus
Voodoo
Walt Disney's Comics and Stories
Web of Evil
Web of Mystery
Weird Fantasy
Weird Horrors
Weird Mysteries
Weird Mystery Tales
Weird Science
Weird Science-Fantasy
Weird Suspense
Weird Tales of the Future
Weird War Tales
Weird Western Tales
Weird Wonder Tales
Weird Worlds
Wendy, the Good Little Witch
Werewolf by Night
Where Creatures Roam
Where Monsters Dwell
Witchcraft
Witches' Tales
The Witching Hour
World of Fantasy
World of Mystery
World of Suspense
Worlds of Fear
Worlds Unknown
Wulf the Barbarian
The Yellow Claw

II. Movie Monster Magazines

Castle of Frankenstein
Chiller Theatre
Chilling Monster Tales
Cinefantastique
Cult Movies
Famous Films
Famous Monsters of Filmland
Fangoria
Fantastic Monsters of the Films
For Monsters Only
Hammer's House of Horror
Horror Monsters
House of Hammer
Kong: The Most Famous Monster of All Time
Mad Monsters
Marvel Movie Premiere
Midnight Marquee
Modern Monsters
Monster Bash
Monster Fantasy
Monster Madness
Monster Mania
Monster Parade
The Monster Times
Monster World (Mayfair)
Monster World (Warren)

MonsterMad
Monsters and Heroes
Monsters and Things
Monsters from the Vault
Monsters of the Movies
Monsters to Laugh With/Monsters Unlimited
Monsterscene
Movie Monsters
Quasimodo's Monster Magazine
Revenge of Dracula
Rue Morgue
Scary Monsters
Science Fiction, Horror and Fantasy
Science Fiction Illustrated
Screen Thrills Illustrated
Shock Tales
Shriek!
Space Stars
Space Trek
Space Wars
Spacemen
Star Battles
Star Encounters
Star Force
Star Invaders
Star Warp
Starblazer
Starburst
Starlog
Suspense
3-D Monsters
Thriller
Warren Presents
Werewolves and Vampires
World-Famous Creatures

III. BLACK-AND-WHITE MAGAZINES

Alien Invasions Comix (Warren Presents No. 7)
Chilling Tales of Horror
Comix Book
Crazy
Creepy
The Deadly Hands of Kung Fu
Doc Savage, the Man of Bronze
Dracula Lives
Eerie
Empire Encounter Comix (Warren Presents No. 12)
Epic Illustrated
Future World Comix (Warren Presents No. 2)
Galactic War Comix (Warren Presents No. 4)
Ghoul Tales
The Haunt of Horror
Heavy Metal
Hell-Rider
Help!
Horror Tales
Kull and the Barbarians
The Legion of Monsters
Mad
Marvel Preview
Masters of Terror
Monsters Unleashed!
Nightmare
1984/1994
Planet of the Apes
Psycho
Ring of the Warlords (Warren Presents No. 5)
The Rook
The Savage Sword of Conan the Barbarian
Savage Tales
Scream
Shock (Chilling Tales of Horror and Suspense)
The Six Million Dollar Man
Space: 1999
*Star*Reach*
Starquest Comix (Warren Presents No. 3)
Strange Stories of Vampires Comix (Warren Presents No. 10)
Sword and Sorcery Comix (Warren Presents No. 13)
Tales from the Crypt
Tales of Terror
Tales of Voodoo
Tales of the Zombie
Terror Tales
Thrilling Adventure Stories
Tomb of Dracula
UFO and Alien Comix (Warren Presents No. 1)
Unknown Worlds of Science Fiction
Vampire Tales
Vampirella
Weird
Weird Tales of the Macabre
Weird Vampire Tales
Witches' Tales

Bibliography

Ackerman, Forrest J. *Forrest J Ackerman, Famous Monster of Filmland*. Pittsburgh: Imagine, 1986.

Cooke, Jon B., and David A. Roach, eds. *The Warren Companion*. Raleigh, NC: Twomorrows Publishing, 2001.

Daniel, Dennis, ed. *The Famous Monsters Chronicles*. Albany, NY: FantaCo, 1991.

Daniels, Les. *Comix: A History of Comic Books in America*. New York: Bonanza, 1971.

DeBord, Guy. *Society of the Spectacle*. London: Rebel Press, 1967.

Fenner, Arnold, and Cathy Fenner, eds. *Frank Frazetta: Icon*. Grass Valley, CA: Underwood, 2003.

Ferry, Ray. *Life Is But a Scream!* North Hills, CA: Karmanirhara, 2000.

Gammill, Kerry, and J. David Spurlock, eds. *Famous Monster Movie Art of Basil Gogos*. Lebanon, NJ: Vanguard, 2005.

Goodstone, Tony. *The Pulps: Fifty Years of American Pop Culture*. New York: Chelsea House, 1970.

Goulart, Ron. *Cheap Thrills: An Informal History of the Pulp Magazine*. New Rochelle, NY: Arlington House, 1972.

Hewetson, Alan. *(The Complete Illustrated History of the) Skywald Horror-Mood*. London: Headpress, 2004.

Hine, Thomas. *Populuxe*. New York: MJF, 1999.

Kane, Brian M. *James Bama: American Realist*. Santa Cruz, CA: Flesk, 2006.

Michelucci, Bob. *The Collector's Guide to Monster, Science Fiction and Fantasy Film Magazines*. N.p.: Imagine, 1988.

Miller, Jim, ed. *The Rolling Stone Illustrated History of Rock & Roll*. New York: Random House, 1980.

Steranko, James. *The Steranko History of the Comics, Volume One*. Reading, PA: Supergraphics, 1968.

Thompson, Hunter S. *Songs of the Doomed*. New York: Summit Books, 1990.

Index

Ackerman, Forrest J 33, 35, 40, 41, 58, 100, 184, 216
Adams, Neal 22, 70–71, 83, 105–107, 127, 137, 157, 179–180, 196–197, 212
Alcala, Alfredo 78, 88, 128–129, 131, 137, 139, 141, 193
Atlas Comics 16, 26–27, 83, 85; *see also* Marvel Comics; Timely Comics
Atlas/Seaboard Comics 28, 52, 54–56, 98, 170
Aurora Monster Models 32, 201

Bama, James 32, 35, 153–154, 201
Beck, Calvin 59–60
Bond, James 25, 77, 87, 152, 202
Burroughs, Edgar Rice 15, 148, 161, 182
Buscema, John 22, 76, 124, 128–129, 131, 137, 140–141, 156

Cardille, "Chilly Billy" 33
Castle of Frankenstein 33, 35, 59–61
Chan, Ernie (Chua) 108, 143, 158
Chaykin, Howard 128, 138, 141–142, 170, 181, 189, 195
Colan, Gene 20, 82, 88, 106–111
Colon, Ernie 171–172
The Comics Code Authority 11–17, 19, 30, 221
Corben, Richard 87, 129, 189, 206
Crandall, Reed 7, 20, 40, 102
Creepy 19, 33, 69–71, 145–147
Cushing, Peter 48–49

Dell/Gold Key (Western Publishing Co.) 28–29
DeZuniga, Tony 128, 130, 137, 156
Ditko, Steve 15–16, 27, 70, 111, 149
Doc Savage 29, 32, 110, 152–158
Dracula Lives! 104–110

EC Comics 7–8, 14, 69, 118, 120
Eerie 22, 71–73, 147
Eerie Publications 63–64, 118–120
Eisner, Will 30
Everett, Bill 9, 74, 96–97

Fabian, Steve 109, 133, 165
Famous Monsters of Filmland 19, 33–41, 58, 104, 184, 187, 212
Frazetta, Frank 7, 57, 70, 71, 73, 124–125, 207–208

Gaines, William 7, 120
Gerber, Steve 74–79
Glut, Don 44–45, 48
Gogos, Basil 35–36, 39–40, 174–175, 184–185, 187, 212, 213
Gonzalez, Jose 101–103
Goodman, Martin 9, 54
Goodwin, Archie 70–71, 100, 172, 190

Harmon, Jim 44–46, 48
Haydock, Ron 44, 46, 48
Heath, Russ 78, 88, 110, 167, 172
Heavy Metal 206–208, 210
Hewetson, Alan 1, 45, 92–97
Horror Monsters 50–51
House of Hammer 64–68, 215
Howard, Robert E. 81, 121–126, 133, 135, 149, 162, 168, 206

Jones, Jeff 50, 71, 98
Jones, Russ 39, 45, 56–58

Kaluta, Michael 128, 151, 167, 179, 210–211
Kane, Gil 22–23, 25, 70, 127, 129, 132, 154, 170, 182

Kelly, Ken 36, 213
Kirby, Jack 10, 15–17, 27

Larkin, Bob 44–48, 84, 88, 90, 157, 159–160, 192
Lee, Bruce 177–180
Lee, Stan 16–17, 19, 41, 59
Lewis, Brian 65–68

Mad 7, 14, 19, 200–202
Mad Monsters 50–52
Marcos, Pablo 73–79, 82
Maroto, Esteban 112, 127, 144, 147, 164, 169, 181, 206
Marvel Comics 1–3, 9, 20, 93, 104, 123, 161–162
Mayfair Publications 61–63
The Misfits 174–176, 216
Monster Madness 41–43, 76
Monster Mania 56–58
The Monster Times 33, 52–53
Monsters of the Movies 33, 43–49
Monsters Unleashed! 2, 80–86
Movie Monsters 54–56, 191

National Comics (DC) 14–15, 19
Neary, Paul 52, 65, 72, 103
Nightmare (Skywald) 115
Nino, Alex 131, 189, 195
Norem, Earl 85, 108, 139–143

Olivia 206

Palmer, Tom 106–110
Planet of the Apes 190–194, 204
Ploog, Mike 20, 24, 85, 88, 192
Psycho (Skywald) 95–97

Reese, Ralph 82, 88, 97, 210

The Savage Sword of Conan the Barbarian 3, 126–144
Savage Tales 140, 163–167

Scream (Skywald) 94, 115–116
Severin, John 7, 26, 50, 127, 138, 169, 182
Severin, Marie 138, 157, 169, 182
The Shadow 150–151
Simon, Joe 10, 15
Simonson, Walter 88, 131, 138, 172, 210
Skywald 1, 27, 92–97, 115–116, 200
Smith, Barry (Windsor) 44, 124, 129, 131, 139, 142, 163, 210, 211
Stanley Publications 4, 117–118
Star Wars 3, 29, 36–37, 183, 187, 204–205
Steranko, James 25, 91, 154, 210

Tales of the Zombie 73–79
Thomas, Roy 22, 44, 123–124, 128–144, 163, 182
Thrilling Adventure Stories 170–172
Timely Comics 9–10, 15–16
Tower Comics 28, 84, 126

Underground Comix 202–203

Vallejo, Boris 2, 75–77, 85, 97–98, 113–114, 126, 134, 136–138, 165–166
Vampira 33
Vampire Tales 112–114
Vampirella 97, 100–103, 147, 181

Warren, James 14, 19, 33–41, 58, 65, 71, 92, 100, 118, 120, 127, 144
Warren Publishing Co. 20, 22, 69, 92–93, 100, 103, 142, 158, 184, 207
Weird Tales of the Macabre 98
Wertham, Frederick 11, 12, 30
Wood, Wallace 7, 15, 39, 58, 73, 81, 145, 169, 184, 207
Wrightson, Bernie 80, 163, 210

Yaple, Robert 130, 131, 133

Zacherley 33
Zombie, Rob 174–175

www.ingramcontent.com/pod-product-compliance
Ingram Content Group UK Ltd.
Pitfield, Milton Keynes, MK11 3LW, UK
UKHW050531150426
5217IPUK00026B/1895